SEARCHING FOR VEDIC INDIA

SEARCHING FOR VEDIC INDIA

DEVAMRITA SWAMI

THE BHAKTIVEDANTA BOOK TRUST

LOS ANGELES   STOCKHOLM   MUMBAI   SYDNEY

Readers interested in the subject matter of this book are invited
to correspond with the publisher at one of the following addresses:

The Bhaktivedanta Book Trust
P.O. Box 34074, Los Angeles, CA 90034, USA
Phone: +1-800-927-4152 • Fax: +1-310-837-1056
E-mail: bbt.usa@krishna.com

The Bhaktivedanta Book Trust
Korsnäs Gård, 147 92 Grödinge, Sweden
Phone: +46-8-53029800 • Fax: +46-8-53025062
E-mail: bbt.se@krishna.com

The Bhaktivedanta Book Trust
P.O. Box 262, Botany, NSW 2019, Australia
Phone: +61-2-96666466 • Fax: +61-2-96663060
E-mail: bbt.au@krishna.com

The Bhaktivedanta Book Trust
Hare Krishna Land, Juhu, Mumbai 400 049, India
Phone: +91-22-6206860 • Fax: +91-22-6205214
E-mail: bbt.in@krishna.com

www.krishna.com

Design by Govinda Cordua. Set in Meridien and Trajan.

ISBN 0-89213-350-3

Printed in Germany

CONTENTS

~

FOREWORD

The ancient Vedic literatures of India tell of a worldwide civilization, with interplanetary connections, that thrived at a time when modern historians would have us believe that humans like us existed simply as hunter-gatherers or had not yet come into being. This Vedic civilization, centered in India, employed technologies based on a scientific understanding of not only the physical elements and forces we know today but also of more subtle material and conscious elements. All of these elements were recognized as having their source in a supreme conscious intelligence. Where modern science sees only ordinary matter and its transformations, the Vedic science saw the action of this supreme conscious intelligence behind everything, and fashioned a way of life that focused less on dominating and exploiting matter and more on elevating each individual conscious self to its original pure state in relation to the supreme conscious self, God.

The history of this remarkable civilization and its knowledge are locked in the ancient Vedic literatures of India, and *Searching for Vedic India*, by Devamrita Swami, gives us the key to it all. Devamrita Swami, who has spent a lifetime in his own search for

Vedic India, is the perfect guide to take us on that journey of intellectual discovery. Devamrita Swami's wit and wisdom combine to make our search for Vedic India not only illuminating but entertaining. He tells us not only the truths of Vedic India, but how they are again coming to be. *Searching for Vedic India* thus takes us not only into the past, but into the future.

Michael A. Cremo
(Drutakarma Dasa)

INTRODUCTION

~

Deep in lost history, did high civilizations and advanced knowledge thrive? Major cultures of the world tell of exceptionally powerful predecessors, far back in time. In the West, of course, a two-hundred-year tradition of mainstream scholarship has completely rejected this possibility. Conservative authorities dismiss the fascinating accounts from other cultures as primitive tales. Liberals agree to grant the ancient information a measure of status—as instructive myth. What properly educated modern would dare take the challenge of an advanced antiquity at face value?

Enter the dawn of the new century. A new breed of researcher combs through earthly and cosmic mysteries. A new stripe of reader relishes the exciting possibilities—ignored for so long by the factories of standardized education.

Leading-edge researchers in the new category sometimes work at prestigious universities. Owing to laurels earned in their past, they can veer off into new radical pursuits without risking their livelihood. More often, however, these knowledge pioneers have to fly solo. Independent of the status quo, they are most effective. Relying upon recognized tools such as geology, astronomy, cartography, and mathematics, the vanguard is uncovering new support for the old views of the ancients.

No longer need an inquisitive audience fear ridicule upon encountering evidence for a brilliant global civilization that disappeared in time. A picture is now emerging that a wiser version of humanity may have walked Earth—many millennia before history, as we currently think it, was constructed.

The matter-bound science prevalent today is under pressure to expand beyond its self-erected barriers. Outside the rusting cage of the Western materialistic paradigm, the sacred science of antiquity beckons us. We are intrigued to find that, whereas the moderns are matter-based, the ancients were consciousness-based.

Up until now, the prevailing notion of human civilization has been a slow linear progression—up from primitive Neolithic beginnings to the technological wonders of today. The greatest drama of the twenty-first century may be the decline and fall of this fundamental belief.

Every society has a particular view of reality, accompanied by attendant patterns for thinking, perceiving, evaluating, and behaving. *Searching for Vedic India* probes the tremors shaking the creed that is the core of the Western attempt at civilization.

The purpose of this book is not to present an airtight case, nailed shut, but to stimulate a poignant awareness of other avenues. Certainly, if we can but shed our inbuilt cultural and conceptual mindset, we are in for a treat. The ancients seem to have mastered dazzling dimensions of awareness—domains impenetrable by the cultural construct we know as the Western scientific method.

I write these words on Easter Island—a remote speck in the midst of the South Pacific, 3,800 kilometers west of South America. The most famous inhabitants are the 600 *moai*, huge stone figures, up to twenty-eight feet high. Until 1971, a U.S. missile-tracking station shared the isle with the *moai*. That station is now abandoned; the missile people are gone. But the megalithic giants remain.

Pause with me, and consider: our type of technological wizardry may be only an eye-blink in an unknown expanse of human history, a span that hides great cultural achievements of a different nature. Today a wealth of literature attempts to introduce the general reader to the eerie knowledge-world of the ancient Egyptians. The mystery-knowledge of the Mayas, though apparently of later origin, is also adequately represented. Where, though, does the spotlight shine on the lost knowledge-world of ancient India? Preserved in the Sanskrit language of the Vedas and in the authentic spiritual traditions that still live today, the profound treasures of remote Indian antiquity are unrivalled.

Searching for Vedic India aims to reveal that Vedic knowledge is in a class of its own. Quietly this book dares to allude that the lost glories of the ancients may have radiated outward from the Indian subcontinent. The search for the headquarters of a missing global civilization should begin with the India that mainstream education has forgotten.

Devamrita Swami
Easter Island
September 1, 2000

CHAPTER 1

BEGINNING THE VEDIC VENTURE

S tanding on the shore of our present conceptions of knowledge, we begin contemplating the vast ocean of India's Vedic culture. Far and wide, our vision lifts and soars, out over the endless waves of fascinating information, up into the horizon of transcendence. Thinking back, we can savor the intuitive curiosity that gently prompted many others like us to embark upon this same venture—exploring the sea of the world's most ancient wisdom.

Increasingly, thoughtful persons graciously accept that the Western process of acquiring knowledge is insufficient and problematic. It has ingrained limitations—as well as some perturbing defects. At the same time, a chronic loss of meaning to life gnaws at the hearts of millions in Europe and America, and nations under their sway. This emptiness, despite the racehorse pace of modern society, has inspired the curious to explore how other cultures attempted the puzzle of life. Particularly appealing are ancient civilizations that approached the world holistically—that is, they adhered to a "whole systems" or "living systems" view of the cosmos. We may gingerly allow ourselves a quiet appreciation of these cultures, which envisioned the universe and nature as a unified living system—pregnant with meaning in every aspect.

Scholars have also contributed to this newfound fascination with the holistic ancients. Archaeologists and palaeontologists seem consistently to march the story of humanity ever backwards in time. They rewrite the chronology of specific artifacts, as well as entire civilizations, further back into what we traditionally call prehistory. Meanwhile, bold nonmainstream researchers suggest that the present version of human society may be just an insignificant episode in a vast but lost span of civilization.

The officially established insights into ancient civilizations are actually very recent. Archaeological labors to document traces of antiquity are approximately only two centuries old. The French emperor Napoleon I, at the start of the nineteenth century, launched the formal era of archaeology, when he sent an expedition to Eygpt. Several archaeologists tagged along, and they recorded the monuments there. Fifty years later, French and British archaeologists began formal research into Mesopotamia.

Even by the mid-twentieth century, knowledge of antiquity was still quite infantile. *Archaeology* magazine, in celebrating its fiftieth anniversary, highlighted a few of the now outmoded beliefs that were accepted as fact just five decades or so ago.[1] When the magazine first appeared in 1948, archaeologists were sure that the history of human beings was little more than 250,000 years old. Farming began in Eygpt only 6,000 years ago. The Maya were peace-loving calendar fanatics. The Stonehenge monoliths in England were an undated mystery. The original North American natives were buffalo hunters who wandered the plains.

In the closing moments of the twentieth century, just five decades later, the glow of these truths had faded into fable. The established version of human history has now been extended back more than 2.5 million years. Agriculture is presently calculated as at least 10,000 years old. The Mayas have been fingered as bloodthirsty killers, and the date for the stone megaliths of Stonehenge has been set at 3000 B.C. Moreover, the story of prehistoric America is now wide open to speculation.

What upheavals in our knowledge of human history will the new century bring? If the discoveries that crowded the twilight of the old century are any indication, the old paradigm is in for a rough ride. In 1996 police in northwestern USA discovered the half-buried bones of what they hoped were the telltale remains of a recent unsolved murder. Upon analyzing the skeleton, however, scientists at the University of California told them their victim was 9,300 years old. Next anthropologists took over, and quickly pointed out that the skeleton did not resemble the bone structure of any people known to have inhabited prehistoric America. Then in 1999 came a clear verdict on the skeleton's identity. America's press announced the end of the investigation: "Lineage of ancient Washington bones points to south Asia." How does present history account for south-Asian related people in North America at that time?[2]

In 1998 the Stonehenge megaliths in England were eclipsed. An ancient astronomical alignment of stones in Egypt's Sahara Desert now holds the distinction as the world's oldest megaliths known today. As reported in the science journal *Nature*, the Egyptian megaliths were given a date of approximately 4000–4500 B.C.—making them at least one thousand years older than the official age now given to Stonehenge. The shock of 1998, however, came from eastern Indonesia. Once again the world's most respected scientific journal, *Nature*, broke the news.[3] Humans seem to have organized sea journeys 800,000–880,000 years ago. Evidence emerged in the form of stone tools found on the island of Flores, 340 miles east of Bali. The trip there, from the Asian mainland, would have required long-distance island hopping. Because of the complexities involved in coordinating such an expedition, scientists concede the use of language as a necessity.

Who were these voyagers, who managed long sea journeys more than 700,000 years earlier than previously thought? Our current standards hold that the only humans existing then were anatomically primitive *Homo erectus*. But boatmaking and sailing are normally attributed only to anatomically modern humans.

Previously, the first major sea journey was fixed at just 40,000–60,000 years ago, when anatomically modern humans are said to have crossed over to Australia from eastern Indonesia. The new discovery has pressured anthropologists to save their theories by drastically upgrading the abilities of *Homo erectus*. Rebel scholars are blowing the whistle. They dare to challenge: why not consider that the seafarers of more than 800,000 years ago were up-to-date humans—that is, *Homo sapiens sapiens*? This plausible angle, however, would force a revolution upon our current ideas of human history.

The Bali discovery would be upsetting enough if merely an isolated challenge. The problem, though, is much bigger. For instance, what do we say about the bewildering find of an anatomically modern human femur in layers 800,000 years old—just next door to Bali, in Java?

Independent investigations are now alerting us to a wealth of evidence that does not fit the accepted theory of human origins. Many of these authentic finds have been politely overlooked for more than one hundred years.

Scholars attending the 1999 annual meetings of both the World Archaeological Congress and the European Association of Archaeologists witnessed the startling resurrection of this most unsettling documentation. A previously untold history of science revealed that in the late nineteenth century, archaeologists and their allied specialists routinely discussed remains of anatomically modern humans found in rock layers of astounding age.[4]

Some finds dated to the Pliocene geological epoch—an interval spanning 2–12 million years ago. Other dates are even earlier. The unavoidable conclusion: because a scheme for human evolution had not yet hardened, scientists of the nineteenth century could approach evidence uninhibited by theoretical preconditioning. Furthermore, the absence of a ruling framework meant freedom from peer pressure to conform.

By the early twentieth century, however, a believable and enthusiastically supported theory of human origins had emerged. Eventually, as the twentieth century came to an end, commitment to a specific evolutionary game plan had successfully erased all memory of any evidence pointing to the existence of modern human bodies millions of years ago.

While conventional professors struggle to ignore the torpedoing of hallowed Western theories, the general public is awash in a tide of alternative knowledge packaged in easy-reading format. This popular surge has moved many seekers to begin their journey to the Vedic ocean. By now, even the so-called average person has gradually become accustomed to hearing notions our grandparents would have considered wacky—if not outright heretical. Search any urban bookstore and you'll find that topics such as reincarnation, near-death experiences, psychic powers, UFOs, aliens, ancient astronauts, extraterrestrial intelligence, parallel universes, the mystery of consciousness, and so forth, are quite the norm—even on bestseller lists.

New books advocating ancient mysteries are fashionable. Their authors drag into the spotlight previously ignored traces indicating that high intelligence, technological prowess, and cosmic knowledge may have existed on Earth many millennia before the supposed dawn of human civilization. When *Fingerprints of the Gods* shot to the top of the British bestseller list in 1995, no one doubted the surging reader interest. To date, the book has sold more than 3.5 million copies in twenty languages.

Television has not been slack to jump aboard. Viewers throughout Europe and America regularly see primetime special telecasts of revolutionary archaeological findings and UFO claims. What we see turns completely upside down the current story of human origins and the cosmos.

Whatever tumult that arrived with the advent of "renegade archaeology" redoubled upon linking with the current UFO boom. The modern UFO era began in the USA in 1947, when a respectable businessman and expert pilot, Kenneth Arnold, declared he saw nine disks in the air, each appearing individually, "like a saucer would if you skipped it across water." The initially doubtful news media became taken by Arnold's solid-citizen credentials, and flashed his story nationwide. Soon the term "flying saucer" entered contemporary vocabulary. Since that time countless reports of sightings, abductions, and governmental cover-ups fill countless books, articles, and videos throughout the world.

The most respected public opinion surveyor in America, the Gallup Organization, revealed that for the last two decades of the twentieth century, American acceptance of UFOs as reality has hovered around 50 percent. Moreover, many more Americans, 72 percent, are now convinced that life exists elsewhere in the universe, though only 38 percent think those life forms will look human. Noting the American public's acceptance of ET life, a spokesperson for NASA, the National Aeronautics and Space Administration, commented: "It could be that the American people are taking two and two and coming up with four."[5]

Most significantly, the Gallup poll, taken in September 1996, showed that 71 percent of America thinks the government is covering up UFO information. In June the following year, a joint poll taken by international network CNN and the international news weekly *Time* magazine disclosed that 80 percent of Americans think the government is hiding knowledge that alien life exists.

Other major nations of the developed world are similar. For instance, in early 1999 a magazine in England polled British acceptance of extraterrestrial life at 50 percent. Paralleling ominous attitudes across the Atlantic, 80 percent said the British government would never inform them of alien evidence.[6] In France, in September 1996, a television poll found that almost half the French people, 48 percent, believe in extraterrestrials, and 33 percent said aliens could benefit Earth with wisdom.[7] Canada, in the same month, polled at 70 percent belief in life on other planets.[8]

One outgrowth of the Western intellect in this century has played a major role in loosening the bonds of conventional thinking. Modern physics, with its perplexing revelations, has confounded our basic understanding of reality. The general public is now more aware that for many years quantum physics has almost completely done away with the universe as the naked human eye sees it. Atoms reveal themselves to be 99.999999999 percent empty space. So-called subatomic particles fade into fuzziness— they become waves.

We are unable to picture what the subatomic world is like. Upon our applying the familiar constructs that serve us well in the everyday world, we are flung headlong into a sea of paradoxes. Harvard University physicist P. W. Bridgeman has explained:

> The structure of nature may eventually be such that our processes of thought do not correspond to it sufficiently to permit us to think about it at all. . . . The world fades out and eludes us. . . . We have reached the limit of the vision of the great pioneers of science, the vision, namely that we live in a sympathetic world in that it is comprehensible by our minds.[9]

At the same time that physics has baffled our minds, ecology has introduced the West to the cosmic beauty of connected organic thinking. True, many still see the universe as an inanimate chunk of matter that we can cut to pieces on a plate and manipulate. But many others relish a new vision of the universe as an interwoven living whole that requires our harmonious participation.

Ecological anxieties have forced us to expand our vision. Through understanding spiritually oriented civilizations, we hope to learn how to interact with nature prudently. Can Earth continue to sustain our frenzied life style and blatant extortion of the environment?

For evaluating the crisis facing humanity in the new millennium, the United Nations Environment Programme (UNEP) completed the most comprehensive and authoritative environmental assessment ever conducted. The unequivocal, emphatic judgment: "The continued poverty of the majority of the planet's inhabitants and excessive consumption by the majority are the two major causes of environmental degradation. The present course is unsustainable and postponing action is no longer an option."[10] The UN report, "Global Environment Outlook 2000," asked, among other things, that industrialized nations cut their resource consumption by tenfold, so that developing countries could have their chance at nature's limited resources.

Remember when, in 1992, over sixteen hundred top scientists, including most of the living Nobel laureates, jointly issued a document, "Warning to Humanity"? They declared that "human beings and the natural world are on a collision course . . . that may so alter the living world that it will be unable to sustain life in the manner that we know." Certainly the future will reveal how time judges the worst-case scenarios.

Ominously, since the pageantry of the 1992 Earth Summit in Rio de Janeiro, where leaders of 178 nations gathered, almost all the international agreements for protecting the environment have turned out to be hot air. The global effort to curtail CFC (chlorofluorocarbon) damage to the ozone is a rare exception.

The general record for international cooperation is so bad that scientists at the European Commission's Joint Research Center in Italy have called for an end to anxiety about saving the world's rainforests. It's too late, they say—the effort is doomed. The Indonesian island of Sumatra won the deforestation world championship. Though an island twice the size of Britain, Sumatra lost almost all its lowland forests in less than twenty-five years.[11]

Erratic and unpredictable environmental change is a daily headache for not only scientists but also politicians. President Bill Clinton announced to the American people in his year 2000 "State of the Union Address": "The greatest environmental challenge of the new century is global warming. . . . If we fail to reduce the emission of greenhouse gases, deadly heat waves and droughts will become more frequent, coastal areas will flood, and economies will be disrupted. That is going to happen, unless we act."

The last two years of the twentieth century had already seen a phenomenal rise in global temperature. Naysayers had asserted that the increase is unrelated to pollution and is a natural fluctuation of the earth's climate. In April, 2000, however, the Royal Swedish Academy announced the results of international scientific research that compared past climates in fifteen sites around the world. Extinguishing the last objections that a similar rise in temperature had occurred in the Middle Ages, the study solidly established that the earth is now hotter than at any time in the entirety of recorded human history.[12]

British and American researchers have observed that the global warming is melting two Antarctic ice shelves. At the opposite pole, scientists discovered something they say has not happened for 50 million years. A voyage to the Arctic, led by Dr. James McCarthy, an oceanographer from Harvard University, found a patch of ice-free water about a mile wide at the top of the world. Disturbed by this dramatic sight of an iceless North Pole, Dr. Malcolm McKenna, a palaeontologist from the American Museum of Natural History, commented: "Some folks who pooh-pooh global warming might wake up if shown that even the pole is beginning to melt at least sometimes, as in the Eocene."[13]

According to current scientific understanding, in the Eocene geological period, about 55 million years ago, water and jungles of tropical vegetation pervaded the Arctic and Antarctic circles.

Can environmental change disrupt the world's biggest economies? The Worldwatch Institute provided statistics demonstrating that in 1998 the cost to the world for weather-related damage jumped by 53 percent beyond the previous record high, of 1996.[14] Looking ahead in the new millennium, the International Red Cross warned, "Super-disasters are coming. Changing climate is no longer a doomsday prophecy, it's a reality."[15]

Millions of people in the First World do realize that humanity's relationship with nature is abysmal. In England, 42 percent of the people surveyed by the *Daily Telegraph* said they would part with all the benefits of modern science and technology to regain a natural way of life in a world free of pollution.[16]

Sad to say, in spite of wholesome sentiments, the current human society can boast of an historic but dubious accomplishment: as we enter the twenty-first century, humanity has become a geophysical force—that is, the effects of our technological advancement have altered the fundamental systems and climate of the planet.

Scientific assemblies such as the Sixteenth International Botanical Congress have amply documented this worrisome achievement. More than four thousand botanical scientists from one hundred countries gathered and issued a statement that the current human impact on nature will lead to a mass extinction of plant and animal species rivalling the greatest extinction events of geological history. The president of the Botanical Congress, Dr. Peter Raven, a world authority on plant conservation, estimated that if current human lifestyles continue, by the second half of the new millennium, between one-third and two-thirds of all plant and animal species now living will disappear.[17]

Surely the time is ripe for wondering why we moderns have

charitably enlarged ourselves—why is it we feel a sense of superiority over anyone and anything in the past. A linear notion of progress has dominated Western thinking for the past two hundred years. Our embracing this concept has led to an almost unshakable faith that—in spite of problems—the modern world has been a much better place to live in than anything preceding it.

Statistics contradict this dream. They expose the twentieth century as the most violent century in known human history. Indeed, three times more people died in wars of the twentieth century than in the entire history of warfare between A.D. 1 and 1899.[18] Will the new century soon suffer a nuclear or chemical brawl that breaks the record again?

"Somehow—in some way—things are better," members of developed nations have struggled to remind one another. Yet more than a few sociologists and psychologists—all with no solution—have warned that the human core of modern society has thoroughly rusted, beset by inner emptiness, existential uncertainty, and cosmic dislocation.

For instance, in 1999 *Time* magazine reported that the USA had undergone a 300 percent increase in teen suicides since the 1960s and a 1000 percent increase in childhood depression since the 1950s.[19] More than three times as many American children now suffer from mental and behavioral disorders as compared to only twenty years ago.[20]

A survey of the brightest American teenagers found that almost a fourth of them had considered committing suicide, and that almost half of them knew someone who had tried. Depression and school pressures were cited as the main reasons for contemplating suicide. Interestingly, less than a fourth of these top-achieving high-school students reported that their families ate dinner together every day.[21]

No one will deny that the particular type of technology pioneered in the West since the Renaissance is incomparable in the memory of humanity. Nevertheless, an essential question nags us: Is this pursuit of production and consumption the only criterion for an advanced civilization? Have we actually witnessed human progress, or only our perverted dream of it—a mirage peculiar to our times and peoples?

Every student knows that the typical tale of human advancement highlights certain key stages, celebrated for their accelerating humanity's relentless march forward, to our current dizzying heights. Historians, except for the postmodern school, more or less agree on the same markers as the most significant moments in the history of humankind.

First, the story begins in prehistoric Africa, where the hominids emerged—apes with brains ("Becoming Human"). Second, the humans discovered agriculture, and then coalesced into the first cities—communities where not everyone was a farmer ("Inventing Civilization"). Third, in the sixth century B.C., religious and moral systems suddenly arose, throughout the civilized world ("Developing a Conscience"). Fourth, the empires of Europe and the Middle East brought forth the notion of world civilization ("Seeking a Lasting Peace").

With the fifth step came the rise of rationalism and empirical science ("Achieving Rationality"). Sixth, at the end of the fifteenth century the human societies in Europe and Africa encountered those in the Americas ("Uniting the Planet"). Seventh, beginning in the eighteenth century, the industrial revolution galvanized the world ("Releasing Nature's Energies"). At the culmination, step eight, the world moved increasingly toward democratic government in the nineteenth century, and toward decolonization and world order in the twentieth ("Ruling Ourselves").[22]

The actual destiny we created now demands ceaseless economic growth. The creature's trail leaves devastated environments and depleted resources (Releasing Nature's Energies?);

intercontinental war zones (Uniting the Planet?); and alienated, emptied people (Achieving Rationality?). How can we actually consider ourselves sensible and rational (Ruling Ourselves?) if we are so woefully unable to manage not only our environment but even our own lives? Keeping this honest and realistic appraisal in mind allows a fruitful acquaintanceship with the ancient culture of India. That world of wisdom is revealed in the Vedic texts.

Notes

1 Bruce Fagan, "Fifty Years of Discovery," *Archaeology* 51, no. 5 (September/October 1998).

2 "Tribe Stops Study of Bones That Challenge History," *New York Times*, 30 September 1996; Timothy Egan, "Lineage of Ancient Washington Bones Points to South Asia," *San Jose Mercury News*, 16 October 1999.

3 M. J. Morwood, *et al.*, "Fission-track ages of stone tools and fossils on the east Indonesian island of Flores," *Nature* 392 (12 March 1998): 173–76. Note that, during the course of geological time, Java and Bali were periodically connected to the Asian mainland. The Wallacean islands, however, which include Flores, are exempted from any land connection. For updated information see, for example, John Mulvaney and Johan Kamminga, *Prehistory of Australia* (Sydney: Allen & Unwin, 1999), pp. 104–5.

4 See paper delivered at the 1999 World Archaeological Congress: Michael Cremo, "Forbidden Archeology of the Early and Middle Pleistocene: Evidence for Physiologically and Culturally Advanced Humans"; and paper delivered at the 1999 European Association of Archaeologists: Michael Cremo, "Forbidden Archeology of the European Paleolithic: A Historical Survey of the Treatment of Evidence for Extreme Human Antiquity in the Nineteenth and Twentieth Centuries," to be published by British Archaeological Reports.

5 Brian Welch, quoted by Associated Press, 15 December 1997.

6 Survey by *Focus* magazine, reported by BBC News Sci/Tech, 13 January 1999.

7 As reported by Reuters newswire, 30 September 1996; the SOFRES poll for the weekly *Tele K7* magazine.

8 The *Globe and Mail*, "Canada's National Newspaper," 11 September 1996.

9 Quoted by Huston Smith in *Beyond the Postmodern Mind* (Illinois: Thesosophical Publishing House, 1989).

10 "Global Environment Outlook 2000" (GEO 2000), available from http://www.unep.org.

11 Reuters, 11 January 1998.

12 Geoffrey Lean, Environment Correspondent, *The Independent* (London), "Earth Hotter Than at Any Time in History," 30 April 2000.

13 John Noble Wilford, "Melting, Scientists Find," *New York Times*, 19 April 2000.

14 *Vital Signs: The Environmental Trends that Are Shaping Our Future*, 1999, Worldwatch Institute (Washington D.C.).

15 International Federation of Red Cross and Red Crescent Societies (IFRC), "Annual World Disasters Report," 1999.

16 *Daily Telegraph* (London), 26 August 1991.

17 Sixteenth International Botanical Congress, held in St. Louis, Missouri, July 1999.

18 Worldwatch Institute, press release, 4 May 1999, based on Michael Renner, *Ending Violent Conflict*, Worldwatch Institute (Washington D.C.).

19 *Time*, 3 May 1999, pp. 38–39.

20 Reuters, 6 June 2000.

21 1998 annual poll by the publishers of *Who's Who Among American High School Students*, Reuters, 12 December 1998.

22 The eight markers of civilization are taken from David Fromkin, *The Way of the World: From the Dawn of Civilizations to the Eve of the Twenty-first Century* (New York: Alfred A. Knopf, 1999).

गं०सं० स्वरूपंवक्ष्यामिभक्तानांशुभदंपरं यद्रूप
३ ध्यानतःपुंभिराषण्मासेत्रिसंध्यतः २७
प्रत्यक्षरूपणिदेवीदृश्यतेमणिकर्णिका
चतुर्भुजाविशालाक्षीस्फुरद्रुद्रसुरलोचना
१८ पश्चिमाभिमुखीनित्यंप्रबद्धकरसंपु
टा इंदीवरवतींमालोद्धतींदक्षिणकरे १९
वरोद्धृतेकरस्येमातुलिंगफलंशुभं कुमा
ररूपिणीनित्यनिसं द्वादशवार्षिकी शुद्ध
२०

गं०सं० तःसिध्येदपिसिध्यष्टकंरूणां ॐऐंह्रींश्री
४ क्लींमंमणिकर्णिकीयेनमः स्कंदउवाच
ॐनमोगंगादेव्यै ॐकाररूपिण्यजरातु
लानेतामृतस्रवा अल्पदारभयाशीकालंक
नेदामृतामला १ अथैनोवत्सलामोघापांयो
निरमत्प्रदा अव्यक्तलक्षणाक्षीभ्यानवछि
लापशजिता २ अनाथनाथाभीष्टार्थसिद्धि ४
दानेगर्विनी अणिमादिगुणाधारात्रगण्या

CHAPTER 2

WHOLENESS AND THE VEDIC EXPERIENCE

~

Before the last two decades or so of the twentieth century, the chosen path for most stories of civilization began at the gates of Greece and Rome. Then the trail ascended through the Renaissance to the Enlightenment. Finally it arrived home, ending in what used to be known as the grand triumph of the West.

Because Western civilization derives from the Greco-Roman era, we often seemed to think any value in other cultures requires the same root. A French scholar of Vedic philosophy, René Guénon, called this slant "the classical prejudice." Elaborating, he described it as "the predisposition to attribute the origin of all civilization to the Greeks and Romans."[1]

Previously, Westerners would become flustered, even thrown off balance, when happening upon comparable civilizations that are far more ancient. About those bound to Eurocentrism, Guénon opined, "It might be said that they are mentally incapable of crossing the Mediterranean."[2]

The past has seen an undeniable tendency to judge other cultures and civilizations as bare-bones forerunners to our deluxe behemoths. At present, though, people do have some understanding that the words "culture" and "civilization" are tainted with racial and ethnic superiority. They no longer see Western fixations—such as obsessive individualism, technological fanaticism, and economic intoxication—as the height of human progress.

An open-minded study of India's Vedic past will reveal that many of the sacred cows of the modern West need to be seen in a relative light. How refreshing it is to explore a knowledge-culture at least as valid as the West's but so radically different. British historian Arnold Toynbee commented, "India is a whole world in herself: she is a society of the same magnitude as our Western society."[3]

Because of the cosmic and extra-cosmic scope of the Vedas, the knowledge-world of ancient India can appear much more expansive and intricate than anything our times can offer. In the Vedic Indians we are encountering not entry-level versions of the mighty moderns but a people probably far more advanced and efficient in ways we have yet to fathom.

Well-read contemporary humans are quite aware that the ancient and the modern visions see from different perspectives. Unlike fifty years ago, few today will deny that Western knowledge is saddled with its own preconceptions. Many of us, however, are still reluctant to take the next step: relegating Western science to the status of a cultural artifact—a powerful peculiarity born of a specific society.

One the one hand, we can see the paradigm of Western knowledge bewildered and besieged. Still, on the other hand, our molding may move us to protest: "Although technology does bring problems, isn't pure science still the best, most objective expressway to truth and reality?" Lingering in our craw is the myth that what we call science embodies universal knowledge for all times, peoples, and places. "No one before ever knew so much."

Discharging the last residues of this hubris nets a big payoff: the doorway out of the sterile, mechanistic concept of the universe swings wide open. A noted historian of science, Paul Feyerbend, commented, "It is good to be constantly reminded of the fact that science as we know it today is not inescapable and that we may construct a world in which it plays no role whatever (such a world, I venture to suggest, would be more pleasant than the world we live in today)."[4]

Putting our science in its place has become the mission of an international vanguard of scholars, labeled "the Edinburgh school" by opponents. "The Edinburgh school does not see itself as opposing science, or questioning the integrity of scientists. But it contends that scientific knowledge is only a communal belief system with a dubious grip on reality."[5]

Although this revisionary spirit is especially attributed to academics based at the University of Edinburgh, the conspirators there have worldwide allies. For example, Andrew Pickering, a sociologist of science at the University of Illinois, writes in his book *Constructing Quarks*, "There is no obligation upon anyone framing a view of the world to take into account what twentieth-century science has to say."[6] He recommends the option of seeing a scientific theory as "a culturally specific product . . . a communally congenial representation of reality."[7]

Certainly our brand of science has been great for manipulating a particular slice of nature. But humility permits us to admit that our matter-bound, reductionist science will never allow us access to the whole of existence. We lack even a single valid reason to think otherwise. Therefore it is a liberating experience to study an entire culture that thrives upon realities our mainstream culture never sees. The Vedic texts usher us into a universe alive with energies outside the tunnel of our limited attempt at science. The ways of the ancient seers may turn out to be more evocative of the totality of human experience and beyond. The Vedic metaphysic may well make for a better fit.

The knowledge-culture of ancient India takes for granted that life—intelligent life—pervades the universe, though the present sensory capacity of humans may not detect it. Furthermore, the Vedic perspective considers knowledge of repeated lifetimes as quite elementary—indeed almost child's play. Our traditional Western standpoint, however, holds that only this planet is likely to contain life, that this unique occurrence of life is a very recent development in the history of the universe, and that one shot at living is all you get. Naturally, these primary cultural assumptions, though certainly weakening, will render our academic models of investigation quite simplistic when compared to India's Vedic modes of analysis and description.

WHAT ARE THE VEDAS?

The Sanskrit root *vid* means "to know." Hence *veda* means knowledge. The term *Vedic* refers to the literature and teachings of the Vedas. These texts are the largest mass of sacred knowledge from the ancient world, and we shall see that they are its most brilliant literary achievement. In the Vedic literature we will find an exquisite *Weltanschauung*, a majestic world outlook followed for millennia by a highly developed civilization.

A superficial approach to the Vedic literature would be to politely grant the texts status as an intriguing corpus of ancient legends and mystical charms. The West, however, would benefit profoundly by seriously exploring the value of the Vedic texts, in revealing a completely different way of seeing the universe. And—most important for our problems today—the Vedas reveal a completely different way of belonging to the universe.

Enthusiasts of the Vedas say they contain all things a human being needs to know for both spiritual and material well-being. The most traditional Vedic adepts will go farther. They hold that anything known as knowledge, whether past or present, ultimately derives its seed from information in the Vedic texts. Orthodox sages, however, do acknowledge that identifying the Vedic origins of every department of human knowledge requires a rare level of skill in Vedic academics.

A large bookstore will contain renditions of only a minuscule portion of the total Vedic library. You'll easily find the *Bhagavad-gita*—especially popular throughout the world. Most Vedic texts, it must be said, are not commonly read in the West.

For a classic summation of what comprises Vedic literature, we can accept the standard given by the most prominent Vedic guides, both ancient and recent. They tell us that the Vedic texts include the predominantly ritualistic and sacrificial guidebooks: the *Rig-veda, Yajur-veda, Sama-veda,* and *Atharva-veda.* These four Vedas are not collections of hymns and prayers that resemble the invocations recited in more recent religions. The texts contain highly esoteric ritualistic techniques said to have effected changes in nature through the precise vibration of sound. The ancient mystics held that different mantras matched up with different phenomena of the universe. This lost art of sonic manipulation aimed at both material and spiritual goals.

Then there are the Vedic histories: the *Mahabharata* and the *Ramayana.* The *Bhagavad-gita* is a chapter in the *Mahabharata.* Vedic literature also includes the metaphysical textbooks: the Upanishads and *Vedanta-sutra.* The cosmological treatises, the Puranas, complete the Vedic library.

The Vedic literature touches upon all aspects of human civilization. Though famous as metaphysical tomes of an exalted caliber, actually the Vedas also deal with fulfilling the routine requirements of everyday life. Fascinating information, in seed form, is given in subjects such as statecraft, military science, astronomy, mathematics, astrology, music, drama, architecture, and subtle—psychic—forms of technology. Of course, the section of the Vedas delineating medical knowledge, the *Ayur-veda,* is currently in the spotlight, as alternative healing disciplines surge into mainstream Western society.

The departments of Vedic material knowledge, we should note, are not strictly secular, in the modern sense. That is to say there is no firewall between mundane "how-to" information and spirituality. Embedded within every area of material instruction are specific directives for spiritual attainment. Consequently, even the most humdrum aspects of human life are construed as instruments for spiritual awakening.

An uncanny confidence permeates the Vedic texts, that the highest reality can be approached via any subject matter. Since everything has emanated from the supreme reality, all subjects of study are considered within the purview of Transcendence. At their full peak of development, all subjects are seen as converging into knowledge of the ultimate, the origin. Consequently, the Vedas mix and match subjects at will. We discover that the reason is not haphazardness, but a profound understanding of both the ultimate ground of reality and the multifarious facets of existence.

The Vedic texts undoubtedly are rich nourishment for the dedicated transcendentalist—the avid explorer yearning for the zenith of spiritual knowledge and experience. Nevertheless, while accelerating the progress of these adepts, the Vedas also clearly recognize that most human beings need a gradual course for rising to the spiritual plane. Therefore the reader will observe that, alongside exhortations to achieve paradisal realms, the literature also emphasizes the best methodologies for living in this world—so that we may then peacefully contemplate the next.

The Vedas equip the pilgrim through the cosmos with an authoritative guide for the trek. Not only does the literature set out markers for the stages of spiritual advancement, but it also, and more importantly, presents the whole of life in a frame enabling every aspect of human experience to become spiritually fruitful. Some Western writers have said that the Vedas reinterpret the world so that it becomes a vehicle for the spiritual path. Reinterpretation, however, is in the eyes of the beholder. The Vedic viewpoint is that the texts present the world as it is, in the clarity of its actual purpose.

The ultimate goal of the Vedas clearly is what we call enlightenment, self-realization. But the Vedas acknowledge that for most of us the path to the supreme truth is a long, winding road. Thus the Vedic transcendental trail is designed to accommodate persons of varying levels of commitment and motivation.

Stored within the Vedas are supermundane accounts of personal existence beyond the clutches of matter, as well as humane advice for living in the familiar confines of time and space. Therefore, while the Vedic literature certainly can be challenging, demanding, and mind-bending, it also can be comforting and familiar. We can profit by understanding that the Vedas are not a doctrine or theology, but a breathing experiential context.

Setting the cosmic wanderer on the right course, the Vedas inform us of the infinite totality containing the spot known as our individual life. Once the living entity is on track, the Vedas supply all necessary knowledge and strength to quickly or gradually achieve life's precious goal: freedom from material illusion, association with pure souls, and finally transcendental love with the Supreme Soul. The path and patterns are well established, but the rate of progress is open to individual expression.

For the layperson, the Vedas first teach how to perform ordinary labor in a methodical way that produces future material benefits. The modern penchant seems to be the opposite: work hard to enjoy now in a way that brings suffering later. As the life of a participant in the Vedic system of work becomes more sober and deliberative, the person is then ready for metaphysical analysis. Through this philosophical discipline, comprehension of what is matter and what is spirit thickens. Then gradually the life style of a full-fledged transcendentalist in devotion becomes attractive.

Finally, the mature pilgrim, on the road to spiritual perfection, learns to focus every aspect of his existence directly on the *summum bonum*, the Ultimate Source.

COPING WITH THE IMMENSITY

For some Western minds, the vast scope of Vedic literature may seem a formidable conceptual barrier. How do these antiquated texts cover so much territory? From the Vedic viewpoint, nature, and the universe as a whole, is a grand hierarchy of living beings—nonhuman, human, and humanoid. Even interplanetary and intergalactic panoramas seem but routine vistas in the Vedic library. Most thrilling are the detailed descriptions of nonmaterial worlds beyond the entire fabric of time and space.

As for everyday human life on earth, the Vedas prescribe a balance between spiritual necessities and bodily requirements. The average human being is guided to satisfy both sides of the scale. For the layperson, overemphasis on one side or the other is said to produce havoc, both individually and collectively. Consequently, the Vedic social system combines material impetus with spiritual dynamics. Judging by the thousands of verses dedicated to explaining how a proper society functions, the Vedic texts obviously place great emphasis on civilization as a precise tool for both material and spiritual upliftment.

Immense scope is not the only asset that sets the Vedas apart. In size the Vedic tomes appear monumental. Quantitatively, the Bible and Koran do not compare, and the Vedas easily dwarf lengthy ancient works such as Homer's epics and the sacred canon of China. The Vedic historical text *Mahabharata* has 110,000 four-line stanzas. That makes it the world's longest poem—approximately eight times as long as the *Iliad* and *Odyssey* combined. The other Vedic history, the *Ramayana,* consists of 24,000 couplets. The cosmological treatises—the eighteen chief Puranas—contain over 400,000 verses. For example, the *Bhagavata Purana* alone (also known as the *Shrimad-Bhagavatam*) has 18,000.[8] The *Rig-veda, Sama-veda, Yajur-veda,* and *Atharva-veda* contain 20,000 hymns. There are 108 main books of Upanishads, philosophical expositions.

The Vedic texts say they derive from an oral tradition, a heritage of profound knowledge handed down for millennia. The books describe that before they were committed to writing, generation after generation of spiritual intellectuals memorized the verses and passed them on intact. The Vedas are not unique in this oral transmission. Originally other ancient information, such as the *Iliad,* the *Odyssey,* and the Germanic sagas, also were never written down, but were passed on from mouth to ear. The qualifications to be a link in the Vedic chain of knowledge, however, are indeed special.

Because *Veda* seemingly refers to any knowledge from India that fosters transcendence, Westerners can have difficulty getting a grip on the term. First, there seems to be an absence of rigid barriers as to what the terms *Veda* and *Vedas* refer to. Several conceptions abound. A technicality has circulated in the West that the designations *Vedic* and *Vedas* only apply to four texts: the *Rig-veda, Yajur-veda, Sama-veda,* and *Atharva-veda.* The *Rig-veda* is occasionally singled out as being in a class of its own. Still others advocate all the above, plus the Upanishads.

This book takes the stance endorsed by the four main schools of spiritual knowledge in India. They accept all the aforementioned texts, with the important inclusion of the Puranas and Itihasas—the Vedic commentaries on historical events. These four main schools authenticate their inclusion of the Puranas and Itihasas with specific citations from the four Vedas and the Upanishads.[9] When classifying the Vedic literature, the main schools in India make only the distinction between what is known as *shruti* and *smriti.* The term *shruti,* "that which is heard," refers to the timeless truth heard by pure Vedic sages. *Smriti*, "that which is remembered," refers to the sages' accumulated elucidations on what they have heard from the *shruti*. Hence, texts such as the *Rig, Yajur, Sama, Atharva,* and Upanishads are known as *shruti*. Histories and commentaries such as the *Mahabharata, Ramayana,* and the Puranas are known as *smriti*. Because Buddhism and Jainism do not accept the authority of *shruti* and *smriti*, their followers are always judged as outside the Vedic purview.

Westerners seem to have a penchant for dissecting and chopping when attempting to grasp something vast. Even scholars often experience difficulty in comprehending a single, united Vedic culture and textual tradition. Furthermore, outsiders may overlook how the authority of the Vedas correlates with the authority of Vedic tradition. To explore the spiritual life of India—both ancient and modern—we need to see how the Vedas and the Vedic patriarchs work together. The two have always been intertwined.

In the sacred knowledge of India, words spoken by the Divine and words spoken about the Divine have an intriguing relationship. It's a two-way street: the pure sages affirm the Divine, and the Divine affirms the pure sages. This unique mutual stimulation makes the Vedic texts and tradition alive with spiritual excitement. The *shruti*—the original sound heard—is compared to our mother. *Smriti* is compared to our sister. The analogy is based on traditional family life: a young child learns from the mother, and then the child reinforces that knowledge by learning it again from the older sister.

Away from the lecture halls of academia and within the Vedic tradition itself, not much fuss is made of the distinction between *shruti* and *smriti*, the two branches of the same tree of knowledge. Among adherents and practitioners, all definitions of *Veda* or *the Vedas* include both elements, *shruti* and *smriti*. Both are seen in a symbiotic relationship of continuing revelation—the living Vedic experience.

A masterly Vedic sage can demonstrate how all the seemingly diverse Vedic elements unite. The individual texts form a remarkably coherent whole, which has maintained its internal integrity over the millennia. This textual harmony is the verdict of the prime Vedic teachers throughout India's history. It would seem that for us to pursue our interest in experiencing an actual palpable taste of the living Vedic tradition, the most appropriate way is to accept the version of the patriarchs who guide India's Vedic culture.

THE VEDAS AND WESTERN SCHOLARSHIP

For the past two hundred years there has been a definite gulf between traditional scholarly approaches to the Vedic literature and the Vedic literature's description of itself. Obviously, Western academics will rely upon a firm stance of what is known as critical scholarship. By their own admission they are steeped in an approach to knowledge known as rational-empiricism. Naturally, therefore, they are inclined to dismiss the Vedic literature's own delineation of its origin, purpose, and scope. More venturesome readers will have to decide for themselves why the Vedic literature's description of itself is necessarily deemed unacceptable. Most scholars operating from a reductionist, empirically bound paradigm rarely discuss the conflict.

Consider the inviolable maxims of the Western monopoly on knowledge, stated baldly:

- The world is ours for the knowing—and especially the taking.
- The only authentic method for increasing our grasp of nature and the universe is through probing measurable aspects of the physical world—the sole tool is instrumentation that assists our physical senses and rational powers.
- There will be no lasting mysteries—in time, our powers of

empirical investigation and logical analysis will solve all riddles of the cosmos.

- Western rational-empiricism is actually universal—all other cultures must recognize this and submit.
- The whole world can experience progress—if all peoples would apply our science, technology, and rationality.[10]

Contrary to stereotyped opinion, approaching the Vedic texts "the Vedic way" does not imply that we discard intelligence and discrimination. Nor does the Vedic approach to itself demand blind faith. What is recommended is a different way of using intelligence. The Vedas present information for the purpose of enlightenment and self-transformation. Consequently, genuine Vedic researchers require a willingness to raise their consciousness and become personally transformed. This flexibility is especially necessary because Vedic knowledge presents much about the universe that our science is in no position to either affirm or deny.

The influential Polish philosopher Henryk Skolimowski has perhaps come closest to elucidating the ideal approach. A Professor Emeritus at the University of Michigan, he challenges that the Western educational system has been rigorously conditioned by what he calls "the Yoga of Objectivity."

To the average Westerner, the term *yoga* means systematically putting the body through an elaborate set of exercises for toning and conditioning. Utilizing this popular conception, Skolimowski asserts that modern education and scholarship impose a stringent set of exercises specific to the mind. Practiced from earliest high school to the completion of the PhD, this long, demanding system of fitness training is designed to whip the intelligence into shape.

Although the term "yoga" may sound strange as applied to the process of imposing the attitude we call "objectivity" on our minds, it is not ill-conceived. . . . The purpose of these exercises is to see nature and reality in a *selective way*. It takes many years of stringent training (just as it does in any other form of Yoga) before the mind *becomes* detached, objective, analytical, clinical, "pure." This frame of mind is seen as essential for dealing with scientific facts and scientific descriptions of reality.[11]

What we took to be universal virtues—so-called objectivity and detached, clinical analysis—upon deeper reflection are seen as hidden cultural operations performed on the brain. Objectivity, though a hope sacred to us, is always bound up with the predominant, though often submerged, fundamental assumptions about the nature of reality. These hidden premises about reality, when shared by an entire culture, shape and color "the pure lens" of objectivity.

In this way, our modern passion for what we call scientific objectivity turns out to be a brilliant method for honing the mind to see the world in a unique way. "The scientific method has molded the mind to be its servant. The scientific view of the world and the objective cast of mind mirror each other. In the scientific world-view the mind has become hostage to a selective vision of reality."[12]

Have you ever wondered why there is no place in that world for the consciousness of the observer? We choose to remove *ourselves*, forcing upon ourselves a severe detachment from what we observe—the greater the distance, the better. Cold clinical analysis—"objectivity"—is the precious experience sought. The ardor is to see things and ourselves as if all exists in isolation.

Leading-edge thinkers are starting to broadcast the problem. Still, twinges of fear linger that if we dare minimize "the Yoga of Objectivity" our intellects will wither away. Skolimowski and his colleagues propose "the Yoga of Participation." This method of acquiring knowledge proceeds from the acceptance of wholeness and interconnection in the universe—and our indelible place in it. We scientifically observe through participation.

In objective research the observer tries as far as possible to separate himself from that which is being observed; by contrast, in participatory research one gains knowledge by identifying with the observed. Rather than objective consciousness, participatory research involves compassionate consciousness. This involves training, but of a very different sort from the training of objective consciousness—a "yoga of participation."[13]

Subjectivity is not taboo in participatory research, especially since Western science has not succeeded in objectifying or quantifying our subjective experience—our consciousness. Participators thoroughly expect that observation will lead to acclimatization, and they are ready to discuss it. Rather than immediately rejecting personal reports of pertinent experience, they try to apprehend them by entering within. Biologist Elisabet Sahtouris alerts us to the creeping presence of participatory approaches even amid mainstream science:

> This concept of partnership between researcher and phenomenon is very interesting and important. My Native American scientist friends say they must integrate with nature to learn from it, but that is a novel idea to most Western scientists. Still, it happens—I think of Barbara McClintock identifying with her corn, Jonas Salk learning to think like a virus, Lynn Margulis discovering the intelligence and consciousness of bacteria.[14]

The biologist Barbara McClintock won a Nobel prize in 1983 for her work. Though certainly no rebel against conventional science, she gives us a personal account that reveals solid inroads by the method of participation. She sought to identify with the object of her research—chromosomes—by observing from within.

> I found the more I worked with them, the bigger and bigger the

chromosomes got, and when I was really working with them I wasn't outside. I was part of the system. . . . it surprised me because I actually felt as if I was right down there and these were my friends. . . . As you look at these things they become a part of you.[15]

The current ruling method for acquiring knowledge has unnecessarily deified the "value-free observer," the unbiased hero who presents nature to us "as it is." The full-blown method of participation, however, does not succumb to this religion. Uncurtailed by the Western fetish for supposed objectivity and exact replication, the participatory method employs other criteria. These alternative standards are especially crucial in our attempts to fathom experiences and perceptions of the cosmos that differ radically from our own. Pioneering intellectuals, seeking to transcend the limitations of the current scientific method, have come up with benchmarks such as "trustworthiness." That means a way to establish reliability through multiple tests—even though the trials are not strictly precise.

Instead of fanatically insisting upon controlled experiments that are rigidly replicable, a naturalistic mode of inquiry would also avail itself of other guidelines. For instance, a suitable procedure for investigating Vedic knowledge would include tests for credibility, dependability, transferability, and confirmability.[16] There must be an effective system of expert judges and vigilant consensual verification. In this way the researcher could gain access to "all the evidence" in the cosmos. That means not just the cold, quantifiable data empiricists adore, but also the "warm data"—the subjective reports of inner exploration generated by erudite spiritual voyagers.

The Vedic texts clearly warn that much of their information and teachings is extraterrestrial, and therefore beyond the range of ordinary sense perception. Yet, at the same time, the Vedas present methodologies for enhancing perception and verifying what lies beyond the ordinary grasp. Empirically immersed scholars, however, seem to make light of epistemological barriers. Understandably, to remain true to their calling, they must assume the Vedas are mythology and then assign themselves the task of analyzing and demythologizing. Perhaps their occupational conscience allows them no alternative.

In the past, institutionalized scholars have correctly assumed that readers will always accept their version, because of the reputation of Western academics, stemming back two or three centuries. After all, who would not have wanted to survey ancient history and culture from what was considered the inherently superior and objective modern vantage point? The times, however, are swiftly changing. Reductionist modalities of thought are losing their glamor; academic biases are standing out more visibly; and, for many open-minded persons, the so-called paranormal is on its way to becoming a normal paradigm.

Notes

1   R. Guénon, *Introduction to the Study of the Hindu Doctrines*, (London: Luzac, 1945), p. 38.

2   Ibid., p. 38.

3   A. Toynbee, *Civilization on Trial and the World and the West* (New York: Meridian Books, 1958), p. 257.

4   Paul Feyerbend, "Consolation for the Specialist," in *Criticism and the Growth of Knowledge*, ed. Imre Lakotos and Alan Musgrave (Cambridge: Cambridge University Press, 1970), p. 228.

5   Kurt Gottfried and Kenneth G. Wilson, "Science as a Cultural Construct," *Nature* 386 (10 April 1997).

6   Andrew Pickering, *Constructing Quarks: A Sociological History of Particle Physics* (Chicago: University of Chicago Press, 1984).

7   Ibid.

8   The total number of verses in the *Bhagavata Purana* can seem to vary according to how the lines of Sanskrit verses are divided.

9   For example, the *Atharva-veda* (11.7.24) states: "The *Rig, Sama, Yajur,* and *Atharva Vedas* manifested from the Supreme Lord along with the Puranas and all the demigods of the heavenly planets."
The *Brihad-aranyaka Upanishad* (2.4.10) states: "Just as a fire kindled with wet fuel sends out clouds of smoke, so the Supreme God has breathed out the *Rig-veda,* the *Yajur-veda, Sama-veda, Atharva-veda,* Itihasa, Puranas, science of knowledge, mystic Upanishads, succinct verses, codes, elaborations, and commentaries. He, indeed, breathes all these out."
Two verses in the *Chandogya Upanishad* (7.1.2,4) both refer to the Puranas and Itihasas as the fifth Veda that accompanies the four Vedas.

10 List based on Henryk Skolimowski, *The Participatory Mind* (London: Penguin Books, 1994), pp. 68–69.

11 Ibid., p. 148.

12 Ibid.

13 Willis W. Harman, *A Re-examination of the Metaphysical Foundations of Modern Science* (California: Institute of Noetic Sciences, 1991), p. 95.

14 Willis W. Harman and Elisabet Sahtouris, *Biology Revisioned* (Berkeley, California: North Atlantic Books, 1998), p. 20.

15 In Evelyn Fox Keller, *Reflections on Gender and Science* (New Haven: Yale University Press, 1985), p. 165.

16 Yvonna S. Lincoln and Egon S. Guba, *Naturalistic Inquiry* (New York: Sage Publications, 1985).

CHAPTER 3

INTO THE UNKNOWN: TRACING THE VEDAS

~

Today's science often becomes tomorrow's fable. Similarly, today's mythology can become tomorrow's history. Sometimes ancient texts formerly considered total myth attain the status of fact. For example, before archaeological discoveries in the Middle East, strict scholarship would sometimes dismiss biblical accounts as mere legend. Excavations, however, corroborated some of the people, places, and events of the Bible.

For example, though scholars disagree whether the story of Exodus ever happened, they do agree that the Book of Exodus names the city of Ramses as a site where the Israelites slaved. In the 1970s excavations located Ramses near the city of Qantir. Moreover, ancient records from Egypt do tell of slaves fleeing into the Sinai Desert on an escape route similar to the one described in Exodus. Naturally the public is keenly interested. German writer Werner Keller described favorable findings in his book *The Bible as History*, which has sold over ten million copies, in twenty-four languages. David Rohl, Britain's most high-profile archaeologist, wrote the best-selling *A Test of Time:*

The Bible From Myth to History. The focus of much academic infighting, Rohl advocates a new chronology for Egypt that allows a fresh look at Biblical history.

Then there is the classic case of Troy, the city mentioned in Homer's *Iliad* and *Odyssey.* In 1829 a seven-year-old German boy gazed at a picture his father had given him of the legendary Troy in flames. Unable to rid his mind of the scene, the wee lad vowed to himself that one day he would actually discover Troy. Forty-four years later Heinrich Schliemann did just that. Though scholars initially snubbed his work, Schliemann—the first "archaeologist for the masses"—directly communicated to the world the exciting progress of his quest. His media were popular books and newspaper dispatches. In 1873 the Troy of Agamemnon, though previously deemed myth, entered the pages of acceptable history. Schliemann fulfilled his childhood ambition by unearthing the city's ruins, proving beyond a doubt that the Homeric epics had historical basis.[1]

Schliemann was the first to test a literary tradition through excavation. Before his success, nothing existed of Greek prehistory except what were thought to be romantic tales. Almost nothing was known about the Aegean Bronze Age. The common assumption was that Greek culture began around 776 B.C., the year of the first Olympiad. The German pioneer pushed that date back by half a millennium.

The ancient Mesopotamian city of Ur had predominantly mythic credentials until the British archaeologist Leonard Woolley, beginning in 1923, excavated the city. His work allowed scholars to fully authenticate the existence of Ur. Tracing its existence from 4000 B.C. to 400 B.C., they derived a thorough picture of everyday life in the city. Personal inscriptions established the real existence of King Sargon I, ruler of Akkad. Formerly thought to be a legend, Sargon I is now known to have reigned in 2400 B.C. Furthermore, Woolley uncovered geological evidence of a great flood, suggesting a potential correlation with the disaster described in Genesis.

A more recent example of myth becoming history emerged in September 1997, with the discovery of a Viking longship. Scholars had already documented smaller Viking boats, but they had always deemed the superboats described in Norse sagas as myth. The supposed length of these boats defied modern credulity. The Viking references to these boats as dragons further certified them as imaginary. Yet, during the dredging of a harbor in Denmark, a sunken longship of the fantasy class came to light—ironically right in front of the world-famous Viking Ship Museum. The immense war boat, 114 feet long, proved the Norse sagas accurate in their chronicling of "great ships," the biggest class in the Viking fleet.

Marine archaeologists scored their biggest triumph in May 2000, when they lifted three Egyptian cities from the pages of mythology to the journals of authorized history. On the Mediterranean seabed, they found the 2,500-year-old remains of Pharaonic cities that for moderns had only existed in Greek tragedies, travelogues, and legends. These ancient texts glorified the importance of the cities Menouthis, Herakleion and Canopus, but no physical evidence could be found.

The famous ancient Greek historian Herodotus visited Egypt in 450 B.C. and wrote about the city Herakleion, with its temple dedicated to Hercules. All three cities are named in Greek tragedies. Mythology tells us a story of Menelaos, the king of Sparta. During his return from Troy with Helena, he stopped in Herakleion. While there his helmsman Canopus was bitten by a viper and then transformed into a god. Thus Canopus and his wife Menouthis were immortalized by two cites named for them. The Greek geographer Strabo presented a geographic location for the cities. He described the opulent life style, while Seneca, the Roman tragedy writer, condemned the cities as decadent.

French underwater explorer Franck Goddio based his mission

upon these ancient hints and then relied upon electronic technology, including magnetic waves, to scan the seabed for possible signs that the cities actually existed. Working for two years under coastal waters twenty to thirty feet deep, Goddio's team found the cities "frozen in time," at the bottom beneath five feet of silt.[2]

The Middle East, Scandinavia, Greece, and Egypt are all areas well within the Western comfort zone. That is, we feel no qualms about sifting for our cultural roots and history there—even amid what we think is just myth. The Middle East gave us our religions. Besides the lands of the Bible, Mesopotamia also figures prominently in Western religious heritage. The region fostered both the Babylonians and Assyrians of Old Testament fame. Ancient Greece gave us our intellect. The Vikings, of course, are homeboys. India, however, is far from our sphere of familiarity—a distant land where everything is completely strange.

Moreover, the old culture of India regards Europe as insignificant. India has its own vision of world history, a unique and highly articulated view of antiquity that has prevailed for thousands of years. The Vedic version of ancient India has had a rough ride in the West, perhaps because Western empathy for the mysterious subcontinent is so difficult to muster. In the modern academies, few have felt the need to search for serious truth in "the Indian myths." Consequently, the history of Vedic India continues to reign as the biggest enigma of myth versus fact.

The marked absence of cultural empathy between India and the West combines with an even greater barrier: ancient India's notorious lack of a historical tradition that the West will accept. History—as moderns like to read it—began with the Greeks. The first efforts of Greek historiography culminated in Thucydides (460–400 B.C.) and Herodotus (490–409 B.C.), known as the fathers of Western history. The Romans followed, initially in the Greek language, later with major authors like Livy (59 B.C.–A.D. 17) writing in their own Latin.

Even early China had an approved historiographical tradition. The post of Shih, the official archivist, existed as far back as anyone knows about Chinese history. The Shih kept detailed daily records of events. The currently recognized father of Chinese historiography, Ssu-ma Ch'ien, is said to have composed his Shih-Chi (Historical Records) around 100 B.C. In India, though, apparently no great historian recorded the Vedic period—that is, in terms conforming to our current models of history. It was not until the first millennium A.D. that South Asia came up with a historiography that scholars accept.

HISTORY AND THE VEDAS

Exasperation with India's lack of an ancient history deemed suitable goes a long way back. The first recorded complaint dates in the eleventh century A.D., when the Arab savant of India, Alberuni, criticized: "Hindus do not pay much attention to the historical order of things, they are very careless in relating the chronological succession of their kings, and when they are pressed for information and are at a loss, not knowing what to say, they invariably take to tale-telling."[3]

In the nineteenth century, after an early period of fascination with Indian antiquity, Euro-American scholars took up the same chant, which began loudly in their time and quietly continues today. For example, the major Sanskritist Arthur A. Macdonell rendered this typical judgment: "History is the one weak spot in Indian literature. It is, in fact, nonexistent. The total lack of historical sense is so characteristic that the whole course of Sanskrit literature is darkened by the shadow of this defect, suffering as it does from an entire absence of exact chronology."[4]

Closer to our day, the scholar D. D. Kosambi declared: "India has no historical records worth the name."[5] The current dean of Western archaeologists studying India, F. R. Allchin, considers

Kosambi his teacher and the inspirer of the present generation of scholars attempting to reconstruct India's early history.[6] Kosambi directed:

> In India there is only vague popular tradition, with very little documentation above the level of myth and legend. . . . there is no Indian history worth reading. Any work where the casual reader may find such detailed personal or episodic history for ancient history should be enjoyed as romantic fiction (like some Indian railway timetables!), but not believed.[7]

Staring down at what appears to be the ahistorical, irrational, and mythic world of the Vedas, the latest wave of Indic scholars in the West have adapted to the nationalistic sensitivities of a former colony. Rather than directly reproaching the ancient Indian version of history, they quietly shake their heads in disbelief. Sometimes modern Indian scholars, embarrassed, seek to eloquently absolve the Vedic Indians for their failure to produce a historical work that Western academia will recognize: "Historical facts seem to dissolve in the hands of ancient Indians, changing into epic poetry, sagas, mythology, and legends. Time was unreal and of secondary importance."[8]

The ancient Egyptians, Sumerians, Babylonians, and Assyrians all left tablets that give a glimpse into aspects of everyday life. For ancient China, the scholar can peruse inscriptions on oracle bones, graves, and royal annals. Also available is the work of a few early recorders, especially that of Ssu-ma Ch'ien. All together these sources are said to give a modest idea of early China back to 1400 B.C. While Greek and Roman historical sources do not reach so far into the past, their quality is considered far superior.

On the other hand, the original Vedic civilization of India has left behind scant records that can whet the Western historical appetite. Nothing of Vedic India seems to conform to Western empirical standards. The earliest specimens of accepted historical writing in South Asia do not appear until A.D. 4, in the form of chronicles written by Sri Lankan Buddhist monks. Why did the ancient Indians apparently pay no attention to chronology?

Immediately we can rush to judgment and assume that the Vedic Indians' seeming disinterest in history—as we know it—owes to a primitive inadequacy. Most likely they just could not keep records, we could surmise. More dexterous scholars have started to grasp the unconventional truth: the Vedic Indians considered precise philosophical insights more important than chronological order and the routines of daily existence. Also, the ancient Indians accepted the planetary and cosmic accounts in Vedic knowledge as sufficient satisfaction for their own type of historical appetite.

All history, no matter how conceived, is selection. Histories are compendiums of selected events and perceptions. Rather than accuse the ancient Indians of having no grasp of "the true historical science," we could choose to recognize that they kept records of what they felt was significant, according to a method they found appropriate for their purposes.

Additionally, as we shall discuss more fully in chapter 10, if a people's conception of time is cyclic rather than linear, they may well accept the implications of "what goes around, comes around" in a very full and fascinating sense. In other words, there is indeed nothing new under the sun. Birth is going on, death is going on, then the cycle repeats. Hence, why pay so much attention to the sequence of mundane events on the revolving wheel of existence? After moving through different phases, soon things will be back to the way they started—according to where you were on the wheel when you first took note of them. Better to concentrate on exemplary personal traits and life-styles, especially those that directly foster freedom from the wheel of time.

From the conventional viewpoint, it is true that we would be hard pressed to find a more ahistorical people than the ancient Indians. Yet, we may do well to ask, What is the convention responsible for our viewpoint? The lauded archaeological team of C. C. Lamberg-Karlovsky and J. A. Sabloff taught an introduction to archaeology at Harvard University. In their standard text, *Ancient Civilizations*, before describing the peoples of antiquity, they considered it necessary first to equip the reader with a "history of history." Even the educated are often surprised to learn that history is a many-splendored relative thing. What history is and how history should be composed are issues that undergo great change over the centuries.

> In dealing with texts from the remote past, the modern reader meets with conceptual barriers which become a constant source of misunderstanding and misinterpretation. Just as the physical plan, the social structure, the economic foundations—and almost every other aspect of a civilization—have varied from one culture to another over time, so has the way people think.
>
> This is especially true of perceptions of history. The historical consciousness as we know it is a recent development. Only in the past few hundred years have the study and placement of historical processes in their "proper" sequence and perspective been a concern of history and science. Even now our understanding of the historical process continues to change from one generation to the next.[9]

In the Greeks, the West finds its first historical security. Unlike our understanding of the ancient Asians, the Greeks directly sought to establish historiography—the tactics and theories that should govern historical writing. They wanted to erect an intellectual framework for studying the past. Curiously, the Greek pursuit of history also echoed major themes of ancient India. The majority of the classical historians embraced the cyclical nature of life. Patterns of events repeat themselves; therefore history repeats itself. Also, like the Vedic Indians, the Greeks cherished inquiry into origins.

The ascendancy of Christianity brought the first major shift to historiography as handed down by the Greeks. Rejecting the cyclic understanding of existence, Augustine (A.D. 343–430) saw history as moving in a linear path, purposely from point A to point B. Furthermore, each succeeding civilization was an improvement over its predecessors. Augustine's notions have now influenced the West for more than fifteen hundred years. Even the atheistic Marx took shelter in history as a straight line with purpose—a workers' paradise, not Christian redemption.

The Italian Vico of Naples (1668–1744) began the era of modern historiography. He believed in the necessity of laws to govern history just as laws govern in science. In the nineteenth century, major thinkers such as Comte, Hegel, and Marx put forward their own visions of history, and in the twentieth century Spengler, Kroeber, and Toynbee predominated.

Interestingly, though a key modern-day historical thinker, Oswald Spengler seems to have shared the same perceived problem as the ancient Indians. He did not organize his presentations of historical data according to "proper historical sequence." Spengler saw in each civilization a defining gestalt—an overall form and style that characterized the culture. The historian's job was to divine that gestalt and depict it.

Moreover, Spengler refused to grant Western culture a superior position over other cultures. His most famous work, *The Decline of the West*, presents an inevitable disintegration of civilization as Westerners know it. He considered that each civilization "passes through the age phases of the individual man. It has a childhood, youth, and old age."[10] We can note that once again, even in modern times, the ancient outlook of history moving in cycles still demonstrates its attractiveness.

The Dating Game

Chalking out a timeline for the chronology of spiritual knowledge in India is a renowned dilemma. Archaeology has sought to shed some light on the history of the texts. Finds of pottery, coins, and especially inscriptions are combined with textual evidence—the hints contained within the texts themselves. Gallant efforts aside, dating the first recording of the knowledge in the texts is a major headache. None of the texts give the year they were written. Sometimes if one text is quoted by another text, then academics venture to say that the quoting text must be later. Apart from educated hunches, though, scholars know precise dating is not feasible.

The appearance of Buddha has been grasped upon as a lifeline for establishing a chronology of India's spiritual literature. Buddha's days are the first in Indian history that are somewhat lit. Moreover, the cities of his time are the first urbanism, so far, that can be traced by history. Recently, some scholars have revised the dating of Buddha from 566 to 486 B.C.[11] The other major beacon for dating India is the invasion by Alexander the Great in 326 B.C. The lives of both Buddha and Alexander the Great, however, are both very late markers in a vast unknown expanse.

In the first century A.D, Indian Buddhist itinerants went to China as missionaries. Chinese pilgrims, in turn, visited Buddhist sacred places in India. The Chinese gave dates for when the Indian Buddhist texts were translated into their language. Scholars deem these dates reliable. Preceding these, however, are secure dates from the time of Emperor Ashoka in the third century B.C. The famous stone inscriptions of that time mention some of the early Buddhist canons.

Events and texts in relation to Buddha have been helpful for solidifying the history of Buddhism—a comparatively recent phenomenon. But these Buddhist aids provide scant help for probing the depths of Vedic antiquity.

India's lack of an acceptable historiography that critical scholars will accept has rendered the dating of Sanskrit texts problematic. It is academically acceptable today to assert that the Vedic era began two thousand or so years before Christ. The internal perspective of the Vedas, however, would consider this officially allotted timespan a mere pittance. Nevertheless, some scholars seem to have felt that this short span is an uncomfortably vast expanse of time. Therefore they have theorized classifications of the Vedic civilization into arbitrary periods, and they have coined names that have stuck.

These periods are based on a theoretical historical order in which some believe certain books of the Vedas appeared. The supposition is understandable, founded as it is upon the linear assumption that, during the progression of hundreds and thousands of years, new forms of Vedic philosophy must have evolved. This view is especially popular with those who see the Vedic literature as a potpourri of accumulated diversities, with no singular origin or comprehensive master plan.

Owing to this conjecture, theoretical appellations for broad divisions of Indian history have assumed the garb of fact. The unsuspecting reader will find that catchy tags such as "Chandra, Mantra, Brahmana, and Sutra," or "Vedic, Epic, Sutra, and Scholastic," have become common fare in books introducing the ancient history, religion, and philosophy of India. Yet there is little evidence available for reconstructing approximate periods during the expanse of Indic antiquity. These attempts at classification are educated visualization at its best—the paucity of ordinary historical evidence allows for little more. It should be noted, however, that the Vedas do contain lists of dynasties and rulers, but the information does not always confirm current formulations of India's distant past.

Modern Indologists like to date the origins of the Vedic knowledge to anywhere from 4000 B.C. to A.D. 900, according to the particular branch of the Vedas under analysis and the particular scholar attempting to fix a date. Western scholars will generally hug the latest dates; many Indian scholars, as well as a few daring Western pundits, reach for the earliest dates. Indologists do agree, however, that the Vedic literatures incorporate material much older than the guesses at when they were first written down.

The first scholar to take a real stab at dating the Vedas was the most dominant figure in nineteenth-century Sanskrit studies. Friedrich Maximilian Müller, known to the English world as Max Müller, is certainly the godfather of Indology. His legacy still looms today, though contemporary scholars, when pressed, mildly distance themselves. Müller was recruited by the British colonial regime in India. The chairman of the Education Board arranged that Müller would receive funds from the British East India Company to translate the Vedic texts in a way that would destroy the Indians' reverence for them. The money was never paid in full, but with paltry help from the British government, the German Müller, basing himself in England, would go on to produce an amazing output: fifty-one volumes of his monumental series *Sacred Books of the East*.

A stern fundamentalist Protestant, Müller left written tracks of his scholastic motives. He took no pains to hide his agenda— much more evangelical than colonial. In 1868, writing to the Duke of Argyll, then Secretary of State for India, Müller proclaimed, "The ancient religion of India is doomed, and if Christianity does not step in, whose fault will it be?"[12] While publishing his many translations of Vedic texts, still in use today, Müller explained his mission in an 1896 letter to his wife:

> I hope I shall finish the work, and I feel convinced, though I shall
> not live to see it, yet the edition of mine and the translation of the
> Veda will hereafter tell to a great extent on the fate of India. . . . It
> is the root of their religion, and to show them what the root is,

I feel sure, is the only way of uprooting all that has sprung from it during the last three thousand years.[13]

As the most influential Sanskritist of his century, Müller was the first heavyweight to venture into Vedic chronology. He decided to assign the *Rig-veda* to 1200 B.C., and then he hypothesized periods for each branch of the Vedic texts. Because of Müller's towering presence in the field, even some of today's scholarship, and certainly most popular books on India, are encumbered by his shot in the dark.

We need to know about Müller and his motives because everywhere you'll find books positing that the Vedic texts sprang up around 1200 B.C. or so. Many present-day Indologists admire Müller's calculation as reasonable and even shrewd. For example, a contemporary reputable scholar affirms, "Max Müller's chronological estimate, though not devoid of weak points, has [despite his own reservations] . . . often been more or less tacitly regarded as nearest to the mark."[14]

A much-touted introductory university textbook, published in 1996, courteously pushes aside attempts to date the Vedas earlier. It maintains, "The more sober chronology proposed by Max Müller suggests a date of 1500 to 1200 B.C."[15] However, what we almost never hear is that Müller himself later disowned his own guesswork. Near the end of his life, he candidly confessed in print, "Whether the Vedic hymns were composed 1000, 1500, or 2000 or 3000 B.C., no power on earth will ever determine."[16]

In the first quarter of the twentieth century, the German scholar Moriz Winternitz, who for several decades held the Chair of Indology at the University of Prague, dismayed at the reality still attributed to Müller's foundational speculation. Winternitz, one of the most prominent scholars of his time and discipline, observed, "It is remarkable, however, how strong the power of suggestion is even in science. Max Müller's hypothetical and purely arbitrary determination of the Vedic epochs, in the course of the years, received more and more the dignity and the character of a scientifically proven fact, without any new arguments or actual proof having been added."[17]

Reminding academia of the clouds surrounding Müller's guesstimate, he explained that any attempt to reconstruct the Vedic period and its literature through empirical methodology is unscientific. Winternitz—in this instance the most honest of the modern moguls of Indology—elaborated upon his assessment: "[The Vedic period's] actual history is still to a great extent wrapped in darkness and unexplored. Above all, the chronology of the history of Indian literature is shrouded in truly terrifying darkness, and most of the riddles still remain to be solved by research."[18]

Furthermore, Winternitz pointed out that, especially when writing handbooks for nonspecialists, it would be so gratifying and convenient to divide the Vedic literature into three or four periods and assign dates. "But every attempt of such kind is bound to fail in the present state of knowledge, and the use of hypothetical dates would only be a delusion, which would do more harm than good." He cited a popular maxim, circulating among the specialists of his time, stated by the American Sanskritist W. D. Whitney: "All dates in Indian literary history are pins set up to be bowled down again." Winternitz concluded, "For the most part this is still the case."[19] Whitney's primer on Sanskrit grammar, first published in 1879, is still in use today. And Winternitz, though regarded as outmoded in some respects, is still relied upon by current scholars. After all is said and done, the verdict of Whitney and the conclusion of Winternitz still prevail today as the safest course—though certainly not the course always taken.[20]

In the inner rooms of Indology, scholars may admit they have no real idea when Vedic texts originated. But the public wants to hear dates—life must go on. D. K. Chakrabarti, of Cambridge

University, warns, "The simple truth is that after more than two centuries of modern textual research we have nothing more than general—and very contested—chronological limits for most of our early texts."[21]

LINGUISTIC ANALYSIS

More than a few of us know that India predates civilization in Europe by thousands of years. Less than a few know that India is also the oldest continuous civilization in the world. No traces of Pharaonic Egypt will we find in modern Egyptian life. Sumer has long disappeared, and the Maya—forcibly converted to Christianity five centuries ago—have little connection with their ancient roots. The first Europeans to enter India found that the culture possessed a full sense of its own antiquity—a sense of origin extending farther back in time than what most mainstream scholars are presently willing to concede. That same continuity of cultural identity still thrives today.

During the two or three hundred years before the first successful archaeological excavations, the Sanskrit language itself was the only substantial relic available for the scrutiny of curious Europeans. Hence, the linguists and their interpretations set the context for understanding India's past—an inheritance of conjecture that grips Indology even today.

Sanskrit, the language of the Vedic texts, first became known to Europeans early in the seventeenth century. The first serious study of Sanskrit began after the British had subjugated all of India, late in the eighteenth century. Pressed by the enormity of ruling India, the British strove to acquaint themselves with Indian history, law, and literature. Just who were these Indians? The British had to figure out the Indian niche in the scheme of civilization—as Europeans knew it.

A few of the scholarly inclined colonizers tried their hand at translating Vedic texts. Amid this minor intellectual flurry, a colonial judge, Sir William Jones, entered the pages of academic history. A brilliant Oxford linguist, Jones had learned twenty-eight languages by the end of his short life—mostly by teaching himself. Financial problems, though, had forced him to study law. In 1783, duly knighted, he arrived in Calcutta as judge of the Supreme Court. After four months of studying Sanskrit, in 1786 he announced to the newly formed Asiatic Society of Bengal his famous discovery that Sanskrit was related to Latin and Greek, as well as Persian, Celtic, and Gothic:

> The Sanskrit language, whatever its antiquity, is more perfect than the Greek, more copious than the Latin and more exquisitely refined than either; yet bringing to both of them a stronger affinity than could have been produced by accident; so strong that no philosopher could examine all three without believing them to have sprung from some common source, which perhaps no longer exists.[22]

Jones was the first to put forward a full theory that the similarities were no coincidence, that the languages shared ancestry. Initially his observation was just another academic diversion for classical scholars, who delighted in a new linguistic and philological tool, "the common source." In 1816 an Englishman, Thomas Young, dubbed the proposed linguistic family "Indo-European," and later, in 1833, German scholar Franz Bopp pushed it. At the time, the European nations seemed to be locked into an identity crisis. Each nation searched intensely for superiority over the other. For completing the Indo-European linguistic hypothesis, it was found convenient to materialize a people who spoke that conjectured tongue. Hence the mystical advent of the Indo-European race, whom we read about to this day.

The nineteenth-century intellectuals were bandying about

new concepts of competition between races. Fascinated by the spread of European colonies all over the globe, they assumed that the expansive European cultures were the zenith of the human species. If indeed linguists were indicating a unique primal language spoken by a single tribe that fathered the modern Europeans, then that tribe had to be the "purest Europeans." Who (in Europe) was it? Most importantly, where was the prestigious homeland of that distinguished original race, with its primeval language and culture?

The Indo-Europeans were envisioned to have migrated— around 1500–1200 B.C.—from Europe or its immediate vicinity, through the mountain passes of Afghanistan into northwestern India. Sweeping down onto the Indian plains with horse-drawn chariots and superior iron weapons, these light-skinned nomads were pictured to have overrun the dark-skinned inhabitants and then organized their communities. It was figured that upon the arrival of these migrants or invaders—often referred to as Aryans—civilization in India swiftly followed.

A bullish academic growth industry sprang up around the quest for the Indo-European homeland. The Indo-Europeans, or Aryans, it was conceived, brought Sanskrit with them to northern India and, after conquering the lowly inhabitants, imposed Sanskrit and Vedic ways upon them. Since its beginnings in the early nineteenth century, the Indo-European ploy became much more convoluted and complex. Some early scholars of Indic studies had looked to India as the original home, because it appeared to offer the oldest language.

Later in the nineteenth century, though, as the British Raj set in, scholars like Max Müller generalized the location to "somewhere in Asia." After the first half of that century, any importance of the Indo part of the appellation faded. In 1851 the linguistic scholar Robert Latham put forth the first serious proposal of a European homeland. He really got the ball rolling. Consequently, since that time no one really visualized the Aryans as having any consequence for the world while within India—the primal tribe was too busy on crucial business in its fatherland, Europe.

By the first decades of the twentieth century, when Hitler pronounced the Germans as the true heirs of the original Aryan glory, most scholars knew exactly what he meant. The same hypothetical race was now under an exclusive contract to the Nazis, who had no doubts what exact part of Europe was the *Urheimat*, the original home.

As the sons of the Allies marched off to war, their scholars began to reconsider how an originally academic linguistic speculation—presented in relation to Sanskrit literature—transformed into a creed of European racial superiority. What British Nobel laureate Rudyard Kipling had crowned "the white man's burden" bounced back as bombs raining on London. The Indo-European and Aryan dogma had mutated into the Nazis' private biological weapon.

In a seminal work titled *Aryans and British India*, Thomas Trautmann, a professor of history and anthropology at the University of Michigan, points the finger:

> It is hardly surprising therefore that the use of "Aryan," so popular up to World War II, is now poison for linguists and has given way completely to "Indo-European" . . . The Aryan concept is the central idea of twentieth-century fascism, and the fact that it was developed by scholars raises the question of the role scholars have played in preparing the way for these appropriations.[23]

BAKING THE PIE

Upon discovering the commonality Sanskrit had with Greek and Latin, and its more distant resemblance to modern tongues of

Europe, linguistic scholars in the nineteenth century were able to sketch out surprising groupings of languages and peoples. Six years before Darwin's *The Origin of Species* appeared, a German linguist, August Schleicher, published his family-tree diagram of Indo-European languages. Utilizing the concept of a genealogical chart to show the relationships among Indo-European (IE) languages, Schleicher depicted the trunk of an original language, with other languages branching from it. The branch languages further divided into subbranches.

The tree diagram purported a geographical reality: branch and subbranch languages spread out across Eurasia and gradually mutated. The common root of the whole tree is a hallowed mystery. This origin is called PIE, an abbreviation for Proto-Indo-European. It is a scholarly hunch for which there is no direct evidence. PIE was baked by inference—very learned supposition though. The undeniably common features of the tree's branches seem to call forth an ancestral language, hidden at the root. The consensus of scholars who support PIE feel overwhelmed by the surety that PIE had to have existed somewhere, at some time. There is no other way, they say, to explain the many similarities among the various IE languages.

Language groups of the world do fall outside the *Stammbaum*, the family-tree model. For example, Semitic languages such as Hebrew and Arabic do not grow on it. The common response from the historical linguistic school is to say these outsiders must have a historical relationship to IE at a deeper level—at a now unknown substratum deeper than the PIE root of the IE tree. Ultimately the fervent goal of the historical linguistic project reaches far beyond the IE idea. The hope is to merge all the languages of the world into one grand family tree.

Forthright linguistic specialists, however, have their deep reservations about the tree, even as it is grown and carefully pruned today. Although a monument to more than a century of brilliant development, it ails from many shortcomings. These deficiencies are technical details for nonspecialists but major drawbacks for candid experts.[24]

The generally educated person should at least grasp that the now firmly established tree conveniently projects from the present into antiquity. First, it assumes a particular conception of how language originates and spreads. Then, in fact, it bakes a conjecture—out from the oven comes a proto-language, PIE. Then what was conceived of as merely an analytical, hypothetical tool becomes an actual tongue—spoken by real people, living in real communities at a special unknown locale.

Skeptical scholars point out that the noble calling of historical linguistics unfortunately becomes ahistorical. It flounders when eager linguists apply it to a remote past for which we lack historical documentation. No highly educated person will fail to appreciate the discipline's prodigious research of speech and word patterns in the past and present. Yet, without historical backing, the PIE unfortunately is in the sky. The Indo-Europeanist O. Szemerenyi wryly noted the following: "Indo-European was discovered exactly 150 years ago by a young German scholar, Franz Bopp, not, as one may have expected, in some unknown part of the world, but in his study."[25]

Though almost every linguistic scholar certainly respects the sheer explanatory power and scope of the IE hypothesis, even its dedicated advocates squirm uncomfortably at the necessary search for its required proto-people. Indeed, the missing IE proto-people have plagued scholars for at least 150 years. A current pillar in the field, J. P. Mallory, states:

> We call the people who spoke this ancestral language the Indo-Europeans or Proto-Indo-Europeans. But although we can give them a name, they are unlike almost any other ancient people we are likely to encounter. As the linguistic ancestors of nearly half

this planet's population, they are one of the most important enti-ties in the prehistoric record—and yet they are also one of the most elusive. No Proto-Indo-European text exists; their physical remains and material culture cannot be identified without exten-sive argument; and their geographical location has been the sub-ject of a century and a half of intense yet inconclusive debate.[26]

This quest for the origins of the Indo-Europeans has all the fascination of an electric light in the open air on a summer night: it tends to attract every species of scholar or would-be savant who can take pen to hand. It also shows a remarkable ability to mes-merize even scholars of outstanding ability to wander far beyond the realm of reasonable speculation to provide yet another ex-ample of academic lunacy. . . . One does not ask "where is the Indo-European homeland?" but rather "where do they put it now?"[27]

Valiantly projecting into the past is apparently part of the sci-entific halo that comparative linguistic analysis has attained. The presumption that the varieties of linguistic processes present now must have also existed in the past has acquired the aura of hard science. Erudite yet more restrained linguistic scholars remind their colleagues of the elusiveness of human reality: the probabil-ity generated by statistical models does not always coincide with history. In other words, "the improbable" usually happens some-where. The Indo-European researcher Raimo Anttila has ac-knowledged: "History can play tricks on us."[28]

Few academics deny that the unearthing—or perhaps desktop reconstruction—of a proto-language is made necessary by the family-tree model. Nevertheless, the big question is that, although tentative attempts to reconstruct the long-sought PIE are almost obligatory, why should these theorizations, gropings, be exalted to the status of actual tongues spoken in remote antiquity? Reality may have been quite different.

Summing up the PIE, for almost two centuries the academic world has seen brilliant Indo-European linguistic analysis. The tools of the trade fashion linguistic reconstructions. Those reconstructions in turn grow branches and subbranches on the family-tree model. But what the general nonspecialist public is never told is that the tree has severe limitations. Moreover, beyond a certain point in time, linguistic reconstruction loses its luster. Though academia is supposed to be empirical, its linguistic experts have catapulted far into the remote past, far free of empirical verification. Hence, although doubtlessly a compelling and intellectually tasty calculation, the current PIE is ahistoric. The straightforward conclusion is that Proto-Indo-European exists on a pastry shelf far from history—with no sign of coming to the historical table.

INTO INDIA, OUT FROM INDIA, OR BOTH?

The unknown should probably be left unknown, and that would save us much brain energy. But intelligent men and women seem unable to resist the clarion call to build castles in the sky. Therefore, the vacuum of the historical unknown continuously fills with intriguing speculations.

"Aryan Comings and Goings" is now the biggest football game in Indology town. Scholars line up on both sides of the divide: Aryans into India or Aryans out. Western Indologists predominantly defend the "into-India" goal. Some Indian Indologists vehemently defend the "out-from-India" goal. Most Indian scholars, however, just want to shut down the West's dominance of the tourney—or at least establish a level playing field. Then there are neutral observers on the sidelines. They implore that all the gladiators just admit they really do not know what transpired thousands of years ago.[29]

The ball was kicked into play in the nineteenth century by the Western linguistic scholars. By tracing Sanskrit and its related European tongues back to the PIE, their overwhelming judgment concluded that Sanskrit was not native to India, and that the Vedic Indians came from outside. They insisted that an original Indo-European tongue developed into Vedic Sanskrit and then into the classical Sanskrit familiar today. For almost two centuries, these Western linguistic superstars have dominated the match—nay, defined the match.

Now the Indian scholars are hungry for an upset—they want to take possession of the game. After all, most popular books on India written for educated people imply that blue-eyed warriors from near Europe conquered the South Asian region and then mixed with the backward natives to create the Vedic tradition and modern India.

A few of the stars in the Indian lineup share obvious nationalistic motives. Most, however, are just convinced that the "Aryans-in" hypothesis is ill-conceived. They are weary of every known fact about ancient India becoming forced into the straitjacket of a theory that has produced no new insights for a century.

The Western titans shoot back that it is highly probable, if not almost certain, that the Aryans were coming in—even if we do not know when, how or why. Any other view, they feel, has to reek of contemporary South Asian nationalism and politics. Meanwhile, in the awesome Western ranks, significant dissension has appeared, which will be discussed under archaeology.

Any empathic discussion with scholars at every university in India reveals the overwhelming dismissal of the Aryan-immigrant theory. Only a tiny minority supports it. Most of the Indian scholars simply feel that there is no evidence that the Indo-Aryans pushed their way into the subcontinent from outside. Few of them, however, will rush to the opposite pole and declare that the Aryans went out from India, to civilize the rest of the world. Neutral experts find it interesting to note that the arguments of the indigenous-Aryan advocates rest not on imagination but on alternative explanations of the very same evidence the Aryan-in team uses to insist on an external origin of the Aryans.

The data and interpretations of modern comparative linguistics have rigidly defined the quandary: either Sanskrit was imported into India from abroad or it was exported from India to abroad, as an indigenous product. Take your choice, linguistic scholars command. Most scholars in India, however, feel that a profound lack of evidence renders the entire issue inconclusive. They want a reconsideration and reexamination of the immigration theory and its justification.

Moderate Indian academics respectfully maintain their inability to feel comfortable with the Aryans-in theory. Understandably, they wonder why they should uncritically inherit a version of their remote antiquity assembled for them by their former colonial lords. They want to erect a post-colonial era of Indian scholarship, unencumbered by excess baggage from the British Raj.

Western scholars were the founders of the linguistics, philology, and archaeology used to reconstruct India's lost ancient history. Hence, Indian brains feel the need to reclaim their intellectual sovereignty, so to speak. They want the reins for the historical reconstruction of Indian antiquity, and are rushing to reformulate the current paradigm by mastering the same academic methods and tools that gave birth to it.

Attempts by Indian scholars to establish the so-called indigenous-Aryan paradigm set off a mighty uproar in Western arenas. Immediately the Western opponents cry, "Foul play—nationalism." Unfortunately, sometimes even moderate attempts just to question the incumbent Aryan immigration model—not replace it—risk swift chastisement. No doubt, a belligerent streak of nationalism does mar counter-immigration scholarship. But Western Indologists are gradually realizing their mistake in offhandedly dismissing all revisionist efforts as nationalist politics. In looking for politics and its effect on "pure scholarship," judges should not mistakenly focus upon the current tumult raised by a few very vocal Indian researchers who double as ideologues. After all, the whole Aryan notion has been politically tinged from its very inception 150 or so years ago.

Although sometimes the opposing sides of academia can barely talk to each other, several top-ranked scholars in the West are mediating the hot war between the Aryan-ins and the Aryan-outs. A few patient Western scholars have begun the inevitable process of sifting through the rival positions, pointing out examples of valuable scholarship in both.

Western Indologists bristle at the thought that their Indian counterparts may see them as neo-colonialists. "What do they want from us?" the Western academy often complains. "We're just doing our venerable job—honestly gathering data and objectively interpreting it." Nevertheless, decreasing numbers of Western scholars are willing to deny that what we now call India's ancient history was largely the product of the nineteenth-century climate of European politics and religion.

The British regime had a huge stake in the Aryan notion. By asserting that the ancient Aryans intruded into India from Europe, or nearby, the British arrival could be seen as the modern reenactment of an ancient drama. Instead of colonialism, Indians were witnessing the natural return of long-lost Aryan brothers. Therefore, while it is true that Indian scholarship has to carefully steer clear of modern politics, neutral parties in the academic clash point out that Western scholarship has utterly no grounds whatsoever for condescension. Its closet is full of skeletons.

In deflecting the thrusts of the anti-invasion team, the Western side has put forward a new twist: migration instead of invasion. Hence these Aryans-in scholars perhaps sidestep the attack on their goal by claiming that the anti–Aryan-invasion camp is railing against an outdated notion. The news is spread that the concept of "invasion" was retired many decades ago. The new term "migration" is trotted out when the pressure on the goal mounts. "We envisage a situation in which groups of Indo-Aryan speakers arrived in an area where another language or languages were prevalent and, living there for a period of interaction with the existing population, became involved in a process of acculturation."[30] This new wrinkle has a slow influx of Aryans gradually co-opting the locals. The upper crust of the Aryan immigrants amalgamated with the upper crust of the late Indus Valley Culture. Thus we have the "acculturated-Aryan migrant" rather than the Aryan conqueror.

Actually, some recent books by the most eminent scholars still use the word invasion. Furthermore, neutral parties on the sidelines remind the agile Aryans-in defenders that "migration" is in the eyes of the beholder. The American pioneers of the Wild West generally saw their entrance as a migration—they were peaceful farmers, with guns, settling free land in the American West. The indigenous Americans, however, certainly saw the white man's influx as an invasion—not a process of acculturation. Scholars in India, and Western supporters, point out that cleaning up the vocabulary of the Aryan-intruder side does not extinguish the fiery controversy: Aryans in, out, both, or none?

Indologists have tacitly clung to the Aryan-entrance idea in the same way biologists seem to hold tight to Darwinism. In the natural sciences, Darwin's basic model is generally accepted without question, but the details are regularly discussed and modified. Likewise, although the Indological trend these days is to speak of linguistic migrations instead of militaristic invasions, we should note that most of the bricks and mortar of the present Indic-studies edifice were solidly put into place a century or so ago. Therefore gallant debunkers understandably choose to attack the established structure, not its latest fittings.

We should remember that, by assembling the Aryan-invasion theory, colonial scholars more or less declared war on the traditional historical narrative of Vedic, Sanskritic culture. Rather than always unilaterally demanding the ancient Vedas prove themselves, wouldn't it be interesting to challenge the other side? For refreshing scholarship, why not consider the colonially derived Aryans-into-India notion as the newcomer that has to run the gauntlet? Indeed, now even some prestigious Western scholars, behind the scenes, are quietly beginning to question their own side.

ARCHAEOLOGICAL RESEARCH

Archaeology is a prime tool for unearthing the secrets of past great civilizations. We know that Vedic historical records give little vision of Vedic civilization that would satisfy an entrenched empiricist. Similarly though, modern archaeological digs have also not provided much to fill in an officially acceptable picture. In fact, until the 1920s the archaeological prehistory of India was a blank. True, the geographical sites mentioned in the Vedas are still known today. Perhaps a mental block against seriously considering the historicity of the Vedas prevents the funding needed to make possible extensive research at these sites.

The Indus Valley Breakthrough

Bounteous days for archaeologists in India finally began in 1921. In that decade, under the direction of Sir John Marshall, the cities Harappa and Mohenjo-daro were exhumed. Separated by forty miles, lying along the Indus River in what is now Pakistan, the two cities were the earliest proof of advanced civilization to emerge from the soil of India. Whereas previously India's prehistory was commonly conceived as dark and barbaric, now India was certified as having a civilized prehistoric past dating back at least 4,500 years.

In the late 1800s British historian and archaeologist Alexander

Cunningham began research at Harappa. Marshall, however, was the first to organize systematic excavations in the Indus area. As director-general of the Archaeological Survey of India, in 1924 he announced to the world the discovery of a new civilization. He irrevocably turned the tide in his three-volumed report *Mohenjo-daro and the Indus Civilization:*

> One thing that stands out clear and unmistakable both at Mohenjo-daro and Harappa is that the civilization hitherto revealed at these two places is not an incipient civilization, but one already age-old and stereotyped on Indian soil, with many millenniums of human endeavor behind it. Thus India must henceforth be recognized along with Persia, Mesopotamia, and Egypt as one of the most important areas where the civilizing processes of society were initiated and developed.[31]

Prior to the Indus Valley evidence, the prevalent belief was that all civilization had arrived with invaders from the vicinity of Europe. No one would have thought that something native had preceded the envisioned Indo-European wave of civilization. Yet the discoveries of the 1920s, called the Indus Valley Culture, established India as the oldest known living civilization.

Though the script found on seals has yet to be deciphered, there is evidence that fastidious attention was paid to the household bathrooms, the drains, and the Great Bath at Mohenjo-daro, and all have obvious continuity with later elements in the Indian civilization. To this very day in India there are the same kind of boats and bullock carts with a framed canopy, little changed from the Indus Valley artifacts. In analyzing the finds, researchers with an eye for detail have noted that the absence of pins and the fondness for bangles and elegant nose ornaments are all uniquely Indian.

The excavated "lost cities of the Indus" were a fabulous archaeological find. They evinced an extraordinary precision in town planning and a fascinating array of household amenities. The same sophistication of town planning and civil engineering would not appear again until two thousand years later, in the Roman civilization.

> Each settled area had streets running on a north–south and east–west grid, with smaller roads and alleys connecting neighborhoods to main thoroughfares. Streets led from gateways into the heart of the city, effectively dividing it into neighborhoods. Many Harappan houses were two-storied and appear to have had open courtyards, living rooms, bathing platforms (watertight floors with drains), and latrines. Most dwellings were connected to an elaborate citywide drainage system that reflects a well-organized civic authority.[32]

Some researchers perceive that awesome structures such as the Great Bath of Mohenjo-daro and the large reservoir at Lothal would have required advanced knowledge of mathematics, especially geometry. Where did it come from? The Great Bath is estimated to have been built in 2200 B.C. It is a pool 39 feet long, 23 feet wide, and 8 feet deep. Bitumen sealed the brick walls, and the floor slants to a drain in the corner. Two flights of steps took bathers down into the tank. In 1998, at a site in Dholavira, amid what is now desert, the remains of a huge 5,000-year-old dam were discovered. Although the most spectacular Indus Valley site within what is now India, Dholavira is 30 miles from the border with Pakistan, in a sensitive military zone. Hence, red tape impedes research.

Archaeological evidence reveals that the Indus Valley Culture covered a huge territory. To date, researchers identify more than 1,500 Indus-era cities and towns, in an area spanning from the mountains in northern Afghanistan south to the Arabian Sea, and from the coast near the present Mumbai (Bombay) east to New

Delhi, in central India. The urban and village network covers an area that researchers say extended more than 250,000 square miles. Thus in this region we have by far the largest known cultural domain of those times (more than double the area of the Egyptian and Sumerian cultures).

Most noteworthy is the unity of culture that seemed to have spanned the vast area. Art, script, technology, and even weights and measures were uniform. These major indicators of a unified material culture were in place as early as 2600 B.C. The latest studies reveal the Indus cities to have been political and economic centers. Although some of the culture's characteristics, such as script and standardized weights, faded away in prehistory, other elements—especially the style of arts, crafts, and agriculture—remained into the historic period.

Amazingly, some of the ancient Indus technologies are present today in South Asian urban centers. Much of the same methods for making pottery, beads, and jewelry are still essential to everyday Indian life. Gold jewelers still use the same weight system. Today in South Asia, the design of ox-carts and certain agricultural implements, as well as ways of fishing and animal husbandry, all demonstrate the Indus legacy.

Current finds have pushed back India's archaeological history of continuous settlement much further than the famous sites of Mohenjo-daro and Harappa. Excavations at Mergarh, 125 miles west of the Indus River in west-central Pakistan, revealed an agricultural community dated to between 7000 and 6500 B.C. This site ranks as the earliest archaeological evidence in India of developed culture and economy. A team of French archaeologists, headed by Jean-Francois Jarrige of the Musée Guimet in Paris, dated the Mergarh site. They also established a general continuity of culture from its origin until what appears to be the later, full onset of the Indus Valley civilization. Jarrige combined with Richard H. Meadow, of Harvard University, to explain in *Scientific*

American, "Step by step one can see the stage being set for the development of the complex cultural patterns that became manifest in the great cities of the Indus civilization in the middle of the third millennium B.C."[33]

The most recent finds at Mergarh drove home deeper a fundamental point that the first Indus Valley discoveries had already revealed. That is, cultural diffusion—whether from Europe, southern Russia, Sumer, or Egypt—was not a prerequisite for civilization to develop in India. What archaeologists had uncovered was doubtlessly a segment of India's own indigenous past.

The acclaimed scholar V. Gordon Childe, trained both as an archaeologist and philologist, wrote in his work *New Light on the Most Ancient East*:

India confronts Egypt and Babylonia by the third millennium [B.C.] with a thoroughly individual and independent civilization of her own, technically the peer of the rest. And plainly it is deeply rooted in Indian soil. The Indus civilization represents a very perfect adjustment of human life to a specific environment. And it has endured; it is already specifically Indian and forms the basis of modern Indian culture. In architecture and industry, still more in dress and religion, Mohenjo-daro reveals features that have always been characteristic of historical India.[34]

At the start of the twenty-first century, the latest archaeological finds now push back the dates of the Indus Valley Culture beyond those Childe cites. Instead of the third millennium B.C., now scholars openly discuss artifacts from near the middle of the fourth.[35]

Indus Enigmas

The hope that the Indus digs would throw substantial light directly on the origin of the Vedas themselves remains unfulfilled.

The Indus excavations have given scant evidence for reconstructing the period in which the Vedic literature was composed. Puzzling over the problem, some scholars, such as Wilhem Rau, a notable German historian of Vedic material culture, wonder if a "Vedic archaeology" is even possible. Discouragement comes easy, since so little material remains have been recovered. A new breed of researchers, however, maintain that no one is seriously looking in the right places.

Undoubtedly, the Indian tropical climate was not conducive to the survival of any written material—whether on bark, cotton, palm leaves, or wood. Nor would that environment favor the preservation of other artifacts. In Egypt, however, except around the Nile Delta, conditions allowed even highly perishable materials to survive. Therefore many Egyptian texts, of all types, lasted through the ages.

Searching for magnificent tombs that might reveal crucial information is significantly irrelevant to the Vedic past. Unlike the people of Pharaonic Egypt, Vedic Indians did not bury their dead (though some primitives and outcasts on the social periphery of Vedic civilization may have done so). The Vedas prescribe cremation—still practiced by most Indians to this day. Therefore skeletal remains from antiquity are rare. The Indus Valley region shows an absence of large cemeteries. Moreover, nowhere have bones appeared that would allow scholars to say with confidence, "These belong to the skeletons of the actual people who composed the Vedas."

Though no one today denies that India had an indigenous civilization thousands of years ago, the essential question still stands: what, if any, is the relationship between the Indus Valley Culture and Vedic civilization? Aryans-in fans are quick to argue that the Indus Valley Culture was non-Vedic. This position leaves the door wide open for the Indo-European Aryans to enter India and work their wonders. As the newcomers spread across the fertile plains of northwestern India, they also released into India the entirety or at least the roots of Vedic culture and Sanskrit. Soon the new Vedic ways from abroad would predominate, as the Indus Valley natives declined.

Aryans-out fans are quick to protest. They want to establish the Indus Valley Culture as a Vedic forerunner. In this way they can effectively oust the conceptualized hordes of Indo-European immigrants. No intruders would be needed to account for Vedic culture—it developed from the Indus Valley civilization.

The Indus Valley mystery, however, is greater than even the widely separated goals of the Aryans-in or Aryans-out contest. Neutral observers on the sidelines just want to establish that no one knows for sure. Whether the Indus Valley people were Vedic or not is not yet clearly discernible either way, so all the combatants should back off and fight about something more verifiable.

Vedic sympathizers looking to establish the historical authority of the Vedas may well find the Indus Valley mystery irrelevant. The enigmatic Indus culture could easily have been marginal to the apparently missing, highly advanced Vedic civilization—so extensively described in the Vedic texts. In other words, though the Indus people may have been "not so Vedic," the Vedic people were still around.

Artifacts have made it obvious that the Indus Valley people gave significance to the bull, the tiger, and the elephant. Yet, where are the horses that play such a major role in the Vedas? The horse has become the most important missing person in ancient India. Were they there in the Indus Valley Culture or did the envisioned Indo-European Aryans introduce them, along with all the other gifts attributed to them? Indeed, horse-bone fights are common in academia, as each side tries to assert or deny indigenous evidence of horses in India before the second millennium B.C.

The indicators of religion in the Indus region are also hotly contested. While undoubtedly they directly point to elements extant in later Indian civilization, whether they point to the Vedas is not yet clear from the evidence available. Both sides of the debate pin their hopes on the translation of the Indus script, found on soapstone seals, tablets of copper and clay, utensils, and pottery. The earliest agreed-upon samples of Indus script are from pottery fragments dated to 2800 B.C.[36]

Some archaeologists note images on seals that suggest a seated yogi and objects resembling paraphernalia used in Shiva worship. Other researchers say nothing is clearly specific to the Vedas. Further excavations at Kalibangan and Lothal uncovered what even some Western Aryan-intrusion scholars say are clearly Vedic altars for fire sacrifices. But they also reason that their Aryans must have intruded much earlier than the current theory allows, and that this early-bird version of the Aryans then coexisted with the Indus folks for a long time, before eventually diminishing them.

Most Aryans-in proponents are certain the Indus fireplaces indicate not Vedic rituals, but native kitchen practices. Neutral bystanders say the identification of the so-called fire altars is weak and not worth arguing over.

The Indus Valley Culture suddenly declined, as accounts have it today, around 1800 B.C. A former interpretation was that invading Aryan warriors finished the natives off quickly. At the Mohenjo-daro site, a few skeletons were found in excavated buildings and streets. The context of these remains, it was thought, indicated an unexpected violent death at the hands of the mighty Aryan intruders from abroad. These bones are still cited in books for the general public as a proof for the Aryan invasion. That detail, however, has been eased out of the current academic migration version. Drastic environmental changes—flooding and aridity—are now the recognized terminators of the Indus people.

The ancient Greek geographer and historian Strabo (63[?] B.C.–A.D. 21[?]), though living much later than the Indus Valley

Culture days, seems to have provided a significant clue about earlier geological upheavals. In his *Geography*, he recorded information gleaned from a companion of Alexander the Great (356–323 B.C.) named Aristoboulos:

> He says that when he was sent upon a certain mission he saw a country of more than a thousand cities, together with villages, that had been deserted because the Indus had abandoned its proper bed, and had turned aside into the other bed on the left that was much deeper, and flowed with precipitous descent like a cataract, so that the Indus no longer watered by its overflows the abandoned country on the right, since that country was now above the level, not only of the new stream, but also of its overflows.[37]

Current research by Louis Flam of the City University of New York indeed shows that the Indus River drastically changed its course. Mohenjo-daro and Harappa survived, owing to their position on high ground; other settlements were flooded, and then silt from the river buried them.

DISSENSION: ARCHAEOLOGY VERSUS LINGUISTICS

Unity is a luxury no longer afforded in the Western study of ancient India. The smug confidence radiated by linguistic scholars starkly contrasts with the stern defiance put up by prominent archaeologists. This split in the ranks translates into exciting public disputes. On one side, most linguistic scholars are sure about the intrusion of the Aryans. On the other side, important archaeologists are just as sure no archaeological evidence for the theory exists.

A venerable Sanskritist of Oxford University fame bared his heartfelt confidence: "The Aryan invasion of India is recorded in no written document, and it cannot yet be traced archaeo-logically, but it is nevertheless firmly established as a historical fact on the basis of comparative philology." Continuing his unabashed conviction, T. Burrow—oft quoted in both academic and popular books on India—explained: "So far we have had to rely entirely on linguistic relationships to account for the origin and early movements of the Aryans."[38]

With all due respect for the brilliantly creative work in linguis-tics, dissenting archaeologists point to the concrete and there take a firm stand. Nowhere in the South Asian archaeological record, they declare, is there any evidence of the linguists' pet scheme. That is, there is nothing indicating a west to east movement of peoples permanently settling India—during either the so-called prehistoric or the proto-historic period.

The first European scholars of India happened to be brilliant linguists. Sanskrit and its relation to classical European tongues fascinated these men of the eighteenth and nineteenth centuries. Indeed, besides the Vedic texts they had no other relics from India to interpret. Therefore, as a direct result of their pioneering sup-positions, for several centuries an intricate tradition of linguistic hypothesis has prescribed and virtually defined attempts to con-struct the history of Vedic India.

Archaeology, a relative newcomer to the scholarly world, bore no fruit in India until the first part of the twentieth century. Hence, archaeological researches into Vedic India, as well as stud-ies of Vedic astronomy and mathematics, have grown up like fledglings under the broad wings of comparative linguistics. Pro-testing the burden of conjectures imposed by Western Sanskritists and philologists, the American archaeologist Jim Shaffer labeled their effect upon Indological research "linguistic tyranny."[39]

He gives this summary of the major plight of Indology and the internal clash between its archaeological and linguistic components:

The Indo-Aryan concept was never subjected to rigorous valida-
tion beyond the field of historical linguistics. Linguistic reconstructions were used to interpret archaeological materials, which
in turn were used to substantiate the original cultural reconstructions.

The Indo-Aryan invasion(s) as an academic concept in 18th
and 19th century Europe reflected the cultural milieu of that period. . . . What was theory became unquestioned fact that was
used to interpret and organize all subsequent data.

Current archaeological data do not support the existence of
an Indo-Aryan or European invasion into South Asia any time
in the pre- or proto-historic periods. Instead, it is possible to
document archaeologically a series of cultural changes reflecting
indigenous cultural developments from prehistoric to historic
periods.[40]

The archaeologists' complaint is that in many instances scholars of comparative and historical linguistics have allowed their
assumptions to predetermine their results. Though they purport
to be empirical, they frequently operate beyond the realm of the
history. Consequently, the ingenious outcomes they sincerely devise—the "reconstructions" and their "proto-language"—remain
mere calculations. Who can resist the compelling elegance of a
proto-language, gradually diffusing from an original, ancestral
staging ground? And, most importantly, who can renounce such
a golden opportunity for scholastic industriousness?

The unfortunate result is that honest attempts to understand
India's past have been restrained by a taut circular harness. First,
linguistic data was employed to paint a theoretical vision—an
Aryan invasion of India. Second, linguistic scholars felt pressed by
their own theories, "the reconstructions," and they visualized into
Vedic texts the Aryan-invasion scenario—how Sanskrit emerged
in India. Third, any archaeological evidence that emerged was

interpreted through the same lens—through the Aryan-intrusion filter.

Even a nonspecialist can anticipate what transpired. As time passed, non-historically based linguistic conjectures piled atop one another—seemingly like the immense granite blocks that form the pyramids. Scenarios were visualized that stretched back four, five, and six millennia. Yet none of these majestic schemes have any correlation with an archaeological culture. The actual result, prominent archaeologists protest, has been almost two centuries of academic mist and fog. Shaffer, seeking to break through the clouds, states:

> We reject most strongly the simplistic historical interpretations, which date back to the eighteenth century, that continue to be imposed on South Asian cultural history. These still prevailing interpretations are significantly diminished by European ethno-centrism, colonialism, racism, and anti-semitism. Surely, as South Asian studies approach the twenty-first century, it is time to describe emerging data objectively rather than perpetuate interpretations without regard to the data archaeologists have worked so hard to reveal.[41]

Another prominent Western archaeologist adding to the dissent is Jonathan Mark Kenoyer of the University of Wisconsin. A specialist on the Indus Valley Culture and head of the current excavations at the Harappa site, he dismisses the theory that incursions of Indo-European Aryans overpowered the Indus Valley cities and brought about their demise.

> There is in fact no archaeological or literary evidence for invasions during the period of the Indus civilization's decline. Current theories take into account many factors that would have contributed to the fragmentation of the society, including the break-

down of agricultural life, the migration of people following changes in river courses, and the failure to maintain political and economic control over the vast region.[42]

A major archaeologist who does not rock the boat is F. R. Allchin, the aging dean of the South Asian field. Resting his assurance on—need he say it—linguistic studies, Allchin feels secure in pursuing archaeology according to the Aryan-incursion paradigm. He notes that loyal adherence to that hypothesis flourishes—among almost all linguistic scholars dedicated to explaining Indo-European languages and their spread.[43]

Indo-European specialist Bruce Lincoln offers this wry analysis of the relationship between archaeology and its domineering big brother:

> Archaeology can offer nothing new to the study of Proto-Indo-European civilization. For any candidate culture advanced by archaeologists as the Proto-Indo-European culture, only two types of evidence can be offered: evidence that conforms to the evidence offered by linguists, which will be tautological . . . or evidence that differs from the linguistic evidence, which will then call into question whether the candidate ought not to be rejected in favor of another that better fits the linguistic evidence.[44]

Linguistic scholars are not taking the conflict with the eminent but rebellious archaeologists lightly. Often they aggressively counterattack by minimizing the value of archaeology. It cannot stand on its feet without them, the linguistic experts assert. It is subordinate, they say, because, after all, artifacts like pottery and tools do not talk. Another shortcoming of archaeological material, they add, is that you have to find it. So much is lost forever, and therefore archaeological evidence—or its lack—cannot stack up against the power of linguistics. Some linguistic scholars feel emboldened enough to declare that, since the Aryans-in theory is indeed a linguistic affair, only linguistic "evidence" really counts—archaeological support is not really relevant. They argue that only when there is a great mass of archaeological material can the interpretations of linguistics begin to recede into the background.

Meanwhile, other scholars remind both sides and the spectators in the arena that the linguistic hammerlock is actually quite weak because no singular, ruling linguistic theory exists. Every few decades major changes in the classification of languages occur. Right now leading linguists are once again proposing several major overhauls.

In this way the battle continues, an academic skirmish that pits not only the West against India, but also the West against the West. The *Encyclopaedia Britannica* quite succinctly calls our attention to the dense billows of confusion due to the Indo-European invasion/migration device:

> Theories concerning the origins of the Aryans, whose language is also called Aryan, relate to the question of what has been called the Indo-European homeland. . . . European scholars who first studied Sanskrit were struck by the similarity in its syntax and vocabulary to Greek and Latin. This resulted in the theory that there had been a common ancestry for these and other related languages, which came to be called the Indo-European group of languages. This, in turn, resulted in the notion that the Indo-European-speaking people had had a common homeland from which they had migrated to various parts of Asia and Europe. The theory stirred unlimited speculation, which continues today, regarding the original homeland and the date of the dispersal from it. The study of Vedic India is still beset by "the Aryan problem," which often clouds the genuine search for historical insight into this period.[45]

WRITING WHEN?

There was a time when the story of writing was cut and dried. What archaeologists dug up indicated that the Sumerians were first off the mark, with clay tablets recording commercial and administrative matters, dated to 3200 B.C. One or two hundred years later the Egyptians were to have followed suit, with a system of pictorial hieroglyphics. On the Indian subcontinent, the Indus Valley Culture joined the club in 2500 B.C., using ceramic seals in business. Then came China, in 1500–1200 B.C., with its divinations inscribed on turtle shells and ox bones. Mesoamerica brought up the rear; Olmec, Mayan, and Zapotec writing is dated at 250–300 B.C.

Though the general public still gets to enjoy this popular history, behind academic doors the theory is now hotly dissected. A pivotal international symposium on the origins of writing, held at the University of Pennsylvania, could reach no conclusion for solving the most important questions of how and why writing was born. None of the assembled archaeologists, historians, and other experts could agree whether writing first came from pictures or numbers, or whether early writing systems developed independently or through cross-fertilization.[46]

Even the glory of the Sumerians was under attack. Dr. Günter Dreyer, director of the German Archaeological Institute in Egypt, had put forward hieroglyphic inscriptions from tombs dated as early as 3200 B.C. and possibly 3400. Now it was an open question, he said, who scored first—the Egyptians or the Sumerians. Upon the news of Dreyer's discovery, Vivian Davis of the British Museum declared outright that the Egyptian writing system had beaten the Sumerians' by at least 150 years. A colleague at the Museum, Sumerian scholar Christopher Walker, refused to turn the other cheek: "If they [the experts on Egypt] think they have evidence of a fully developed script at that point, we would start looking for earlier stages [in Sumeria]."[47]

Meanwhile, from the Indus Valley, a new challenger entered the arena. Indus Culture experts Kenoyer and Meadow distributed on the Internet pictures of marks on potsherds they felt could indicate proto-writing by Indus folk as early as 3300 B.C. If their educated hunch proves correct, the Indus Valley would thereby garner a birthdate of writing that is at least contemporaneous with the origin of writing in both Egypt and Sumeria. Another Indus specialist, Gregory L. Possehl of the University of Pennsylvania, urged caution. He was not yet convinced that the markings indicated symbols leading to full-blown writing.

Regardless of how the new Indus Valley controversy winds down, no scholar thinks that Indus writing owes anything to Sumeria. Scholars such as Asko Parpola of the University of Helsinki have conclusively shown that no relation exists between Indus script and Sumerian writing. An interesting sidenote is that, although a few scholars in India propose a connection between the Indus Valley script and the Sanskrit of the Vedas, currently almost all of their Western brethren are not impressed.

Vedic Writing

To this day, the origin of Vedic information remains perplexing and controversial. In particular, the dating of the scripts used in the literature has long been an academic battlefield. The traditional perspective is that the Vedas, as a body of knowledge, are originally a revelation that cannot be found in time. Skeptics, no doubt, would object that ancient spiritual traditions generally exaggerate their age. Modern Vedic partisans are quick to counter that modern materialists drastically minimize the timespan of human presence on Earth.

When scholars study the written language of each Vedic text, they see symptoms of compilation over a long time. Observing the differences in the Sanskrit, scholars posit a development of the Vedic language inside the texts. Some feel that this development is

a safe guide for establishing an approximate sequence of the actual texts. For example, Sanskritist Michael Witzel of Harvard
University theorizes five stages of Sanskrit needed to get from the
language of the *Rig-veda* to that of the Upanishads.

Scholars sympathetic to the Vedas, while noting the inarguable differences in language of the Vedic literature, remind us
that language and the knowledge that it conveys are two different things. Obviously, the message need not share the same date
as the medium. The Vedas are a corpus of information orally
derived. Hence, the written language, in which we now find this
oral knowledge, primarily indicates the form of Sanskrit script
prevalent when each Vedic component of knowledge entered
the page.

The advanced memory skills of both ancient and modern India
are well attested, even to the satisfaction of Indologists. Even
skeptics accept that at least part of the Vedic literature has been
orally transmitted with astonishing accuracy for three thousand
years. Students had to learn the knowledge word for word, with
no errors in pronunciation or accent.

The *Rig-veda* especially is famous for its system of double-
checking. Specially trained reciters memorized it in two ways:
they could recite it according to certain Sanskrit grammatical rules
and without certain rules. This process insured the changelessness
of the words and even the accents of the *Rig-veda*. Early in the
twentieth century, Winternitz, in his *History of Indian Literature*,
judged: "There can be no doubt that this kind of oral transmission
gives a greater guarantee for the preservation of the original text
than the copying and recopying of manuscripts."[48]

The oldest known writing materials used in India were palm
leaves and birch bark. Both materials are fragile and easily perish
in the Indian climate. The earliest manuscripts found date in the
first millennium A.D. They have been found inside and outside
India, even as far as Japan. Most of the manuscripts used today

can be traced to paper originals. Paper, however, was introduced by the Muslims circa the thirteenth century A.D.

Few now make light of the Indian ability to pass Vedic knowledge down intact over huge expanses of time. The scholar Richard Salomon, in a definitive study hailed as the standard, surveyed current research on communicating the Vedas. He particularly singled out works by the Germans Oskar von Hinuber and Harry Falk as the current pacesetters. Salomon states: "It is certainly true that intellectual activity in India has always strongly favored oral over written means of expression, and both von Hinuber and Falk have effectively put to rest the already discredited skepticism about the possibility of oral composition and preservation of the Veda."[49]

The scholars surveyed take the position that no writing occurred in India before 300 B.C. King Ashoka, whose empire covered most of the Indian subcontinent in the third century B.C., had his edicts inscribed on rocks and pillars. His royal message, exhorting his people to live virtuously, still reigns as the earliest specimen of writing scholars will accept without controversy. Salomon provides us that information and then adds his own deep afterthought:

> According to the position espoused in these books—which, given the authority of their authors and the quality of their scholarship, is likely to be hereby established as the currently prevailing point of view, at least in the West—the heartland of India was preliterate until the 3rd century B.C. But can we imagine such a state of affairs, given what we know (admittedly not too much) of the state of society and culture in India, especially in the northeast, before this time?[50]

Cautiously he goes on to point out that the conclusions of recent scholarship do really seem a likely scenario—that is, when based on what he calls "the grounds of the unfortunately meager evidence that is left to us." Hence he concludes his review of the field by offering sincere appreciation to his academic colleagues for their labors, followed by pessimistic homage to the actual mystery of it all:

> Still, we should not fall into the trap of thinking that the last word has been spoken. Admittedly, it hardly seems likely, after all the years of waiting, searching, and the dashing of false hopes, that some major archaeological discovery will reveal a whole new picture of the origins of writing in the Indian heartland, or reveal a sustainable (rather than purely hypothetical) connection with the Indus script. Nevertheless, it would be unwise to rule out surprises in the future, and we should leave the door open, as does Falk ... But we must also agree, if reluctantly, with his final sentence: "Zur Zeit erscheint dieser Fall jedoch kaum zu erwarten." [However, to date we can hardly expect this to happen.][51]

Putting it all in ordinary parlance, what we are being told is this: "Based on very few shreds of actual evidence, what we have here is first-class scholarship. It successfully renders a brilliant scenario that faithfully adheres to the scant facts presently available."

It certainly seems that since the bygone days of Müller and Winternitz, nothing major has changed. For the best scholars, dating the Vedic literature is still a trip into the "truly terrifying darkness"—a verdict on dating the Vedic literature declared many decades back.

As Seen from Space: Vedic India

Recently, satellite technology has contributed a major discovery—too new for inclusion in all but the most up-to-date books on India's past. The Vedic texts mention an abnormally wide river named Sarasvati, which flowed from the Himalayan mountains to the sea. Sarasvati is the principal river in the *Rig-veda*, which contains fifty references in forty-six hymns to her. For example, in one verse the *Rig-veda* describes the Sarasvati River as "pure in her course from the mountains to the ocean."[52] In other Vedic literature you can read of Vedic sages convening metaphysical dialogues on the banks of this river. They also frequented pilgrimage sites along its course. Where is that river, mentioned so many times in the *Mahabharata* and the *Bhagavata, Vamana,* and *Padma Puranas*? We don't see it today.

Archaeologists, in their quest for the lost past, are now supplementing their shovels with scanners in space. In 1972 NASA, the American government's space department, launched the Landsat program, to scan and study agricultural areas from satellites. Because vegetation would reflect infrared rays, scientists could estimate crop yields. By the late 1970s geologists, geographers, and archaeologists began to climb aboard, and to use the technology to glean geologically hidden information about ancient societies. For example, the Great Wall of China—visible with the naked eye from a space shuttle—shows up on imagery scans as a thin orange band. From the space images, scientists detected two generations of the Great Wall.

Some researchers employed Landsat imagery to pinpoint the location of Maya ruins in the Yucatan jungles and prehistoric structures in the plains of what was once Mesopotamia. In 1981 the space shuttle *Columbia* aimed its imaging system at the major deserts of Earth. The images brought to light ancient riverbeds in the Sahara, buried in bedrock ten to fifteen feet below the sands on the surface.

In 1986 the French introduced the next breakthrough in satellite remote sensing. Whereas the Americans ventured their Landsat program as a tentative experiment, the National Center for Space Study in France designed the new technology, named

SPOT, to be fully operational from the outset. Able to capture objects or areas as small as thirty feet wide, the multispectral imagery and panchromatic data used by SPOT—though not offering the fine detail of aerial photographs—covers much wider areas.

An Indian and French archaeological field team on the ground, coordinating with a French SPOT satellite in space, has ascertained that the Sarasvati River, as described in the Vedas, is fact, not mythology. Vividly exposing the signatures of old rivers and their branches, data from SPOT shows that the Sarasvati did exist. The satellite's sensors and pointable optics reveal the dried bed of a river extending from the present Ghaggar River and flowing four miles wide, in the region of India west of what is now Delhi. In what is now Punjab, satellite imagery has shown the Sarasvati's bed to be twelve miles wide. From space, researchers can detect that the Sarasvati had many tributaries, which obviously watered an immense area of fertile soil. Traces of artificial canals, directing water to more remote agricultural locations, are also visible.

After the first archaeological breakthrough in India, at Harappa in 1921, the findings were accepted as evidence of what was called the Harappan culture. Then, in the same decade, another major site surfaced at Mohenjo-daro. Both cities, lying along the Indus River, were rechristened the "Indus Valley Civilization." Since the 1950s, more major sites have been located. The distinctive feature of this new breed—Lothal, Rupar, Dholavira, and Banawali—is that they all lie on or near the banks of the newly discovered Sarasvati River. In 1992 a Pakistani archaeologist, Rafiq Mughal, discovered at Guneriwala—across the Rajasthan border—a site on the dried riverbed of the Sarasvati that apparently is as large as Mohenjo-daro.

In this way we can see that the discovery of the original 1,000-mile Sarasvati River has put the sites excavated on the Indus River in a new perspective. A much larger concentration of sites—more than 1,000—has been detected along the old Sarasvati riverbed, buried under the sands of the Thar Desert. This number contrasts with the approximately 100 sites found directly on the Indus River and its tributaries. Consequently, the culmination of all the archaeological work done in northern India so far has prompted many Indian scholars to rename the Indus Valley network of sites as the Sarasvati-Indus Civilization. Objectors, minimizing the importance of the Sarasvati's discovery, say that the cultural contents exhumed at the Sarasvati sites do not yet compare in significance with those of the well-known Harappan sites. At any rate, those abreast with current scholarship now know the entire Sarasvati-Indus cultural milieu covered a far greater area than originally thought.

Flowing from the Himalayas, the rediscovered full course of the Sarasvati roughly parallels the Indus River to the Arabian Sea. This monumental find has a more startling corollary, intuited back in the latter half of the nineteenth century by the Sanskritist Max Müller.

To his credit, Müller, despite lacking the technology available now, did glimpse the shake-up a future resolution of the Sarasvati legend would bring. In his *Sacred Books of the East*, he recorded his anticipation:

> Though it may not be possible to determine, by geological evidence, the time of the changes which modified the southern areas of the Punjab and caused the Sarasvati to disappear in the desert, still the fact remains that the loss of the Sarasvati is later than the Vedic age, and that, at that time, the waters of the Sarasvati reached the sea.[53]

For Vedic investigators, there is a crucial question: When exactly was the heyday of the Sarasvati River's mighty flow? And when were the various stages of its drying up? Current technology is now capable of ascertaining when geological changes forced the Sarasvati to disappear. More time is still needed, though, to fine-tune the data. Satellites alone cannot clinch the geochronology. Some grey areas still exist, and certainly scholars always need time to assimilate the conclusions, unavoidable though they seem to be. High-tech work on the ground has to nail the case shut.[54]

The Indo-French combined satellite and field study attests that parts of the river began to dry up as early as 3000 B.C. Dates by others put the complete disappearance anywhere from 2500 to 1700 B.C. Western academics currently consider the dating work by the Pakistani archaeologist Rafiq Mughal to have the most potential. He says the river flowed as a perennial in the fourth and early third millennium B.C., and then disappeared at the end of the second millennium.[55]

Many of the more than one thousand archaeological sites discovered on the Sarasvati's banks allow carbon-14 dating. Since the sites adhere to the course of the river, dating them gives a key to the life of the river itself. So far, sites downstream, near the river's mouth in the sea, give approximate dates of 3000 B.C., and as you move upstream, towards the Himalayas, the dates become more recent, ranging to 1300 B.C. We should bear in mind, however, that carbon-14 dating is no longer a cutting-edge technology, though it is still a traditional mainstay in archaeology. It is now known to generate younger dates.

Most significantly, many archaeological sites are directly on the old Sarasvati riverbed itself. All researchers agree this inarguable fact shows that parts of the river certainly had to have dried up long before the people constructed dwellings there. Sites found on the riverbed are carbon-14 dated at 3000 B.C. Paul-Henri Francfort, leading the French scientific team, certified in the journal *Eastern Anthropologist* that, at the time of these first sites on the riverbed itself, "no large perennial river had flowed there for a long time."[56]

Vedic literature, however, does describe the flow of the mighty, ocean-bound, perennial river. Lovers of the epic *Mahabharata*, which contains the *Bhagavad-gita*, will recall intriguing passages such as "The holy flow of the Sarasvati joins the sea impetuously." (MBh 3.88.2) Other verses describe Sri Balarama's pilgrimage tour inland, along the Sarasvati River. For example: "The procession moved swiftly to the pilgrimage sites at the time of the war of the Kurus; going upstream along the Sarasvati, from the ocean onwards." (MBh 9.34.15–18)

Then we have the stanza in which Sri Balarama's upstream tour reaches the river's source: "While ascending the Himalaya, prominent with the Sarasvati River, Balarama saw Plaksha Prasravat." (MBh 9.53.11) Other Vedic histories, the Puranas, also echo this geography.

We are left with a startling conclusion: the Vedic texts are obviously describing the geography of India as it was circa 3000 B.C. and probably earlier—when the Sarasvati River emanated from the Himalayas and flowed majestically all the way into the Arabian Sea. That means the Vedic people and their advanced culture were around back then, coexisting somehow with the mysterious Indus Valley tribes. Thus we can safely contemplate that in some form—oral or otherwise—the Vedas did exist around 3000 B.C. As a result, we can be confident that Vedic culture, with its religion and philosophy, is the oldest living culture in the world.

Notes

1 There are those who doubt Schliemann's portrayal of his childhood ambition, but this is indeed the account as he tells it. For the doubts, see David Traill, *Schleimann of Troy: Treasure and Deceit*.

2 Associated Press, 3 June 2000.

3 Alberuni, *Kitab-Ul Hind*, trans. E. C. Sachau, vol. 2 (London reprint, 1983), pp. 10–11.

4 A. A. Macdonell, *Sanskrit Literature*, p. 10, quoted in F. E. Pargiter, *Ancient Indian Historical Tradition* (London: Oxford University Press, 1922), p. 2.

5 D. D. Kosambi, *The Culture and Civilization of Ancient India* (London: Routledge and Kegan Paul, 1965), p. 9.

6 F. R. Allchin *et al.*, *The Archaeology of Early Historic South Asia* (Cambridge: Cambridge University Press, 1995), p. 329.

7 Kosambi, *Ancient India*, pp. 10, 23.

8 D. P. Singhal, *India and World Civilization*, vol.1 (Michigan: Michigan State University Press, 1969), p. xvii.

9 C. C. Lamberg-Karlovsky and J. A. Sabloff, *Ancient Civilizations: The Near East and Mesoamerica* (Menlo Park, Ca.: Benjamin/Cummings Publishing Co., Inc., 1979), p. 3.

10 O. Spengler, *The Decline of the West* (New York: Knopf, 1926), vol. 1, pp. 104 ff.

11 The revision of Buddha's dating is the work of Richard Gombrich and Heinz Bechert. See Bechert, "The Date of the Buddha Reconsidered," *Indologica Taurinensia* 10 (1982), pp. 29–36.

12 Max Müller, *Life and Letters*, vol. 1, ed. Georgina Müller (London: Longmans, 1902), pp. 357–58.

13 Ibid., p. 328.

14 J. Gonda, *Vedic Literature* (Wiesbaden, Germany: Otto Harrassowitz, 1975), p. 22.

15 Gavin Flood, *An Introduction to Hinduism* (Cambridge: Cambridge University Press, 1996), p. 37.

16 Moriz Winternitz, *A History of Indian Literature*, vol. 1 (New Delhi: Oriental Books Reprint Corp., 1927, 1972), p. 293.

17 Ibid.

18 Winternitz, *A History*, p. 25.

19 Ibid., p. 25.

20 Currently, the most conservative academic position on the dating of the *Rig-veda*, as especially championed by Michael Witzel of Harvard

University, has been that the *Rig-veda* is a bronze age text that precedes the iron age. It is said to derive from the Greater Punjab area of the Indian subcontinent.

This position also holds that the date of the *Rig-veda* must come after the dissolution of the Indus civilization (ca. 1900 B.C.), since the cities of the Indus civilization cannot be discerned in the *Rig-veda*. In this way, the time frame of the *Rig-veda* is restricted to 1900 B.C. as the upper limit and 1200 B.C. as the bottom.

The *Rig-veda* mentions horses, spoked wheels, and chariots. To date, conservative scholars see no satisfying evidence that all three of these had appeared in the Indian subcontinent before circa 1900 B.C. Thus, they currently say, the *Rig-veda* could not have originated before then. Horses are not accepted to have been in South Asia before 1700 B.C. Some reported finds are considered to be from archaeologically unacceptable sites (unstratified or badly recorded excavations).

Other reported finds of horse are said to have confused horses bones with those belonging to the native half-ass, which is very similar to a horse.

Chariots of "the Indo-Aryan type" are judged to have first appeared around 2000 B.C., in the area surrounding the Ural mountains.

Thus, based on the clues currently available, the conservative position feels confident in theorizing a group of newcomers that arrived in India bringing with them the horse-drawn chariot, speaking a language derived from Indo-Iranian/Indo-European, and composing an Indo-Iranian/Indo-European type of intricate poetry. All of these are theorized to have been introduced into the Greater Punjab only after the demise of the Indus civilization. That civilization is presently seen by conservatives as being devoid of chariots and horses, as well as Indo-European types of language, religion, and rituals.

21 D. K. Chakrabarti, *Colonial Archaeology* (New Delhi: Munshiram Manoharlal, 1997), p. 153.

22 Sir William Jones, *The Works of Sir William Jones*, ed. Anna Marie Jones, 13 vols. (London: John Stockdale and John Walker, 1807), 3:34–35.

23 Thomas R. Trautman, *Aryans and British India* (Berkeley: University of California Press, 1997), pp. 14–15.

24 The tree scheme ignores the mutual influences among the various branches after they separate; it makes no allowance for interactions between the speakers of Proto-Indo-European and the speakers of other language families; it does not give proper consideration to time

depth—that is to say, its offspring languages lack sufficient chronological space to exist.

25 O. Szemerenyi, "The New Look of Indo-European Reconstruction and Typology," *Phonetica* 17 (1967): 65.

26 J. P. Mallory, *In Search of the Indo-Europeans* (London: Thames and Hudson Ltd, 1991 ed.), p. 7.

27 Ibid., p. 143.

28 Raimo Anttila, *Historical and Comparative Linguistics* (Amsterdam and Philadelphia: John Benjamins, 1989), p. 387.

29 In the words of veteran Indic scholar F. R. Allchin, "At one extreme there is the conservative Indian view which regards the Aryans and their languages as indigenous to South Asia; at the other, broadly stated, is the view of Western philologists that the Indo-Aryan languages were carried to South Asia around the middle of the second millennium B.C., as part of the much wider dispersal of the IE languages." (Allchin, *Archaeology*, p. 41)

30 Ibid., p. 43.

31 John Marshall, *Mohenjo-daro and the Indus Civilization*, vol. 1 (London: Oxford University Press, 1931), p. viii.

32 Jonathan Mark Kenoyer, "Birth of a Civilization," *Archaeology* 51, no. 1 (January/February 1998): 58.

33 J. F. Jarrige and R. H. Meadow, "The Antecedants of Civilization in the Indus Valley," *Scientific American*, August 1980.

34 V. Gordon Childe, *New Light on the Most Ancient East* (New York: W. W. Norton & Company, 1953), pp. 183–84.

35 In 1999 Dr. Richard Meadow announced the discovery of a pottery shard with a probable date of between 3500 and 3300 B.C. The shard has markings on it that some eminent scholars, including Meadow, say are proto-writing samples, whereas other South Asian archaeologists, such as Gregory Possehl, are more hesitant to classify the markings in this way.

36 Ibid.

37 Strabo, *Geography* 15.1.19.

38 T. Burrow, "The Early Aryans," in *A Cultural History of India*, ed. A. L. Basham (Oxford: Clarendon Press, 1975), pp. 21, 23.

39 Jim Shaffer, "Indo-Aryan Invasions: Myth or Reality?" in *The People of South Asia*, ed. John Lukacs (New York: Plenum Press, 1984), p. 88.

40 Ibid., pp. 81, 88.

41 Jim Shaffer, "Migration, Philology, and South Asian Archaeology," in

Aryan and Non-Aryan in South Asia: Evidence, Interpretation and History, Opera Minora, Harvard Oriental Series, vol. 3, ed. Johannes Bronkhurst and Madhav M. Deshpande (Cambridge: Harvard University, 1999).

42 Kenoyer, "Birth of a Civilization," p. 55.

43 Allchin, *Archaeology*, p. 45.

44 Bruce Lincoln, quoted in Mallory, *In Search*, p. 186.

45 "India: the Early Vedic Period," in *Encyclopaedia Britannica* [CD-ROM] (Encyclopaedia Britannica Inc., 1998).

46 See John Noble Wilford, "Who Began Writing? Many Theories, Few Answers," *New York Times*, 6 April 1999.

47 Discovery News Briefs [cited 15 September 1998]), available from http://www.discovery.com/ (original story from the *Times* [London], 14 September 1998).

48 Winternitz, *A History*, p. 37.

49 *Journal of the American Oriental Society* 115, no. 2 (1995): 271–79.

50 Ibid.

51 Ibid.

52 *Rig-veda* 7.95.2

53 Max Müller, *Sacred Books of the East* (xxxii, p. 60)

54 An example of lingering resistance is a feud over the Sanskrit word in the *Rig-veda, samudra,* such as RV 7.95.2. Both Vedic sympathizers and many Western scholars accept, without controversy, its meaning as "ocean": in other words, the Sarasvati flowed into the ocean. Some scholars, however, perhaps as a thinking exercise, like to make problematic the word *samudra,* saying it might mean other things. For instance, see T. Y. Elizarenkova, "The Concept of Water and the Names for It in the Rgveda," *Orientalia Suecana,* Uppsala, vols. 45–46, (1996–97): 21. Also, some Indologists like to point to Afghanistan, where there is the river known in Iranian as Harahvaiti, now as Helmand. Everyone agrees that two rivers with the same name (Sarasvati = Harahvaiti) is the result of the usual process of colonists transferring a name from their old place to their new site (e.g., Paris, France, to Paris, Texas). Thus the question, for a few, is: Did Indians bring the name to Afghanistan, or did Afghans bring it to India? It must be said, however, that most scholars do accept that the obvious location of the Sarasvati described in the *Rig-veda* is in Haryana-Punjab-Rajasthan, India. Generally, the nitpicking, or "thinking exercises"— about what and where "Sarasvati" really refers to—manifest whenever

Indian scholars trumpet too loudly the major ramifications of the *Rig-vedic* Sarasvati's obvious location in India.

55 M. R. Mughal, "Recent Archaeological Research in the Cholistan Desert," in *Harappan Civilization*, ed. G. Possehl (New Delhi: Oxford & IBH, 1982), pp. 85–95. *Ancient Cholistan: Archaeology and Architecture* (Rawalpindi: Ferozsons Ltd, 1997), p. 26.

56 Paul Henri Francfort, "Evidence for Harrappan Irrigation System in Haryana and Rajasthan," *Eastern Anthropology* 45 (1992): 91.

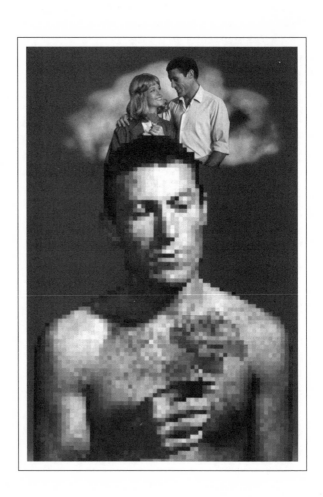

CHAPTER 4

VEDIC SELFHOOD

The ancient covenant is in pieces: Man at last knows that he is alone in the unfeeling immensity of the universe, out of which he has emerged only by chance. Neither his destiny nor his duty has been written down.[1]

A stark beginning for our entry into Vedic selfhood, but this famous declaration by French Nobel Laureate Jacques Monod highlights the radical difference between Western science and the experiential knowledge of the ancient Vedic sages. Certainly not everyone in the modern world will swallow molecular biologist Monod's chilling assessment. But few will deny that the barrenness he and his fellows celebrate has driven countless millions of humans to despair, despite technological development.

"Where did the self go?" is the obvious question a Vedic intellectual, transported from the past, would ask upon reviewing the present knowledge and flavor of humanity. "What do people live in relation to?" he would wonder, aghast.

"Never mind," we'd reply as we pushed the old sage aside. "Have you ever seen such mighty economic booms, and busts, like ours before? Get a real job, and we may slow down to hear you—never before has there ever been a culture so practical, innovative, and free."

Whether ancient or contemporary, humans expect society to serve the individual in the quest for subsistence and happiness. Society, comprised of people with desires and needs, is supposed to satisfy its members' desires and needs. That we all agree. But it would seem obvious that in order to satisfy its people, society must address knowledge of the self. This is the Vedic imperative we will explore.

Any attempt to satisfy the self that is not based on correct knowledge of the self must fail, the Vedas assert. Indeed, it does seem that we will have more than a few problems in satisfying ourselves if we are not clear what we are. If the individual is the building block of society, it would seem to follow that without a proper understanding of the self, all attempts to organize and maintain society will miss the mark.

C. G. Jung, the Swiss psychiatrist who began the analytical school of psychology, had much to say on the inner emptiness of Western society. Quite popular these days, his thoughts on dream analysis and what he called the "collective unconsciousness" contribute weightily to the current boom in what are known as contemporary spirituality and alternative healing.

Society, Jung maintained, is just the sum total of individuals in need of purification. The ancient Vedic vision shares this well-stated preliminary outlook on self and society. But then the Vedas plunge much further ahead. They precisely delineate the nature of the self—uncharted waters for Western science and religion.

In a famous comment to a Chicago newspaper, Jung revealed, "Among all my patients in the second half of life . . . every one of them fell ill because he had lost what the living religions of every age have given their followers, and none of them has really been healed who did not regain his religious outlook."

A social worker, Ruth Topping, wondered what he meant by "religious outlook." Was it the usual Judeo-Christian standard of piety? she queried him. Not quite, intimated Mr. Jung, in a letter from Zurich. He replied:

When you study the mental history of the world, you see that people since time immemorial had a general teaching or doctrine about the wholeness of the world. . . . This has been the case in primitive tribes as well as in highly differentiated civilizations. . . . In our civilization this spiritual background has gone astray. Our Christian doctrine has lost its grip to an appalling extent, chiefly because people don't understand it any more.

As these views deal with the world as a whole, they create also a wholeness of the individual. . . . People are no longer rooted in their world and lose their orientation. They just drift. . . . The problem cannot be settled by a few slogans.[2]

We can see that, on the one hand, moderns have been ritualistically sprinkled with the simple platitudes of the Semitic religious systems. Conventional Judaism, Christianity, and Islam, while skimping on analytical knowledge of the self, effectively drill us in basic morals. On the other hand, we are barraged by the boasts of superstar scientists like Monod, who seek to teach us childish rhymes that we are meaningless matter, driven by chance, in the vast cosmic emptiness.[3]

Though accurately fingering the Western dilemma, Jung himself gave no definitive knowledge of the self or of the Whole. Because of his lack, as well as the shortcomings of Western religionists, ecologists, doctors, and scientists, our transported Vedic sage would wonder how anyone could ever become holistic—despite the enormous popularity of the word. If the ancient Vedic seers could journey forward into our time, surely they would want to know, "Where in your civilization is comprehensive knowledge of the part—the individual self—and the all-encompassing Whole it belongs to?"

CONSCIOUSNESS, THE MISSING LINK

Restoring the ancient covenant has to begin with understanding consciousness. The mystery of the conscious self, seconded perhaps by the riddle of the cosmic origin, lies beyond the limits of present intellectual capacities. Although the quest to know consciousness withers the brains of our best researchers and theoreticians, the Vedic texts seem to thrive on the challenge. Therefore the enigma of the conscious self is a quite befitting place to start our investigation of Vedic antiquity.

How can ancient texts, we may ask, deal with such an advanced topic? Actually, when we rise above our prejudices and embarrassment, the question probably should be how did modern civilization, for so long, not deal with consciousness.

Nothing in our life provides us with a greater first-hand experience than our own consciousness. Yet, in spite of its paramount familiarity, it is also the foremost modern mystery. Certainly, then, it is a suitable barometer for gauging the intellectual strength of the Vedas. To catch a glimpse of consciousness and its relation to selfhood, as presented in the Vedas, we can try four very brief and simple experiments, all based on the Vedic method of personal analysis.

Experiment 1: Slow down for a moment and feel from within the parts of your body. Whose limbs and senses are they?

We say without hesitation, "This is my hand opening, my nose smelling, my stomach rumbling." No one says in English, German, or Russian: "I hand, I nose, I belly." The obvious assumption, both in our language and everyday experience, is that something mysterious claims proprietorship over the various limbs, senses, and organs. Everything is "my," but where am I?

While that something is indeed registering user's rights over the organism and its parts, the entire body is constantly changing. What we casually refer to as growth and aging, the Vedas know as changing bodies.

Scientists put forth an estimate that roughly 60 trillion cells compose the human body. Yet, though every type of cell is replaced periodically, still our basic core identity remains the same. Vedic education begins with this observation: something does not change though the body is changing.

Experiment 2: Try to take a look "inside yourself." Gently endeavor to feel out the very root of the personal "I," the underlying nucleus of your subjective experience. What is the core of this "I-ness?" Try to discover it.

You may say that when you "look inside," when you introspect, all you "see" are various psychological states. That mental stuff is I, you may think. But what is doing the looking? Just as there is the undeniable sense of an observer different from the physical body, similarly there is also a perceiver of the psychological content. "My moods, my fantasies, my thoughts," we say. In other words, that which witnesses is always different from that which is witnessed. You can't get your fingers on the witness of our emotions and mental phenomenon, and you can't see it, but it is there as the experiencer and perceiver.

We know the witness by being it. We can't know it by "stepping back" to observe it, because it always "steps back" with us, to look at anything. We can further clarify our little experiment by mentally peeling away the socially and individually induced layers covering this root of our subjectiveness. In the background of what we think is our selfhood, we will find the inescapable factor taken for granted in all our witnessing: conscious awareness.

Experiment 3: You know what it's like to lay down to sleep in a completely dark room. Try it tonight. You can't see a thing with your eyes. But your conscious awareness is still there. It witnesses an endless parade of the mind's contents. Thoughts, memories, desires, and fantasies appear and disappear. Though the objects of consciousness are always moving in and out, the ground of consciousness itself remains.

Experiment 4: Next, while you are laying in total darkness, try to "jump out of" your conscious awareness, to study it from an "outside vantage point." Obviously you cannot jump outside of your own consciousness, because consciousness is the experiencer even of attempts to understand itself. Without your consciousness, there is no experience of existence.

> As the sun alone illuminates all this universe, so does the living entity, one within the body, illuminate the entire body by consciousness. (*Bhagavad-gita* 13.34)

All awareness of our surroundings and us owes to our possessing consciousness. Though consciousness is so essential to our existence, for Westerners it is still an immediate and ultimate mystery. Modern thinkers have great difficulty just conceptualizing about consciousness. In fact, scientists themselves admit that until recently, those wanting to research consciousness had to disguise their work, so they would not lose academic respect and funding.

The ancient Vedic sages would certainly agree with the obvious: we cannot account for the cosmos without accounting for the accountant. Fifteen centuries ago, the Catholic founding-father Augustine wondered, "What we are looking for is what we are looking with." Modern scientists have not been able to come to his rescue. Perhaps because consciousness is the most intimate thing in our life, "prepackaged" in our every thought and action, many scientists still find it so hard acknowledging the reality of consciousness. First, many of them have to admit it exists, in of itself. Then they can start their attempts to find its source. The German sage of quantum physics, Max Planck, noted, "Science cannot solve the ultimate mystery in Nature. And it is because in the last analysis we ourselves are part of the mystery we are trying to solve."

A serious student of the Vedic texts will soon see that consciousness is to Vedic sages as snow is to Eskimos. It's the predominant reality, and they know they can't get away from it. In fact, the ancient Vedic scholars easily accepted the obvious: that is, "the stuff" of our world—the materiality—is only experienced as an appearance within consciousness. Therefore, rather than running away from the consciousness mystery, we might grant some credit to the way the Vedic literature unravels it. The Vedic methodology begins by accepting the obvious: consciousness is foundational, and all else supplementary. From that basis, everything proceeds.

Night Dream, Life Dream

Let's return to our quick experiments, for further insight into the Vedic mode of analyzing the self. We can easily see that within our conscious experience there is room for physical objects. But our problem actually may be something else. We have to decide if there is room for experience within physical objects. In other words, how can what we understand as physical objects produce conscious experience? You'll find that the Vedic texts condemn blind dogmatic faith in physical matter "in of itself," as if matter were an empowered substance, with inconceivable potencies.

At least in the beginning of our quest for self-knowledge, the Vedas can actually goad us to make use of an empirical approach. You do this by starting from all that you've actually got—conscious experience. Next, you pursue knowledge of what it is and why you have it. Then you try to understand the physical or mental objects that arise within consciousness.

We should bear in mind that naive realism has no value in the Vedic texts. Only a fool is said to believe the world exists directly as his senses perceive it. Because human vision *feels* so simple, we have the tendency to think that the image we see is directly the world "outside ourselves." Though at one time, vision specialists did believe in a one-to-one correspondence between the image flashed on the retina and the image registered by the brain, they have long discarded this idea. In other words, no photographic-like image is projected into the visual cortex of the brain. That means when the eye sees a circle, the subsequent electrochemical activity in the brain does not "possess the form" of a circle.

When you behold a green tree, what is happening? Assorted frequencies of light bounce from the tree to the retina of your human eye. There the cells react to the amount of light according to three frequency ranges, which correspond to three primary colors. Then electrochemical impulses are shot back to the human brain. Next comes perplexity. Somehow, mysteriously, into your consciousness—a mystery itself—emerges an image, what humans accept as "a green tree."

The Vedas assume we understand that the world as we perceive it—or think about it—depends on our states of consciousness, our levels of awareness. The texts point out that we are only dealing with appearances—the effects of something upon our consciousness. That something is—in of itself—unknown to us, because of the filtration done by our senses, combined with the mediation done by our states of consciousness.

Directly given to any human, whether scientist or layperson, are only consciously experienced appearances, filled with sense data and their relationships. Regardless of how brilliant we may be, can we rely upon these phenomena and the hypothesized relationships between them, without understanding consciousness? The answer comes to us when the alarm clock rings in the morning.

While sleeping, we can directly experience vivid dreams filled with what we take to be independently existing physical objects. We cavort with obliging lovers and fight off horrible attackers.

But as our consciousness enters the state of wakefulness, the dreamtime world suddenly disappears.

> When a person is in deep sleep, he dreams and sees in himself many other objects, such as great mountains and rivers or perhaps even the entire universe, although they are far away. Sometimes when one awakens from a dream he sees that he is in a human form, lying in his bed in one place. Then he sees himself, in terms of various conditions, as belonging to a particular nationality, family and so on. All the conditions of deep sleep, dreaming and wakefulness are but energies of the Supreme Personality of Godhead. One should always remember the original creator of these conditions, the Supreme Lord, who is unaffected by them. (*Shrimad-Bhagavatam* 6.16.54)

How do we understand the dreaminess of perceptions we have while sleeping? Certainly it's not by how they look. The objects and persons that populate our dream world appear to us as true as the components of our wakeful world. We judge the difference by duration. Dream stuff vanishes in time, when we wake up. Awake stuff—though we forget about it when we fall asleep— sticks around day after day, to greet us when we arise. But awake stuff also vanishes in time. Vedic teachers describe that the moment of death is very much like the moment a dream breaks. Hence, it seems that all we can honestly say is that some dreams last for a night, some for a day, and some for a lifetime. Consequently, the Vedas maintain, how can we ever consider either night-dream or daydream perceptions as bedrock truths of existence?

THE UNKNOWN KNOWER

A main impediment to our benefiting from Vedic knowledge is the Western determination to agonize over how nonphysical conscious experience supposedly arises from a physical world. Our best brains wonder, "How is it that some complex physical processes let loose with this strange stuff 'consciousness', and some don't?"

Scientists of this particular calling start their research with a belief in a physical world that exists in of itself, and then they try to understand how consciousness arose from it. The British philosopher J. J. C. Smart effectively communicated their conviction: "By 'materialism' I mean the theory that there is nothing in the world over and above those entities which are postulated by physics (or, of course, those entities which will be postulated by future and more adequate physical theories)."[4] Actually, only because of the ultimate riddle—subjective consciousness—do our scientists have the capacity to attempt probing their so-called physical objective world.

> This body is called the field, and one who knows this body is called the knower of the field. (*Bhagavad-gita* 13.2)

Up until very recently, mainstream scientists often publicly ridiculed persons and cultures opting for a nonmaterial explanation of the conscious self. "There you go again, chasing that *ghost in the machine*," was a common barb they threw. But as the twenty-first century begins, the entrenched materialist myths of the modern West have lost much ground. The shoe is now on the other foot. These days even laymen can point out that the problem for Western science is not the ghost in the machine, but *the machine in the ghost*. The age-old Vedic challenge is that things accepted as rock-solid fact are being perceived by an unknown!

A much easier pathway into the Vedic world is to avoid dogma. Instead, we start with only what is *directly* and indisputably given in our own experience—consciousness. Certainly it is refreshing to take as given only what is given, and leave as inference what is inferred. As should be clear now, without understanding consciousness, the worlds of both the layperson and the Nobel-prize winner are occult.

As long as we have no ultimate foundation for any of our Western forms of knowledge, we will have to live our lives trying to float calmly in the darkness atop a turbulent ocean of puzzles. Therefore, invoking a lack of empirical grounding seems an invalid argument for rejecting the Vedic presentation. Perhaps we moderns are the ones who should try to be a little empirical! We can try to accept from the outset the only thing we are sure we experience, and then be open to information—no matter how ancient—that unabashedly focuses on it. Probably there is no need becoming too anxious about the Veda's apparent lack of a foundation that agrees with our current concepts—all of which certainly have no foundation.

Unburdened by Western superiority complexes, our journey to the sea of the Vedas can proceed rapidly. We approach the Vedic Experience as consciousness—the sole thing we are directly experiencing—and then we build upon that. A mindset free of what we might call modern occultism will properly position us. Then we can forge ahead to figure out what we mean by the external world of common sense, as well as the strange subatomic world of modern physics. Moreover, then we can also analyze what we mean by the existence of other conscious experiences. We can try to comprehend other consciousnesses beyond our own—finite or even infinite:

> You should understand that I am also the knower in all bodies,
> and to understand this body and its knower is called knowledge.
> That is My opinion. (*Bhagavad-gita* 13.3)

From the ancient Vedic perspective, modern psychologists and philosophers mistakenly confuse the contents of consciousness with consciousness itself. They cannot discriminate between consciousness and the transformations of physical and mental—material—personhood. But the Vedic texts hold that consciousness is fundamental to all content—whether physiological, psychological, or combinations of both.

The Vedas teach us that before progressing further, we must at least comprehend that consciousness is always a constant, regardless of changes in the body and mind. That means consciousness is never lost or altered. Certainly the Vedic texts accept that our perception and awareness of the external world can vary by altering the body, mind, and senses. But basic consciousness is said to always be steady.

We should note that to move forward in our acquaintance with Vedic knowledge of the self, we must bear in mind the correlation it presents between consciousness, the contents of consciousness, and mind/body change. Upon our becoming comfortable with this principle, we can then easily venture ahead to explore not only the Vedic self but also the Vedic universe.

> As one can understand the presence of the air by the aromas it carries, so, under the guidance of the Supreme Personality of Godhead, one can understand the living soul by these three divisions of intelligence: wakefulness, dreaming and deep sleep. These three divisions, however, are not the soul; they are constituted of the three modes of material nature and are born of material activities. (*Shrimad-Bhagavatam* 7.7.26)

The first two of these three operational categories of conscious experience are more or less as we understand them in our everyday experience. The third—deep sleep—may require some explanation. Even during so-called "unconsciousness," we always have consciousness. Deep sleep refers to the state in which experience of all mental and physical phenomena shuts down, so much so that even dreaming stops. Sometimes we may be medically classified as "unconscious," or comatose. Doctors use the Glasgow Coma Scale to measure the depth of coma. Still, the Vedic point is that this state is just another phase of conscious experience.

In all three states of consciousness—wakefulness, dreaming and deep sleep, we have different experiences. The Vedas present the *atma*, the soul, as the neutral observer of these three states of material existence. The activities of the body and mind, though based on the energy of the soul, are distinguished from the activities of the soul.

Because the subject of the *atma* is difficult to understand, the Vedic texts give many definitions by negation. That is, they introduce the soul by explaining what it is not, or what cannot happen to it. For example, I may describe an apple by saying, "It is not purple, it is not prickly," and "It never ponders." But this analysis by negation does not directly tell you what an apple is.

The Vedic methodology of logical negation is known as *neti neti:* "It is not this, it is not that." It is especially helpful when dealing with inconceivable things. First, the *neti neti* process clears out the weeds of preconception. Then the truth of what something is may sprout upon fertile ground. The Vedic texts known as the Upanishads specialize in this tactic. Their main contribution is to establish the living entity and the Supreme as nonmaterial.

For example, Brahman, the Supreme Absolute Truth, is described as incomprehensible, beyond words, without qualities or form. By describing the antimaterial quality of the Absolute, the *neti neti* process of the Upanishads paves the way for the most difficult subject matter: spiritual form, spiritual qualities, spiritual activities, and spiritual personality. Generally people reason from their limited experience that individuality, activities, and qualities automatically imply material existence. Hence they speculate that spiritual perfection must be the opposite: no personality, no form, no activities, and no qualities.

Naive readers of the Upanishads often become confused by the abundance of impersonal descriptions of the living entity and the Supreme. Thus they miss out when the actual conclusion drops. They can't find their way through the intense *neti neti* to see the verses revealing the inconceivable personal reality of transcendence. Amid the impersonal statements, meant to drive away our material preconceptions, an adept student of the Upanishads will certainly find the culmination. The soul is clearly stated as personal, and in its perfect capacity it interacts with the Supreme Soul, which is also personal.

The *Bhagavad-gita* is also known as *Gitopanisad*, because it gives the essence of Vedic knowledge and is one of the most important Upanishads. In the *Gita,* as the text is known for short, Krishna gives many negative definitions of the soul. "It does not take birth, nor does it die. It has not come into being nor will ever come into being. Unbreakable and insoluble, it can't be cut, burned, moistened, or withered. It is immutable and indivisible." In this way, based upon our immediate experience, we can first visualize all the things the soul is not.

But directly what is the *atma,* the soul? The *Bhagavad-gita* gives several explicit, direct hits: "It is eternal, ever-existing, and primeval. Always the same, it is fixed in its constitutional nature. It is present in all environments."

The Vedas teach us that consciousness indicates the presence of the nonmaterial living entity, the soul, just as sunshine or light indicates the presence of the sun. We cannot see the wind, or the mind, or time; yet we understand the presence of these invisible things symptomatically, by indirect evidence. Sometimes when we wake up in the morning, clouds or fog cover the sun. Nevertheless we see a glimmer of sunlight and feel confident the day has begun and the sun is present. Likewise, by observing the evidential symptoms of the soul, we can understand its presence.

SOUL SEARCH

Proponents of Vedic wisdom are certain that, if we like, we can derive substantial confirmation for our intuition that there is indeed a unitary conscious self, a soul generating our life symptoms. The overwhelming strength of this immediate, everyday experience nags at the heart of more than a few scientists, though their laboratory research for the soul comes up empty-handed.

Because Western culture *seems* to be based on "seeing is believing," naturally we may wonder why we have not caught a glimpse of the soul. Some researchers have even gone after the soul with a PET scanner, looking to apprehend it in the brain. Modern physiology and cognitive science have searched in vain for a physical location of a transcendent identity. Lacking any direct evidence, generally the conclusion is that there is no essential self—no inner "screen" of experience and no inner experiencer.

In fairness to the Vedic view, however, we must remind ourselves that much of our current scientific theories indeed base themselves on indirect evidence of things never directly seen. For instance, no scientist will argue to banish the word electron because it refers to no directly observed thing. At a university lecture a physics professor may say to us, "Here we can see an electron." But all we can actually observe is a streak of condensation in a cloud chamber. Authorities, however, instruct us to be confident that the symptoms indicate an electron.

The secure, visually verifiable world of the ordinary person has long ago given way to increasingly strange and magic-like constructs of physics. The theoretical explorations of subatomic matter are certainly fascinating. But they offer scant confirmation for reality as our senses directly perceive it. The Nobel laureate Richard Feynman, known in academia as "the physicist's physicist," commented, "[our current physics] describes nature as absurd from the point of view of common sense. And it agrees fully with experiment. So I hope you can accept nature as she is—absurd."[5]

Physicists say it takes eight to ten years just to train a recruit to comprehend fundamental reality according to the chimera of quantum mechanics. Not only does the candidate for initiation have to accept that the world buzzes with components that are intrinsically unobservable, but also the inductee has to hold to waves and particles that have no single objective reality until an attempt is made to measure for them.

> An expert geologist can understand where there is gold and by various processes can extract it from the gold ore. Similarly, a spiritually advanced person can understand how the spiritual particle exists within the body, and thus by cultivating spiritual knowledge he can attain perfection in spiritual life. However, as one who is not expert cannot understand where there is gold, a foolish person who has not cultivated spiritual knowledge cannot understand how the spirit exists within the body. (*Shrimad-Bhagavatam* 7.7.21)

Materialists, as mechanists, flaunt their conviction that life is matter. They are sure that the same fundamental laws known to govern nonliving substances also control the living. Savor this recent eulogy of Jacques Monod and his famous book *Chance and Necessity*, cited at the start of this chapter: "Monod died in 1976, but molecular and cell biologists continue to cite his book as an outstanding exposition of a philosophy that accepts a mechanistic view of life and celebrates its resultant glory—the entire living world of Earth."[6]

Materialists assure themselves that everything about a living system can be reduced to billiard balls of matter and nothing more. They denigrate as vitalists those who hold that living organisms differ from inanimate matter because of the presence of a life force, a special energy.

In the first half of the nineteenth century, vitalism was actually accepted knowledge. A well-read overview of cell biology reminds us: "Although it is tempting to ridicule such views, in the days before there was any significant knowledge about cells, the theory of vitalism was mainstream science. . . . As scientists gradually demanded more evidence for their theories, the concept of vitalism slowly faded."[7] For the past 150 years, vitalism has been effectively ousted from the official canon of Western scientific knowledge. Nevertheless, more than a few major scientists, including Nobel laureates, continue to at least flirt with it. Some, out of exasperation, unofficially entertain it.

Holdouts for a material solution to life, of course, have not faded. They still proudly rule the laboratory—without demanding evidence for their theories. Take for example Duke University cell biologist Harold Erickson.

> The secret of life is not a secret any more. We've known for twenty or thirty years now that life is not more mysterious than the chemical reactions on which it is based. There's an incredibly complex set of chemical reactions, but they're all logical and understandable. We don't yet understand them all but we do understand a lot of them and it's not hard to see that eventually we should know them all.[8]

But this postdated check—"payment not quite now, but surely in the future"—can fly much higher in the sky. For instance, in the hands of Tom Pollard, a cell biologist who heads the world-famous Salk Institute in California, wishful thinking ascends to the rank of arrogant Western fables. Pollard, a former president of the American Society for Cell Biology, wonders when the masses will wake up to *the certainty* that life is just a globule of chemistry and physics: "What molecular biologists have believed for two generations is now generally regarded as *proved beyond any doubt.* Life is entirely the result of physics and chemistry inside cells and among cells. I wonder whether the general public is prepared to sign on?"[9]

More honest scientists have already signed off. Nobel Prize–winning chemist Albert Szent-Gyorgyi is a classic example. Seeking to understand the mystery of life, he began his quest by studying organisms in their natural environment. Next he switched to studying cells. Then he moved to the chemistry of proteins. Finally he settled upon electrons, hoping they would be the clues to life. Nearing the end of his life, he poignantly confessed, "In my search for the secret of life, I ended up with atoms and electrons, which have no life at all. Somewhere along the line, life ran out through my fingers. So, in my old age, I am now retracing my steps."[10]

Another Nobel laureate, Eugene Wigner, says that the possibility of a self-duplicating unit emerging on its own is zero. Since the ability to reproduce is one of the fundamental characteristics of all living organisms, Wigner concludes that our present understanding of physics and chemistry does not enable us to explain the phenomenon of life.

America's National Academy of Sciences established a committee for reviewing origin-of-life research. Its chairman, Harold P. Klein, concluded, "The simplest bacterium is so damn complicated from the point of view of a chemist that it is almost impossible to imagine how it happened." After reviewing the latest batch of theories, his committee, unable to endorse any of the competitors, hoped that much more research would save the day.[11]

Remember the famous primordial soup theory for the origin of life? Textbooks still teach that in 1953 Stanley Miller vividly demonstrated in his laboratory how the first chemicals of life arose on their own. From a froth of basic chemicals likely to have been present on the primitive Earth, self-replicating molecules were to have emerged spontaneously. For his bestowing upon us a brilliant chemical solution to the riddle of how life began, Miller was revered. Forty or so years later, in his old age, Miller himself has admitted his fabled experiment has led nowhere.[12]

Even the avowed materialists among the top-ranked scientific aces confess their bewilderment, though they won't drop their faith. Lamenting that the awesome tools of biotechnology still cannot produce life out of inanimate matter, Francis Crick, the Nobel laureate of DNA fame, complained that the origin of life seems "a miracle, so many are the conditions which would have to be satisfied to get it going."[13]

As Sure As Death

Since a thorough search of memoirs and musings reveals that, even in hallowed scientific chambers, vitalism will not die, we might benefit by looking to the Vedas for a more satisfying version of it. The Vedic texts do not shirk from declaring that the soul is undetectable by material methods. Through the naked senses or technologically assisted senses, no one, we are informed, can directly see the soul. Yet the Vedas insist that through preliminary application of common sense, graduating to advanced techniques of spiritual discipline, a thoughtful clear-brained person can receive verification that the soul exists and that it is the crucial agent activating the body.

Resonant with anyone's experience, the Vedas point out that death is the biggest incentive for wondering about biological life. What happens when a creature dies? The body has the same weight, shape, and material constituents—dead or alive. Yet when dead, its growth, metabolism, and other functions completely halt. Unless you keep the lifeless body on ice, it immediately starts to decay.

The Vedic perspective prods us to consider: What is the difference between a living body and a dead body? What is the active agent responsible for the body to grow from infancy to maturity—without which a new baby is pronounced stillborn, though all the necessary organs are intact? If life is merely a biochemical machine, then we should inject the right chemical formula and repair the faulty mechanism. To be honest, only when the dead body comes back to life again will we have verified this theory.

The Vedic conclusion is that life transcends whatever we know from our modern physics and chemistry. Upon the death of a loved one, our ordinary parlance reveals our resonance with the Vedic literature. We say, "She's gone," and "He's passed on." But what has departed? The same body that you hugged and squeezed lies there waiting, but now you are not attracted. What's missing? Now we just want to get rid of the body—after the appropriate rituals, of course. That necrophilia is certainly revolting implies that the real person we loved we never saw. The Vedic conclusion is that the mysterious entity now missing we never actually saw or touched. So why all the tears?

> O lamenters, you are all fools! The person for whom you lament is still lying before you and has not gone anywhere. Then what is the cause for your lamentation? Previously he heard you and replied to you, but now, not finding him you are lamenting. This is contradictory behavior, for you have never actually seen the person within the body who heard you and replied. There is no need for your lamentation, for the body you have always seen is lying here. (*Shrimad-Bhagavatam* 7.2.44)

The countless testimonies of near-death experiences (NDEs) have rocked the materialistic faith. NDEs challenge the notion of death as the utter end—the termination of bags of biochemicals that were formerly alive. So widespread are books describing

NDEs that there is no need to duplicate their efforts here. In short, in many cases, though the body is pronounced clinically dead, its occupant hovers above the operating table, watching the surgical team acknowledge defeat. Later, the person is able to describe exactly what went on in the operating room, from a vantage point above the scene—though he or she was obviously unconscious and often pronounced dead.

Surprisingly, from the Vedic perspective, NDEs are not spiritual experiences. They involve what is known as the subtle body, in its ability to function—with the soul—separately from the gross body.

> There are two kinds of bodies for every individual soul—a gross body made of five gross elements and a subtle body made of three subtle elements. Within these bodies, however, is the spirit soul. One must find the soul by analysis, saying, "This is not it. This is not it." Thus one must separate spirit from matter. (*Shrimad-Bhagavatam* 7.7.23)

The above verse gives us a succinct presentation of the Vedic self, both internal and external, or essential and superfluous. Material existence means that a gross covering and a subtle, or astral, covering surrounds the spirit soul. The gross physical body is composed of ingredients we know from ordinary earthly experience: solid matter, liquid matter, gaseous matter, radiant energy, and space. But then there is also a subtle body—the psychic body—composed of finer substances enumerated as mind, intelligence, and false ego. This is the vehicle responsible for so-called astral projection, astral travelling, and NDEs. And this is the aura-producing field.

Just as the soul uses the physical body as a mechanism, it can also travel in the subtle astral body, without the physical covering. Either by training or special circumstance—such as a near death—this wandering can happen. Moreover, many people can travel astrally in dreams, whether they are aware of it or not. In any case, from the Vedic vantage point, there is no question of mind over matter, because mind is matter.

Remnants of the Vedic delineation of the spirit soul covered by a gross and subtle body show up in Egypt and Greece. To Vedic patriarchs this is not surprising; they consider Egyptian and Greek civilization to be expatriate Vedic offshoots.

The Egyptians accepted that everyone had several bodies, ranging in function from gross and subtle material to completely spiritual. The physical body was called *khat,* a word indicating "that which must decay." The *khat* received all the efforts at mummification and preservation that every schoolchild today reads about. But actually the Egyptians did not expect the physical body to rise again, leaving the tomb, though their efforts at mummification figure so prominently in our fascination. They accepted that beyond the gross physical body there were subtle astral layers, one of which, the *ka,* could travel independently of the gross body. Ultimately the soul, the *ba,* was the unit of eternality, meant to dwell in the heavens. Controversy exists about the functional differences and terminology of the several intermediary subtle aspects because Egyptologists have not found definitions clear enough for them.

The so-called mystery religion of the Greeks seems obvious in its derivation from Vedic knowledge, probably via Egypt, if not India directly. The scholar G. R. S. Mead openly suggests that the Egyptian, Chaldean, Bacchic, Orphic, and Eleusinian "mystery cults" all came from the same source.[14] The Greek Orphic mystery knowledge taught that there are three bodies: an ethereal, an aerial, and a terrestrial. The ethereal meant nonmaterial; the terrestrial was the physical form; and the aerial was the subtle astral intermediary. Terrestrial life meant the interplay of all three, and the goal of life was to free the soul from its coverings. Plato obviously inherited much of his description of the soul from the Orphic knowledge base. Of all the Greek mystery schools, the Orphic line was distinguished by its asceticism, celibacy, and its prohibiting of meat and wine.

The Great Brain Hope

We may laugh at the labor the Egyptians invested in mummification, but how many of us know that just as Russian communists preserved the body of Lenin, and the Chinese government, the corpse of Mao Zedong, so Western scientists have preserved Einstein's brain? The pickling of his gray matter is fitting because, in their avoiding the ancient Vedic science of the soul and its consciousness, moderns have rushed to brain research as the last resort. In this way the study of the self has turned into the study of neurons.

The Canadian surgeon Dr. Wilder Penfield, a Nobel Laureate in physiology and medicine, did his own version of soul searching, while operating on people's brains. With an electrical probe he would stimulate areas of their motor cortex, to discern which part of the brain controls which part of the body. Upon his stimulating a particular place in the motor cortex, the patient's arm would start to lift. Penfield would ask the patient to describe his situation. "My arm is rising," was the response. But the person would deny he had made the decision to move it. Then Penfield would request the patient to move the arm in another direction. The arm would move, as the patient confirmed he had made the choice.

Looking with the best instruments technology can offer, neuroscientists can never find the decision-maker, who recognizes he had not chosen to move his arm when the surgeon's probe stimulated the corresponding part of the motor cortex. Likewise, no neuroscientist can track down the agent who did make the deliberate decision to lift the arm. Scientists can find the correct area in the brain where the decision is executed, but the thinker behind the thought, the commander behind the choice, always escapes their detection. In fact, when Penfield stimulated the temporal lobes of human brains, he set off a flood of experiences from the past—replete with authentic sights, sounds, and smells. A boy heard his mother talking to him on the phone and could repeat the entire conversation; a woman saw herself in her kitchen and could hear her son frolicking outside. But in each case, when the person experimented on was asked, "Are you there in these scenes," the person replied, "No, I'm on the operating table, witnessing these experiences." Where in the brain is the witness, the discriminator?

When Penfield first began the experiments, he had thought his discoveries would reveal a physical window, through which the conscious self could be observed and quantified. Four decades of brain research later, Penfield concluded that no neurological explanation would suffice—the self was of a different ilk. "The form of that energy is different from that of neuronal potentials [electrochemical activity] that travel the axone [nerve] pathways. I am forced to choose the proposition that our being is to be explained on the basis of two fundamental elements."[15] A few days before his death in 1976, he gave his final pronouncement: "The brain is a computer. . . . But it is programmed by something that is outside itself."[16]

Another Nobel Prize winner, Sir John Eccles, in 1965 wrote in *The Brain and the Unity of Conscious Experience*, "I believe that there is a fundamental mystery in my existence, transcending any biological account of the development of my body (including my brain)."[17] Sixteen years later the neurophysiologist told an interviewer, "If you look at most modern texts on evolution you find nothing about mind and consciousness. They assume it just comes automatically with the development of the brain. But that's not the answer."[18]

We have seen that after more than forty years of investigation,

Wilder Penfield relinquished his hopes for the brain. He accepted that the secret of selfhood entails another fundamental element—beyond matter. Sir John Eccles too, at the end of his career, made no secret of his final conclusion. Summing up his life's work in his 1985 book *The Wonder of Being Human*, he declared that each person has a "divinely created psyche."[19] But if we judge by the current thunder in brain hope, we might infer that sentimentality had overtaken these Nobel Prize winners in old age. Today, among hard-core reductionist scientists, the brain reigns supreme—like never before.

Often laypersons are surprised to hear that scientists holding to an exclusive faith in matter calmly refer to themselves as materialists. Because these very learned specialists are absolutely sure the nonmaterial does not exist, they infer no negative implications from the designation "materialist." In fact, they wear the hat rather proudly. Everything in existence, they believe, consists of matter. The cosmos and life—everything, including so-called spiritual knowledge—have all evolved from physical processes of matter, they say. Chance is the almighty instigator, in association with "natural laws"—which somehow are also matter.

Attempting to build upon their certainty that life emerges from matter, the diehard materialistic scientists—now more than ever—brilliantly strive to explain the self and consciousness strictly in terms of mechanistic events in the brain.

The peerless DNA giant, Francis Crick, has placed himself solidly at the forefront of this last ingenious gasp. Because he is the codiscoverer of DNA structure, when he switched to consciousness research as his final frontier, he bestowed matchless stature and prestige upon the field.[20] The well-seasoned Crick, nearing ninety years, works in tandem with his young German prodigy, Christof Koch. Together they broadcast throughout the world their burning conviction that consciousness emerges from electrical oscillations in our neurons.

Hardcore reductionist scientists like Crick and Koch publicly declare their determination to exterminate any alternative to materialistic explanations. Crick trumpeted his arrival on the consciousness battlefield. In his book *The Astonishing Hypothesis: The Scientific Search for the Soul* he proclaimed, "You, your joys and sorrows, your memories and ambitions, your sense of personal identity and free will, are, in fact, no more than the behavior of a vast assembly of nerve-cells. As Lewis Carroll's Alice might have phrased it: 'You're nothing but a pack of neurons'."[21]

The bravado is impressive. A dispassionate analysis, however, clearly reveals something else. Just as modern medical advances in understanding the human body by isolating its biochemicals have not yielded any breakthroughs in creating life, similarly, the latest breakthroughs in understanding the physical processes of the neural system have also failed. Brain science still has not brought consciousness within our grasp. As in previous decades, it's the same old story: no branches of modern knowledge have allowed us to cross the eerie canyon between physical description and subjective, conscious reality. In fairness to the ancient Vedic knowledge, we should admit that, though the clouds of latest research may thunder, still no rain falls. Why?

Moreover, how much do we know about the brain and the self anyway? Of all the cells in the body, neurons, we have been told, generally do not change. What you get during prenatal months are, for the most part, the neurons you can expect to have for the rest of your life. Suddenly, however, in 1998, that scientific tenet tottered and sagged. A science writer for the *New York Times* reported:

> For years neurobiologists clung to a fundamental truth: once animals, or people, reach adulthood, they may lose brain cells but they can never grow new ones. . . . But now, in experiments that experts call amazing, that dogma has been overturned. Scientists

have found that monkeys are constantly making new brain cells in the hippocampus, an area of the brain used for forming long-term memories. Moreover, they report, the production of new cells is squelched when the animals are under extreme stress. Experts say they fully expect that humans are no different and that they, too, make new brain cells in adult life.[22]

Dr. Elizabeth Gould of Princeton University and her colleagues made the discovery. Gould explained the barrier of tradition she had to break through: "People believed that in order to store memories for a lifetime, you need a stable brain. If cells are constantly dying and new ones being produced, how would that be possible?"[23] Dr. Arturo Alvarez-Buylla, at Rockefeller University, recalled one of his research associates entertaining the idea that an adult brain can form new neurons. But, he said, "People thought that was bordering on fantasy."[24]

In the last months of the twentieth century, neuron surprises continued. Besides arriving every day in the hippocampus region of the brain, now thousands of fresh neurons were caught entering daily into the cerebral cortex, the outer part of the brain related to intellectual functions and personality.

"The scientific community can easily believe something it is 50 percent ready to absorb, but not something that comes out of left field," said Eric R. Kandel, a well-known neuroscientist at Columbia University. "But here, we are prepared for it."[25]

Kandel compared the changes set in motion by the revolutionary research to the paradigm shifts made famous by the historian of science, Thomas Kuhn. A major scientific theory, Kandel noted, is about to disintegrate—making way for a new vision.

Scientists easily concur that the neuron news, though based on research in monkeys, will prove true of people, too. As fellow primates, humans generally follow suit. A team of scientists from Harvard University, the Salk Institute, and the Sahlgrenska

University Hospital in Sweden is now confirming Gould's work by experimenting upon human brains directly, rather than extrapolating from research on animal brains. The team wrote in the journal *Nature Medicine*, "Our study demonstrates that cell genesis occurs in human brains and that the human brain retains the potential for self-renewal throughout the life."[26]

The neurons in human beings have turned out to be inconstant. Therefore, before investing any further doctrinaire convictions in them, we'd do well to ask ourselves an irksome question: Can the consciousness of the living entity survive without its neural hardware? Or, put another way, does consciousness absolutely require neurology? A few cases from England expose more of our deep ignorance, despite assurances from neurological scientists.

The medical study of hydranencephalics emerged in the 1970s and 1980s. A scholarly journal, *Developmental Medicine and Child Neurology*, first broke the news. In England, neurologist John Lorber of the University of Sheffield was studying two children who had water not "on the brain" but in place of a brain. A light shone onto one side of their skulls would have cleanly passed through to the other. Though neither child had any cerebral cortex whatsoever, both were normal in their mental functions.[27] How can this be? How can you be a "whole person"; how can you think properly?

After a minor flurry in popular science magazines, the discovery faded. Might the implications have been just too daunting for further deliberation? Meanwhile, as conventional brain science continued its way, the work on no-brain humans quietly proceeded. Other cases turned up. Soon Lorber assembled a test group of patients in which more than 95 percent of their cranium was devoid of brain substance. In other words, it would not be hyperbole to say their skull was empty. Some of the persons were severely disabled, but half of them had IQs greater than 100.

The greatest challenge to brain dogma, however, graduated

from the very same University of Sheffield—with highest honors. A brilliant student happened to visit his doctor. Noticing the young man's head was larger than normal, the doctor referred him to the specialist John Lorber, simply out of curiosity. The neurologist's routine brain scan revealed jolting evidence: inside the future mathematician's head something essential was missing.

Lorber documented the case: "There's a young student at this university," he certified, "who has an IQ of 126, has gained a first-class honors degree in mathematics, and is socially completely normal. And yet the boy has virtually no brain." [28]

Still, advocates of the consciousness-from-brain belief blindly march on. They feel that as the essential, tofulike grey substance evolved through neo-Darwinism, at some critical point it must have manifested the "secondary phenomenon" known as consciousness. In other words, when matter gets complicated enough, the conscious experience appears—whether from brains, or maybe from computers!

A growing number of contemporary scientists, however, have concluded otherwise. They protest that even the most brilliantly detailed knowledge of the brain would still fail to resolve the fundamental question: Why should brain matter give rise to consciousness? They say it is one level of challenge to analyze the cognitive processes of the brain. But to demonstrate that subjective, conscious awareness emerges from physicality is another venture altogether.

The ancient Vedas can help us to clarify this real issue. The Vedic agility in analyzing existence can richly frame the context of our present scientific crisis. For Western systems of knowledge to survive in their present state, they must first admit to and then solve an extraordinary internal problem. That is, how can subjective, conscious experience be explained as arising from *any physical system*—brain or otherwise?

Whether our hope lies in the electrochemical processes of neurons, or in the more diminutive world of subatomic particles, or in magical quantum fields, the same impasse blocks our way. Perhaps, by urging us to look somewhere else, the primeval wisdom of the Vedas can save us centuries of groping in darkness.

The standard reductionist approach of modern science gave us a technology that showered upon us many conveniences. But there are increasing tremors beneath the cathedrals of learning and the temples of research. Let's give credit where credit's due. The ancient Vedic knowledge seems to clearly spotlight the epicenter of a long overdue quake in Western science, philosophy, and religion. That is, our present fund of knowledge simply makes no provision for nonphysical phenomena that are not ultimately composed of physical constituents—be they atoms and molecules, or particles and waves. The Vedic axioms do not waffle in their handling of this crucial issue. They hit it head on.

The Western Quake

We are witnessing both the collapse of classical empiricism (how we get our knowledge) and the collapse of metaphysical realism (the world is as our senses perceive it, and science describes it as it is.)[29]

While the academic establishment generally continues to plow straight ahead, seldom acknowledging the fissures widening around them, the nonspecialist people are apparently changing course.

If we judge by the popularity of alternative science, alternative history, alternative medicine—in short, alternative forms of almost every traditional discipline—it does seem that a new paradigm is emerging, in spite of the mulishness of institutionalized scholarship and research. Books, videos, and CD-ROMS document the heaps of what used to be known as "anomalies," but which are now coalescing into their own impressive branches of study. The Internet zips around the earth the probes and finds of a global army of alternative researchers and nonmainstream intellectuals.

Barring a worldwide technological breakdown, the global communications system does seem to be spearheading a global paradigm change. We might bear in mind, though, that developed countries, with only 15 percent of the world's population, use the vast majority of all telephone lines. Furthermore, statistics taken at the start of the new century show that the USA, Japan, the UK, and Germany accounted for two-thirds of all Internet usage. Worldwide, only 2.5 percent of the world's people access the Internet, a number that will certainly but slowly increase.[30]

The USA easily surpasses any other nation in numbers of Internet users. The think-tank Stanford Research Institute International researched the psychology of American Internet users. It found that a segment of the population labeled "the actualizers"— well educated and keen on self-actualization—formed 10 percent of the American adult population but remarkably 50 percent of Internet users.[31]

Among the educated, are we about to see a major shift in the conceptual patterns underlying human civilization? After studying the classic periods of change in the Western world, the acclaimed historian Lewis Mumford noted, "Every transformation of man has rested on a new metaphysical and ideological base . . . a new picture of the cosmos and the nature of man."[32] Historians generally agree that there have been four or five major transitions in the Western attempt at civilization. Since the fall of the Roman Empire, the end of the Middle Ages has been the most recent watershed. Usually such pivotal periods happen only once or twice a millennium.

Is the Western world indeed changing from one type of civilization to another? Or, as we lurch into the new century, are we undergoing typical millennial fits of uncertainty? Many say things are completely atypical. For example, a prominent spokesperson on the international New Age scene, Jean Houston, seems ready for drama on the high seas: "Other times in history thought they were it. They were wrong. This is it! We are living in a huge mind/body quake, moving towards levels of ourselves that we never thought to have. We are in whitewater all the time. It's no longer a quiet pond."[33]

Crystalline messengers of the "New Millennium" exhort us that what they call "the deep collective unconsciousness" wants a total transformation of humanity. Some statistics may bear these prophets out. The World Values Survey covered forty-three nations—70 percent of the world's population. Its global coordinator, Ronald Ingelhart, concluded that a dozen or so nations were undergoing what he called the "postmodern shift": a declining trust in the traditional modern bulwarks of government, science, economics, and religion, combined with a newfound penchant for personal growth and inner development. England, Canada, Scandinavia, the Netherlands, and the USA led this new wave.[34]

In the USA, studies have revealed that 44 million American adults form a flourishing segment of society called the Cultural Creatives.[35] Espousing ideals of spiritual transformation, personal development, and ecological sustainability, this 24 percent of the population has its eyes wide open to new paradigms of thought, including syntheses of the East and West. Anthropologist Anthony C. Wallace called such potential agents of change "cultural revitalization movements." These are the advance guard, he says, who wake up an entire culture to see that the old story doesn't work any more and a new story is needed.[36] Keenly hopeful of the future, the revitalizers announce that we require a new image of "who we are" and a new way to fit into life.

The reputable American pollster Dan Yankelovich discerned that in the USA, the percentage of the people who see spiritual development as an essential for their lives has jumped from 53 percent to 78 percent in three years. Significantly, only 6 percent of this large majority consider themselves "New Age."[37] Noting this poll, many perceive the predominance of a spiritually minded mainstream.

But can the "actualizers," the "Cultural Creatives," the "post-moderns," and even a "spiritual mainstream" make a dent in the classic set of human problems? Since the Renaissance, both the traditionalists and moderns have grappled with the basic social challenges: how to divide wealth, eradicate disease, provide necessities for an increasing population, handle social complexity, and shape a global ethic. What is the crucial knowledge the great new hope bears that will make a difference?

Whether or not the transmoderns in the Western world can mobilize themselves and society, the Vedas stand ready with the standard: profound and comprehensive knowledge of the self and its consciousness. Restoring the ancient covenant would seem to begin with the best knowledge of the self that either antiquity or the present world can offer. Then the West, filling the huge hole in its Semitic religions and empirical science, literally can finally begin to deal with itself.

Nobel Laureate brain scientist Roger Sperry points out: "Beliefs concerning the ultimate purposes and meaning of life and the accompanying worldview perspectives that mold beliefs of right and wrong are critically dependent . . . on concepts regarding the conscious self."[38] Our social values, he explains, directly and indirectly depend on what we think consciousness is.

The Vedic seers call for a civilization molded so that its members can soberly ponder and act upon the deepest issues of life. The Vedic view is that the nonmaterial particle, the spirit soul, is striving for freedom from the material, and that overindulgence in temporal demands blunts our spiritual sensibilities. For the man and woman of the Vedas, the perfection of science is to know the qualities of the material and the nonmaterial, and to free the spirit soul from the nonpermanent atmosphere.

The conclusions of the Vedas urge that a society inspire its people to realize, "I don't know who I am, where I've come from, and what my purpose is in the cosmos. Why must I suffer physical, mental, and environmental disturbances? Why are old age, disease, and death forced upon me, though I don't want them? Where shall I go after leaving this present body? Or, is death the absolute end?"

Spiritual pragmatism is the Vedic legacy for self and society. A civilization certainly cannot ignore the people's routine requirements for food, shelter, and similar necessities. Yet, massive problems arise when leaders mistake symptoms of our innate human hunger for profound spiritual knowledge and experience as cravings for better material facilities and sensuality. Hence, both ancients and moderns require precise knowledge—not postmodern sentiment—so that a society can establish the most favorable social conditions for spiritual growth.

Notes

1 Jacques Monod, *Chance and Necessity*, trans. Austryn Wainhouse (New York: Alfred A. Knopf, 1972).

2 Letter dated 12 November 1959.

3 Monod's pioneering, widely read book *Chance and Necessity* introduced modern molecular biology and evolutionary theory to the general public.

4 J.J.C. Smart, *Essays Metaphysical and Moral* (Oxford: Blackwell, 1987), chap. 16.

5 Quoted in Abraham Pais, *Niels Bohr's Times in Physics, Philosophy, and Polity* (Oxford: Clarendon Press, 1991), p. 349.

6 Boyce Rensberger, *Life Itself: Exploring the Realm of the Living Cell* (Oxford: Oxford University Press, 1996), p. 24.

7 Ibid., p. 25.

8 Ibid.

9 Ibid.

10 Albert Szent-Gyorgyi, *Biology Today* (California: CRM Books, 1972).

11 *Scientific American*, February 1991, p. 104.

12 John Horgan, *The End of Science* (New York: Broadway Books, 1997), pp. 138–39.

13 Ibid., p. 141.

14 John M. Watkins, *Orpheus* (London: John M. Watkins, 1965), p. 153.

15 Wilder Penfield, *The Mystery of the Mind* (Princeton, N. J.: Princeton University Press, 1975), p. 48.

16 *MacLean's* Magazine, 17 April 1976.

17 Sir John Eccles, *The Brain and the Unity of Conscious Experience* (Cambridge: Cambridge University Press, 1965).

18 *International Herald Tribune*, 31 March 1981.

19 Eccles, *The Wonder of Being Human* (Boston: Shambala Publications, 1985), p. 176.

20 *Scientific American*, July 1994, pp. 72–78.

21 Francis Crick, *The Astonishing Hypothesis: The Scientific Search for the Soul* (London: Simon & Schuster, 1994).

22 Gina Kolata, "Studies Find Brain Grows New Cells," *New York Times*, 17 March 1998.

23 Ibid.

24 Ibid.

25 Nicholas Wade, "Brain May Grow New Cells Daily," *New York Times*, 15 October 1999.

26 As reported by Maggie Fox, health and science correspondent, Reuters, 2 November 1998.

27 As reported by David Darling, who holds a degree in physics from the University of Sheffield and a Ph.D. in astronomy from the University of Manchester, in his book *Soul Search* (New York: Villard Books, 1995), pp. 82–83.

28 Quoted in John Lewin, "Is Your Brain Really Necessary?" *Science* 210 (12 December 1980): 1232–35. The original article, "Is Your Brain Really Necessary?" by neurologist John Lorber, alluded to in this *Science* article, is published in a German book called *Hydrocephalus im frühen Kindesalter*, ed. D. Voth (Stuttgart: Ferdinand Enke Verlag, 1983). Neurological fanatics will find no peace of mind in the minute details of the case: the brilliant math graduate had a fleck of grey matter inside his skull—a tiny rind 1 millimeter thick. That is approximately 2 percent of what normally should be inside the cranium. Thus, the appropriate pronouncement: no brain. Physicalists, however, will always indeed look for a physical explanation. Desperately grabbing on to the 2 percent fleck, they will empower it with miraculous abilities. And if the 2 percent speck was missing, they would empower the walls of the empty skull. And whatever happened to evolutionary expediency? Why do we carry around such a big brain, if a speck of grey matter will get the job done with honors?

29 Henryk Skolimowski, *The Participatory Mind* (London: Penguin Books, 1994), p. xiii.

30 National and global Internet usage statistics from *Vital Signs 1999*, Worldwatch Institute (Washington D.C.).

31 *American Demographics*, July 1996, p. 41.

32 Lewis Mumford, *Transformation of Man* (New York: Harper Brothers, 1956).

33 Radio interview, "New Dimensions," recorded on tape-set "The New Millennium" (Ukiah, California: New Dimensions Tapes).

34 Ronald Ingelhart, "Changing Values, Economic Development, and Political Change," *International Social Science Journal*, no. 145 (September 1995): 399.

35 Paul Ray, "The Integral Cultural Survey: A Study of Values, Subcultures, and Use of Alternative Health Care in America," delivered to the Fetzer Institute in October 1995.

36 "Cultural Revitalization Movements," *American Anthropologist*, 1961.

37 Reported in the *Noetic Sciences Review*, 25th anniversary issue, 1998, p. 22.

38 Roger Sperry, "Changing Priorities," *Annual Review of Neuroscience* 4 (1981): 1–15.

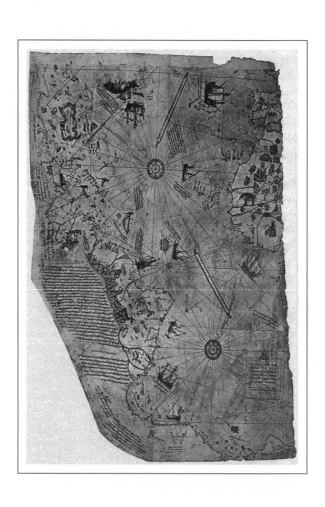

CHAPTER 5

MAKING AND
CHANGING HISTORY

~

Ancient history departments at universities are usually cozy, comfortable nooks. The dust of inertia seems to have long settled on the books and their theories. Certainly the very nature of antiquity—so distant and far-removed—has allowed its professors to feel shielded from the challenge of fresh winds, which can ventilate academic areas closer to the pulse of modern life.

Actually there is no academic or popular literature more in need of revision than books on India's Vedic past. Though the British era at the beginning of the eighteenth century has long passed, the evangelical and colonial motives linger, in the form of a compounded inheritance. Consequently, while the motives of Westerners have changed, this cumulative legacy from the Old World continues to deaden our present awareness of ancient India.

A complete revision of Indology, though essential, is an arduous task. Masterly interpretations by successive academic generations are lodged atop one another. Hence Indology, difficult enough because its secrets are locked away in a mysterious oral and written tradition—or buried in the sands of the Thar Desert—becomes even more perplexing due to the intricate inheritance of conjecture.

The German master of quantum physics, Max Planck, once noted, "A new scientific truth does not triumph by convincing its opponents and making them see light, but rather because its opponents eventually die, and a new generation grows up that is familiar with it."

Planck's wryness applies even more to the study of ancient India. For a bold newcomer in the field to challenge the inertia, hoping for a shake-up, is institutionally unacceptable. The candidate has to grapple with the entire accumulated stock of past linguistic formulations. Then the daring savant must refute each of the successive layers, which have encrusted a rickety or even imaginary historical framework over the past two hundred years. Finally, in old age, an energetic nonconformist scholar may hang on in life long enough to wield the stature required for introducing just a modest revision. The study of India's past, however, desperately requires a monumental revolution.

Recent unexpected upheavals in the study of ancient America demonstrate what fresh eyes and hands could accomplish with India's past. Who were the first people in the New World? The prehistory of the Western Hemisphere used to be a cakewalk for scholars. Now it is a quagmire.

Formerly, until the mid-1990s, scholars were sure that no people were in the Americas in the millennia before circa 11000 B.C., because two massive sheets of ice covered what is now Canada and the northern USA. The glaciers retreated around 11000 B.C., allowing the ancestors of the indigenous Americans to cross the Bering Straits. These people were assuredly North Asians from Siberia.

The first tremors signaling the end of this assurety came when the famous Spirit Cave mummy—discovered in Nevada in

1940—had its age radically revised by the University of California. Employing new dating methods, scientists recently pushed the age back from 3,000 years to 9,415 years. Hence the problem: the mummy does not have indigenous American ancestral features. It resembles South Asian folk.

Closely following the heels of the Spirit Cave revision came the Kennewick man. Found on a riverbank in the state of Washington, the skeleton was in such good condition that police thought it to be a recent murder victim. The University of California, however, determined their suspected victim was 9,300 years old. Hence another problem: the Kennewick man, like his Spirit Cave counterpart, is not a North Asian ancestor of the indigenous Americans. He also hails from somewhere in South Asia.

Go to any bookstore or library and you will see that all mainstream books on New World prehistory say that the Western Hemisphere was populated exclusively by indigenous Americans with roots in North Asia. Now arises proof of a South Asian connection. That evidence could easily mean that two diverse peoples inhabited the Americas, and that one of those two is now lost to modern history.

The bones of the Arlington Springs woman have just entered the spotlight and are shaking the stage. Given an age of 13,000 years, these remains are the oldest in North America, to date. Although found in 1949, they have just undergone DHA and radiocarbon tests unavailable at the time of their discovery. The bones come from California's Channel Islands. Therefore they complicate theories on America's settlement by indicating that at least some of the first Americans may have come by sea—not via a land bridge from Asia.[1]

In southeastern Brazil a 13,500-year-old skeleton was recovered in 1998. This find also refutes the idea that the first Americans originated only in Siberia and migrated over the Bering land bridge only between 11,000 and 10,000 years ago. The skeleton resembles Africans and Australian aborigines—not Asians or Native Americans. According to University of Sao Paulo anthropologist Walter Neves, the skeleton makes evident that another people were in the New World before the Mongoloids are said to have crossed over the Alaskan–Asian land bridge.[2]

Another radical discovery in Monte Verde, Chile, during the 1970s, took twenty years to triumph over resistance. An ancient campsite was discovered that scientists date at 14,700 years old—now the oldest accepted site of human habitation in the Americas. In 1998, after two decades of work, a team of American and Chilean scientists swept away the last skepticism about the site's age. The problem with the campsite was its location—12,000 miles way from the proverbial land bridge. Scholars confidently informed the annual meeting of the American Advancement of Science that unless the migrants had made an astoundingly frantic beeline down to Chile after the glaciers receded, they must have been on the continent for tens of thousands of years.[3]

Geologists were willing to allow 2,000 years for the quickest nonstop trip down from the Bering Strait. Indeed, to reach Monte Verde, Chile, the ancient campers had to traverse 12,000 miles of mountains, plains, and jungles, through climates ranging from arctic to tropical. Upon adding minimal travel time to the campsite's age, the resulting date of 16,700 years ago would put the settlers squarely amid the massive glaciers that covered much of the continent. Hence, the trek must have been even earlier, before the ice converged circa 18000 B.C.

Several geneticists, including Theodore Schurr of the Southwest Foundation for Biomedical Research in San Antonio, Texas, and Douglas Wallace of Emory University, are asserting a far earlier migration based on research of genetic diversity. They compared several DNA markers found in modern Native Americans and modern Siberians, and then calculated that the Siberian ancestors left for the New World at least 30,000 years ago.[4]

Linguistic scholars were not to be outdone. They advocated that the most compelling evidence is, of course, linguistic. Based on the conjectured evolution of languages in the New World, they joined the rush to push for an older date of entry into the Americas.

At a news conference, Johanna Nichols, a language expert from the University of California at Berkeley, added to the new scientists' conclusions the linguists' verdict that the more than 140 languages spoken by indigenous Americans needed tens of thousands of years to develop: "The linguistic population of the New World is 40,000 years old or something like that."[5]

Whether we stress the physical or the linguistic side of the discovery, the unsettling implications are that the non-Mongoloid people of the settlement were in place at least before the most recent Ice Age.[6] Interestingly, a scholar from the venerated Smithsonian Institute in Washington D.C. alerted the media that final acceptance of the Monte Verde site would immediately hasten the emergence of more evidence. Why? Dennis Stanford explained that many scientists who had uncovered sites older than 10,000 years had been afraid to come forward—they feared ridicule.[7]

When we turn to Indian prehistory and the possibility of major revision, the task is daunting. Contrasted with the Western Hemisphere's prehistory, the archaeological record for India's antiquity is comparatively barren. As discussed in chapter 3, the linguistic scholars have tirelessly filled the vacuum for almost two hundred years. Therefore all roads to revision, they assert, run through them.

We should always remember that the incumbent Aryan invasion/migration theory is primarily a linguistic model. This verdict no one denies. Linguistic scholars defend their configuration by attesting that the lack of archaeological evidence simply means the right proofs haven't turned up yet. Some of them boldly say the archaeological absence may mean that nothing is actually there to be found. Perhaps invading armies or migrating peoples leave no trail of artifacts, they reason.

Detractors to the Aryans-in theory like to deride the linguistic scholars' iron grip on Indology. But merely deriding linguistic studies will not suffice, its supporters complain. They challenge that the revisionists must come up with a better model, a new Great Theory. To be acceptable, this replacement must attempt to explain the entire Indo-European appearance of languages spreading and culture diffusing. The invasionists/migrationists feel that they have proffered a satisfactory scheme and that therefore they need not heed the revisionists, who have failed to manufacture a counter-model. In other words, either put up a Grand Theory or shut up. Neutral observers of the fray, however, raise a crucial question: Does any of the venerable linguistic evidence apparently supporting invasion/migration allow other interpretations?

In response, cutting-edge scholars have demonstrated that all the much-vaunted linguistic data can be reconfigured in ways that do not support the classic Aryans-in hypothesis. Though these alternative reconfigurations do not sink the incumbent model, they clearly reveal that its supposedly firm foundations are alarmingly pliant. The same data employed to support it can point several other ways. Consequently, within Indic studies, a new protocol emerges: just calmly admit that ready conclusions about India's prehistory are not yet possible.

Storm watchers should keep their eyes fixed on the dating of Vedic literature. Here is a major field of ancient study ripe for a blast. Steady momentum is gathering to review the current notions. Certainly, in the twenty-first century, we can look forward to major revisions. What makes this impending overhaul so dangerous for the status quo is that all theories of intelligence as a recent development in human history would have to go right out the door. And there lies the rub. It's too much, too great a price to pay.

The academic establishment has staked its very existence on the gradual evolution of human intellect and achievement, from utter primitiveness to advanced modernity. But the Vedas fly right in the face of this conception. Hence, for many decades the dust has been left to settle on the Vedic texts—in the sense that they are not treated as compendiums of valuable information about the planet and the universe.

Let's take a quick look at themes in the Vedas that have so doomed them to rejection as serious treatises—or at best, relegated them to the mythology department:

- Earth has been populated with intelligent life for millions of years.
- The technology available on this planet thousands of years ago was far more advanced and subtle than the crudities we have now.
- The present version of humanity—that is, the strain occupying Earth for approximately the past 5,000 years—is debased, in behavior and intelligence. Many previous cultures, lost to current versions of history, were much more advanced in every respect.

Few mainstream academics will take these Vedic assertions seriously. Meanwhile, mainstream television treats the masses to a cornucopia of anomalies, which challenge the most securely established notions. The standard scientific idea has been that humans like us are fairly recent arrivals. Before about 100,000 years ago, only more apelike ancestors are said to have existed. They are said to have originated about four to five million years ago. Before them, about forty to fifty million years back, the primeval ancestors—primitive apes and monkeys—appeared. Life itself began by chance two or three billion years ago.

Despite the candied simplicity of this story, trouble is brewing—especially in the normally placid discipline of ancient studies.

Documented cases reveal that *humanity could be millions of years older* than the theory of evolution allows. Simultaneously the general public is becoming aware that knowledge contrary to the predominant mindset has been filtered out—even sometimes suppressed.

HIDDEN HUMAN HISTORY

In autumn 1993 an estimated 33 million Americans watched televised evidence dating the Sphinx back thousands of years earlier than the academically accepted date of 2500 B.C. A geology expert from Boston University, Dr. Robert Schoch, got inside the fence surrounding the Sphinx—before having his permission revoked by the Egyptian government's academic wing. He had enough time, though, to confirm a nonacademic's hunch.

An independent American researcher, John Anthony West, had read in an obscure book by French mathematician R. A. Schwaller de Lubicz that water, not wind, had eroded the Sphinx. When in the history of Earth had there been enough water or rain in arid Egypt to wear down the Sphinx? The Sahara Desert represents millennia of dryness. Therefore, West rightfully concluded:

> If the single fact of the water erosion of the Sphinx could be confirmed, it would in itself overthrow all accepted chronologies of the history of civilization; it would force a drastic reevaluation of the assumption of "progress"—the assumptions upon which the whole of modern education is based. It would be difficult to find a single, simple question with graver implications.[8]

Schoch confirmed the cause of the erosion: rainfall—not even flooding. Schoch had earned his Ph.D. in geology and geophysics at Yale University, where he specialized in rocks eroded by weather. He knew that the heavy precipitation resulting in the erosion patterns on the Sphinx had ceased thousands of years before the Egyptologists' accepted date for the Sphinx of 2500 B.C.

Official history has given the Sphinx an age of 4500 years. For most of that allotted time it has been buried up to its neck in sand. Egyptologists have always enforced their official explanation for the scars and fissures all around the Sphinx and on the inside walls of its enclosure. Though not rock specialists, they established harsh desert winds as the culprit. Schoch, however, used geological knowledge to point out the real perpetrator of the scars and cracks: torrents of rain for thousands of years. His solid presentation, to this day, has withstood the counterattacks from conventional Egyptologists. He explains:

> As a geologist I come to Egyptology as an outsider. By and large, Egyptologists don't use this kind of scientific evidence; they rely instead on a mix of methods that includes historiography, archaeology, anthropology, philology, and literary analysis. Geological analysis is an alien form of thinking, one that Egyptologists are likely to reject because of their own lack of familiarity with it.[9]

To find in Egypt a climate wet enough to weather stone over thousands of years, we have to retreat to at least the 3,500-year span occurring between 8000 and 4500 B.C. At that time, the eastern Sahara was completely different: a savanna lavished by the kind of constant rainfall that inundates tropical regions. Schoch, demonstrating the guardedness of an established scholar, took care to offer the most conservative date possible: back to 7000 B.C.

Those more bold—like the expedition's inspirer, West, argue for the rainy period preceding 10000 B.C. These less-constrained voices argue that, among other points, no archaeological evidence exists yet of any high civilization in Egypt between 7000 and 5000 B.C. No Pharaohs are known to have lived then. Conventional scholars say that only primitive agricultural communities characterized the eastern Sahara and the banks of the Nile at that time. How could these farming enclaves muster the motivation and technology to engineer and erect colossal stone monuments? For this and other reasons, the challengers conclude that the civilization responsible for the Sphinx must have existed in the rain period preceding 10000 B.C. and disappeared long before the later era of downpours.

In the case of either projection—conservative or bold—the reaction of mainstream Egyptologists was the same: furor exploded. How dare these outsiders trespass on their domain. They publicly stormed and raged: Who was this wayward, though highly reputed, geology scientist, aided by a jack-of-all-trades non-scholar of no repute? Expecting this inevitable response, West had wisely arranged to film the entire geological examination of the Sphinx, for direct presentation to the people on nationwide television. "Since we could expect nothing but opposition from academic Egyptologists and archaeologists, a way had to be found to get the theory to the public."[10]

An archaeologist at the University of California's Berkeley campus got right to the point: advanced intelligence and antiquity do not mix. "There is no way this could be true," declared Carol Redmont. "The people of that region would not have had the technology, the governing institutions, or even the will to build such a structure thousands of years before Khafre's regime [2500 B.C.] . . . [The assertion] flies in the face of everything we know about ancient Eygpt."[11] At Boston's Museum of Fine Arts, the assistant curator of the Egyptian Department, Peter Lecovara, stood up for the academic establishment: "That's ridiculous! Thousands of scholars working for hundreds of years have studied this problem and the chronology is pretty much worked out. There are no big surprises in store for us."[12]

Schoch presented his research to the 1992 Convention of the Geological Society of America. Upon earning the hearty approval of his peers, in that same year he went on to the Annual Meeting of the American Association for the Advancement of Science. Firmly standing up to the Egyptologists attending, he pointed out that his job was neither to enrage them nor to coddle them:

> I've been told over and over again that the peoples of Egypt, as far as we know, did not have either the technology or the social organization to cut out the core body of the Sphinx in pre-dynastic times. . . . However, I don't see it as being my problem as a geologist. . . . If my *findings* are in conflict with their *theory* about the rise of civilization then maybe it's time for them to reevaluate *that theory*. . . . I'm just following the science where it leads me.[13]

While Schoch dutifully presented the most cautious explanation of the research, his cohort, West—unencumbered by academic necessities—advanced the bold import:

> We are told that the evolution of human civilization is a linear process—that it goes from stupid cavemen to smart old us with our hydrogen bombs and striped toothpaste. But the proof that the Sphinx is many, many thousands of years older than the archaeologists think it is, that it preceded by many thousands of years even dynastic Egypt, means that there must have been, at some point in history, a high and sophisticated civilization—just as all the legends affirm.[14]

At the turn of a new century, the "Sphinx Battle" has settled into an impasse. Egyptologists cannot refute the geological evidence signaling a major revision. They opt to ignore it.[15]

The producers of the television special *Mystery of the Sphinx* won an Emmy Award, the top prize in America for television. Back again they came, in February 1996, with their documentary *Mysterious Origins of Man*. This time the information was even more revolutionary. Millions in the USA were astounded to learn, among other shocking things, that more than a century ago, in mining shafts at California's Table Mountain, modern-age tools as well as human bones had been found in rock strata ranging in age from 9 million to 55 million years.

J. D. Whitney was the official geologist for the state of California during the time of the extraordinary discoveries. He gathered and authenticated the findings of several decades. Producing an authoritative, thorough report entitled *Auriferous Gravels of the Sierra Nevada of California,* Whitney presented a powerful case for "Tertiary Man"—humans existing in the geologic period from 65 million to 2 million years ago.

In 1879, at the time of the report's completion, the president of the American Association for the Advancement of Science, O. C. Marsh—a preeminent paleontologist of his day—addressed the association and gave his verdict: "The proof offered by Professor J. D. Whitney in his recent work is so strong, and his careful, conscientious method of investigation so well known, that his conclusions seem irresistible. . . . The existence of man in the Tertiary period seems now fairly established."[16]

The cofounder of the theory of evolution, Alfred Russell Wallace, gave considerable credence to Whitney's documentation of the stone artifacts and human fossils found in the gold-bearing gravels of California. Wary of the knowledge filter that had begun to afflict the study of human origins, he lamented that evidence for anatomically modern humans existing in the Tertiary was increasingly "attacked with all the weapons of doubt, accusation, and ridicule."[17] Disturbed by the trend, Wallace admonished his fellow scientists:

> The proper way to treat evidence as to man's antiquity is to place it on record, and admit it provisionally wherever it would be held adequate in the case of other animals; not, as is too often now the

case, to ignore it as unworthy of acceptance or subject its discoverers to indiscriminate accusations of being imposters or the victims of imposters.[18]

Wallace was describing the state of affairs among his peers at the end of the nineteenth century. As the twentieth century progressed, however, Tertiary Man didn't even merit a controversy. The grip of social convention had become a vice—contrary findings and their perpetrators were silenced.

More than a hundred years after J. D. Whitney's painstaking efforts to call attention to human artifacts and skeletal remains in layers ranging from 9 to 55 million years old, his work has been forgotten, and references to it in textbooks have become extinct. Though Harvard University published his treatise in 1880, the implications of the evidence have never been addressed or followed up by twentieth-century scientists. The artifacts still exist, at the Phoebe Hearst Natural Museum, at the University of California, Berkeley. When assembling the documentary *Mysterious Origins of Man*, the television network—an American national giant—applied for permission to film them for nationwide exposure. The museum refused.

Upon the airing of the special documentary, academics saw red again. They protested that the information was presented by researchers who did not hold academic degrees in their fields of investigation, and therefore true scientists cannot take their findings seriously. After all, Michael Cremo had studied political science in his university days and, although his cohort Richard Thompson holds a Ph.D. from Cornell University, it is in mathematics, not anthropology or palaeontology. Nevertheless, these two independent scholars had combined to produce a hefty 952-page tome, the now famous *Forbidden Archaeology*, chronicling the establishment-imposed blinkers that impede objective knowledge of humanity's origins.

After the nationwide telecast, a flood of mail from the academic community accused the documentary's producers of destroying the intelligence of the nation and propagating "bogus science." The NBC network, capitalizing on the success of the first telecast, later the same year followed with a second. This time mainstream academia mobilized beforehand, as the Internet rang with calls to battle. Dr. Jere H. Lipps, a paleontologist at the University of California, rallied his colleagues: "If you are worried about science in America, tell your local NBC station, NBC, and its various sponsors that you object to the portrayal of this program as science. America must get smart, and we can make a difference!"[19]

Dr. Allison R. Palmer, president of the Institute for Cambrian Studies, which specializes in the geological period 570 to 500 million years ago, turned to the government for help. Seeking to pressure the Federal Communications Commission—the American agency that grants licenses to television networks—he demanded, "At the very least NBC should be required to make substantial prime-time apologies to their viewing audience for a sufficient period of time so that the audience very clearly gets the message that they were duped. In addition, NBC should be fined sufficiently so that a major fund for public science education can be established."[20]

The producers of *Mysterious Origins* calmly directed the enraged scholars to the cases they had aired that did involve degree-holders in the particular fields—and they reminded academia of their fate.

For example, Dr. Virginia Steen McIntyre holds a Ph.D. in geology. She was a fellow with the United States Geology Survey when she did her fieldwork in Mexico, and the National Science Foundation funded her research. She presented careful conclusions about advanced stone tools found at Hueyatlaco. She dated the layers containing the implements at 250,000 years B.C.

Moreover, two other USGS academically certified members, using four different methods of dating, backed her up. Their work did more than challenge the standard story of New World anthropology. Since toolmaking humans were not due on Earth until 100,000 years ago in Africa, the radical findings also threatened the traditional story of human origins. The result? In spite of McIntyre's impeccable credentials, her findings were ignored and her career was ruined.

The uncompromising book *Forbidden Archaeology* and its abridged version, *Hidden History of the Human Race*, carefully document hundreds of cases demonstrating that humans like ourselves have lived on Earth for millions of years. For instance, in 1979 in East Africa, the renowned archaeologist Mary Leakey and her team found footprints embedded in deposits of hardened volcanic ash dated 3.7 million years old. The footprints—discovered at Laetoli, Tanzania—are just like those a modern human would leave. Scientists tell us that the prints belong to ape-men who had feet just like ours. Sharp "alternative researchers," however, remind the public that the ape-men of that far distant time, called australopithecines, had feet quite unlike ours. All scientific side-stepping aside, the only creatures now known that had the feet to make those footprints are humans like ourselves. But remember the standard story: humans like us only came to be about 100,000 years ago.

Let's turn back again to forgotten geological work in the previous century. In 1862 *The Geologist*, a scientific journal, documented a human skeleton dug up from ninety feet deep, in the state of Illinois.[21] More than two feet of unbroken slate rock directly covered the skeleton. Once again, an official state geologist handled the case. He dated the geological layers embedding the skeleton at 300 million years old. Shortly before the Illinois find, in 1852, the journal *Scientific American*—a mainstay even back then—reported construction workers finding something quite odd in Boston. While excavating the foundation for a building, under fifteen feet of solid rock, they uncovered a metallic vase, with inlaid floral designs of silver.[22] Michael Cremo, coauthor of *Forbidden Archaeology*, checked modern geological surveys, to learn the age of the rock containing the vase. Current science dates that rock layer at over 500 million years.

Chapter 1 presented the upsetting discovery that at least 800,000 years ago, toolmaking humans journeyed by sea to the island of Flores, Indonesia. Previous conceptions held that anatomically modern humans had made the earliest major sea crossing, between just 40,000 to 60,000 years ago. Boatmaking and sailing are usually attributed to modern human bodies. Yet, rather than choosing to christen the Flores people *Homo sapiens sapiens*, scientists immediately labeled them as the anatomically primitive *Homo erectus*. In this way, drastically elevating the capacities of *Homo erectus*, they detoured an explanation that would devastate the current conceptions of human history.

Cremo turned the spotlight on this deft maneuver in his address to the World Archaeological Congress in January 1999. Lest anyone think the Flores boating problem is an isolated occurrence, Cremo also presented other disturbing finds, related in time:

> Anatomically modern femurs of the same age from Java offer corroborating evidence. [Furthermore] in 1997, H. Thieme reported advanced wooden hunting spears in German coal deposits about 400,000 years old. Spears are normally associated exclusively with anatomically modern humans. Thieme chose to raise the cultural status of European *Homo erectus*, but another possibility is to posit anatomically modern humans.
>
> Discoveries of anatomically modern human bones by Boucher de Perthes at Abbeville, France, in deposits the same age as the German spears, offer corroborating evidence.[23]

Vedic sympathizers are well positioned to handle any drastic revisions to the standard saga of human origins. The evidence that challengers have brought to light is consistent with Vedic information. *If only our Indologists knew!*

MAPS TO AN UNKNOWN INTELLIGENCE

A professor of the History of Science, Charles Hapgood, through an unusual route, found his way to intriguing signs that an intelligent ancient civilization had preceded dynastic Egypt. Filed away in the US Library of Congress are hundreds of medieval maritime maps. Called portolans, meaning "port to port," these maps have been known to scholars for centuries. But, constricted by the convention that any map from medieval times must be full of gross inaccuracies, the academic community paid little attention to the potential treasure.

Hapgood, educated at Harvard University, was the first to conduct a comprehensive study. His interest ignited in 1956 when he heard a radio discussion of an ancient map known as the Piri Reis map, a copy of which had been presented by a Turkish naval officer to the US Navy Hydrographic Office earlier in the year. The original had been found rolled up on a dusty shelf in the Topkapi Palace in Istanbul in 1929. Painted on a gazelle skin, with a date of 1513, the map showed a portion of the western coast of Africa on the right, the eastern coast of South America on the left, and what seems to be the northern coast of Antarctica at the bottom.

But Antarctica was not discovered until 1818, more than three hundred years after Piri Reis drew the map. The astonishment, however, does not end there. Indicating that major problems may afflict our current historical conventions, the map seems to show part of Antarctica's topography free of ice.

The Antarctic ice cap contains 90 percent of Earth's total ice.

Covering about 98 percent of the Antarctic continent, the ice cap is Earth's largest. It is also considered the oldest. Scientists opine that Greenland was glaciated 7 million years ago and that Antarctica has probably been iced, at least partially, for 35 million years.

Currently there is an academic debate over whether any warming affected the Antarctic ice cap during its theorized 35-million-year existence. A group of scientists led by Peter Webb, of Ohio State University, assert they have discovered evidence of a glacial meltdown 3 million years ago. Other scientists, such as George Denton and David Merchant, say no.

Our predicament is that on the one hand, we have the Piri Reis map, which apparently depicts Queen Maud Land at the South Pole with bays free of ice. If indeed the map depicts Antarctica, then we must go to the other hand. We have to cope with contemporary scientific opinion that has not seen evidence for an ice-free Antarctica before at least the controversial date of 3 million years ago. Finally, we have the most important questions: what civilization, lost in time, was able to chart the Antarctic coastline? Moreover, how and when could its people see Antarctica without ice?

The Piri Reis map certainly has its problems. A few of its details seem more medieval or Renaissance than ancient. Also, historians know that at the time Reis wrote the map, European mariners were trading rumors that a body of land existed below South America. For example, Amerigo Vespucci, blown far off his course, spotted land. Maybe it could have been the Falklands or maybe even Antarctica, as some scholars theorize. Finally, Hapgood himself recognized the problem that the map shows South America and Antarctica as one continuous coastline, as if the two continents were adjoined rather than separated by 600 miles of ocean. Some say that perhaps what we see as Antarctica is actually what Reis meant to be Patagonia—the bottom of the Argentine coast.

Robert Schoch, the Yale geological scholar who set off the

Sphinx battle, has declined to embrace the Reis map. He does, however, freely admit its challenge. "I continue to find Hapgood's ideas fascinating and tantalizing, but the evidence is less than cogent. The Piri Reis map contains no information of indisputably ancient origin, and the supposed coast of Antarctica could well be the lower reach of South America."[24] Those who see Antarctica in the Reis map do have major supporters, renowned for their technical expertise and concern for every square mile of the planet. In a letter to Charles Hapgood, the US Air Force affirmed the scholar's analysis and its consequences:

8 Reconnaissance Technical Squadron (SAC)
United States Airforce
Westover Airforce Base
Massachusetts

6 July 1960

Subject: Admiral Piri Reis World Map
To: Professor Charles H. Hapgood
                 Keene College
                 Keene, New Hampshire

Dear Professor Hapgood
    Your request for evaluation of certain unusual features of the Piri Reis World Map of 1513 by this organization has been reviewed.
    The claim that the lower part of the map portrays the Princess Martha Coast of Queen Maud Land, Antarctica, and the Palmer Peninsula is reasonable. We find this is the most logical and in all probability the correct interpretation of the map.
    The geographical detail shown in the lower part of the map agrees very remarkably with the results of the seismic profile

made across the top of the ice-cap by the Swedish–British Antarctic Expedition of 1949.

This indicates the coastline had been mapped before it was covered by the ice-cap.

The ice-cap in this region is now about a mile thick.

We have no idea how the data on this map can be reconciled with the supposed state of geographical knowledge in 1513.

Harold Z. Ohlmeyer
Lt. Colonel, USAF
Commander[25]

The Air Force reconnaissance expert certainly knew that cartography is a complex activity requiring a sophisticated level of civilization. High-ranking US Air Force officers undergo years of rigorous studies, comparable to what only the best civilian universities can offer. Academia, if it chooses to recognize the challenge, would have to find the ancient people directly or indirectly responsible for the map—at a time when historians acknowledge no development of civilization. Typically we would look for the tail end of this advanced civilization—its last days. Then, according to our Western linear conception, we would have to go back in time at least a few thousand years more, to allow such a civilization to attain the required level of geodesy and cartography.

Piri Reis is a documented historical person. An admiral in the fleet of the Ottoman Turks, amid his naval battles he wrote a famous sailing text of his day. The manual described the navigational intricacies of the Aegean and Mediterranean seas. In notes on the now famous Antarctic map, Reis wrote that he did not do any of the surveying, but derived the map from a collection of earlier sources—some dating back to the fourth century B.C. He did not mention anything about the identity of the earlier cartographers.

Reis was beheaded in 1554 or 1555 by his superiors. Professor Hapgood seems to have accrued a small measure of Reis's hapless fate. No academic praise came his way—no recognition for making a major, well-researched, and original contribution to the study of antiquity. Worse yet, until his death most of his scholarly peers shunned him and ridiculed his work. The American nationwide telecast *Mysterious Origins of Man* and several nonspecialist books have postmortem established his reputation, citing him for his possibly overturning the conventions of world history.

The subglacial profile of Queen Maud Land, Antarctica, lay hidden under ice until 1949, when a combined British–Swedish reconnaissance team conducted a seismic survey. As Hapgood discovered in his research at the US Library of Congress, Piri Reis's map was not the only portolan to indicate ancient knowledge of an ice-free Antarctica. The professor found the Oronteus Finaeus Map of 1531, which, in addition to Queen Maud Land, showed amazing details of mountains, estuaries, inlets, and rivers in several other areas. These details so finely accorded with contemporary scientific analyses of what lies below the ice that Hapgood had to conclude that ancient men had visited Antarctica and perhaps lived there before the glacier completely swallowed up the land.

Like the Reis map, the Oronteus Finaeus map has its problems. Missing is the Palmer Peninsula, which extends out from the Antarctic mainland toward South America for almost 500 miles. Also, much of what the map shows as solid land, such as Wilkes Land and the Amery Basin, would theoretically be underwater in the absence of the glaciers. The ever-cautious Robert Schoch concludes: "The Oronteus Finaeus map may be a representation that is partly accurate and partly hearsay. This raises a tantalizing question about explorations of the southernmost continent that are lost to history." Richard Strachan of the prestigious Massachusetts Institute of Technology went further. He confirmed the close correspondence of the Oronteus Finaeus map with the latest surveys through the ice cap.

The most famous cartographer of the sixteenth century is renowned for the Mercator projection—to this day still used on most maps of the world. Gerard Kramer, known as Mercator, in 1569 included the Oronteus Finaeus map in his *Atlas*, and also presented Antarctica on several of his own maps—with details even more distinctly recognizable.

Then in the eighteenth century—still long before the official discovery of the icy continent—French geographer Phillippe Buache apparently surpassed all the aforementioned maps by presenting his cartography of an entire Antarctica free from ice. Modern science did not have an entire subglacial topography until 1958, when a full seismic survey of Antarctica was performed. The modern survey seems to have generally confirmed what Buache had done back in 1737. What are the primary sources of the Finaeus, Mercator, and Buache maps? What people in remote antiquity originally could have possessed all this knowledge?

Like the other maps, the Buache map has its supporters and detractors. Buache added more wonders to the riddle. His map reveals an ultimate challenge: an ice-free waterway across the Antarctic continent, thus dividing it into two main landmasses. Though modern maps show Antarctica as one mass, the 1958 seismic survey shows it is a hidden archipelago of large islands, with mile-thick ice wedged between them.

We should note that orthodox geologists say the latest date when these waterways were clear is millions of years ago. But what humans were around millions of years ago to witness and map Antarctica with its land completely free of glaciers and its waterways completely unobstructed with ice? Who passed this knowledge down? If the Buache map, like the others, at least partially holds up, then undoubtedly we will be told that there must be another explanation.

"A Civilization that Vanished"

Hapgood tracked down and analyzed more maps, suggesting knowledge of other parts of the world, such as South America and northern Europe. The reader may consult his *Maps of the Ancient Sea Kings* for the complete presentation. His final chapter, entitled "A Civilization that Vanished," points the open-minded in an revolutionary direction:

> The evidence presented by the ancient maps appears to suggest the existence in remote times, before the rise of any known cultures, of a true civilization, of an advanced kind, which either was localized in one area but had worldwide commerce, or was, in a real sense, a *worldwide* culture. This culture, at least in some respects, was more advanced than the civilizations of Greece and Rome. In geodesy, nautical science, and map-making it was more advanced than any known culture before the 18th century of the Christian era.[26]

While the public, with little help from the scholastic establishment, tries to find its way through all this astounding information that overturns the established story of human origins and civilization, the Vedic texts have been waiting for their day in the sun. The Western world has known about the revolutionary contents of the Vedas for almost two centuries, but rare is the Western Indology expert who considers the texts a reasonable documentation of human civilization. Even Indian scholars have been trained to feel apologetic or disdainful about what has come to be viewed as the Vedas' gross exaggerations and fantasies concerning the ancients. A. L. Basham, who wrote the popular classic *The Wonder that Was India*, is one of many.

For a quick glimpse at what unsung surprises may lie in the Vedas, let us consider these renditions from the *Yajur-veda* and

Atharva-veda, for instance. Here are the possibilities of verses when in the hands of a sympathetic Sanskrit translator:

> O disciple, a student in the science of government, sail in oceans in steamers, fly in the air in airplanes, know God the Creator through the Vedas, control thy breath through yoga, through astronomy know the functions of day and night, know all the Vedas, *Rig, Yajur, Sama* and *Atharva*, by means of their constituent parts.
>
> Through astronomy, geography, and geology, go thou to all the different countries of the world under the sun. Mayest thou attain through good preaching to statesmanship and artisanship, through medical science obtain knowledge of all medicinal plants, through hydrostatics learn the different uses of water, through electricity understand the working of ever lustrous lightening. Carry out my instructions willingly. (*Yajur-veda* 6.21)

> O royal skilled engineer, construct sea-boats, propelled on water by our experts, and airplanes, moving and flying upward, after the clouds that reside in the mid-region, that fly as the boats move on the sea, that fly high over and below the watery clouds. Be thou, thereby, prosperous in this world created by the Omnipresent God, and flier in both air and lightning. (*Yajur-veda* 10.19)[27]

> The atomic energy fissions the ninety-nine elements, covering its path by the bombardments of neutrons without let or hindrance. Desirous of stalking the head, i.e., the chief part of the swift power, hidden in the mass of molecular adjustments of the elements, this atomic energy approaches it in the very act of fissioning it by the above-noted bombardment. Herein, verily the scientists know the similar hidden striking force of the rays of the sun working in the orbit of the moon. (*Atharva-veda* 20.41.1–3)[28]

Sanskritists will fight over translations. Needless to say, rare is the Western scholar who will let these verses speak in this way. To calmly admit that the *Yajur-* and *Atharva-veda* speak of electricity, nuclear energy, and aircraft is to violate every bias and preconception that forms the edifice of our Western creed. Whether the people these verses refer to were supposed to have lived millions of years ago or 10,000 years ago or just 5,000 years ago, it all has to be wrong.

The Western attitude toward Vedic literature, however, was not always so insensitive and dismissive. The first nineteenth-century European scholars to encounter the Vedas often brimmed with awe and admiration. Whether these original European savants of India understood the full ramifications of the Vedic world view is, of course, doubtful. But certainly they were deeply moved by the philosophical wisdom, breadth, and eloquence of Vedic knowledge. The prime concern of Europe with India, however, was commerce.

THE EUROPEAN QUEST FOR INDIA

In the beginning, European interest in India centered exclusively upon trade. Marco Polo, the thirteenth-century explorer, gave Europeans their first authoritative information of East Asia. He described India as one of the wealthiest countries in the world, and particularly referred to Cambay, a city in west-central India, as a busy port. Later, Christopher Columbus would pour over *The Travels of Marco Polo*, as well as Cardinal Pierre d'Ailly's *Image of the World*. But Columbus's main inspiration was more esoteric. He was a firm devotee of the Second Book of Esdras, an apocryphal book very popular in the early Christian Church. It primarily told of a future age that would succeed the world order existing at the time the Romans conquered Jerusalem.

The system of ideas Columbus derived from 2 Esdras included

a round Earth; a very great land distance between the edge of the West (Spain) and the edge of the East (the Indies); and a short sea distance between Spain and "India." So Christopher Columbus set out to the west, searching for a shorter route to the Far East, and he ran into the New World instead. Consequently the Spanish flag flew in what was later to be named the "West Indies." Later, 2 Esdras would lose out to the reforming Council of Trent (1545–63). The Roman Catholic Church, refusing to certify it as canon, sent it to the back of the Latin Bible, as an appendix to the New Testament.

When in 1498 the Portuguese navigator Vasco da Gama landed at Calicut, now Kozhikode, in southwestern India, he was restoring a direct economic link between Europe and the East that had ceased about one thousand years earlier. After the decline of the Roman Empire in A.D. 4, Greek overland merchant activity faded. Since that time, Arab intermediaries had brokered any overland trade with the East. They often made business quite dangerous—or stopped it completely. Upon the arrival of the Portuguese at the start of the sixteenth century, the first European commercial settlements in India began. The European powers at that time saw India mainly as a land of spices, and to a lesser extent as an exotic realm, mystified by imaginative Greek authors. The Indians, from their side, saw the Europeans as *yavanas:* strangers to proper human culture.

The Portuguese, on the southwestern coast of India, encountered the Christians of St. Thomas. These devotees were enclaves of Indians who claimed that St. Thomas had converted them. At first the Portuguese missionaries professed friendship. Then, suspecting the Indian Christians of heresy, the Portuguese forced their church to accept the jurisdiction of Rome. All their rites were latinized, local bishops were replaced with Portuguese ones, and the Inquisition was installed. As for the multitudes of non-Christian Indians, the cruel tactics of the Portuguese, combined with their missionary zeal and intolerance, earned them little sympathy.

Battles in Europe had a great effect on who would dominate the future of India. In 1580 Spain annexed the Portuguese kingdom. Eight years later, the British navy forced the Spanish Armada to retreat to Spain in defeat. The Armada's disappearance on the open seas meant the naval route to the East was now open for the Dutch and the English. The Dutch arrived first. Their primary concern was neither empire nor religion. Monopoly was their speciality—not imperialism or conversion. The British and French followed. Even a Danish East India Company gave business a try.

The British, after establishing their first trading post in India in 1600, competed with the French and Portuguese for commercial control of port cities. The British East Indian venture at first met with determined Dutch opposition, and then it had to confront the French East India Company. The Seven Years War between Britain and France (1756–63) knocked the French out of the competition for India's resources. At the same time, British military triumphs over the rulers of Bengal provided Britain a massive increase in territory. Wielding a huge army of mercenaries, the British East India Company defeated an Indian army in 1752 and gained the upper hand—guaranteeing its future supremacy.

The British Crown granted the British East India Company an official monopoly on India. Eventually the Company succeeded in completely pushing out all its international rivals. The Fourth Anglo–Dutch War (1780–84) permanently ended the Dutch naval threat; and the end of the Napoleonic Wars (1815) removed any last fears of the French bouncing back. Consequently, through treaties and military coercion, the British East India Company finally achieved control over the whole subcontinent of India. In the year 1818 the British Empire in India became the British Empire of India.

During the preceding centuries of international jousting for the control of commerce in India, Europeans had become aware of Sanskrit, the language of the Vedic texts. Now that Britain's naval might had swept the seas clean of mercantile competition for India, some of the intellectual members of the British military and bureaucracy began to learn the local languages. Their official goal was to help establish an efficient and lasting regime in India. A few of them took an interest in the religious texts of India.

In 1784 the Asiatic Society of Bengal was established in Calcutta, to publish and disseminate historical, linguistic, and literary studies. William Jones, Charles Wilkins, and Thomas Colebrook emerged as the pioneers of Western Indological studies. Charles Wilkins had been the first to learn Sanskrit, and he busied himself studying with pundits in Benares and translating Sanskrit works. In 1785 he published his rendition of the *Bhagavad-gita.*

Several of the scholarly inclined British colonizers began to intuit that perhaps they had stumbled upon the primeval religion, predating anything from the Middle East. In 1786 the linguistically brilliant judge Sir William Jones announced to the Asiatic Society of Bengal his famous discovery that Sanskrit was related to Latin and Greek, as well as Persian, Celtic, and Gothic.

To be precise, Jones was not the first to notice similarities. One hundred years earlier, a Florentine merchant in Goa, Filippo Sassetti, and an English Jesuit, Thomas Stevens, had independently detected the same phenomenon. Jones, however, was certainly the first to make a full scholarly presentation. And he forthrightly proclaimed a heartfelt attraction to Vedic literature and philosophy:

I am in love with Gopia, charmed with Crishen [Krishna], an enthusiastic admirer of Raama and a devout adorer of Brihma [Brahma], Bishen [Vishnu], Mahiser [Maheshvara (Shiva)]; not to mention that Judishteir, Arjen, Corno [Yudhisthira, Arjuna,

Karna] and other warriors of the *M'hab'harat* [*Mahabharata*] appear greater in my eyes than Agamemnon, Ajax and Achilles appeared when I first read the *Iliad*.[29]

Jones described himself as "a devout and convinced Christian,"[30] and like modern scholars he viewed the *Bhagavata Purana* as "a motley story."[31] Yet, remarkably ecumenical in his outlook, he did not hide his appreciation of the Vedic knowledge of reincarnation: "I am no Hindu but I hold the doctrine of the Hindus concerning a future state to be incomparably more rational, more pious and more likely to deter men from vice than the horrid opinions inculcated by the Christians on punishment without end."[32]

The German Romance with India

The work of the Asiatic Society of Bengal became the highbrow talk of Europe. The Society's journal attained immediate fame, and the English translations by its Calcutta Sanskritists were rendered into German and French. German scholars, in particular, lost no time accelerating into this new intellectual frontier. Sanskrit and Vedic philosophy became a prime delight for many German romanticists. Whereas the British relationship with India quickly entered the mold of colonialism and conversion, the Germans—with no economic or political interests in India to tend—freely plunged into a lively intellectual and emotional attachment.

The first to incite the German passion for India was Johann Gottfried von Herder, a philosopher and writer whose advocacy of intuition over rationality greatly influenced the famed Goethe. From von Herder came many of the ideas that formed the basis of German Romanticism, and he fired the imaginations of his literary fellows to venerate Mother India. "The Brahmins [the spiritual intelligentsia of India] have wonderful wisdom and strength to form their people in great degrees of gentleness, courtesy, temperance, and chastity. They have so effectively established their people in these virtues that, in comparison, Europeans frequently appear as beastly, drunken or mad."[33]

Friedrich von Schlegel, another philosopher and writer whose essays contributed to the intellectual basis of German Romanticism, took to studying Sanskrit. Beginning in 1805, he used his newfound knowledge to teach a series of lectures at the University of Cologne. "Everything, absolutely everything, is of Indian origin," he exulted.[34] He attributed the Egyptian civilization to missionary seeds from India, and asserted that the Hebrew nation based itself on remnants of Vedic metaphysics. In 1808 Schlegel published his *Essay on Language and Wisdom of the Indians*. The first two sections of his book glorified the beauty and antiquity of the Sanskrit language, as well as its brilliance in conveying profound philosophical concepts. In another section he advocated that a migration of talent and intellect from northern India had introduced civilization to Europe.

To their intense appreciation of India, the German Romanticists grafted a love of Germany as the first European recipient of civilization. "If the regeneration of the human species started in the East, Germany must be considered the Orient of Europe," said Friedrich von Schlegel's brother, August Wilhelm von Schlegel.[35] An influential scholar in his own right, August Wilhelm became the first professor of Sanskrit at the University of Bonn. In 1823 Julius von Klaproth coined the term "Indo-Germans," and many German writers picked it up. Naturally, non-German intellectuals of the time quickly began to prefer the term "Indo-Europeans," and Franz Bopp, in 1833, established that preference even east of the Rhine.

The Prussian minister of education, Wilhelm von Humboldt, began studying Sanskrit in 1821. Also renowned as a founding father of linguistics, Humboldt published an extensive study of the *Bhagavad-gita*. He described the *Gita* as "the deepest and loftiest thing the world has to show."[36] The rampant fascination with India affected also the famed composer Ludwig van Beethoven. His manuscripts contain fragments of selections from the Upanishads and the *Gita*.

The philosopher Georg Hegel compared the discovery of Sanskrit to the beholding of a new continent. He felt it established "historic ties between the German and Indian people."[37] Though the complex Hegel admitted to no great love for India, and criticized Romantics for idolizing it, nevertheless in his classic *Lectures on the Philosophy of History*, he eulogized the Indian subcontinent as the "starting-point for the whole Western world."[38]

Another famous German philosopher, Arthur Schopenhauer, became completely enchanted by the Upanishads. Upon reading a translation into Latin, he called them "the production of the highest human wisdom."[39] Considering the Upanishads to contain almost superhuman conceptions, Schopenhauer said, "It is the most satisfying and elevated reading (with the exception of the original text) which is possible in the world; it has been my solace in life and will be the solace of my death."[40]

So internationally known was the magnitude of the German immersion in Vedic studies that, when in 1871 the various German states finally consolidated into the German Empire, some British authorities in India attributed the unification to the pervasive German love for Vedic knowledge. Though an exaggeration for sure, the notion does indicate Germany's reputation then for relishing ancient India. Sir Henry Maine, a scholarly member of the Viceroy of India's council, dramatically declared, "a nation has been born out of Sanskrit."[41]

The energetic German commitment to Indic studies continues to this day. Almost every serious German library features a special collection of books on India. Every university maintains a departmental library of Indology. Chairs of Sanskrit are maintained at six universities: Bonn, Tübingen, Hamburg, Munich, Marburg, and Göttingen. Almost every university offers Sanskrit instruction in its department of comparative linguistics. Three German universities publish their own magazine on Indology.

Other Nations Jump Aboard

The French were not to be left out of the rush to embrace India. Voltaire, the quintessential Enlightenment thinker, became fascinated. In 1775 he asserted, "I am convinced that everything has come down to us from the banks of the Ganges: astronomy, astrology, metempsychosis, etc."[42] He too seemed to think everything about Adam and Genesis actually derived from India.[43] Diderot, the French philosopher and writer famed for his work on the *Encyclopédie*, suggested in his article on India that the "sciences may be more ancient in India than in Egypt." In Paris, the first university chair for Sanskrit was established in 1816. Quickly French scholars translated the works of India-loving Germans. Jules Michelet, the French historian known for his spirited seventeen-volume *Histoire de France*, felt certain that India was "the womb of the world."

The Slavic peoples also wanted in. At the beginning of the nineteenth century, questions of Slav roots concerned scholars of the various Slavic regions. Some would publish works comparing words in Sanskrit and Slavic languages. The Czech scholar Pavel Shafarik wrote that the Slavic peoples originated in India. A Polish scientist, Valentin Mayevsky, elaborately described the connection between the Slavic peoples and ancient Indians. Russia published its first Sanskrit text in 1787. N. I. Novikov translated Charles Wilkins's rendition of the *Bhagavad-gita* from English. An Asian Academy was established at St. Petersburg in 1810, with a Sanskrit professorship. Russia would go on to produce famous nineteenth-century Indologists such as V. P. Vasilyev and V. P. Minayev. The Hungarian Csoma de Körös (1784–1842) visited India and studied language and literature there.

Across the Atlantic the Americans kept up with the Vedic bonanza. Formal Indic studies began there at Yale University in 1841. Elihu Yale, a former governor for the British East India Company at Madras, had funded the university in 1718, with the help of gifts brought over from India. The new university, rewarding his patronage, took on his name. At Harvard University, in 1836, a group of authors and poets gathered to found the Transcendental Club of America. The cream of America's literary world—Ralph Waldo Emerson, Henry David Thoreau, Walt Whitman, and others—studied the Vedic texts available, as well as ideas from Goethe, Kant, and the ancient Egyptians, Greeks, and Persians.

The American transcendentalists, as they are now called, located and studied English translations of the *Bhagavad-gita*, Upanishads, and the *Vishnu* and *Bhagavata Puranas*. Emerson issued forth his classic praise of the *Gita:* "I owed a magnificent day to the *Bhagavad-gita*. It was the first of books; it was as if an empire spake to us, nothing small or unworthy, but large, serene, consistent, the voice of an old intelligence which in another age and climate had pondered and thus disposed of the same questions that exercise us."

Henry David Thoreau, the still venerated author of *Walden*, is on record expressing intellectual euphoria: "What extracts from the Vedas I have read fall on me like the light of a higher and purer luminary, which describes a loftier course through a purer stratum." Also, "In the morning I bathe my intellect in the stupendous and cosmogonal philosophy of the *Bhagavad-gita*, since whose composition years of the gods have elapsed and in comparison with which our modern world and its literature seems puny and trivial."

Anointing the *Gita* as the best intellectual treat, Thoreau said, "The reader is nowhere raised into and sustained in a bigger, purer or rarer region of thought than in the *Bhagavad-gita*." For an

American of his very conservative and Christian time, he made a bold evaluation: "The religion and philosophy of the Hebrews are those of a wilder and ruder tribe, wanting the civility and intellectual refinements and subtlety of Vedic culture."

Other giants of the American literary world who acknowledged influence from Vedic philosophy were T. S. Eliot, Paul Elmer, and Irving Babbitt. They had all studied at Harvard under the renowned Sanskritist Charles Rochwell Lanman, who taught for over forty years and published books on Sanskrit and Vedic philosophy. Another factor contributing to Vedic interest in America was the founding, in 1842, of the American Oriental Society.

Certainly amid all the nations cited above, scholars with negative and even racist perceptions of the Vedic texts could be found. What is monumental, though, is the unique freshness and headiness that the very first winds of Indology blew through most academic chambers in the first half of the nineteenth century. "India, yes! The Vedas, yes!"

Especially at the junction of the eighteenth and nineteenth centuries, European intellectuals expected an "Oriental renaissance." The idea was that, just as the study of Greek had paved the way for the first Renaissance, so the study of Sanskrit and the Vedas would launch the second. The older Orientalism—based on European studies of Arabic, Persian, and Hebrew—had given way to India and the Vedas as the standard bearer.

Unencumbered by biases, the original reactions of European scholars are a testimony to the intellectual joy a fair-minded approach to the Vedas can bring. But the breezes of profound appreciation that swept the European continent did not last. After all, the British Crown had serious business to tend in India—with immense consequences for the study of India's past.

Mainly the Calcutta-based British intellectuals had sparked Europe's enthusiasm for India. In their homeland, however, the boom was modest. Some intellectuals in the British Isles were charmed by the ancient wisdom of India—its Sanskrit, astronomy, and geography. Some even sought to find a connection between ancient India and the Celts. The enthrallment did not last, in the downpour of realpolitik.

> But the fire in England was soon damped. Great Britain could not, or would not, be the hearth for such a renaissance. Thereafter . . . the Victorians procured their best workers only by appealing to the German universities. . . . It was, above all, the case with Max Müller, who was born in Dessau in 1823 and died a professor of comparative linguistics at Oxford in 1900. Ultimately, England was to welcome many more Orientalists than she gave birth.[44]

By the time the nineteenth century turned into the twentieth, almost all the benign attitudes spurring Western scholars' unbiased appreciation of Vedic knowledge had turned into ice. No independent India would be born of Sanskrit knowledge. The British goal, stated and unstated, was to eradicate any notions that India had knowledge in remote antiquity.

The Legacy of the British Empire

In the early nineteenth century, while the British consolidated their hold on India, a great debate enveloped Britain about the purpose of its government there. At that time the East India Company still had exclusive rights to India. Naturally the mercantile outfit wanted India to remain its private fief, to harvest for maximum yield. When the merchants' profits increased, the land was deemed well governed. Though this approach enlivened the Company's investors, obviously those not in a position to reap profit would have had other ideas.

The liberals wanted a British government that accepted

responsibility for the welfare of the Indian people. Riding on this tide, the evangelicals, both Anglican and Baptist, added that British responsibility included India's spiritual welfare as well. A burgeoning force in England, the evangelicals wanted the government to educate the Indians in a way that prepared them for conversion.

The Utilitarians were also on the rise. These followers of Jeremy Bentham and John Stuart Mill wished to experiment on India, as a laboratory for their social theories. They yearned to transform India through legislation. Then there were radical rationalists eager to apply the doctrine of human rights they had picked up from France, and also British entrepreneurs lusty to break the monopoly the East India Company enjoyed.

At first the British government in India actively sought to prevent Christian missionaries from proselytizing. Incendiary preachers could ignite the masses, the administrators feared. The evangelists, however, were unstoppable. Preaching without the required sanction, they would sometimes even smuggle themselves into the country. In Britain they waged a fierce campaign to end the official policy of neutrality in Indian religious affairs, and finally forced the government to grant them an open field. In 1813 the East India Company lost its commercial monopoly over India, and missionaries could enter freely. Government fears that any appearance of religious coercion would set off violent uprisings proved well founded. In 1857 religious strife helped set off the Indian Mutiny. Afterwards, the British Crown, relieving the East India Company, completely assumed all governmental power.

Representing the best (and only) religion, the best civilization, and the best race, the British were confident in their application of superior intelligence. "A central issue for the British in their arguments over Indian policy was how the Indians might be made to love the British regime."[45] In stooping to interact with the pagan races, they had no doubts as to the status of the native population. For example, quite in line with the norm, the governor general the Marquis of Hastings, upon arriving in India in 1813, noted, "The Hindoo appears a being merely limited to mere animal functions, and even in them indifferent . . . with no higher intellect than a dog."[46]

Though shocking to our modern sensibilities, we have to hear these words through the ears of the typical Englishman of the day. The British knew who and what they were dealing with—no modern egalitarianism complicated life then. They had a job to do in India, and trendy intellectual fascination was not to interfere. The historian and anthropologist Thomas R. Trautmann, in his impressive study *Aryans and British India*, cut right to the core:

> British Indomania did not die of natural causes; it was killed off. The Indophobia that became the norm in early-nineteenth-century Britain was constructed by Evangelism and Utilitarianism, and its chief architects were Charles Grant and James Mill. The key texts are two: Grant's "Observations on the state of society among the Asiatic subjects of Great Britain, particularly with respect to morals; and the means of improving it" (1796), and Mill's *History of British India* (1817). They require our close attention.[47]

"Observations," Seen by Charles Grant

The first of the two terminators, Charles Grant, served in the East India Company and then returned to Britain. A Scottish evangelical who had achieved ideological prominence with the Company while in India, back home Grant penned a massive policy paper, "Observations on the . . . Asiatic subjects of Great Britain." Published in 1796, it set the agenda for British rule and also justified it: the sacred mission was to reform the Indians. Casting out the Orientalists who wanted to respect Indian culture, religion, and society, Grant argued for aggressive conversion to both Anglicism and Christianity. A direct assault on Indian civilization and its European admirers, Grant's lengthy treatise had immense influence. From it derived the "reform policy" of the British. They were in India to dispense the twin benedictions of Anglo refinement and Christian salvation. Historians say it would be difficult to overemphasize the effect of Grant's work, especially since some form of his ideas guided British rule for 150 years—until India's independence in 1947.[48]

Grant crafted his offensive mostly in 1792, in the wake of the Calcutta Sanskritists and their international success. When Grant published in 1796, his work marked the turning of the tide. Though modestly regarded at first, the "Observations" became the favorite warhorse of the Evangelicals in Britain. They demanded of the Crown that India yield to the Cross. The East India Company's territories had to open for unrestricted proselytizing. In Grant's work, the pro-missionary lobby found a perennial winner. During the first half of the nineteenth century, when the Evangelicals waged constant campaigns in Britain, every time they mounted Grant's manifesto and rode, the power of its effect increased.

Straightaway, the "Observations" did away with the Orientalists' mystique:

> It has suited the views of some philosophers to represent that people as amiable and respectable. . . . The generality, however, of those who have written concerning Hindostan, appear to have concurred in affirming what foreign residents there have as generally thought, nay, what the natives themselves freely acknowledge of each other, that they are a people exceedingly depraved.[49]

Minimizing a popular notion that the tropical climate in India fostered decadence and sloth, Grant transferred the blame from nature to the Indians themselves: their government, laws, and religion. He explained that the Hindus, throughout their history, have always lived under despotism, which has profoundly affected their character. Continuously forced to grovel under tyrants—both native and foreign—the Hindus never could develop fortitude, integrity, and brotherhood. "They have had among themselves a complete despotism from the remotest antiquity; a despotism, the most remarkable for its power and duration that the world has ever seen. . . . as a people, [they are] void of public spirit, honor, attachment; and in society, base, dishonest, and faithless."[50]

When targeting the laws of Indian society, Grant launched the "evil priestcraft" weapon, perfected by centuries of Protestant campaigns against Catholics. All the social law of India, he proclaimed, is "the work of a crafty and imperious priesthood, who feigned a divine revelation and appointment, to invest their own order, in perpetuity, with the most absolute empire over the civil state of the Hindoos, as well as over their minds."[51]

Grant skewered the religion of India with Protestant misunderstandings, built on a missionary tradition of damnation that continues to this very day. The religion of India propounded fatalism, superstition, and ritualism. Moreover, the gods were licentious, and their worship lewd.

Since the disease of India was moral—depraved government, laws, and religion—Grant's panacea was also moral: "The true cure of darkness, is the introduction of light. The Hindoos err, because they are ignorant; and their errors have never fairly been laid before them. The communication of our light and knowledge to them ... would have great and happy effects upon them, effects honorable and advantageous for us."[52]

The "Observations" concluded with a dramatic insistence that the Indians were "every way different" from the British. The two peoples had absolutely nothing in common. In this way Grant sought to drive away from his countrymen the devil of Orientalist sympathy and appreciation. Only an aggressive cleansing—led by the arts, philosophy, and especially the religion of the British— could reverse India's woeful plight. The work of Charles Grant indeed became the British policy of love: merciful colonizers would wash away Indian sins with the potent detergent of Western knowledge.

History, According to James Mill

The *History of British India*, written by James Mill and published in 1817, was the paramount literature for purging British appreciation of India. A Scottish intellectual, Mill traded a career as a Presbyterian minister to become the chief promoter of Jeremy Bentham's Utilitarianism—a popular philosophy that stressed material progress and the greatest good possible for the greatest number of people. James Mill's eldest son was the even more celebrated Utilitarian John Stuart Mill.

The evangelically fired "Observations" of Charles Grant became the stuff of the masses. James Mill's work, however, was the wine and cheese of the intellectual elite. Instead of Grant's cureall—Christian conversion—Mill prescribed secular modernization. In three volumes, the *History of British India* was the first full account of the British domination of India. It was a systematic, detailed approach to ancient India and its relevance to British rule. Book 2 of his three-volumed work was entitled *Of the Hindus*. In its ten chapters Mill presents his date and conclusions. What follows is a taste of the wonders.[53]

In Chapter 1 he examines "the chronology and ancient history of the Hindus." Dismissing as empty boasting any notions that India had a glorious past, Mill wonders aloud why Europeans of his time respected such foolish vanities. Chapters 2–5 discuss his perceptions of the gross flaws in the traditional Indian economic, political, and legal structures. Mill saw crudity in the traditional system of occupational divisions, tyranny in the brahmins, absoluteness in the monarchy, and a legal system that reflected "the state of law among a rude and ignorant people."

Chapter 6 confronts religion. Mill explains that no intelligible system of belief can be detected in the wild, impenetrable legends, made even more obscure by "the language of the brahmins . . . the vast multiplicity of their fictions, and the endless discrepancy of their ideas." Chapter 7 is an outstanding portrayal of Indian character. A quick sample:

> The vices of falsehood, indeed, they carry to a height almost un-exampled among the other races of men (p. 324); no other race of men are perhaps so little friendly and beneficent to one another as the Hindus (p. 326); a timid being (p. 329); listless, apathy and corporeal weakness of the natives of Hindustan (p. 333); the lan-guid and slothful habits of the Hindu (p. 334); avarice forms a more remarkable ingredient in the national character of the Hin-dus, than in that of any other people (pp. 336–37).

Mill turns to the arts of India in chapter 8. The Hindus "little courted the pleasures derived from the arts," he noted. The sculpture, painting, and music never progressed beyond levels normal for a primitive society. The artifacts "are not merely void of attraction; they are unnatural, offensive, and not infrequently disgusting." In general the level of fine arts was lower than "the height of even of the Egyptians, much less of the Greeks and Romans." Chapter 9 dismisses Indian literature, poetry, and science: the literature was unattractive; the poetry was enthusi-astic exaggeration; and all the so-called scientific knowledge "derived from other nations more advanced in civilization than themselves."

Mill called Chapter 10 "General Reflections." There he pre-sented his mission statement: "To ascertain the true state of the Hindus in the scale of civilization" was of pressing importance to the British people, because they were empowered "with the government of that great portion of the human species." For aiding the great British mission to clarify the true worth of India, Mill left some concluding principles. First, he explained, India's history, like that of any uncivilized area, was a boiling cauldron of petty states—the wars cooling only by the occasional imposition of a larger political entity. Second, India attained a high degree of civilization only when dominated by foreigners. Third, even Europe in the Dark Ages was superior to the best India could offer: "The Gothic Nations, as soon as they became a settled people, exhibit the marks of a superior character and civilization to those of the Hindus." Fourth, the general character of the Indian is deceitful and treacherous.

No brief flash in the sky, by 1858 the *History of British India* was into its fifth edition. The work solidly established Mill as an India expert, and it became required reading for British students preparing for civil service in India. Mill, one of the original contributors to the *Encyclopaedia Britannica* of his day, receives this evaluation in the *Encyclopaedia's* current edition: "The work itself and the author's official connection with India during the last 17 years of his life effected a complete change in the system of government in that country."

The official vision enshrined by Charles Grant, James Mill, and others extended through the nineteenth century to the mid-twentieth. Needless to say, scholars today vehemently condemn the racism of their nineteenth-century predecessors. Without a doubt they would all find Mill's language quite revolting. Yet, as in the past, almost none of them take seriously the Vedic contention that—hidden in antiquity—a highly advanced Vedic civilization thrived. Rather than openly deriding the Vedas' version, however, Indologists quietly dismiss it—while politely complementing the Vedic texts for their attractive and colorful legends.

Even merely to say that the Vedic presentation of ancient humanity may be worth investigating is considered ridiculous. If a scholar who says so is Indian, immediately they are branded a right-wing cultural nationalist. This political bent may be true in some cases, but it does not automatically render all the work of such scholars completely useless. Or, if the researcher is a Westerner, they best have independent funding and career plans. Anyone seen to defy the academic establishment in this most critical area—the official version of human ancientness—is both blackballed and mothballed. Like so many of the contrarian scholars who research humanity's mysterious origins, unless you find nonacademic means for airing your findings, you remain an intellectual outcast. This is the state of affairs as we enter the twenty-first century.

Oxford's Chair and Müller's Ghost

Indology in the English language formally began at Oxford University. Here mobilized the intellectual response to the sudden popularity of the Vedic texts. A Colonel Boden bequeathed his entire fortune to the university for promoting knowledge of Sanskrit texts among the British. The specified goal: "to enable his countrymen to proceed in the conversion of the natives of India to the Christian religion."[54]

In 1833 H. H. Wilson became the first occupant of the Boden Chair of Sanskrit, after outmaneuvering his friend, the famous German philosopher and linguist August Wilhelm von Schlegel. Though Schlegel's trusted friend, Wilson campaigned against him behind his back, by covertly sending derogatory letters about Schlegel's skills to key persons at Oxford. Wilson went on to translate several Vedic texts. He is sometimes described as the greatest Sanskritist of his time, but modern scholars have documented evidence showing that Wilson plagiarized manuscripts of deceased authors and avoided research. "He wrote an analysis of the Puranas without reading them."[55]

Oxford University offered prizes for the works that attacked Vedic knowledge. Wilson, the first Boden professor, described a series of lectures he gave to prepare the contestants: "These lectures were written to help candidates for a prize of 200 pounds . . . for the best refutation of the Hindu religious systems."[56]

Wilson urged the British government not to forcibly convert the Indians. Though he was a moderate—compared to the evangelicals—he made his program clear:

> From the survey which has been submitted to you, you will perceive that the practical religion of the Hindus is by no means a concentrated and compact system, but a heterogeneous compound made up of various and not infrequently incompatible ingredients, and that to a few ancient fragments it has made large and unauthorized additions, most of which are of an exceedingly mischievous and disgraceful nature. It is, however, of little avail yet to attempt to undeceive the multitude; their superstition is based upon ignorance, and until the foundation is taken away, the superstructure, however crazy and rotten, will hold together.[57]

Rather than force-feeding the Indians, Wilson thought that a full exposure of Vedic fallacies would speed the triumph of Christianity. Astute enough to realize that the people of India would not easily abandon Vedic knowledge and traditions, Wilson advocated a shrewd ploy:

> The whole tendency of brahminical education is to enforce dependence on authority—in the first instance upon the guru, in the next upon the books. A learned brahmana trusts solely to his learning; he never ventures upon independent thought; he appeals to memory; he quotes texts without measure and in unquestioning trust. It will be difficult to persuade him that the

Vedas are human and very ordinary writings, that the puranas are modern and unauthentic. . . . As long as he opposes authority to reason, and stifles the workings of conviction by the dicta of a reputed sage, little impression can be made upon his understanding. *Certain it is therefore, that he will have recourse to his authorities, and it is therefore important to show that his authorities are worthless.*[58]

Wilson proved right. The best way to tame India was by presenting Vedic tenets as a motley bag of vivid legends, propounded by foolish teachers to a gullible public. By spotlighting Vedic knowledge dashed upon the rocks of Western empiricism, a vivid lesson would etch itself in the people's mind. Then they would abandon the chains of their past heritage.

The biggest name in nineteenth-century Indology turned out to be Max Müller. As a young scholar in Germany, Müller got his first big break from Thomas Macaulay. Though Lord Macaulay is most famous for his five-volumed classic *History of England*—an immensely popular work throughout the nineteenth century—he also served on the Supreme Council of India and took on colonial education as part of his portfolio. In 1836 he asserted, "It is my belief that if our plans of education are followed up, there will not be a single idolator among the respectable classes in Bengal thirty years hence. And this will be effected without any efforts to proselytize, without the smallest interference with religious liberty, by natural operation of knowledge and reflection."[59]

Lord Macaulay had a plan to dissipate the darkness of Vedic India with the torchlight of Western knowledge. Upon his returning to England, he cast about for a powerful scholar who could translate the Vedic texts in a way that anyone could see their innate foolishness. H. H. Wilson turned him down, but recommended a young German scholar named Friedrich Maximilian Müller.

In 1854 the Prussian ambassador brought the thirty-one-year-old Müller to see Macaulay. The lord told him that the East India Company would fund him with a grant of ten-thousand pounds sterling—if Müller would translate the Vedas in a way conducive for reorientating the Indians. Bear in mind that the average university professor back then made five hundred pounds a year. Müller, in short, had broken into the big time.

But first he had to survive Macaulay. The following year he had to sit silently for one hour while Macaulay poured upon him the fire of antiheathen zeal. Unable to get a word in, Müller, by his own admission, submitted, taking the import deep in his heart: "I went back to Oxford a sadder man and a wiser man."[60]

Two years later, in the wake of the Indian Mutiny, the East India Company dissolved. India was now directly in the hands of the British Government.

Müller had received only part of the sum promised for his publishing appropriate versions of the Vedas. But with amazing tenacity and willpower, he pushed on, taking whatever financial support he could receive from the Crown. In his almost fifty years of labor, he produced an astonishing output: the *Sacred Books of the East*, in fifty-one volumes.

Müller left no doubt about his view of the people into whose texts he poured his life: "A people . . . never destined to act a prominent part in the history of the world. Social and political virtues were little cultivated, and the ideas of the useful and the beautiful hardly known to them."[61] In 1876 Müller wrote to a friend that, rather than going to India as a missionary, dependent on the government, he would opt for a different strategy: "I should like to live for ten years quietly and learn the language, try to make friends, and then see whether I was fit to take part in a work, by means of which the old mischief of Indian priestcraft could be overthrown and the way opened for the entrance of simple Christian teaching."[62]

Producing built-to-purpose reconstructions of the Vedic texts suited Müller's modus operandi just fine. In fact, he never once laid foot in India. His letter to his wife, as quoted in Chapter 3, is blatant enough to merit a second look:

> I hope I shall finish the work, and I feel convinced, though I shall not live to see it, yet the edition of mine and the translation of the Veda will hereafter tell to a great extent on the fate of India and on the growth of millions of souls in that country. It is the root of their religion, and to show them what the root is, I feel sure, is the only way of uprooting all that has sprung from it during the last three thousand years.[63]

Today, in various Indian metropolises, the German Government has named its centers "Max Müller Bhavan" (Max Müller House), in honor of its mighty son. Though the current generation of scholars has eased Müller out of Indology's pantheon, his ghost still dominates the literature available to the nonspecialist public. Think of Müller whenever you pick up an introductory university text or Time-Life illustrated book and read a cute story like this: "By rigorously analyzing the linguistic characteristics of the Vedas, and comparing them to those found in later, Buddhist literature, the date assigned for the composition of the Vedas is about 1200 B.C. This therefore indicates a date three hundred years earlier as the time when the Aryans invaded India and imposed the Vedic religion and culture upon the conquered tribes."

Müller, as explained in Chapter 3, repudiated his own speculation—but obviously to no avail, as we can see more than a hundred years later. His monumental series *Sacred Books of the East* is out of print—except, ironically, in India—but shadows of his work march on.

The third titan of nineteenth-century Indology was Sir Monier Monier-Williams. His *Sanskrit–English Dictionary* is still widely used by scholars today. Upon the death of H. H. Wilson in 1860, Monier-Williams acceded to Oxford's Boden Chair. But first he had to beat off the other leading contender, Max Müller. The supporters of Müller let all of British academia know that Müller's Sanskrit was world class. Moreover, they charged that Monier-Williams could not properly read Sanskrit, except in transliteration: "The eyes of Europe are on our election. Shall we elect a man . . . who cannot read a Sanskrit manuscript?"[64]

Monier-Williams, however, excelled at academic infighting. He knew the minds of the electors—about fifteen hundred of them. After glorifying Müller's work to them, he pointed out that more money was spent to bring out Müller's *Rig-veda* than was ever spent to publish an edition of the Bible. Furthermore, he claimed that Müller specialized in obscure, archaic Vedic texts, whereas he wisely focused upon popular Sanskrit literature. The candidate with greater expertise in the literature of the masses would prove of superior value—especially for the missionaries, in their uphill fight against the Hindu mind. That battle, Monier-Williams reminded them, was what the Chair was all about.

Müller went down in ignoble defeat, by two hundred votes, to a relatively unknown but cagey rival. Neither of the two scholars forgot the battle for the rest of their lives.

Upon his inauguration, the triumphant Monier-Williams gave an address entitled, "The Study of Sanskrit in Relation to Missionary Work in India." A few modern historians opine that, unlike Müller, Monier-Williams lacked real evangelical fire. They say his occasional "down with the Vedas, up with the Cross" exhortations were just academic posturing, meant to keep his funding intact: "When the walls of the mighty fortress of Brahmanism are encircled, undermined, and finally stormed by the soldiers of the cross, the victory of Christianity must be single and complete."[65]

This statement of policy, and his other battle calls like it, perhaps may indicate Monier-Williams' doing the needful, to guarantee his income and academic stature. Yet we must not fail to note his reflections as an old man, looking back over his years: "Yes, after a lifelong study of the religious books of the Hindus, I feel compelled to publicly express my opinion of them. They begin with much promise amid scintillations of truth and light and occasional sublime thoughts from the source of all truth and light, but end in sad corruptions and lamentable impurities."[66]

EXTERMINATING VERSUS DISCREDITING

Modern scholars of the Vedas certainly aren't missionaries on a crusade to convert the heathens. And certainly there have been much more brazen efforts to modify an indigenous culture than what the British did. When the Spanish conquistador Cortés defeated the Aztecs in 1521, he ordered the wholesale destruction of the capital Tenochtitlan. Because the Aztecs sacrificed humans, it is sometimes hard for us to sympathize with them. Still, the Spanish destruction of Mesoamerican cultural achievements has proved a terrible blow to historians' solving the puzzle of human antiquity.

In Mexico both the Church and the State combined to annihilate the past. Any written records the Spanish could get their hands on were destroyed. Statues were smashed, burnt or melted down. If the statues were too big for these honors, they were buried. Montezuma, the Aztec emperor, had given Cortés two circular calendars, one of solid silver, the other of solid gold. As large as cartwheels, the calendars were beautifully engraved with hieroglyphs—a sure treasure for scholars. Cortés immediately had the artifacts melted down into ingots.[67]

The newly colonized people of Mexico were ordered to convert to Catholicism or die. Furthermore, they were forbidden to write in their own language and were forced to learn Spanish. As an official policy, the Church and the regime sought to prevent scholars from publishing anything that might indicate Mexico had any worth as a civilization before Cortés invaded.

Throughout the Central American region of Spanish conquest, enthusiastic friars carefully gathered and burned entire storehouses of ancient knowledge.

Fr. Diego de Landa torched thousands of Mayan scrolls made of deerskin, inscribed with hieroglyphs and story paintings. He explained: "We found great numbers of books, but as they contained nothing but superstitions and falsehoods of the devil we burned them all, which the natives took most grievously, and which gave them great pain."[68]

The Catholic bishop of Mexico, Juan de Zumarraga, congratulated himself for destroying, he said, twenty thousand idols and five hundred temples. Amassing the fruits from eleven years of conquistador historical plundering, he built up a huge pile of astronomical writings, manuscripts, paintings, and hieroglyphic scrolls and burned them all.[69]

In 1529 a Franciscan friar, Bernardino de Sahagun, learned the native's tongue and scoured Mexico for knowledge of its past. Accumulating twelve volumes worth of information from his Indian friends, he was the first to discover that, before the Aztecs, the Toltecs occupied the land. Though in his books he made sure to minimize accounts of Spanish atrocities, still he could not openly publish. Eventually his suppressed works disappeared completely, until an incomplete copy of his manuscript surfaced in 1808.[70]

In 1697 a priest named Don Carlos de Sigüenza y Gongora, having made friends with the Indians, accumulated an extraordinary collection of manuscripts and paintings, which had escaped the mass burnings 150 years earlier. Researching the chronology of ancient Mexico, he concluded that before the Toltecs were another people, the Olmecs. Following Sigüenza's death, however, the Inquisition got hold of his priceless archive and dispersed everything or destroyed it. Later, in 1767, when the Jesuits were expelled from Mexico, many of the scrolls they had patiently collected also disappeared.

The purposeful eradication of ancient Mexico by the Spanish still impedes modern attempts to reconstruct the past. Countless archives, monuments, and artifacts of the ancient peoples of Central America are gone for good. Even languages were lost, during the forcible conversion to the Catholic catechism and the Spanish tongue. How many written records survived the Spanish tornado of destruction? The joint campaign by the Church and State left us with less than twenty original codices and scrolls.[71]

Obviously, to their credit, the British in India were much more gentlemanly and subtle. Rather than destroying, the British had a different style: "Discrediting is the better part of valor." Initially, at the end of the eighteenth century, the first British to study Vedic texts tried to consider the literature and its stated antiquity seriously. But their appreciations were drowned out by the uproar of negative scholarship that so characterized the bulk of Indology's development in the English language.

James Mill, in his *History*, brought out in 1817, took special care to remove the halo around William Jones, the internationally acclaimed Calcutta Sanskritist and linguistic scholar:

> It was so unfortunate that a mind so pure, so warm in the pursuit
> of truth, and so devoted to oriental learning, as that of Sir William
> Jones, should have adopted the hypothesis of a high state of civi-
> lization in the principal countries of Asia. This he supported with
> all the advantages of an imposing manner, and a brilliant reputa-
> tion; and gained for it so great a credit, that for a time, it would
> have been very difficult to obtain a hearing against it.[72]

From the year 1823 we have the words of an early British Indologist, John Bentley, thrashing an Englishman who had dared to write in praise of the Vedic texts:

> By his attempt to uphold the antiquity of Hindu books against absolute facts, he thereby supports all those horrid abuses and impositions found in them, under the pretended sanction of antiquity. . . . Nay, his aim goes still deeper; for by the same means he endeavors to overturn the Mosaic account, and sap the very foundation of our religion: for if we are to believe in the antiquity of Hindu books, as he would wish, then the Mosaic account is all a fable, or a fiction.[73]

We should not misconstrue the Calcutta Sanskritists' passion for India. They had no doubt that the European civilization of their day was superior. What distinguished them from the Mills and the Grants was their willingness to credit India with ancient glories. Jones, Colebrooke, Wilkins, and other British doyens of the Oriental renaissance were convinced that within the Vedas dwelt an ancient and primeval truth—the remote source of all religion and civilization. They knew Europe was certainly the zenith for everything—except, perhaps, creative imagination. Still, the Calcutta crew reveled in the hidden marvels of Indian antiquity.

Mills, however, with his Utilitarianism, punctured the Orientalist euphoria and slashed it to pieces. Ancient humanity was crude, barbaric, and ignorant. Forcing this edict upon Indic Studies, Mills urged modernization as the key for rescuing India from its dark past. Meanwhile, Grant called on Britain to save India's soul. Both of these justifications for colonization carried the day. Indian culture and knowledge was redefined as primitive and wicked. Consequently, a deliberately constructed negation of Indian civilization became the British social norm.

Now and Then: Any Difference?

Certainly, academic institutions no longer offer prizes for the best demolition of the Vedic tradition. And surely no respectable scholars would dare employ the invective their nineteenth-century predecessors wielded. Yet, because scholarship generally builds upon the work done by past authorities—especially when archaic languages are involved—the heritage of the forefathers is not easy to jettison. Consequently perspectives born of the pioneers in Indology continue to pop up—it can't be helped. "The foundations for the recovery of India's past were laid by certain eminent classical scholars, including Sir William Jones, James Prinsep, H. T. Colebrooke and H. H. Wilson . . . the debt owed these men is great."[74]

We should have the sensitivity to realize that modern Indologists feel insulted to be impugned as a bunch of geriatrics who lack the critical acumen to drop old theories and prejudices. When backed up against a wall, they distance themselves from Müller and company.

Many current Indologists protest that the past is over. They say their predecessors are relics of bygone days—fresh blood entered the field long ago. Other scholars, who have taken the trouble to survey the sociology and history of Indic Studies, from its beginnings to the present day, say otherwise. The extent of the problem, they assert, is much greater than their colleagues acknowledge. After a thorough study of British Indology, Thomas Trautmann, a reputable mainstay at the University of Michigan, gave his verdict:

> By century's end [the nineteenth century], a deep and lasting consensus was reached respecting India, which I call the racial theory of Indian civilization: that India's civilization was produced by the clash and subsequent mixture of light-skinned civilizing invaders (the Aryans) and dark-skinned barbarian aborigines (often identified as Dravidians). The racial theory of Indian civilization has proved remarkably durable and resistant to new information, and it persists to this day. It is the crabgrass of Indian history, and I should like to uproot it.[75]

Then there is the work of anthropologist Bernard S. Cohen. Exploring what he calls the construction of the colonial sociology of India, Cohen published a span of papers, such as "Notes on the History of the Study of Indian Society and Culture" (1968), "The Command of Language and the Language of Command" (1985), and "The Consensus, Social Structure, and Objectification in South Asia" (1990). Cohen's well-received work drove home the conclusion that academic knowledge of India is still largely the product of colonialism and its effects.[76] Another example is David Lorenzen's treatise "Imperialism and the Historiography of Ancient India" (1982).[77]

The name Edward Said often whips up the biggest storm among Indologists. Said's fame or notoriety derives from his successfully revealing that the massive errors of the colonial scholars still linger. Concentrating mainly upon the Middle East, Said also touched upon India, in his book *Orientalism*. Western Indic scholars generally loathed and sometimes praised him for his demolishing their assurances of "that was then and this is now." To the contrary, he demonstrates that "all academic knowledge about India and Egypt is somehow tinged and impressed with, violated by, the gross political fact."[78]

Said's work is a polemic—a highly successful agitator, scattering academic discussions in new directions. Favorable Indological scholars sought to buttress Said's precepts by firmly grounding them in the Indian context. A noted example came out of the 1988–89 South Asia Seminar at the University of Pennsylvania. The scholars Carol Breckenridge and Peter van der Veer edited a collection of papers entitled *Orientalism and the Post-Colonial Predicament* (1993). The preface of this pro-Said elucidation relays how it finally emerged—from within a sea of turmoil and opposition. Evidently, academia does not like its dirty laundry washed in public. Indologist-bashing is a serious offense, even for members of the guild.

Often mainstream Indic scholars assure us that "certain eminent classical scholars" of the colonial period have been retired—replaced by more contemporary aces. Nevertheless, a casual visit to a local library or bookstore demonstrates the actual predicament: scant scent of any supposed change has drifted down from the ivory towers to the nonspecialist public. Furthermore, at the universities themselves, life is not so flexible. Academic habit is a powerful tide.

Thus a skilful observer will note that modern scholars of ancient India—though not on a Christian mission—indeed do evidence a tacit resonance with the ways of their predecessors.

The onward trudge of intellectual labor has a way of perpetuating itself, by feeding on fealty and conformity. As Thomas Kuhn pointed out in his classic treatise *The Structure of Scientific Revolutions*, once a paradigm—with all its attendant sub-assumptions and nuances—hardens like concrete, to remove all traces of it is very difficult. Of course, now the crusading fire of Christianity at Western universities, when compared with the past, shows only a few embers. The current campus proclivity is not "evangelism" but "empiricism." Added to the burden of colonialist baggage, the modern yoke of mechanistic scientism is what the Vedic literature struggles with today.

Where did the human race come from, and what is the real account of its remote past? Although, up until now, mainstream academia has effectively banished the Vedic version, have we received a solid theory to cling to in its place? We expect that the evidence scientists and historians have gathered is based on what they observe. But what happens when evidence pops up that completely disintegrates pet theories?

Today we must answer not only to the ancient assembly of Vedic sages but also to a new breed of scientific researchers. Detouring the traffic jams of academia, both the Vedic seers and the new wave of independent scholars assert that the history of humanity on this planet radically differs from the story we've been told.

Notes

1 *Los Angeles Times,* 11 April 1999; Associated Press, 12 April 1999.
2 Sasha Nemecek, "Who were the First Americans?", *Scientific American,* September 2000.
3 Reuters report by Maggie Fox, Health and Science Correspondent, Philadelphia, 16 February 1998.
4 Nemecek, Ibid.
5 Reuters, Ibid.
6 This was the verdict of mainstream archaeologists at the 63rd annual meeting of the Society for American Archeology, March 1998. Also see D. J. Meltzer, "Monte Verde and the Pleistocene Peopling of the Americas," *Science* 276: 754–55.
7 Fox, ibid.
8 John Anthony West, *Serpent in the Sky* (Illinois: Quest Books, 1993), p. 186.
9 Robert Schoch, *Voices of the Rocks* (London: Thorsons, 2000), p. 50.
10 West, pp. 226–27.
11 *Los Angeles Times,* 23 October 1991.
12 *Boston Globe,* 23 October 1991.
13 Extracts from the AAAS meeting quoted in Graham Hancock, *Fingerprints of the Gods* (London: Mandarin, 1996), p. 447.
14 *Mystery of the Sphinx,* NBC-TV, 1993.
15 A typical ploy used by mainstream Egyptologists against Schoch is to attack his work as it is presented in the popular video *The Mystery of the Sphinx* rather than as it is presented in technical articles. For example, see Zahi Hass, *The Secrets of the Sphinx: Restoration Past and Present* (Cairo: American University in Cairo Press, 1998).
   Mark Lehner, James Harrell, and K. Lal Gauri have also tried to counter Schoch's work. An independent study by geologist David Coxill ("The Riddle of the Sphinx," *InScription: Journal of Ancient Egypt,* spring 1998, pp. 13–19) has confirmed Schoch's conclusions.
16 Michael Cremo and Richard Thompson, *Hidden History of the Human Race* (California: Govardhan Hill Publishing, 1994), p. 149.
17 Ibid., p. 101.
18 Ibid.
19 Michael A. Cremo, *Forbidden Archeology's Impact* (Los Angeles: Bhaktivedanta Book Publishing, 1998), p. 518.
20 Ibid., p. 534.
21 *The Geologist* 5 (1862): 470.
22 *Scientific American,* 5 June 1852.

23 Michael Cremo, from abstract of paper, "Forbidden Archaeology of
    the Early and Middle Pleistocene: Evidence for Physiologically and
    Culturally Advanced Humans," given at the 4th World Archaeological
    Congress, Capetown, South Africa, January 1999.
24 Schoch, p. 103.
    In his book, Schoch presents an overview of possible technical
    objections to the portolans. Ice sheets does not come off of land like
    glass comes off a picture. If the estimated 30 million billion tons of ice
    covering Antarctica melted, the land would rise up—a process geolo-
    gists call isostatic rebound. Also if the ice cap melted, the sea level
    would rise dramatically. Theoretically, a rising sea level combined with
    isostatic rebound would produce a continent looking dissimilar to
    today's version with the ice neatly subtracted.
25 Letter reproduced in Charles H. Hapgood FRGS, *Maps of the Ancient Sea
    Kings* (Philadelphia and New York: Chilton Books, 1966), p. 243.
26 As quoted in Colin Wilson, *From Atlantis to the Sphinx* (London: Virgin
    Books, 1997), p. 98.
27 *Yajur-veda*, trans. Devi Chand (Delhi: Munshiram Manoharlal, 1980).
28 *Atharva-veda*, trans. Devi Chand (Delhi: Munshiram Manoharlal,
    1980).
29 S. N. Mukherjee, *Sir William Jones: A Study in 18th Century British
    Attitudes to India* (Hyderabad: Orient Longmans, 1987), p. 107.
30 "Jones Tradition in British Orientalism," *Indian Arts and Letters*, 20
    (1946): p. 10.
31 Sir William Jones, *The Works of Sir William Jones* (London, 1807), p. 395.
32 Mukherjee, p. 108.
33 J. G. von Herder, *Outlines of a Philosophy of the History of Man*, 2 (London,
    1803): 34.
34 Letter to Ludwig Tieck, 15 December 1803, cited in *Vorlesungen über
    Universalgeschichte—1805–1806*, ed. Worke J. J. Anstett, 14 (Munich,
    1960): xxxi.
35 Quoted by René Gérard, *L' Orient et la pensée romantique allemande*,
    p. 132.
36 Moriz Winternitz, *A History of Indian Literature*, 1 (New Delhi: Oriental
    Books Reprint Corp., 1927, 1972): 15.
37 Georg Hegel, *Die Vernunft in der Geschichte*, ed. Hoffmeister (Hamburg:
    n.p., 1955), p. 158.
38 Hegel, *Vorlesungen über die Philosophie der Geschichte* (Stuttgart, Germany:
    Reclam, 1961), p. 215.
39 Winternitz, *A History*, p. 20.
40 Ibid. pp. 266–67.

41 Reference from S. Sathe, *Aryans: Who Were They?* (Mysore: Bharatiya Itihasa Sankalana Samiti, 1991), p. 13.

42 Letters from Voltaire, 15 December 1775.

43 "Adam and Eve," *Dictionnaire Philosophique*.

44 Raymond Schwab, *The Oriental Renaissance*, trans. Gene Patterson-Black (New York: Columbia University Press, 1984), p. 43.

45 Thomas R. Trautmann, *Aryans and British India* (Berkeley: University of California Press, 1997), p. 17.

46 Quoted in R. C. Majumdar *et al.*, eds., *History and Culture of the Indian People*, 10 (Bombay: Bharatiya Vidya Bhavan, 1965): 348.

47 Trautmann, *Aryans*, p. 99.

48 Ainslie Thomas Embree, *Charles Grant and British Rule in India* (London: George Allen & Unwin, 1962), p. 157.

49 Charles Grant, "Observations on the state of society among the Asiatic subjects of Great Britain, particularly with respect to morals; and the means of improving it," p. 20. Printed as Appendix I in *Report from the Select Committee on the Affairs of the East India Company 1831–32*, pp. 3–92. Facsimile reprint, *Irish University Press Series of British Parliamentary Papers*, vol. 5, *Colonies: East India* (Shannon: Irish University Press, 1970).

50 Ibid. p. 32.

51 Ibid. p. 35.

52 Ibid. p. 60.

53 The quotations are all from the fifth edition: James Mill, *History of British India*, facsimile reprint (New York: Chelsea House Publishers, 1968).

54 Sir Monier Monier-Williams, *A Sanskrit–English Dictionary,* 1899; facsimile reprint (Delhi: Motilal Banarsidass, 1970), p. ix.

55 "H. H. Wilson and Gamesmanship in Indology," *Asian Studies* 3 (1965): 303.

56 Horace Hayman Wilson, *Emminent Orientalists* (Madras: G. A. Natesan and Co.,1992), pp. 71–72.

57 H. H. Wilson, *Works*, 2 (London: Trubner and Co., 1862): 79–80.

58 Ibid., pp. 80–81.

59 John Clive, *Macaulay, The Shaping of the Historian* (New York: Viking, 1975), pp. 412–13.

60 Max Müller, *Life and Letters*, vol. l, ed. Georgina Müller (London: Longmans, 1902) *Life and Letters of Max Müller*, vol. l, chap. 60, p. 171.

61 Max Müller, *Chips from a German Workshop*, vol. 1 (London, 1867), p. 66.

62 Nirad C. Chaudhuri, *Scholar Extraordinary* (Oxford: Oxford University Press, 1974), p. 325.

63 Max Müller, *Life and Letters*, vol. l, ed. Georgina Müller (London: Longmans, 1902), pp. 357–58.

64 Ibid., p. 228.

65 Monier-Williams, *Modern India and the Indians*, 3rd ed. (1879), p. 261.

66 Monier-Williams, *Religious Thought and Life in India* (Oxford: Oxford University Press, 1885), p. 10.

67 Peter Tompkins, *Mysteries of the Mexican Pyramids* (London: Thames and Hudson, 1987), p. 7.

68 Friar Diego de Landa, *Yucatan before and after the Conquest*, trans. William Gates (Merida, Mexico: Producción Editorial Dante,1990), p. 104.

69 Tompkins, *Mysteries*, p. 21.

70 Ibid., p. 24.

71 Constance Irwin, *Fair Gods and Stone Faces* (London: W. H. Allen, 1964), p. 34.

72 Mill, *History*, 2: 109.

73 John Bentley, *Historical View of the Hindu Astronomy* (Osnabruck: Biblio Verlag, 1825, reprinted 1970), p. xxvii.

74 William Theodore de Bary, et al., eds., *Approaches to Asian Civilizations* (New York: Columbia University Press, 1964), pp. 34–35.

75 Trautmann, *Aryans*, p. 4.

76 See Bernard Cohen, *An Anthropologist Among the Historians and Other Essays* (Delhi: Oxford University Press, 1990).

77 David Lorenzen, "Imperialism and the Historiography of Ancient India," in *India: History and Thought: Essays in Honour of A. L. Basham*, ed. S. N. Mukherjee (Calcutta: Subarnekha, 1982), pp. 84–102.

78 Edward Said, *Orientalism* (New York: Pantheon Books, 1978), p. 11

LIFE AND DEATH: THE WHEEL OF SAMSARA

~

T he crucial difference between Vedic culture and our present edition is not about the value of acquiring information or knowledge. The immense gulf between the two modes of living concerns what actually is valuable information; what is essential knowledge. The Vedic view never casts out knowledge of matter. It simply puts mundane knowledge and information in its proper place. If the body is indeed secondary—incidental to the real self, the soul—wouldn't it follow that knowledge of manipulating matter is inferior and auxiliary? Knowing the glories of spiritual science, who would want to overdose themselves with information on material transformations and permutations?

Without a doubt, the civilization presented in the Vedic literature does alert its members to the futility of temporal progress in a temporary world. At the same time, however, the Vedic conclusion never says this world is false, or nonexistent. Just as a mirage, though merely a reflection of light on sand, has a reality, similarly material existence, though fleeting, is factual. At night we forget our daytime reality and ply the world of dreams. During the day we forget our activities in dreams and wrestle with our responsibilities in wakefulness. Both environments are ephemeral; yet they exist. What is false, the Vedas state, is our misuse of them. That mistake comes from two more fundamental errors: first, thinking the body and mind of matter are the self; second, perceiving the cosmos of matter and spirit as our property.

The Vedas remind us quite graphically: What is the value of a temporary body, flapping in the breeze for a few moments, though decorated with high technology? The next life is fact, the Vedas declare. Therefore we should use this temporary body to secure the eternal. If we lack the gumption to strive for putting a complete stop—in this very lifetime—to our material existence, then at least we can use the body to make gradual spiritual advancement. While doing so, we can lay up for ourselves a better standard of material happiness in the next life, with improved facilities for spiritual cultivation.

In other words, Vedic civilization has something for everyone: the gradualists and the transcendentalists. Both parties know that this life is a preparation for the next. According to their measure, they act with intelligence and vigor now. Meanwhile, they keep an eye open for the effects of their present consciousness on future births.

The gradualists know the art of sorting themselves out progressively. The transcendentalists, though, abandon all mundane ties to accomplish liberation as soon as possible. The crucial common ground is that all see the present life as part of a sequence. From the Vedic perspective, no one should foolishly chop this life out of the fabric of continuity and idolize it as the all-in-all. Therefore, even participants in Vedic culture who don't have their eyes irrevocably fixed on transcendence still follow the Vedic injunctions. Although they opt for the slow train, not the express, they want to live this life so that the next one is an improvement.

Vedic culture exalts knowledge for its transformational power. The current penchant for worshipping at the altar of material information is considered debased and dehumanizing. Where is the potency of materialistic education and knowledge to transform, to purify, the Vedas ask? Herein lies the heart of the Vedic challenge to our modern world. What is the actual effect of what you know? The Vedic texts deem as most precious that information able to transform not only the present life but also the next one. The prize transformation is to completely escape the cycle of birth and death.

Nontranscendentalists want to tarry, because they are attached to material attractions. Nevertheless, they do not want to ruin their future lives. Even today in India you will find that persons suffering material difficulty know their problems stem from faulty actions in their previous life. Those enjoying the high life, with its attendant temporary luxuries, know their comforts result from pious acts in their past life.

On the surface, the Vedic universal law of karma smacks of fatalism. Superficially, Vedic life can seem predestined and unalterable: with your ball and chain, you resign yourself to slogging along in the mire as best you can. Some critics blame Vedic cosmic statutes for what they perceive in modern India as a chronic lack of material spunk. The folk notion in the West is that to compete effectively—whether in the marketplace, the factory, or the research laboratory—we require solid acceptance that "it's absolutely all on my shoulders." We exhort ourselves that our mighty abilities will make the difference between victory or defeat, wealth or poverty, the Nobel Prize or academic anonymity.

French philosopher and humanitarian Albert Schweitzer decried the Vedas as "world- and life-negation."[1] Overwhelmed by the Vedic pronouncements that life in the realm of matter is temporary, insubstantial, and troublesome, some readers may react as he did. Upon viewing the Vedas more patiently, however, we certainly find not spinelessness but savvy—relentless drive and stamina for attaining permanent bliss in full knowledge. The ancient texts urge us, "Don't be bought off by the phantasmagoria of material existence. With pure consciousness arise and conquer death." Even those unready to abruptly halt their pursuit of material happiness receive appropriate medicine. For them, the Vedas prescribe a methodical, incremental progress. While living out material ambitions and attachments, those still tethered to material fulfillment can gradually acclimate themselves to the spiritual reality.

The Vedic version works to persuade us that "world- and life-negation" actually means to suppress the soul, to stifle the real self. When we identify the temporary body with the self, consider the temporary world of matter to be our only home, and venerate the temporary stimulations of our body and mind as life's pinnacle, the Vedas say we have indeed negated life—we have destroyed ourselves.

The negators of the self are those who waste their human life and the valuable advanced consciousness it allows.

The *Brhad-aranyaka Upanishad* (3.8.10) describes the killer of the self:

> He is a miserly man who does not solve the problems of life as a human and who thus quits this world like the cats and dogs, without understanding the science of self-realization.

Vedic literature such as the *Ayur-veda* advocate that life spans are longer when the Vedic formulas for natural living and high thinking are followed. Still, longevity—though hallowed today—is not the foremost Vedic goal. Since life-after-life is a Vedic fact, the major emphasis falls upon the lasting benefit we can accomplish for our consciousness, moment to moment.

Try envisioning the monumental change in society once the feverish, desperate clinging to one life as the all in all subsides. Far from nullifying all ambition and achievement, the knowledge that this life is but one in a series invokes accountability, soberness, and genuine long-range planning. That we can see by studying the Vedic cosmological treatises, the Puranas.

As we drive our body through material existence, the Vedic historical perspective offers us a rearview mirror, and seeks to persuade us to look in it occasionally. Although our just due may not catch up with us in this lifetime, we can learn to see the reactions trailing our actions, for our future experience. For those who choose to accept that they can't get away with anything, the Vedas present precise guidance as to how we can arrange society, so that while fulfilling the immediate needs of the body, we can also benefit ourselves in our future births—not suffer. Even we can opt to stop birth, if we have the determination.

> What is the value in this world of a prolonged life that is wasted by years of inexperience? Better a moment of full consciousness, because that gives us a start in searching after our supreme interest. (*Shrimad-Bhagavatam* 2.1.12)

The Vedic message is that my present consciousness will generate my future. Even death does not wipe the slate clean. We will face the reactions to our actions, whether good karma or bad. Real progress begins when we become conscious that we are accountable for our consciousness. Consequently, the Vedas enjoin us to use our human intelligence to find out the universal law of action and reaction, and adhere to it.

From the Vedic standpoint, nothing about life is clear until we can understand our existence independent of the current body. Then we can inquire into the system that governs our changing from one body to another.

OUT OF THE BODY:
WORLDWIDE ACCEPTANCE

Can I really travel out of my body? How can I be "me" without it? In Chapter 2 we discussed the Vedic concept of the subtle body: a psychic, astral layer composed of finer matter than the gross components of the physical layer that we easily see. Though some people, especially some healers, can perceive aspects of the subtle form, most cannot. The Vedic texts explain that every living entity possesses this subtle body. Composed of mind, intelligence, and false ego, the subtle body can exist even when separate from the gross physique. By understanding the relationship between the soul, the gross body, and the subtle body, then we can easily comprehend out-of-body experiences, or OBEs. The full Vedic picture of the self and its coverings is far more profound than any naive dualism. The Vedic science of the self is "interactionism" at its best, especially since all the components emanate from the same ultimate controlling source, and all their possible interactions are fully documented.

Throughout human history, we will find accounts of OBEs. The Hebrews, the Chinese, the Egyptians, indigenous North Americans, the South Pacific peoples, the Greek philosophers, and the alchemists in medieval times all knew about it. A study published in the Journal of the Society for Psychic Research found that of 44 non-Western societies, all except three accepted OBEs.[2] In another cross-cultural study, the anthropologist Erika Bourguignon looked at approximately half of all the known human societies, and ascertained that out of the 488 peoples she studied, 437 had something about OBEs in their culture.[3]

For those who don't know, a typical OBE goes like this: during sleep, trauma, or purposeful concentration, a person feels his mind separate from the body. While he or she floats off to somewhere else, the person can even look down and see the gross body. The stuff of witchcraft-laden primitive societies, you say? But the modern West also has its share. For instance, university students polled in England also affirm OBEs. Cecilia Green, in the 1960s Director of the Institute of Psychophysical Research at Oxford, surveyed 115 students at Southampton University. Of them 19 percent admitted to an OBE experience. Upon her polling 380 Oxford University students, 34 percent said yes.[4] Now what in the official Western religious or scientific knowledge system can explain such a rather prevalent experience? What stumps our professors, however, the so-called mythological Vedic texts easily handle.

NEAR-DEATH EXPERIENCES:
A ROUTINE AFFAIR

Near-death experiences (NDEs), though a sensation in the last quarter of the twentieth century, have been with us in the literature of humanity for thousands of years. Lengthy descriptions are found in the *Egyptian Book of the Dead*, the *Tibetan Book of the Dead*, and especially in Canto Six of the *Bhagavata Purana*—the encyclopedic Vedic text. Plato, in book ten of *The Republic*, describes a Greek soldier named Er who "returned to life" just seconds before his funeral pyre was to be lit. Medieval literature is full of NDEs. The Venerable Bede, for example, presents an account in his *A History of the English Church and People*.

As stated in chapter 2, chronicles of NDEs are so common that there is no need to rehash the subject in its entirety. A 1981 Gallup Poll, the most quoted poll in the USA, suggested that approximately one in twenty Americans have gone through a near-death experience. Since the time of that poll, numerous journals, organizations, and counseling groups have sprung up to cope with the demand for understanding NDEs. Major near-death researchers include the British psychiatrist Dr. Peter Fenwick,

Australian Dr. Cherie Sutherland, and a five-star group of well-published Americans, such as Drs. Raymond Moody, Kenneth Ring, Michael Sabom, Maurice Rawlings, and Melvin Morse.

What is of immediate interest for our focus on the Vedic perspective is the dramatic continuation of personal existence—when all vital signs of life are undetectable in the body. NDE accounts describe how the breathing and pulse stop, and all traces of consciousness cease. Electroencephalographs, or EEGs, give readings that are completely flat—they show no brain-wave activity whatsoever. In many cases the persons are officially diagnosed as clinically dead.

Yet during this time of apparent death, many persons undergo extraordinary experiences. Often they report encounters with celestial or hellish beings. Irrespective of the reliability, what is important for the Vedic view is that these incidents reveal acute sense perception and heightened awareness. The experiencers report ordinary situations and objects that investigators can easily verify. Somehow the clinically dead person sees things in his room and even beyond its walls—though the physical body has ceased to function. What is the sensory apparatus that accomplishes these perceptions? Once again we are nudging closer to Vedic knowledge of the subtle body.

Near-death patients recall floating above their physical body. They can often describe all the final efforts of the medical staff—from a vantage point at the top of the operating room. Michael Sabom, a cardiologist and professor of medicine at Atlanta's Emory University, made a study of cardiac-arrest patients who, during NDEs, observed medical procedures and details that they in no way should have been able to see. The patients, of course, had no prior knowledge of these things. Therefore they had nothing to draw upon for fabricating a believable story.[5]

Most NDE tales, however, though retold and rehashed in one best-selling book after another, have turned out to be unverifiable to the standard of precise science. Although the sheer impact of the personal testimony is what carries the day for the layperson, careful researchers seeking to corroborate the claims can have a tough time. The patients either have since become confused about details or have died. Or else the hospital staff was uncertain about the exact medical circumstances of the incident. NDEs are unpredictable, and no specific procedures are in place beforehand to probe them. After all, the job of the medical staff is to stop death, not to monitor bodies after they have been pronounced clinically dead.

One solid account that seems to have withstood the test of time and inquiry is from Kimberly Clark, at the University of Washington Hospital in Seattle. As Dr. Sabom and others have relayed, a woman, known to the public only as Maria, "died" of cardiac arrest and then "came back." Afterwards, she was able to describe the position of an object outside the hospital, at an inaccessible location. She told Clark, a hospital social worker, that she had been out of her body and had "thought herself" out of the hospital building and up its side to another floor. There she had come "face-to-face" with a tennis shoe poised on the window ledge. Clark knew Maria had been admitted at night, and had been completely incapacitated ever since. The doubtful social worker went outside the hospital, looked up at the ledges, but could not clearly see anything from so far down. How could Maria have seen anything from the ground, at either night or day—especially in her immobile, deathly condition. Clark then went inside the building again and up to the third floor. Room after room she investigated, having to press her nose against the narrow windows to see out of them. Finally she saw the shoe and retrieved it. She was shocked to note that the minute details Maria had given about the shoe were, first, completely correct and, second, impossible to see unless someone could float outside at close range—on the shoe's other side.[6]

Most of the scientific and medical disbelievers in NDEs think they are hallucination—the projections of a dying brain. In repelling these skeptics, believers point to the occurrence of NDEs in people with completely flat EEGs. They say the fact that the instrument registered absolutely no brain activity whatsoever shows NDEs are not hallucinations. Usually, a person's dreaming, imagining, or even hallucinating record a huge amount of EEG activity. Naysayers, however, assert that EEGs are inaccurate at low levels of brain activity and also have made some big mistakes—such as getting positive readings from Jell-O.

NDEs are so widespread, with so many persons involved, it is indeed hard to dismiss every aspect of them with a simple flick of the modern empirical hand. And, as already pointed out, descriptions of them are found throughout recorded human history. The problem is the Western knowledge filter. Whenever something—no matter how striking or prevalent—doesn't fit into the current materialist paradigm, it is filtered out. That means among established "careful, rational thinkers" the existence of the abnormal phenomenon cannot be taken seriously. Nevertheless, the Vedic perspective can easily accommodate what should be obvious to anyone—filtered or not. If we set aside the perhaps more sensational, "other-dimension" aspects of NDE narratives, then we can concentrate on what is of urgent concern. What should immediately grab our intelligence is that something with the capacity to move, hear, and see undeniably does separate itself from a physical body that has been rendered completely inoperable.

The disruption for the Western knowledge factories does not end here, though. From the standpoint of modern science it is certainly eerie when a person whose body has been given up for dead perceives from a position outside of it. But this blow to our materialist tradition is compounded when the person seeing from outside the body is physically blind. The NDE researcher Dr. Kenneth Ring has recently concentrated his efforts on experiencers who are completely blind. He was able to interview and study in depth twenty-one of these cases. Of this group, three were positive they could not see anything, three said they were unsure because the experience of sight was so foreign to them, and fifteen immovably declared that during their NDE they had "visual experiences," some in detail. Ring labels this phenomenon "mindsight."[7]

We may be sure we can see only with our physical eyes, but documented evidence persists to the contrary. When we start to consider the Vedic assertion that we have a subtle, astral form that is the template for our physical form, and that the subtle body has its own subtle senses, then we may make sense of the baffling evidence that OBEs and NDEs place under our nose. "Sightless seeing," however, does not restrict itself to experiences outside the body. A clinical researcher at Harvard Medical School, David Eisenberg, presented the account of two young Chinese sisters who could "see" via the skin in their armpits. In this way they could see well enough to read notes and identify colors.[8] A neurologist in Italy, Cesare Lombroso, investigated the case of a blind girl who could see via the tip of her nose and the lobe of an ear.[9] In the 1960s the Soviet Academy of Science certified that a Russian peasant, Rosa Kuleshova, could read newspapers and see photographs via the tips of her fingers. Her abilities were so incontestable that *Life* magazine publicized them in a special article.[10]

TEMPORARY TREE; ETERNAL FRUITS

No longer an esoteric concept outside of the East, reincarnation certainly has become popular in the West. That we have lived before and will live again has become a widespread Western sentiment. In casual conversation often someone quips, "I'm so keen on this hobby or pursuit, I must have done it in my past life." Nevertheless, most of the rush to reincarnation shows itself to be superficial. The average "born-again" supporter has given little thought to what it means to leave the body with its familiar world and accept another one. Whims and fancies aside, is there a repository of actual knowledge explaining the full reality of reincarnation?

Vedic knowledge of the temporary body and our existence beyond it describes how reincarnation affects both the individual and society. The overall vision the Vedas give us is that when a society follows the Vedic working codes for good karma and preliminary transcendentalism, then nature reciprocates by supplying the necessities of material life. In this way prosperous living is said to be inclusive in all Vedic directives. The best wealth, however, is considered something else. Real wealth, in the Vedic sense, means using the temporary to gain the eternal. Though the human body and all its social and economic achievements rise and fall, Vedic ingenuity aims at employing this temporality for eternal goals. The Vedas urge us: invest, transform. Get the right information to use your capital of human life wisely.

> The Vedas enjoin that the factual result of the tree of the body is the good fruits and flowers we derive from it. But if the bodily tree does not exist, there is no possibility of factual fruits and flowers. Even if you think the body is based on untruth, without the help of that bodily tree there cannot be factual fruits and flowers. (*Shrimad-Bhagavatam* 8.19.39)

This verse helps us to understand the human body and its value. In the material cosmos, where spirit soul is embedded within gross and subtle matter, even the factual truth cannot exist without a touch of untruth. In other words, the ultimate truth is certainly the light of spirit—not the shadow of matter. Nevertheless, to realize that eternal truth—the eternal fruits and flowers—we require a temporary device, the transitory tree of the human body.

The Vedas never say that the cosmos is false. Though matter

is deemed the inferior potency of the Supreme, it still has its usefulness. Both the light and shadow have a purpose. In fact the shadow depends on the light for its existence. The Vedic literature instructs us how to use the shadow of matter to align ourselves with the light of spirit. Therefore, even the shadowy realm of gross and subtle matter has its correct purpose. Though inferior—without self-activating potency—it does emanate from the Supreme. Genuine knowledge teaches us to transform even this temporariness into a catapult to the eternal.

The entire Vedic approach to civilization rests on this deft principle of spiritual utility. Matter and its arrangements, when utilized in accord with Vedic directions, can lead to spiritual awakening. This ingenuity is the heart of Vedic culture. Hence, why the accusations of extreme other-worldliness? The Vedic follower certainly seems to have both feet on the ground—with head appropriately in the sky.

The living entity lost in the shadow energy of matter cannot come out of the illusion without the help of the body—itself an element of illusion. We need the facility of the human body to follow not only the Vedic system but also any system of religion and philosophy. Since the flower and fruit of spiritual development have to be obtained via the body, we should not neglect bodily care. An actual human society means the organization of bodies for coordinated spiritual progress. Therefore, we also should not neglect the smooth functioning of human society.

Still, bodily and social maintenance should not consume all of our time and energy. We want to experience the actual fruits and flowers from the tree of the body—and the tree of society. As long as the body lasts, we can thoroughly study the Vedic instructions and strive to achieve perfection. A society coordinated for the same purpose makes attaining that fruit much easier.

Although the body is temporary, not eternal, we learn that a proper human society can help us take from the body the best service and make our life perfect. Or an appropriate society can facilitate our accumulating credits for continued spiritual progress in the next birth. We should remember this point about the civilization chronicled in the Vedas: the individual and the society work hand in hand for a coordinated spiritual evolution—spanning, if necessary, many lives. Therefore, knowledge of the soul's transmigration from one body to another is essential for a Vedic-approved society to achieve its goals.

Reincarnation And The Big Three:
Christianity, Judaism, and Islam

More often than not, someone raised in one of the Semitic religions is surprised to learn that the rest of the world considers reincarnation self-evident. Outside the major belief systems that sprang up near the Mediterranean, religion and reincarnation go hand in hand. Any professor of comparative religion will point out that, from a global viewpoint, we will find no concept in the world's religions more universal than reincarnation. In the societies of both the primitives and the civilized, it's there. Certainly we will find it in the religions associated with India. Both the Vedic-based traditions and those outside—such as Buddhism, Jainism, and Sikhism—all accept reincarnation. Yet it is also there in Pharaonic Egypt, polytheistic Greece and Rome, as well as in Taoism, Zoroastrianism, and a global potpourri of ethnic shamanism and tribal beliefs.

What's even more surprising, though, is to find reincarnation—at different times, in different places—vibrantly residing within the precincts of Judaism, Christianity, and Islam. The Semitic mainstream generally rejects reincarnation, because its traditions believe the soul is not eternal, in that a new one comes into being with each new human life. Nevertheless, within the Semitic camp, strong notions of reincarnation have managed to push up their head.

Mainline Judaism does not formally accept reincarnation. It views all subjects that deal with "the next world" as a mystery inaccessible while we are in this life. Yet the Jewish tradition has an esoteric side—the Kabbalah. Jews conversant with Kabbalistic literature make reincarnation sound almost intrinsic to the Jewish faith. Also connected with Kabbalism are the Hassidic Jews, whose teachings directly affirm reincarnation. Upon turning to the world of broader Islam, we find that the Sufis focus on what they say are the esoteric teachings behind the Koran. Reincarnation tallies prominently with the Sufi masters, and through their great influence they passed the concept into Islamic literature.

In the Christianity that moderns know, reincarnation seems to run into a brick wall. If you go back in time and consider medieval Catholic theologians such as Thomas Aquinas, as well as Reformation chieftains like Luther and Calvin, and then, if you move forward to the average Christian leader today, the concept of a soul changing bodies would prove utterly strange to all. In modern Western Christendom, whether the true believer calls himself Catholic or Protestant, reincarnation has no official place. Yet, when we examine the entire history of Christianity, we find something else.

For the first wave of Christians, reincarnation was a ready option, a prevailing wind in the climate of that day. During the first four hundred years A.D., early Church Fathers such as Clement of Alexandria, Justyn Martyr, St. Gregory of Nyssa, Arnobius, and St. Jerome embraced reincarnationist concepts. Even St. Augustine seriously flirted with the possibility. In his famous confessions, he wrote, "Did my infancy succeed another age of mine that dies before it? Was it that which I spent within my mother's womb? . . . And what before that life again, O God of my joy, was I anywhere or in any body?"[11]

To understand reincarnation's fall from grace, we have to know something about the emergence and demise of Gnosticism—

"secret knowledge." What is now called Gnosticism was not alien to early Christianity, but permeated its history during the first few hundred years. In those early times, Gnosticism had spread throughout the Mediterranean region. The latest textual discoveries reveal an effect far greater than previously thought.

The common misunderstanding, past and present, has been to confuse pro-reincarnation elements in the Church with Gnostics. Thus when Church leaders waged an intense campaign against Gnosticism, people assumed that reincarnation was also taboo. Particularly, reincarnation was closely associated with Origen (A.D. 185[?]–254[?]), by far the greatest thinker and Biblical scholar of his day. Moreover, among all the Christian fathers— with the possible exception of Augustine—Origen is held to be the foremost church genius. Throughout the whole history of Christianity, it is clear that no literature except the Bible itself wielded a greater authority in the Church than Origen's writings did in their time. But some three hundred years after his death, it seemed that a general council of the Church had condemned Origen. Between the emperor Justinian and the Church, the handling of the Origen controversy generated a murkiness about reincarnation that has continued in Christendom to this day.

Many popular books on reincarnation pinpoint the Second Council of Constantinople (the Fifth Ecumenical Council of the Church) in A.D. 553 as the official end to Origen and reincarnation in Christianity. Since Origen was popularly associated with reincarnation, and since he was supposed to have deviated from orthodoxy, people have assumed that reincarnation and Christianity are incompatible. The scholar Geddes MacGregor has given the best blow-by-blow account in his book *Reincarnation in Christianity*.

MacGregor, a Christian theologian and Emeritus Distinguished Professor of Philosophy at the University of Southern California, concludes that the facts do not support a clear-cut resolution of the issue. Certainly one can hardly blame laypersons for any inability to sort through the tedious maze of political intrigue, ecclesiastical powerplays, and theological rivalries that MacGregor relays.

By the sixth century, Origenism had probably become quite remote from Origen himself, much as Neoplatonism went beyond Plato, or neo-Darwinism exceeded Darwin. A monastic community in Palestine known as "New Laura" had become the center for intellectual monks who aligned themselves with the "Origenist movement." Their affinity for doctrines such as those of preexistent souls and universal salvation began to get them into hot water. The monks' opponents succeeded in getting Emperor Justinian to write a letter to the patriarch of Constantinople. The brief named Origen—dead for several hundred years—as one of several pernicious heretics. At the command of Justinian, a synod was convened at Constantinople in 543 and an edict was issued, setting forth a list of errors attributed to Origen. This edict, besides refuting the errors, was supposed to promote peace between East and West. But it only divided them further.

Pope Vigilius initially opposed the imperial order. Consequently he broke off communication with its supporter, the Patriarch of Constantinople. Then the Pope himself arrived in Constantinople, whereupon he suddenly reversed himself. Careful not to allow that the emperor had any clout in theological issues, Pope Vigilius issued a document condemning the writings that Emperor Justinian's edict had already cursed. The Pope's document, however, was vehemently denounced by bishops in Gaul, North Africa, and elsewhere. Consequently in 550, Pope Vigilius withdrew it (just three years before the council that is believed to have finished off Origen).[12]

The story just begins there. Even at this stage, though, MacGregor says it is impossible to peer into all the grand chessplay. The Origenist squabble was a rather minor side issue, amid major geopolitical and ecclesiastical maneuvers. Meanwhile, the monks who called themselves Origenists split into two groups. In 553 Emperor Justinian was ready for action again. He convened the whole Church, in the Second Council of Constantinople—also known as the Fifth Ecumenical Council of the Church.

To delineate Justinian's motives would require a lengthy political analysis. In short, the goal of the emperor's statecraft was to reunite East and West. Coincidentally, he wanted to condemn a doctrine known as Nestoranism. The writings of Nestorius—banned by Justinian back in 543—had nothing to do with Origen. These Nestorian heresies were the stated cause of the convocation, not Origenism.

> The extent, if any, to which Origenism was really condemned at that ecumenical council is, to say the least, questionable. . . . The Ecumenical Council was convened on May 5, 553, under the presidency of the Patriarch of Constantinople; but the Emperor controlled the proceedings. The arrangements were stacked against the West. Of the 165 bishops who signed the acts of the Council at its final meeting on June 2, not more than six would have been from the West. In protest against that and other irregularities, Pope Vigilius refused to attend. The Three Chapters [by Nestorius] were anathematized; but, as we have seen, they had nothing directly to do with Origen. Of the fourteen anathemas pronounced by the Council, Origen's name is mentioned in one, among a list of heretics; but there is some evidence that justifies a belief that this is an interpolation.[13]

Note that the Pope was not even present at this historic event. He had completely opposed the emperor's convening this council. Refusing the emperor's call to Constantinople, Pope Vigilius secluded himself in a church sanctuary. The council went on without him, in May and June 553. The Pope hid from May to

December. Finally, the next year, on 23 February 554, he surrendered. He officially ratified the council's verdict of the previous year. The result? Chaos. The churches in the West rebelled. Some dioceses even closed communication with Rome until the seventh century. In Africa imperial troops had to force acceptance of the edicts.

The overall outcome was so inconclusive and dubious that some modern Catholic scholars question whether the anathemas laid down by that particular Council are actually binding on Catholics. Yet the tragedy is that, ever since, Christians have taken it for granted that reincarnation is a forbidden doctrine. They hear that the Fifth Ecumenical Council slammed the door on a whole caboodle of Gnosticism, Origenism, reincarnationism, and other deviancies of the day, all lumped together.

By the time of the Council of Lyons in the thirteenth century and the Council of Florence in the fourteenth, it was assumed that the body of beliefs handed down by the apostles denied reincarnation. Thus, these councils insisted that the soul goes nonstop to heaven or hell—or else purgatory, to further prepare for heaven. The Protestants dropped purgatory, the Catholics kept all three, and that's where things stand today.

Christians must find their way to accept that the soul does not exist before birth. This notion, of course, leads to the question how and wherefrom a soul manifests every time a new baby is born. Regardless of the attempted answer, one shot to stay out of everlasting damnation is all the soul gets.

Though the fullness of what Origen believed about reincarnation is not always clear, his sympathies are obvious to all who study his works. The exact scope of his beliefs is clouded—more by his future friends than enemies. After Origen's death, wary scribes allowed potentially radical passages to disappear. Exercising a sort of informal censorship to protect Origen's stature, they did not copy anything that might subject the departed leader to charges of heresy. According to the *Catholic Encyclopedia,* what Origen taught closely resembled what the Platonists, Jewish mystics, and Vedic sages accepted.[14]

Here is a passage that remains:

> By some inclination toward evil, certain spirit souls come into bodies, first of men; then, due to their association with the irrational passions after the allotted span of human life, they are changed into beasts, from which they sink to the level of plants. From this condition they rise again through the same stages and are restored to their heavenly place.[15]

Was Origen actually or properly condemned for teachings like this? Some say that the process of anathema was never applied, or it was revoked, or it was illegitimately executed. Additionally, the reluctant Pope Vigilius is said to have had no real gripe with Origen. The Pope is even said to have opposed nailing Origen— until caught in the emperor's web of theo-politics.

Owing to this fog surrounding Origen's fall from grace, today some Christians conclude that they may safely adopt Origen's concepts. The *Catholic Encyclopedia* acknowledges this stance—in other words, it does exist.[16] In modern times the internationally known Cardinal Désiré Joseph Mercier was among those who say reincarnation has never been formally condemned by the Roman Catholic Church.[17] It would seem that anyone can read the Bible and see that, like the doctrine of the Trinity, the Bible neither explicitly promulgates reincarnation nor directly objects to it. Some verses, though, seem to acknowledge it.

As of yet, few Christian scholars have felt motivation to review the place of reincarnation in the official belief system of Catholicism or Protestantism. Hans Küng, the prominent Swiss Catholic thinker, stated that Christian theologians "scarcely take this question [of reincarnation] seriously."[18] Küng, a globally known voice, advocates elevating reincarnation to a central issue in contemporary Christian theology.[19]

Not surprisingly, a twelve-nation Gallup poll found that between 18 and 25 percent of Protestants and Catholics accept reincarnation. The poll covered major European countries, including the UK, Germany, Italy, and France, as well as Canada and the USA. The results, however, were gathered in 1969.[20] The numbers can only be much higher at the turn of the century.

Life after Life

Death is the Vedic acid test. At that time, the level of consciousness we have cultivated during life is examined. This tenet is explained in *Bhagavad-gita* (8.6):

> Whatever state of being we remember when we quit our body,
> that state we will attain without fail.

What is it that is changing bodies, in past, present, and future lives? The imprint and modus operandi of the soul are visible, though the soul itself is invisible to direct material vision. The next verse of the *Gita* counsels:

> He who dwells in the body can never be slain. Therefore you
> need not grieve for any living being.

The Vedic texts give us precise information how the living entity, the spirit soul, transfers from one body to another. The Vedic laws of the cosmos said to govern this transmigration are certainly far from the purview of our empirical science. It seems natural, however, that eventually we will turn our attention to these laws. Then we will discover more about the Vedic social ramifications of life after life. In other words, that this life is one of many is not just a personal reality—it is a social reality as well. We don't have to be sociologists or psychologists to perceive that knowledge of *samsara*—the wheel of birth and death—can shape the entire organization and thrust of society.

Silly stories of reincarnation are standard fare in tabloids and gossip magazines, but an increasing number of erudite researchers are quietly accumulating a stunning mass of evidence that points to previous lives. Hypnosis is one area of investigation. The clinical work of rigorously scientific hypnotists is said by them to far surpass the attempts of unskilled practitioners, who do not know techniques to prevent them eliciting fantasies. Dr. Joel Whitton, a professor of psychiatry at the University of Toronto Medical School, is one of several highly accredited researchers who use hypnosis to study what people unconsciously may know of their past. Research has shown that more than 90 percent of all hypnotizable persons furnish memories that apparently indicate previous lives.[21]

Spending thousands of hours recording everything hypnotized volunteers would say about alleged previous existences, Whitton found an unusual correlation between these memories and the current experiences of the subject. For example, a psychologist born and raised in Canada had spoken with an inexplicable British accent as a child. He feared breaking his leg and air travel, he constantly bit his nails, and he was strangely fascinated with torture. Once he had a strange vision of being in a room with a Nazi officer, just after operating the pedals of a car. Under hypnosis, the man related memories as a British pilot flying over Germany during World War II. Antiaircraft bullets broke his leg and consequently forced him to lose control of the foot pedals. After he crash-landed, the Germans captured him, tortured him by pulling out his nails, and then he died. Whitton also recorded subjects speaking in archaic languages that only linguists could recognize as Old Norse and a Mesopotamian tongue extant between A.D. 226 and 651.[22]

Dr. Brian L. Weiss, a graduate of Yale School of Medicine and chairperson of psychiatry at Mount Sinai Medical Center in Miami, wrote a best-selling book, *Many Lives, Many Masters.* Here he describes his conversion from a skeptic to a supporter of reincarnation. One of his patients, while under hypnosis, started having a past-life regression. The spontaneous incident propelled Weiss into further investigation. He says that, since publishing his book, he has been flooded with letters from "closet researchers"—that is, fellow psychiatrists who are secret investigators. Weiss says: "There are psychiatrists who write me that they've been doing regression therapy for ten to twenty years, in the privacy of their office, and 'please don't tell anyone, but . . .' Many are receptive to it, but they won't admit it."[23]

The most persuasive and concrete indicators are the work of Dr. Ian Stevenson. A professor of psychiatry at the University of Virginia Medical School, he has an impeccable academic reputation for thorough, labored investigation. Rather than hypnosis, his specialty is interviewing young children who spontaneously, consciously remember previous lives. He rightfully urges caution in admitting evidence from guided past-life regressions. When the mind opens to hypnotic trance, a small spark of a minor cue can ignite a blaze of vivid imagery—completely imagined. Stevenson, therefore, favors memories that rise unsought, and which can be verified through historical research.

During the past thirty-five years, he has collected over 2600 cases of past-life memories, of which sixty-five detailed reports have been published. Collecting evidence from every continent, he says these cases are so common that his staff cannot keep up with the workload. Cases are especially frequent in Hindu and Buddhist countries of South Asia, among the Shiite peoples of Lebanon and Turkey, among the tribes of West Africa, and, interestingly, in the American Northwest.

Usually the children are between the ages of two and four

when they spontaneously start talking of a previous lifetime. Because often their memories are so detailed, Stevenson is able to track down the identity of their previous birth and confirm the particulars. Sometimes he has even taken children to the general vicinity of the precise spot they talked to him about—where his investigation had already uncovered a person who lived and died exactly as the children described. As Stevenson observed, the children effortlessly picked their way through a strange neighborhood, and correctly identified their previous house, possessions, relatives, and friends.

To date, Stevenson has enough data and case histories to fill eight present volumes, with several more to come. He has published studies showing that in a test batch of 387 children who claimed to remember a previous life, 141 of them had phobias that nearly always corresponded to the exact mode of death documented for the previous identity the child recalled. The phobias usually manifested between the ages of two and five, sometimes even before the child had begun to speak about a previous life.

Pursuing a different angle, Stevenson has presented findings from an investigation of nine hundred cases involving biological correlation. He found that 35 percent of the children who remembered a past life had birthmarks or birth defects related in some way to a violent death that could be documented according to their accounts. For some cases he presented striking photographic evidence of the phenomenal correlation between the child's birthmarks or birth defects and the actual fatal wounds of the person whose life and violent death the child recalled.[24]

Stevenson's full work on this latest project was published in 1997. The unabridged documentation, *Reincarnation and Biology*, required two volumes, of more than one thousand pages each.[25] Lest the cynics think that the correspondence between birthmarks and a previous death is just chance, Stevenson divides the average-sized adult body into a grid of 160 boxes, each ten centimeters square. Plotting the skin marks on this grid, he convincingly demonstrates that the odds against a single aberration corresponding with a single wound are 1/160. However, what about cases where more than one wound and skin mark coincide? He documents eighteen cases in which a child remembers death by gunfire and has two birthmarks corresponding to the bullet's point of entry and exit. Two birthmarks correlating with two wounds increases the odds to 1/160 x 1/160, or 1/25,000.

The odds against a chance occurrence soar astronomically in the case of a Turk named Necip Ünlütaskiran. Of his seven birthmarks, six coincided exactly with wounds described in a medical document for the remembered deceased person. Furthermore, Necip claimed that he had stabbed his wife of a previous life in the leg, and the wound had left a scar. The woman was identified, and the telltale scar was there.

Besides his discovery that biological characteristics can furnish strong evidence for reincarnation, Stevenson also found clear inference that some kind of intermediate, subtle body exists, which transfers certain characteristics from the past life to the next one. He states:

> It seems to me that the imprint of wounds on the previous personality must be carried between lives on some kind of an extended body which in turn acts as a template for the production on a new physical body of birthmarks and deformities that correspond to the wounds on the body of the previous personality.[26]

Though Stevenson's work shakes the foundations of modern science, the care and precision of his research have brought him accolades from the most conservative sectors of the scholarly world. Prestigious scientific periodicals such as the *American Journal of Psychiatry,* the *Journal of Nervous and Mental Disease,* and the *International Journal of Comparative Sociology* publish his findings.

Even the American Medical Association—unchallengeable in size, influence, and tradition—officially stated in its journal that Stevenson had "painstakingly and unemotionally collected a detailed series of cases in which the evidence for reincarnation is difficult to understand on any other grounds. . . . He has placed on record a large amount of data that cannot be ignored."[27]

Modern science's pursuance of reincarnation should bring open-minded researchers face to face with the awesome scope of the Vedic social system. How intriguing and stirring are the accounts of the way an entire society can gear itself for practical necessities in both this life and future births! We can only benefit from insight into the broad Vedic social ramifications of life after life.

What follows is a summary of a section in the chief Vedic cosmological treatise, the *Bhagavata Purana*, also known as the *Shrimad-Bhagavatam*.[28] It narrates a dramatic episode that can give us deep insight into the Vedic vision of reincarnation. Particularly we may note the age-old Vedic knowledge of mind–body interactionism. Now, treatment of the body and mind together— "holistic health"—is the vanguard of modern medical research.

At the close of the nineteenth century, the psychologist and philosopher William James foreshadowed the current boom: "No mental modification ever occurs which is not accompanied or followed by a bodily change." In our time, Norman Cousins highlighted the new emphasis on mind–body research by coining the apt phrase, "Belief becomes biology."

Ian Stevenson's treatise *Reincarnation and Biology* contains a chapter entitled "Bodily changes corresponding to mental images in the person affected." The most thorough examination, to date, of the connections between mentality and physiology, the book presents cases from official medical sources. Some of the numerous examples cited are stigmata, alteration of bodily functions by hypnosis, and bodily effects produced when memories of extreme injuries and traumas are relived.

Now that investigating the mind's effect on the physical body is a major field of medical research, we should have no hesitation to consider the ancient Vedic science of how mental states indeed transform into biology.[29]

DEATH ON A WEDDING DAY

A prominent member of the Vedic royalty named Vasudeva had just married Devaki, a royal princess. Their nobility was not in name only. Both were highly qualified descendants of Vedic martial and administrative families. After the gala marriage ceremony, the new husband and wife departed on a chariot, to begin their new home together. A convoy of hundreds of chariots—accompanied by horses, elephants, and maidservants—surrounded the couple. All vehicles and animals were laden with gold, because the wealthy father of the bride had bestowed upon her a large dowry.

The Vedic system for marriage was that the father would give his daughter as much wealth as possible on her wedding day, because she would never inherit his wealth. Property was always bequeathed to the sons. Modern women may consider this unjust, but we need to know more about Vedic customs before we pass judgment. In Vedic culture the women considered their children to be their wealth—more valuable than any amount of gold and land. Obviously, then, their psychology was somewhat different from their modern counterparts.

The bride, Devaki, and groom, Vasudeva, rode in a chariot driven by the girl's brother, Kamsa. Traditionally the brother of the bride would escort his sister on the trip to her new home so that she would not feel uneasy leaving the protection of her father's house for the first time.

As the massive regal procession accompanied the newlyweds to their destination, musicians playing conchshells, bugles, drums, and kettledrums filled the air majestically. The brother Kamsa, controlling the reigns of the horses, guided the chariot on its way. Suddenly a mysterious voice boomed from the sky, directed specifically to Kamsa. "You fool! You are calmly driving the chariot of your sister and new brother-in-law. But you do not know that the eighth child of this woman will kill you!"

Kamsa, though born into a Vedic noble family, had managed to amass within himself all the terrible qualities of a cruel despot. Upon hearing the omen from the sky, without hesitation he dropped the reigns. With one hand he grabbed his sister's hair and, with the other, pulled out his sword to cut off her head.

Vasudeva, the husband, was an extraordinarily qualified statesman, a paragon of Vedic excellence. Though his wedding festival had instantly transformed into utter catastrophe, he displayed astonishing sense, control, sobriety, and equipoise. Immediately acting to pacify and control Kamsa with words, he calmly spoke to his abominable brother-in-law: "My dear Kamsa, you are the pride of your dynasty. All heroes praise your fame. How can such an aristocratic person as you kill a woman, your own sister, on her wedding day?"

Any one of these three factors would ordinarily suffice to halt a potential aggressor. The Vedic injunctions forbid, under any circumstances, attacks upon women, old men, children, cows, and brahmins, the Vedic spiritual intellectuals. Yet Kamsa was prepared to immediately behead a woman—his own sister, another man's wife—on the auspicious day of her marriage. Kamsa was exhibiting, in high relief, the materialistic mentality of demonic selfishness: "I live, you die." One moment he had been affectionately driving his sister; the next, he was ready to kill her. If anyone's existence—even his sister's—seemed to threaten his own, then that person had to be terminated. Employing flattery and reason, Vasudeva struggled to defuse his brutal brother-in-law.

O mighty warrior, why are you so afraid of dying that you are about to perform such a horrid act? Death is sure for us all—it's packaged with our body at birth. Every moment, every hour you are dying, since the time you were born. If you are twenty years old, that means you are twenty years dead. The final blow may come now or in a hundred years. Death is inevitable for everyone. Why are you so afraid?

Vasudeva is pointing out that nothing can actually stop death. We may go either today or after a few days. Hence, futilely attempting to save our skins, why should we embroil ourselves in sinful karma?

Seeking to counteract the dangers of this world, Kamsa was prepared to destroy his family's reputation and the happiness of his next birth. The Vedas admonish us to use our precarious time in this world to stop the cycle of *samsara*—not continue it, or worsen it. According to the ancient texts, by scientifically elevating consciousness to the pure spiritual plane, anyone can make a real solution to the real problems of life.

Upon reminding Kamsa of both the inevitable demise of the body and the vainness of a sinful struggle to avoid it, Vasudeva next sought to teach him a crash lesson in what we popularly refer to now as reincarnation. Vedic teachers prefer a more precise term, transmigration of the soul.

Death means the finale to the soul's stay in a particular body. As soon as the body collapses, material nature reclaims the ingredients. Then the living entity moves into another body, awarded by the laws of nature according to karma.

During the course of one lifetime, the eternally living soul is moving from body to body. Vedic commonsense prods us to see that the stages of infancy, youth, and old age are a sequence of different bodies, like the individual frames of a filmstrip. What we call death is simply another move for the eternal soul—a transmigration to another new body. Just as the soul has transmigrated through the biological stages of one lifetime—from infancy to youth, and so on—similarly it moves from death to birth, accepting another lifetime.

For the ordinary person, everything is a mystery: not simply how the soul moves to a fresh body after death, but also even how in the present lifetime the soul dwells in the series of bodies. The Vedic summary text *Bhagavad-gita* explains transmigration with an analogy:

> As a person puts on new garments, giving up the old ones, similarly, the soul accepts new material bodies, giving up the old and useless ones. (*Bhagavad-gita* 2.22)

Vedic civilization, as presented in the texts, recognized the existence of universal laws that govern the soul's changing bodies. Directed by these laws, the living entity automatically receives a new body according to his past activities, desires, and ambitions. Living under the control of nature means living under these statutes of *samsara*—they control the sequence. Hence the process of bodily change will proceed automatically, in accord with our karmic activities.

Vasudeva urged his brother-in-law to thoroughly consider the law of karma. He wanted to impress upon Kamsa that if he went through with the abominable killing of a woman, the body he was sure to get in his next life would be even more conditioned to misery and ignorance. We can see that Vasudeva, a member of the Vedic ruling elite, was most skilful at disaster management. Amid such a rapidly accelerating calamity, he soberly applied his intelligence and knowledge to push back imminent doom. Now he will give Kamsa a graphic explanation of the soul's transmigration.

When we walk, we put the front foot down, and when confident of our footing, lift the rear foot up. Similarly the soul moves into the new body and abandons the old one. Haven't you noticed how worms on a plant carefully transfer themselves from one leaf to another? In the same way, the living entity changes bodies, as soon as the karma of the present body runs out. His new karma awaits him—in the shape of another body.

Vasudeva is emphasizing to Kamsa that the transmigration of the soul is not haphazard. The laws of nature orchestrate the entire process. The Vedic texts assert that every human deed cuts one of two ways. Either it resonates with the universal laws emanating from the Supreme, or it violates them. Unlike dull creatures in other species, the human being has sufficient intelligence to freely accept or reject cosmic statutes that govern the expression of consciousness.

This freedom of action entails responsibility for the effects. The profound reality the Vedas reveal to us is that the gift of developed consciousness brings accountability along with it. That accountability of consciousness manifests to our eyes as the body—the gross materialization of our actions and reactions.

The Vedic science of transmigration tells us that in the present human body we are undergoing the reactions from deeds of our past life. From that perspective, "body" means the embodiment of reactions to past karmic activity. Meanwhile, we are busy acting again—business as usual. That means, while we undergo our past karma, we simultaneously pile up new karma, which will greet us in our next birth. When the soul moves from the dead body to the new one, it is actually moving from a withered field of spent karmic reactions to a fresh field of ripe ones.

Vasudeva, a shining exemplar of the Vedic martial and administrative class, certainly knew the intricacies of *samsara*, repeated birth and death. Otherwise how could he govern and protect the people? Kamsa was expected to know these cosmic principles too, but had obliterated his intelligence through a life of hedonism. Thinking he was a law unto himself, he felt justified doing anything necessary for advancing or protecting his immediate sense gratification. Therefore Vasudeva continued his valiant instruction, to save both his wife and Kamsa from impending horror.

> Sometimes during the day we lose ourselves in daydreams or contemplation. We create these mental situations by what we have seen or heard. Absorbed in thought, we surrender our consciousness to these visions, completely forgetting our present body and circumstances. Likewise, at night we lose our waking body in dreams. While sleeping we see ourselves act in so many new bodies, in varied exotic ways. All the bodies—of both the day and night dream—are creations of the mind. Our states of consciousness are the secret of the soul's transmigration.

Vasudeva's explanation is progressing from the physical to the mental. In the previous two verses he stressed the physical reality of death and bodily change. Here he gives us a brilliant elucidation of the mind at work—the engine of transmigration. Using the known, Vasudeva is teaching us something unknown. Our mind has the ability to wholly absorb our attention, even at the expense of physical awareness. If we think carefully about this tendency, we may then appreciate the Vedic information that from the mind develops different physiologies, different bodies.

We all have experience of becoming enthralled by a particular mental fascination. Even during the day we can become so engrossed in a thought or memory that we forget our physical body and its surroundings. At night this amnesia, as we might call it, is even more obvious. During dreams, attractive sex partners envelop us; tigers swallow us. Meanwhile we have completely forgotten about the body lying asleep in the bed. Thus, our own daily experience, both day and night, easily demonstrates the inherent power of the mind. It can take us to places, transform circumstances, override the physical—even dictate the physical.

What may be harder for us to comprehend is the Vedic point that this same potency or velocity of the mind carries the soul through the death of one body to birth in a fresh one. Out of the magic hat of the mind comes a new physique that did not exist before. The Vedic literature makes clear to us that the activity of the mind at the time of death is the telltale sign of the next birth.

> The nature of the mind is flickering—it changes to and fro. Impelled by whim or deliberation, the mind changes. Therefore the body changes. According to our mental proclivities at the time of death, material nature offers another body. In other words, in *samsara* new bodies develop according to the movements of our mind. Otherwise the soul could remain free of material coverings, in its original, spiritual body.

What Vasudeva is explaining is that just as the body moves, the mind moves also. The Vedas say the motions of the mind are threefold: thinking, feeling, and willing. By adopting the Vedic perspective of categorizing the mind as a sense, we will probably have an easier time seeing this modus operandi: how it considers things, feels them over, and then wills—spurring the body into physical action.

Acceptance and rejection is another Vedic way of looking at the sensory activity of the mind. We all have experience of the mind grabbing on to an idea or situation and then tossing away the very same thing. Day and night, the mind constantly operates like this: seizing something and letting it go. In the same way, Vasudeva tells us, the soul—through the mind—accepts new bodies and rejects old ones.

The flavors of consciousness, mental transits, actually create gross material bodies in different lives. Again, if we can begin to discern the velocity and intensity of the mind, we can begin to understand the Vedic presentation of samsara.

> Sometimes luminaries in the sky reflect themselves in liquids. When the liquid moves, the reflection moves, bending into different shapes. For example, the moon casts its reflection on a pool of water, and the wind blows the water. As the reflected moon moves with the water, it assumes various shapes—sometimes roundish, sometimes oblong. Though the windblown water, with its deformed moon, may make us think the moon in the sky is also distorted, that is not actually the case. Therefore I implore you: remember your original pure spiritual identity. Do not become demonically contorted by sudden gusts of the material energy. The illusory influence of this energy has manifested as the external body and mind.

Some people today are fond of saying that all of us, collectively, are the universe. Through us, they say, the universe is experiencing itself. As we learn and grow, the universe evolves toward perfection. Vasudeva's classic Vedic presentation to Kamsa steers clear of these reveries. His profound metaphor emphasizes to Kamsa that we don't belong at all in the material atmosphere— whether our hometown, nation, planet, or universe. Mistakenly we think, "I am a human; this is my neighborhood. I am an Australian (or American), a part of planet Earth. What's more, I belong to the universe."

The moon, shining in the sky, does not belong in the water— indeed only its reflection is there. Similarly, Vasudeva wants to point out that we, as pure spirit souls, have an original spiritual existence, though we have forgotten it. Instead of living in our natural spiritual glory, we absorb ourselves in an illusory identity, a material selfhood that is a mere reflection into the temporary realm of material nature.

Enchanted by the ever-shifting waters of the material cosmos, we think we are also shifting—we identify with the permutations of material existence. As a result, when the winds of material change blow, as they must, we change shapes—we change bodies, families, and planets. Nevertheless, all this cosmic commotion in the ocean of *samsara* has nothing to do with the real person, the spirit soul, eternally situated beyond all material contamination.

Vasudeva has given us a lucid picture of how the soul seems to take up various positions in the cosmos. He diligently persevered in his philosophical attempt to prevent his brother-in-law from killing his own sister. If Kamsa could understand the immense consequences of his submitting to the agitating winds of material nature, he could avoid worse turbulence in future births.

> Therefore, since malicious, pungent karma produces a body that undergoes much suffering in the next life, how can it be in your self-interest to violate the universal law of karma? Considering your own benefit, you should not envy anyone, since an envious person must always live in fear of retribution, in this life and the next.

The Vedic civilization that we read of considers ignorance of the law no excuse. The human body brings advanced consciousness, and it also brings responsibility to know the cosmic statutes. Either we must know them ourselves or find out from someone who knows. That burden to know or find out rests on every human being. We can probably sympathize with the Vedic standard if we remember that, when travellers arrive in a foreign country, they are expected to know the road code before driving. In fact, a foreigner is expected to conform to all the laws of the land.

From the Vedic perspective, human action without full existential knowledge or access to full existential knowledge is ludicrous.

Government edicts bind, but a lawbreaker can escape detection. Also, sometimes an innocent person can face criminal charges. Universal law, as presented in the Vedic texts, suffers no such faulty applications, because the authorities said to enforce it are much more powerful than human beings.

Vasudeva concluded his emergency lessons with an appeal to Kamsa's heart for mercy:

> Your younger sister, poor Devaki, is like your own daughter. She deserves your affection—not your sword. We know you are merciful. Please spare her life.

Tragically, Kamsa was not hearing any of Vasudeva's eloquence. No good instruction, philosophy, fear, or guilt would deter him. A powerful man who adhered to no divine authority, Kamsa couldn't have cared less about the effects of karma in this life or the next. Using his limited sense perception, he had instantly calculated: "A voice from the sky has tipped me off—the eighth child of my sister will kill me. Acting decisively I will immediately kill her, neatly eliminating any future problems. This is the reality. I see no other; therefore I care for no other."

Kamsa was an aberration in Vedic civilization. We shudder to think how close to the norm his judgment and behavior may be in society today. Vasudeva, though exceptionally sagelike and wise, was also pragmatic. Seeing Kamsa's unwavering determination to consummate the heinous act, he thought of another approach that might stop his demonic brother-in-law.

We may note that Vedic knowledge of predestined happiness and distress did not weaken the intensity of Vasudeva's emergency efforts. With utmost dedication he executed his duty to save his new wife, exhausting all means. In Vedic culture duty is foremost, not predestination. The Vedas instruct that as long as we have intelligence and strength, we must try to avoid danger. Then, despite our best efforts, if we succumb to a disaster, there is no fault.

Like any sane culture, Vedic culture concerns itself with the intelligent avoidance of all the usual incidental calamities of life. Yet in Vedic culture there is something much more. Vasudeva could struggle against the imminent death of his wife, and he could also struggle against *samsara* itself. In other words, he had the knowledge to confront and conquer material existence, with its cycle of repeated birth and death.

He thought to himself: "First let me save my wife, Devaki. Who knows? In the future there may or may not be sons. Alternatively, the son may actually kill Kamsa, as the voice proclaimed. Therefore, let me do the necessary to cope with the immediate threat. I will promise to hand over any newly born children to Kamsa for his disposal—if he will spare Devaki now. He may try to kill her again later, but what can I do?"

Carefully crafting his final attempt as far as his intelligence would allow, Vasudeva, though ridden with anxiety, fixed a smile on his face and spoke very respectfully to the shameless Kamsa.

> My dear sober brother-in-law, what danger do you actually risk from your sister? The prophecy you heard said death will result from her sons, not her. There may or may not be sons. But if there are, let me assure you I will present them all to you, for your disposal. Therefore you need not fear.

Vasudeva was such a saintly statesman that even a rogue like Kamsa had faith in his words. Accepting Vasudeva's liberal proposal, he agreed that for the time being he would end his assault upon Devaki. Vasudeva praised his decision, and then the newlyweds entered their home.

Notes

1 Albert Schweitzer, *Indian Thought and Its Development*, trans. Mrs. Charles E. B. Russell (Boston: Beacon Press, 1936), p. 1.

2 Dean Shields, "A Cross-Cultural Study of Beliefs in out-of-the-Body Experiences," *Journal of the Society for Psychical Research* 49 (1978): 697–741.

3 Erika Bourguignon, "Dreams and Altered States of Consciousness in Anthropological Research," in *Psychological Anthropology*, ed. F.L.K. Hsu (Cambridge, Mass.: Schenkman, 1972), p. 418.

4 Celia Green, *Out-of-the-Body Experiences* (Oxford: Institute of Psychophysical Research, 1968).

5 Michael B. Sabom, *Recollections of Death* (New York: Harper & Row, 1982), p. 184.

6 Bruce Greyson and Charles P. Flynn, *The Near-Death Experience* (Chicago: Charles C. Thomas, 1984), as quoted in Stanislov Grof, *The Adventure of Self-Discovery* (Albany, N.Y.: SUNY Press, 1988), pp. 71–72.

7 Kenneth Ring and Sharon Cooper, *Mindsight: Near-Death and Out-of-Body Experiences in the Blind* (Palo Alto, California: William James Center for Consciousness Studies, 1999).

8 David Eisenberg, with Thomas Lee Wright, *Encounters with Qi* (New York: Penguin, 1987), pp. 79–87.

9 Frank Edwards, "People Who Saw without Eyes," in *Strange People* (London: Pan Books, 1970).

10 A. Ivanov, "Soviet Experiments in Eyeless Vision," *International Journal of Parapsychology* 6 (1964); A. Rosenfeld, "Seeing Colors with the Fingers," *Life*, 12 June 1964.

11 The *Confessions of St. Augustine* 1, trans. Edward B. Pusey, Harvard Classics (New York: P. F. Collier, 1909), p. 9.

12 Geddes MacGregor, *Reincarnation in Christianity* (London: Quest Books, 1978), p. 56.

13 Ibid., pp. 57–58.

14 *Catholic Encyclopedia*, 1913 ed., 4, pp. 308–9. See also 11, p. 311.

15 Origen, trans. B. W. Butterworth, *On First Principles* 1, chap. 8 (New York: Harper & Row, 1966), p. 73.

16 *Catholic Encyclopedia* 11, p. 311.

17 See Frederick Spencer, *The Future Life: A New Interpretation of the Christian Doctrine* (London: Hamish Hamilton, 1935). Chapter 11 contains references to a letter by Cardinal Mercier to a Polish Catholic professor Wincenty Lutoslawski, who taught a form of reincarnationism he preferred to call palingenesis. The Belgian

Cardinal acknowledged that belief in preexistence and reincarnation had not been officially condemned by the Catholic Church.

18 Hans Küng, *Eternal Life?* (Garden City, N.Y.: Doubleday & Company, 1984), p. 59.

19 Ibid.

20 Gallup and Proctor, *Adventures in Immortality*, p. 487.

21 H. N. Banerjee, in *Americans Who Have Been Reincarnated* (New York: Macmillan Publishing Company, 1980), p. 195, presents a study done by James Parejko, a professor of philosophy at Chicago State University, which reveals 93 out of 100 volunteers hypnotized produced possible knowledge of a previous birth. Joel Whitton found indications in *all* of his hypnotizable subjects.

22 For Whitton's work, see Joel L. Whitton and Joe Fischer, *Life Between Life* (New York: Doubleday, 1986), pp. 116–27.

23 "Interview: Brian L. Weiss, M.D.," *Venture Inward* 6, no. 4 (July/August 1990): 17–18.

24 For Stevenson's work see Ian Stevenson, *Twenty Cases Suggestive of Reincarnation* (Charlottesville, VA.: University Press of Virginia, 1974); *Cases of the Reincarnation Type*, 4 vols. (Charlottesville, VA.: University Press of Virginia, 1974); and *Children Who Remember Their Past Lives* (Charlottesville, VA.: University Press of Virginia, 1987).

25 Stevenson's latest work is *Reincarnation and Biology: A Contribution to the Etiology of Birthmarks and Birth Defects* 2 vols. (Westport, Conn.: Praeger Publishers, 1997); its abridged version is *Where Reincarnation and Biology Intersect*.

26 Ian Stevenson, "Some Questions Related to Cases of the Reincarnation Type," *Journal of the American Society for Psychical Research* (October 1974): 407.

27 *Journal of the American Medical Association*, 1 December 1975, as quoted in Cranston and Williams, *Reincarnation*, p. x.

28 Tenth Canto, chap. 1. See *Shrimad-Bhagavatam* (*Bhagavata Purana*) by A. C. Bhaktivedanta Swami, for the full rendition, with ample, lucid commentary.

29 Norman Cousins, "Belief Becomes Biology," *Advances* 6, no. 3 (1989): 20–29.

CHAPTER 7

MISSING HUMANS AND ARYAN CONSCIOUSNESS

~

Here's an experiment we all can try: stroll through a museum exhibiting prehistoric man, or peruse an introductory anthropology text. A tidy progression of human development unfolds before your eyes. Watch man evolve, from the grossest, primitive beginnings to the dizzying heights of science and culture we think we have today. Any exhibit, textbook, or multimedia CD-ROM will demonstrate geological and archaeological artifacts neatly falling into place, as if automatically sorting themselves according to the ironclad notion of linear human advancement.

Meanwhile, look around, off the beaten path of standardized conceptions. The Western belief in its unprecedented superiority is falling to pieces; huge abnormalities that defy the accepted tale of human origins have sprung forth from the shadows. Contrary evidence calls us back to the likelihood of advanced civilizations existing far before what our conventions dictate. Generally, establishment intellectuals like to sweep all radical indicators under the carpet. Presently, however, the historical rug is so full of lumps from suppressed anomalies that an unbiased person can no longer walk from one Western credo to another without tripping and falling.

What the orthodox fossil record has supplied us so far is a hypothetical beginning for man about 3.5 million years ago. The remains of a bipedal hominid, called Lucy, with apelike and humanlike features, emerged from Ethiopia in 1974. Most palaeoanthropologists accept her species—*Australopithecus*—as our earliest direct ancestor.

Then, about 2 million years back, *Homo habilis*, the progenitors of our own *Homo* dynasty, left their bones and skulls around as fossils. We moderns are lauded as the jewel of this new *Homo* family. About 1.5 million years ago, it is believed that *Homo habilis* overlapped with *Homo erectus* and then passed the baton to him. No significant evolutionary changes are postulated for another million or so years. Next, about 400,000 years ago, *Homo erectus* is thought to have very slowly, leisurely given way to the archaic sapient-type forefathers—still not identifiable as us.

From 100,000 years to 40,000 years back, the famous *Homo sapiens* subspecies *Homo sapiens neanderthalensis*—popularly known as "Neanderthal Man"—is to have dominated the planet. The exact links during this time—like the other times—are known to be unclear, missing, or highly arguable. But at some time between 100,000 and 40,000 years back, *Homo sapiens sapiens*—modern humans—are to have sallied forth. We replaced the Neanderthals completely about 35,000 years ago. Scientists used to say that folks with the looks and brains like us appeared about 40,000 years ago, but the latest discoveries in South Africa have inspired many authorities to say about 100,000 years back.

Evidence of anatomically modern humans from just a few hundred thousand years ago would decimate this entire game plan. Such data does exist, but has been suppressed or discarded. The more intrepid among us are usually familiar with the controversies in modern physical anthropology. It is outside the possibilities of this book to air them, in all their complexity, or to thoroughly persuade readers this way or that. But since the issue is germane to the Vedic thrust, the best-researched and most lively source books are listed in the bibliography.

The monumental text *Forbidden Archaeology* documents how much of the contrary fossils and artifacts surfaced before two milestone events in the late nineteenth century. The first was the ascendancy of Darwin's theory to an unassailable stature; the second was the discovery of Java man, the earliest protohuman hominid, in deposits generally dated at 800,000 years old. Once these two major events solidified as defining norms and then petrified into fossils, no scientist wanting to survive the establishment would think of finding modern humans in deposits equal in age or older than Java man's strata. If any evidence did turn up, it was turned out as a hoax or a mistake—more by the raw power of ordinary academic social convention than any conscious conspiracy.

Prior to Darwin's coronation and Eugene Dubois' dubious Java find, respected nineteenth-century scientists did put forth surprising discoveries. They reported modern human skeletons, various stone tools, and also animal bones showing human modification. All emerged from very ancient strata.[1]

Even those of us who feel no need to question the current predominant but ailing paradigm of human origins will find it stimulating to know the vibrant, well-documented minority view. As the upstart, challenging paradigm gains ground, certainly the ancient Vedic version will become an alluring alternative.

As discussed in Chapter 5, the Vedic literature unambiguously presents three remarkable themes:

- Earth has been populated with intelligent life for billions of years.
- The technology available on this planet thousands of years ago

was far more advanced and subtle than the crudities we have now.

- The version of humanity occupying the Earth for approximately the past 5,000 years is the lowest, in behavior and intelligence. Many previous cultures were much more advanced in every respect.

In the nineteenth century, these formidable Vedic motifs were dismissed as aboriginal babble. Then in the last half of the twentieth century, these Vedic principles occasionally managed to ascend to the rank of delightful myth. Now sometimes they are said to be radiant with creative symbolism and esoteric meaning.

ANCIENT MYTHS, SYMBOLS, AND VEDIC KNOWLEDGE

A popular contemporary concession is that although modern man has mastered fact, he suffers a lack of imagination. Therefore, though we cannot deign to admire Vedic man for his factual presentation of reality, we can certainly revel in his fancy. Indeed, according to this fashionable view, there is no need to appreciate fact in the Vedas, because fact is of little importance in the literature anyway. But the Vedas as myth, we are exhorted, have great redeeming value. Moreover, because myth unzips the timeless patterns welling up from the depths of the collective human psyche, myth is what we desperately need.

This line of thinking owes much to the modern master of myth, Joseph Campbell. Markedly influenced by the scholar of comparative religion Mircea Eliada and the psychoanalyst Carl Gustav Jung, the prolific Campbell saw myth as depicting humanity's quest for transcendence of itself. Due to his international popularization of mythic thought, Westerners can cling to their surety that they've precisely understood reality like never before. Simultaneously they can combine that assurance with a humble confession: we are suffering a decline in the richness of creative imagination. Upon acknowledging this minor ailment, we undisputed champions of fact can then allow ourselves to rejuvenate our right brain. We can stoop to bathe it in the swirling, murky waters of Vedic legend, and other freestyle visualizations.

Differing from the approach of Joseph Campbell is the work of Giorgio de Santillana. Before his death he was an authority on the history of science at Massachusetts Institute of Technology, arguably the foremost university of scientific research in the USA. Teaming up with Hertha von Dechend—also a professor of the history of science, at the J. W. Goethe Universität Frankfurt—Santillana published in 1992 *Hamlet's Mill*. This unusual work argues that what we call ancient myth actually hid advanced scientific knowledge. The two erudite authors say that the ancient chronicles of the world contain images referring to cosmic events and that the language employed, though archaic, is "immensely sophisticated" science. "This language ignores local beliefs and cults. It concentrates on numbers, motions, measures, overall frames, schemas—on the structure of numbers, on geometry."[2]

When did this encoded language prevail on earth? The scholars say "awe-inspiring antiquity"—at least 8,000 years ago. What culture known to conventional historians could have deployed such sophistication in scientific communication? The two professors explained they are not referring to anything on the current list of approved ancient peoples, but are indicating a forgotten period of advanced humanity—"some almost unbelievable ancestor civilization" in what are considered now as prehistoric times.

Among other things, *Hamlet's Mill* reveals that many ancient cultures possessed sophisticated knowledge of the heavens, which modern science has only recently equaled—upon the advent of computers and satellites. The lost heritage left behind by these peoples is stated to clearly entail science, astronomy, and mathematics. This knowledge—a completely different way of apprehending the universe—has been lost to recent millennia. And the people have disappeared too.

> When the Greeks came upon the scene, the dust of centuries had already settled upon the remains of this great worldwide archaic construction. Yet something of it survived in traditional rites, in myths and fairy-tales no longer understood. . . . These are tantalizing fragments of a lost whole. They make one think of those "mist landscapes" of which Chinese painters are masters, which show here a rock, here a gable, there the tip of a tree, and leave the rest to imagination. Even when the code shall have yielded, when the techniques shall be known, we cannot expect to gauge the thought of these remote ancestors of ours, wrapped as it is in its symbols, since the creating, ordering minds that devised the symbols have vanished forever.[3]

Santillana and Dechend do share with Campbell belief in a single, primordial myth underlying all the diverse mythologies of the world. They three agree that much of what we now consider as multifarious bodies of mythic thought actually derives from one source—what Campbell called the monomyth.

Hamlet's Mill, actually first released in 1969, remained dormant until almost the mid-1990s. Here we have the case of two erudite professors—both specializing in the history of science, and both from prestigious institutions on both sides of the Atlantic—declaring that remote antiquity possessed advanced knowledge thousands of years before the current theories of history allow. The general public took no notice, perhaps understandably. The book does require some prior skill and a deep commitment in time and concentration. But scholars of ancient studies ignored its research also, despite the lofty credentials of its authors. Only recently has the book entered the public eye, after the Western knowledge filter shunted it aside.

Once an intelligent person accepts that some of what we now call myth may be the legacy of a highly advanced civilization, naturally they start listening to the ancients carefully. One independent scholar who reads information from the past as direct, unencoded, literal statement is the controversial Zecharia Sitchin. The author of six books in a series entitled *Earth Chronicles,* along with two more works, Sitchin is a perennial wherever the mysteries of the ancients are discussed, and wherever books of that subject are sold. Many reject his conclusions, but no one argues with his scholarly qualifications—or the remarkable nature of the data he uncovers.

Amassing a vast and detailed history of what he presents as the true account of humanity's origins, Sitchin argues that extraterrestrials jump-started the Sumerian and Egyptian civilization. Furthermore, he accepts that before these star-seeded cultures, there had been earlier and more advanced civilizations. His assertions may sound farfetched until his credentials surface. Few linguists can read Sumerian cuneiform text; Sitchin is one of them. However, he is also an authority in ancient Hebrew as well as Egyptian hieroglyphics.

Needless to say, mainstream academia routinely ridicules and shuns "ancient astronaut" proponents, such as Erich von Däniken. Obviously the theories of these renegade researchers are unorthodox. Sometimes their work is found to be shoddy and sensationalistic. Sitchin, though, often remains above the fire. He attests that his sound, exhaustive research is what protects him: "The only difference between me and the scientific community— I'm talking about Assyriologists, Sumeriologists, etc.—is that they refer to all these texts which I read [literally] as mythology."[4]

Since the nineteenth century when scholars verified the existence of Sumer, hundreds of tablets have been found. Some say these inscriptions relay epic tales of early human history dating back thousands of years before Sumer. Renditions of undiscovered original Sumerian accounts have turned up in the remains of the subsequent Akkadian, Babylonian, and Assyrian civilizations. Especially they are found in the library of Ashurbanipal (668–626 B.C.), an Assyrian king who seemed to collect every tablet he could find. His library—discovered in the remains of Nineveh, north of Baghdad—contained more than 25,000 of them, arranged by subject.

Establishment scholars who have translated and studied the epics generally consider them non-historical. For example, the notable archaeologists C. C. Lamberg-Karlovsky and J. A. Sabloff consider most of the documents as "pure fable." Their judgment is not surprising, since the recorded epics include accounts of extra-terrestrial entities "flying about," and kings whose reigns lasted hundreds and thousands of years.[5] Sitchin, translating these tablets, as well as drawing upon ancient Egyptian and Hebrew sources, claims that what most scholars consider "pure fable" are actually journals of ancient history. He recommends that academics read these accounts as serious historical and scientific documents.

Though the quality of Sitchin's research is often uncontested, even avant-garde historians dispute the conclusions he reaches, by way of his strictly literal approach. Fellow alternative researchers have opined that Sitchin is overly presumptuous and simplistic to think he can discern what they feel are the esoteric symbols and subtleties of the ancients, by his reading them as he would read a daily newspaper.

We should bear in mind that none of the above-mentioned pioneering scholars have tackled the Vedic literature. No alternative researcher has attempted to come to grips with the entire mass of Vedic literature, in a head-on extensive analysis. We may wonder how to approach the tremendous wisdom of the Vedic texts. Are the contents merely refreshing myths, welling up from the Jungian collective unconscious? Is their purpose just to increase our intuition and soothe the right side of our brain? Should we concede that the verses are dressed up with decorative artistry, camouflaging deep scientific knowledge? Or maybe we should access the Vedas as we do the evening news on television—that is, what we immediately see is all that is there.

APPROACHING THE VEDAS: ARYANS ONLY NEED APPLY?

Any Vedic preceptor, ancient or current, will tell us the wealth of the Vedas is actually meant for Aryans. Upon this point we must be clear. But what is an Aryan? On this point Western confusion has overflowed. Regardless of the term's misuse in recent human history, immediately we should be clear that *Aryan*, derived from the Sanskrit term *arya*, does not refer to any biological species or race. That clarification should relieve any unnecessary anxieties, left over from World War II.

Furthermore, *arya* does not refer to the speakers of a particular language. The Sanskrit term *arya* refers to "those who are advancing"—noble souls steeped in spiritual knowledge, qualities, and experience. Monier-Williams, in his still standard Sanskrit dictionary, defines the verbal root related to *arya* as "to move, rise, tend upwards, go towards, reach, raise." These meanings are what the Vedic preceptors stress.

Most Western scholars, however, have passed on to one another a fixation for rendering the word *arya* only as an equivalent for the adjective "noble" or "honorable." They like this slant because it helps them to contrast their ethnic version of the *aryas* with the supposed downtrodden ethnic underlings, known as the Dasas and Dasyus. The Aryan ethnics are to have come into India and conquered or displaced the Dasa and Dasyu ethnics. Totally missing in this mistaken ethnic preoccupation is spiritual *ethics*— the actual Vedic behavioral criterion for discriminating between higher and lower peoples.

An Aryan, as the word has come to be, possesses spiritual valor, developed either in a previous life or the present one. To get a full picture of what an Aryan is, however, we need to get a glimpse of how such a qualified person fits into the Vedic universe. We should know that the human form of life is considered special—in a cosmos full of species. Also, we should be aware that human beings actualize their human potential by gathering knowledge in a specific way. These two Vedic principles, interwoven, lead us to a full understanding of who—according to the Vedas—can actually grasp Vedic information.

Vedic knowledge does not limit consciousness to the human form. Nor does it restrict life to the planet Earth. According to your personal outlook, these two cardinal tenets put the Vedas either far in arrears of modern science or far ahead. The Vedic texts take for granted that everywhere in the universe thrive countless forms of living entities—whether human eyes can see them or not. *Bhagavad-gita* declares that living entities exist everywhere in the cosmos (2.24). Consequently, though an environment may appear hostile to human existence, as well as impenetrable to human perception, nevertheless, the Vedas tell us to rest assured: life is there, somehow, some way.

We may reason that humans are not naturally fit to live in the air or sea, but does their incapability mean no creatures can dwell in these environs? Empiricists protest that though we can see life in the sea or the air, no evidence of life throughout the universe presents itself to our eyes or sophisticated instruments. Vedic teachers, however, delight in pointing out the narrow and faulty range of both human perception and its technological extensions. That we cannot detect life on other planets, they say, should not lead us to the outlandish conclusion that only our planet has life. In the right kind of body, life will manifest anywhere, though not always visible to Earthlings and their gadgets.

The Vedas categorize matter into five gross components: solids, liquids, gases, radiance, and the fabric of space. Just as these ingredients are everywhere, so life is everywhere, in bodies suitable to the predominant component of the environment. On Earth, although water covers most of the planet, solids are the predominate component. Hence the Vedas agree with contemporary humans calling the planet "Earth."

The understanding we are given is that just as living entities with solid, tissue bodies can thrive on Earth, so those with other types of bodies can flourish elsewhere. These other inhabitants of the universe are described as having bodies composed of liquids, gases, radiant energy, or space fabric, according to the environment. Every planet is considered to have populations of living entities with suitable bodies. The Vedic literature prompts us to consider that Earth's array of air-breathing, water-drinking, sun-loving species are not the only forms life can take. The body types of "alien worlds" may not resemble human forms—or even any form of tissue we've experienced.

If the possibilities for living phenomena beyond the range of our senses are endless, how can we learn about this full spectrum of life permeating the universe? A veteran staff writer for the *Scientific American*, John Horgan, noted that scientists "are rarely so human . . . so at the mercy of their fears and desires, as when they are confronting the limits of knowledge."[6] Vedic proponents would concur. The Vedas take the stance that complete knowledge cannot come from human sources. Hence, an actual Aryan acquires knowledge in a special way.

The Vedic texts instruct us that every human being inherently suffers four defects. First, our senses, even when technologically extended, allow only a narrow range of perception. Second, our senses are imperfect—mistakes are natural to life in a body and mind of matter. Third, our mind is prone to illusion—we easily accept one thing to be another. Fourth, we have a propensity for hypocrisy. That means in spite of the other three flaws, we still think, "Let me present my thesis or theory; I will teach others."

Western tradition does confess the failings of sense perception. The poet William Blake put the predicament eloquently: "This Life's dim Windows of the Soul/ Distorts the Heavens from Pole to Pole/ and leads you to Believe a Lie." Western philosophers commonly cite four standard examples:

- A green tree appears black at night—demonstrating that the same object can appear differently to the same person;
- A green tree looks red to a color-blind person—revealing that the same object can appear differently to different persons;
- Our organs of perception and the objects they perceive are just subatomic particles arrayed in empty space—still we use the organs to discern forms and qualities of the objects;
- If sunlight takes eight minutes to reach Earth, we only see the sun as it was eight minutes ago. Hence, what we perceive cannot really be what exists at the moment we perceive it, since perception takes time.

Is there life on other planets? Are earthlings the only intelligent life in the universe? How do we really know what's "out there"? The Vedas will eloquently impress upon us that even our awareness of things we think comfortably within range of our perception is faulty—not to speak of that which lies beyond. The Vedic conclusion is that our only hope for real knowledge is a transcendent source. The entire authority of Vedic knowledge rests on its stated nonhuman, even nonmaterial origins. The applicable Sanskrit word is *apaurusha*: knowledge emanating from beyond time and space, beyond the dimensions of gross and subtle matter.

Naturally, upon encountering such a concept, deeply dyed materialists will balk. Yet the more adventurous among us may be in for an exciting, intellectually stimulating experience. It is not easy for all moderns to hear the Vedic version of its own origins, and to reflect upon the true qualifications of an Aryan, but many post-moderns find it enlivening to ponder. They relish the thought that by developing proper qualifications they may have access to voluminous perfect knowledge, passed down to human society from an omniscient, omnipresent, and omnipotent conscious Godhead.

From the Vedic perspective, searching for life forms on other planets is like searching for insects in the tropics. They are everywhere, without a doubt. The converse is also so: to the Vedic adept, denying life on other planets is as bizarre as denying that the tropics are rife with bugs. The Vedas assert that particular life forms may exist on one planet and not another, but all environs of the universe swarm with life—even the sun.

Our cultural sentiments should not short-circuit when we hear the speaker of *Bhagavad-gita,* Krishna, declare, "I spoke this same knowledge millions of years ago to the chief living entity on the sun." (4.1) The Vedas say that, because the actual living being, the soul, is immune to any material circumstances, it can take bodies that can survive anywhere—even in the radiance of the sun.

With our prisms known as senses—whether aided by technology or not—how much can we see, and how much can we understand? There is always incalculably more to know, while we constantly struggle to revise what little we think we already know. For example, until recently, few bio-prospectors—scientists looking for life—thought to look deep inside the earth. The orthodox magazine *Scientific American* admitted, "Long-standing scientific dogma held that this realm was essentially sterile. But that belief, as it turns out, was wrong."[7] Comfortably dwelling far within the earth are extremophiles—living entities that thrive in what scientists thought were impossible habitats. To date, scientists have now recovered organisms from depths extending to almost two miles under Earth's surface, at temperatures as high as 75 degrees Celsius.

Finding weird forms of life on our planet excites scientists interested in life on other planets. Earth's extremophiles demonstrate that life can flourish in environs once thought absolutely inhospitable to any creature. Heat-loving microbes, called thermophiles, are the best-studied extremists. They can easily reproduce and grow in temperatures exceeding 45 degrees C. Surpassing them, however, are hyperthermophiles, which flourish above 100 degrees C and derive their nutrition from water and rock. Karl O. Setter and his colleagues at the University of Regensburg in Germany have isolated more than fifty species of these super heat-lovers, who live without oxygen or light. The current champion inhabits undersea rock chimneys called smokers. This foremost hyperthermophile, called *Pyrolobus fumarii*, reproduces most comfortably at 105 degrees C, but can get the job done even at 113. Below 90 degrees C, however, it stops growing—it can't tolerate the cold.

Psychrophiles go the other way—they love cold. In July 1997 a deep-sea submarine team observed dense colonies of pinkish worms living inside mounds of methane ice on the ocean floor. The researchers, geochemists from Texas A & M University, had allowed for the possibility of bacteria colonies. But never did they expect to find animals—with a fully developed digestive tract—moving about in these icy deposits, at such high pressure and low temperatures.

Then, in 1999, out from ocean dredgings in the South Atlantic, emerged the largest single-celled organism ever found. Thousands of times bigger than the usual bacteria, at 0.75 millimeters wide, it can be easily seen with the naked eye. Although most forms of life cannot live in an environ of hydrogen sulfide, this entity feasts on sulfur. The scarcity of oxygen is no obstacle—the creature "breathes" nitrates instead, and can store them in a sack.

Upon the start of the new millennium, scientists have discovered colonies of microbes 12,000 feet under the ice of Antarctica.

Not only are these creatures uninhibited by the frigid temperatures, but also they are undeterred by the complete lack of sunlight. Conventional wisdom holds that sunlight is the usual source
of energy for life.

"Extremophiles" are now known to flourish in the most inconceivably hot, cold, acidic, or alkaline environs. While their
choice of neighborhood is perhaps sensational news to the modern world, it's rather humdrum for Vedic partisans.

Equality toward all living entities, regardless of species and
habitat, is an essential Aryan qualification. Aryans seek to avoid
killing insects or plants, let alone trees and animals. The principle
is that all forms of life are entitled to protection—not that my
species of life shall enjoy while yours dies. A verse from the
Bhagavata Purana (6.16.43) describes this Aryan trait:

> My dear Lord, one's occupational duty is instructed in *Shrimad-
> Bhagavatam* and *Bhagavad-gita* according to Your point of view,
> which never deviates from the highest goal of life. Those who
> follow their occupational duties under Your supervision, being
> equal to all living entities, moving and nonmoving, and not con-
> sidering high and low, are called Aryans. Such Aryans worship
> You, the Supreme Personality of Godhead.

Discovering the impossible habitats of bacteria, protozoa, and
small animals is impressive, we will readily concede. Our bump-
ing into these extremophiles, as the creatures have been dubbed,
raises the point that humans who are dogmatic that only Earth
has life may well be the actual extremists. At the 1997 annual
meeting of the American Association for the Advancement of Science, scientists discussed the possibility that life exists underneath
the surface of planets that seem inhospitable on the surface.[8]

Meanwhile, right underneath our feet on Earth, do alien life-
forms exist? Every living entity known to scientists is carbon-

based. A nationally famous American scientist, however, is challenging that deep within the Earth are creatures with a biochemical system based on silicon. Completely alien to the carbon-based life we know, these microorganisms are the brainchild of Dr. Tom Gold, Emeritus Professor of Astronomy at Cornell University. According to research scientists at NASA's new Astrobiology Institute, his theory is treated seriously, owing to his reputation for preposterous hypotheses that later prove correct. David Noever of the Institute confirmed: "It's almost naive to assume all life must be carbon-based; I could possibly make good cases for life based on both silicon and phosphorus."[9]

The public seems ready for the revolution in biology. In a survey conducted in October 1997, 60 percent of Americans polled said they believe intelligent life exists on other planets. Of that affirmative group, 47 percent expect extraterrestrials to be smarter than earthlings, and 40 percent expected the same level of intelligence.[10] Exotic microorganisms on Earth are indeed strange, but where in the universe are the "big life-forms"— significant creatures like us?

Coming to our rescue, the Vedic texts teem with "aliens"— humanlike and non-humanlike beings of various powers and skills. Some moderns say they can communicate with extraterrestrial beings through channeling; others say such entities have abducted them in UFOs. In any case, and to whatever extent governments are covering up alien incidents, these controversies are a non-issue from the Vedic standpoint.

BREAKING THE KNOWLEDGE BARRIER WITH SOUND

The Vedic declaration is that, within a universe swarming with living entities, human life is special because it can tally with *shabda*, eternal transcendental knowledge in the form of sound. It is this concurrence with an absolute standard of knowledge and behavior that distinguishes an Aryan from a non-Aryan. Vedic sonic knowledge presents itself as deriving from no living being with a body of matter, and from no realm composed of time and space.

Just as any household device comes with an instruction booklet, similarly the universe—a cosmic device—is said to come pre-packaged with Vedic knowledge. In the same way that matter and spirit emanate from the supreme source, the Supreme Godhead, so does comprehensive, perfect information.

We know that material knowledge refers to things within the dimensions of time and space. The irony of material existence, though, is that much of even the mundane plane lies beyond our comprehension. The experimental process sometimes provides adequate knowledge of the mundane and sometimes not. Spiritual knowledge purports to focus upon things free from creation and destruction. In approaching the supra-mundane, the Vedas insist we have no choice but *shabda*, spiritual sound. This proper choice—not race or language—is the hallmark of an Aryan.

Hearing in Vedic culture is not haphazard. The aural reception of knowledge must be an authorized and accredited process. For the dispensation of knowledge to be considered perfect, two factors are essential: first, the information must be traceable back to the Supreme; second, the teacher transmitting this information must come from a spiritual lineage traceable back to the Supreme. In the Vedic epistemology we have not the gropings of nomadic tribes, nor the technologically and mathematically enhanced probes of modern humanity. Instead we are handed an extraordinarily sophisticated process for bypassing human limitations.

The Vedic purports clearly explain that we can gain Aryan qualifications, and we can lose them as well. The infamous caste system of classification by birth is a corruption of an ancient system of classification by merit. Obviously, birth in a virtuous family is no guarantee of qualification.

In the beginning of *Bhagavad-gita,* we find Arjuna over-whelmed with lamentation for the bodies of his relatives. For this momentary weakness, Krishna chastises him sharply: "How have these pollutions come upon you? Your present state of conscious-ness is *anarya,* un-Aryan. Do not lament for the temporary!" The cut *anarya* is not a racist denigration but a reference to the loss of higher qualities and intelligence. Identifying with the body and those bodies in relation to one's own body is considered non-Aryan—or lacking in real knowledge. Non-Aryan civilization means advancement in bodily consciousness; Aryan civilization means advancement in spiritual consciousness. From the Vedic standpoint, stamping oneself an Aryan while remaining locked in the darkness of material knowledge is abominable.

The authorized aural reception practiced by an Aryan prom-ises to open up a realm of knowledge beyond human frailties—beyond the mind and senses. Vedic adherents say the trajectory of this fabulous gain in cognition extends far beyond the range of scientific methodology. Yet we should note that Vedic epistemol-ogy insists it does not rest on blind faith. It simply questions the usefulness of our limited sense perception and reason when en-countering both the extraterrestrial and the inconceivable. The Vedic thrust is first to hear—assimilate the real knowledge ema-nating from the perfect source. Then, in accordance with this sonic instruction, apply your senses and logic—as far as you can—to experience the perfection of what you are hearing.

The three waning dogmas of modern knowledge stress:

- Objectivism, the assumption of an objective world that the observer can hold at a distance and study, separate from his consciousness;
- Positivism, the assumption that reality is what is physically measurable, quantifiable;
- Reductionism, the assumption that we best apprehend the truth of a phenomenon by studying the behavior of its minute parts.

The Vedas contend a difference in both the derivation of knowledge and its culmination. They point to a supreme original truth unknowable through material perception or mathematical reasoning—however employed by the above three cultural approaches.

We have already learned that Vedic knowledge describes itself as *apaurusha*: not originating from any created person. The Vedic texts also refer to themselves as *shruti*—that which is received by hearing—and *smriti*—that which once heard is remembered. According to the Vedas themselves, they are absolute and self-authoritative. They do not depend on anything external for interpretation.

For the Vedic Aryan, knowledge derived from authority has no negative connotation. The same cannot be said today. Nevertheless, any attempt, past or present, to acquire knowledge requires that we accept some authority—whether scientists, scholars, the Vedas, or whatever. If we think about it, we will see that, even if, through misfortune, we have been misled, still the necessity of acquiring knowledge from authority remains.

The Vedic attitude of an Aryan moves us to examine the sensory faculties of our sources for knowledge. In other words, we are dissuaded from blindly accepting information originating from sources with imperfect senses and intellect.

The Vedic sages exhort us that if we are going to cast our vote for real knowledge, then we should rally behind the source that champions perfection in sensory capacity—and can demonstrate it. This dedication to the proper reception of genuine knowledge encapsulates the Vedic vision of both full-fledged human consciousness and fully developed human society. This nobility is what is known as Aryan.

The Vedas describe that, just as a person can degenerate from the Aryan standard, similarly someone can rise up to it. Even a dog-eater—considered the lowest stratum of human society—can become elevated to the qualifications of an Aryan:

My dear Lord, one who always keeps Your holy name on his tongue becomes greater than an initiated brahmin [spiritual priest]. Although he may be born in a family of dog-eaters and therefore by material calculation may be the lowest among men, he is still glorious. This is the wonderful effect of chanting the holy name of the Lord. It is therefore concluded that one who chants the holy name of the Lord should be understood to have performed all kinds of austerities and great sacrifices mentioned in the Vedas. He has already taken his bath in all the holy places of pilgrimage. He has studied all the Vedas, and he is actually an Aryan. (*Shrimad-Bhagavatam* 3.33.7)

Nowhere in Vedic literature or the traditional lexicons do we find *arya* defined in relation to race or language. Furthermore, Buddha, whose teachings were a later development in religious history, presented his principles as *arya-dharma*: the noble truth meant for those desiring spiritual advancement. Like the Vedic tradition that he rebelled against, Buddha never used *arya* in referring to either race or language. The emperor of Persia, Cyrus the Great—exalted by his people as well as by the Greeks and others—thought of himself as an *arya*. This self-appraisal meant he was emphasizing his righteous caliber, not his membership of a particular race. According to the Vedic standard, especially as enunciated in the *Bhagavata Purana*, humans enamored with their bodily type and who worship the land of their birth are considered to have the intelligence of cows and asses.

CONSCIOUSNESS DETERMINES BODILY FORM

Vedic biology gradates bodies according to how much consciousness they permit. That means the Vedic approach to biology recognizes consciousness as causal. The lower life forms are aquatics, plants, trees, insects, and reptiles. They display almost no consciousness. The bird and animal forms show more, and the civilized human forms provide an ideal manifestation of consciousness—they offer the opportunity to behave as an Aryan.

The Vedas teach us that from the microbe up, all life forms have some degree of consciousness—though often extremely slight and therefore almost imperceptible. Microbe consciousness is not as outrageous to modern ears as it may seem. The famous American biologist Lynn Margulis told the 1991 annual meeting of the American Association for the Advancement of Science that bacteria and other one-celled creatures behave as if they possess consciousness. After all, microbes can be seen to demonstrate sensitivity to light, chemical gradients, and even gravity, and their behavior may be said to evidence "primitive learning." In her 1995 book *What Is Life?*, Margulis bluntly asserted, "Not just animals are conscious, but every organic being, every autopoietic cell is conscious. In the simplest sense, consciousness is an awareness of the outside world."[11]

We may be surprised to know that microscopic bacteria are mentioned in the Vedic literature. One type of microorganism is known by the Sanskrit name *indra-gopa*. The Vedic list of species includes aquatics, vegetation, insects, animals, and humans. But just as there are many types of plant or insect life forms, the texts state that in the universe there are varieties of human forms—400,000 of them! Like the other forms of life, some human forms may exist on one planet and not on another.

The ancient Vedic principle is that the living entity experiences different degrees of consciousness in different forms. We might consider that we do not expect to find a dog's body displaying the same consciousness as a man's. Moreover, we can note that even within the same life form, there are differences in consciousness, according to the phase of bodily development. A baby's state of consciousness differs from a youth's; a youth's from an adult's. For example, when puberty strikes, the boy or girl's state of consciousness changes. We are not surprised to observe this altered awareness, because the body has changed from prepubescence to adolescence.

The Vedas also uphold the converse of this principle governing life forms. Whenever we see differing levels of consciousness, we are instructed to assume we are dealing with different bodies. In other words, the Vedic classification of life forms uses consciousness as the criterion—even in plants. Early in the twentieth century, scientists took an interest in the work of the German physician and psychophysicist Gustav Fechner. His *Nanna, or the Soul Life of Plants* debuted in 1848 but was reprinted in 1921.[12] The early work most people remember, though, is the famous investigation conducted by the Indian scientist Sir Jagadish Chandra Bose on plant sensitivity to injury.

In recent times, reconsideration of plant consciousness has blossomed, owing to the popular presentation *The Secret Life of Plants*.[13] Also Cleve Backster's article "Evidence of primary perception in plant life," published in the *International Journal of Parapsychology*, helped to stimulate the revival of interest.[14] Most mainstream biologists, ethnobotanists, and ecologists, however, do not take plant consciousness seriously. Of course, how can they, when even the subject of their own human consciousness bewilders them.

Contrary to popular sentiment about reincarnation, the Vedas tell us that we are not guaranteed a human form in our next life. The implications for humanity are immense. Are we ready to come back as an animal or tree? Very few contemporary fans of reincarnation consider this possible danger. Surveys and polls reveal that, as reincarnation surges in acceptance, most people think, "Death is spiritual; there's nothing to fear. I will always be a human and humane." They are confident that taking birth repeatedly is like an adventure, a continuous learning experience.

Based on research into near-death experiences, most admirers of reincarnation feel that a next life of light, bliss, and peace is certain. When the international paranormal magazine *Omni* conducted its 1995 survey on afterlife, the median level of education for those who replied was four years of university study. Of all the responders, 82 percent of them asserted their conviction that the afterdeath is a journey of light, peace, and love. A renowned author and professor of sociology at the University of Chicago, Andrew Greeley, gave *Omni* readers this inside tip for approaching the afterlife: "The only way to prepare for it is to have a great capacity for surprise."[15]

HUMAN RIGHTS AND THE HUMAN FORM

A great possibility is that the difference between what we know as near-death experience and actual death itself is like the difference between a near collision and a fatal head-on crash. As we learned from the intense scene with Kamsa on Vasudeva's wedding day (Chapter 6), the Vedic literature is very sober and precise about *samsara*, the cycle of repeated birth and death. Consciousness is accountable; only a fool leaves the next birth to chance. Therefore the whole Vedic social organization centered on refining consciousness and facing responsibility for it. This focus reveals the true province of Aryanism.

> From the age of five years onward, a genuinely intelligent person should use the human form for its proper purpose. Rarely does the living entity achieve a human body. Although temporary like other bodies, the human form has precious value, because it allows action in full consciousness of the Supreme. Even a slight amount of this activity can give us a start on the road toward complete perfection. (*Shrimad-Bhagavatam* 7.6.1)

Vedic culture focuses upon the special privilege of the human body. Because only the human form gives the chance for consciousness to manifest enough for contemplating enlightenment, the human body brings with it a stern mandate. On the other hand, plants and animals, with their dim display of consciousness, cannot execute spiritual development. Therefore, the Vedas hold that a precious human life squandered on the pursuit of animal objectives is the greatest tragedy.

Appropriate laws of nature are said to manage the soul's transmigration through lower life forms. These lower bodies, unconsciously following nature's dictates, allow no free will. After moving through births in countless lower forms, the soul gets the opportunity of a human form. Then he can choose: What to do with my rare gift of developed consciousness?

In Vedic civilization the human birth is regarded as a junction. Unlike in other births, a human can decide what to focus upon. By striving for the same goals the animals achieve, the soul in human form wastes its opportunity of a human body. Consequently in the next life the soul heads back to lower, sometimes almost unconscious, forms. From this degeneration, the gradual ascent can entail countless nonhuman births, as the laws of nature guide the soul—species after species—back up to the human form. The Vedic attitude is that this ride up and down on the Ferris wheel of *samsara* is a catastrophic waste of time and potential.

We are exhorted that, at the very least, a human should act so as to retain the human form in the next birth. Better yet is getting out of the cycle completely. Vedic civilization accommodated both of these goals. From this ancient perspective, human rights are not simply claims to what nature automatically supplies the animals—that is, mere bodily sustenance and protection. True, our turbulent world puts a premium on basic material necessities. For an Aryan, however, the real human right is enlightenment. The Vedic literature describes that a genuine human society, while certainly fulfilling material requirements, assists its people in attaining this actual birthright. No one should suffer ignorance of the self. Ideally, all the aspects of society aim at producing Aryans—there is no question of a biological monopoly.

THE ARYAN MYTH

Now that we know what real Aryans are, what about the fraudulent conception—the master race, "super biology?" To stick all the blame for Indo-European Aryan mania on the National Socialist party in Germany would be grossly inaccurate. In the nineteenth and early twentieth centuries, the notion of a pure Aryan race was the intellectual darling of the brightest academics. Summoned by scholars themselves, at the dawn of comparative linguistics, the ghost of the false Aryans haunted the Western world until the Nazis met their end.

Equipped with the mandatory blond hair and blue eyes, assured of his mastery over all, and obsessed with guarding his racial purity, the mythical Aryan son of Northern Europe was born of academia's union with racism. Leon Poliakov, in his work *The Aryan Myth*—a standard in the subject—traces the genesis of this delusion, beginning with European nationalism.

Each European people sought to evoke for themselves a glorious pedigree. The Romans had turned to Troy as the illustrious root of their ancestry. In the Middle Ages, Spanish aristocrats would distinguish themselves from the masses by advertising their premium Visigothic blood. The French tried to make up their minds whether their superiority stemmed from Vercingetorix and his Gauls or Charlemagne and his Franks. The English, working hard, had to contrive something better than their motley bag of Briton, Anglo-Saxon, Viking, and Norman forefathers. Hence some Englishmen turned to Israel, seeing their lineage beginning as a lost Hebrew tribe.

The Germans, however, were firmly in the driver's seat. They could see that their history spawned the actual predecessors of the very people their neighbors crowed about—the Visigoths, Franks, and Anglo-Saxons. After all, the Roman orator and administrator Tacitus, known today as the greatest historian in the Latin language, had certified the Germans as pure-blooded—untainted by other races.

Once the Protestant Reformation got under way, the Germans' pride in their local origins magnified. They waged ecclesiastical warfare against what they abhorred as the decadent and alien world of Rome. Later, during the eighteenth and nineteenth centuries, the German-speaking lands underwent rapid industrial and intellectual expansion. This boom increased the necessity for an independent, pure origin—with a mandate for glory.

The trends in both comparative linguistics and physical anthropology reinforced the false Aryan notion. Upon the coming into vogue of race studies, the intellectuals of the day were literally off to the races. First, different races of humanity were isolated; then, the Caucasian race easily found its way to the top of the pile. History was conceived of as a survival-of-the-fittest race, each dominating for some time before yielding to a more dynamic race.

Since nothing like the thriving commercial and academic centers of Northern Europe could be seen anywhere else in the world, naturally Europeans of the time had no doubt that their day in the sun had come. Meanwhile, physical anthropologists busied themselves measuring head sizes and came to distinguish long-headed Nordics from broad-headed Southern Europeans. By the end of the nineteenth century, science looked to the stereotyped Nordic physique as the paragon for humanity.

The contribution of linguistics to the Aryan fantasy stemmed from the monumental discovery that Sanskrit was related to European languages. This breakthrough lead to the construction of an Indo-European language family. As described in Chapter 4, at the beginning of the nineteenth century the vogue was to look toward South Asia as the source of civilization. Though Christianity was the religious norm of society, an intellectual fascination with India flourished—that is, before the British Raj set in.

In addition, European intellectuals at that time, though Christian by culture, seemed weary of having to trace their ancestry to Noah. While holding on to the Bible as truth, the pundits of the day sought to yank the cultural roots of Western European free from Hebrew soil. This jettisoning of Judea as the original home was another reason to lift their glance eastwards, to the Himalayas and the Gangetic plains.

> Thus we see that a wide variety of authors and schools located the birthplace of the entire human race between the Indus and the Ganges. It only remained for linguistics to make its contribution, in a decisive though ambiguous manner, by dispelling with one certain truth a fog of adventurous suppositions, and at the same time advancing a new hypothesis [the Aryan Indo-European construct] as fragile as any of those that preceded it. According to this new theory it was not the whole human race but one particular race—a white race which subsequently became Christian—which had descended from the mountains of Asia to colonize and populate the West. It seemed as if the Europeans of the scientific age, having freed themselves from the conventional Noachian genealogy and rejected Adam as a common father, were looking around for new ancestors but were unable to break with the tradition which placed their origin in the fabulous Orient. It was the science of linguistics which was to give a name to these ancestors by opposing the Aryans to the Hamites, the Mongols—and the Jews.[16]

The new discipline of linguistics furnished what seemed to be a comprehensive, attractive framework for ideas of an original pure race. Doubtlessly, the ethnic and nationalistic fervor of the time helped authorize linguistics as a "scientific" field of study. Assumptions based on biological, cultural, historical, and linguistic data all fused to form an internationally accepted Indo-European or Aryan primeval race. It was left to the linguistic scholars to trace the mysterious movements of this proto-people, especially as this specterlike folk left no conclusive archaeological or historic traces. Hence the emergence of linguistic reconstruction—to divine the secret homeland and to project migration and invasion routes. Through historical linguistics, the Aryans would reveal their magical movements.

> The Aryans left their homes . . . on the 1st of March. This settles the question of the climate of their original home. Had their homes been situated in a moderate zone, the Aryans would never, of their own free will, have made their exodus so early; they would have delayed it, if not until May, at any rate until the middle of April. (Rudolph von Ihering, 1897)[17]

Chapter 5 already discussed how the terms *Indo-European* and *Indo-German* both derived from the early fascination with the Vedas and the discovery of linguistic correlation between Sanskrit and European languages. Later in the nineteenth century, the godfather of Indology, Max Müller, and other linguists pushed the appellation "Aryan" to describe the hypothetical mighty race of antiquity. Never mind that the Vedic texts use the word *arya* strictly to describe spiritually advanced peoples. Never mind the necessary spiritual qualifications. Soon *arya* came to refer to biology and etymology.

From *arya* the scholars constructed "Aryan"—the name both for the lost ancestors of the superior white race and for the language it spoke. We should note that in the nineteenth century this word *Aryan* was used interchangeably with the word *Indo-*

European. Later, in the last quarter of that century, Müller would retract his endorsement of the term—to no avail. Scholars had cast the die, and the Western world irrevocably embraced the myth. Even in this century V. Gordon Childe, distinguished as one of the greatest prehistorians of our time, paid homage to the so-called original Aryan race—"fitted with exceptional mental endowments," and the "promoters of true progress."[18]

Until approximately the 1860s, the belief prevailed that the Aryans were ancestors of the white race who originated from Asia, somewhere around the Himalayas. However, by the end of the 1860s, the Asiatic cradle of the race began to rock. Linguists began to relocate the homeland in Europe, and then the rising discipline of physical anthropology firmly anchored the new primeval home. Lazarus Geiger, arguing that the original race of Indo-Europeans had to be pale and blond, began the push for a Germanic cradle of the Aryans.

In 1878 Theodore Poesch put together research showing that the Aryans were blue-eyed blonds. Seeking the geographical center for the racial archetype, he decided that the homeland had to be the part of Europe with the most albinos. The dart he threw stuck in the Pripet marshes of Eastern Europe. Then in 1883 Karl Penka assembled a multi-disciplinary study to get the primordial master race out of the swamps, into a respectable neighborhood. Southern Scandinavia got the nod. The ideas of both scholars, Poesche and Penka, echoed by other anthropologists, gained wide acceptance.

The most famous propagator of Aryanism as a political science was probably Comte de Gobineau, a French ethnologist and social thinker. He wielded his many years of historical, ethnological, and anthropological studies to lay down a theory of racial determinism that effected all of Western Europe. In his most famous work *Essay on the Inequality of Human Races,* he described the mastery of the white race over all others and crowned the Germanic peoples as "the Aryans," the pinnacle of human civilization. He warned that an Aryan society retains its inherent power only as long as strains from other races are kept out. Race-mixing spells doom; an Aryan people weakened by interbreeding sinks into abomination.

Gobineau, it must be said, was absorbed in the scholarly study of "Aryanism" as a social principle—not a political program for action. But his disciple—a British-born, naturalized German named Houston Stewart Chamberlain—carried the "Nordic," or "Aryan Germanic," banner into the twentieth century. There, Hitler's National Socialist movement hoisted the same colors, and paraded them throughout the land. The Nazis clad themselves in "Aryan" rhetoric and brandished the ancient Indian swastika. And why not? "Aryan" referred to the original pure European race, of which the Indians were a talented though wayward splinter group.

In the first decades of the twentieth century, scholarly journals of linguistics and anthropology regularly featured intellectual explorations of Aryan-supremacy themes. Far from being an extremist doctrine, the fermentation was quite widespread—until the brew ignited into World War II. Linguistic speculation had coupled with anthropological guesstimate, and then—borne by the winds of popular prejudice—the resultant germs rapidly multiplied. In this way the Aryan myth eventually exploded into an epidemic. How all this educated but deadly concoction could derive from the Vedic texts, the Sanskrit language, and the Sanskrit word *arya*, only Western civilization knows.

This Aryan family of speech was of Asiatic origin. (A. H. Saycee, 1880)

This Aryan family of speech was of European origin. (A. H. Saycee, 1880)

So far as my examination of the facts has gone it has led me to
the conviction that it was in Asia Minor that the Indo-European
languages developed. (A. H. Saycee, 1927)[19]

PURSUING THE VEDIC LITERATURE

Anthropologists and archaeologists use the word *civilization*
most often in the sense of "life in cities." Viewing a people as "civilized" in the sense of their having attained a supposed universal
standard of civility is now considered a value judgment. To avoid
ethnocentrism, the "rise of civilization" generally refers to the appearance of urban development, and further entails steps toward
complex social organization and economies, record-keeping,
writing and arithmetic, plus some impressive buildings of any
type. We should mark, however, that these attributes are external. That is to say, they may not reveal to us the core purpose—
the inner goal—of the organized human life, especially if it is a
highly spiritually motivated society.

Our modern absorption in technology and economy may
blind us to the dynamics of the ancients, especially in regards to
such an internally sophisticated people as the Vedic texts reveal.
When we drag ancient scriptures and culture through our filter of
conscious and unconscious modern assumptions, naturally the
existential views of the ancients on the self and the cosmos can
appear primitive and nonsensical. Yet, judged according to the
arya standards of remote antiquity, Western civilization certainly
appears barbaric and ignorant.

Contemporary critical scholarship is a laudable and necessary
exercise, of course. Modern Western scholars of the Vedas are often astonishingly meticulous at grammatical and etymological
analyses. Yet, at the same time, they are often brazenly coarse in
probing the Vedic mindset and the core meaning of the texts. In
fact, our academics rarely seem to get their hands on the internal

dynamics. Therefore they conclude that the Vedic texts, though "rich with imagery," are ultimately confused and motley.

Hopefully this book will work to discourage dissecting Vedic literature with the modern knives of false assuredness. As one American professor of India's religions commented, "Much academic scholarship is like the proverbial medical example: the operation is successful, but the patient dies. Traditions that are healthy never take scholarly diagnosis too seriously, and they stay alive by staying off the operating table."[20]

The modern West is just beginning to grope for the nature of the eternal conscious self, extraterrestrial life, cosmic origins, and the realm beyond time and space. When we categorically dismiss these Vedic themes, however, we should know that we utterly lack any bedrock understanding of our own to erect in their place. This dearth is a major embarrassment, despite the chest-thumping pride of our biggest brains. And it is this scholarly lack that blunts Western intellectual diagnosis of the Vedic texts. Consequently, many intelligent Westerners are now no longer taking academic analyses seriously. This post-modern trend generates much consternation in the campus world of erudition.

Persons pursuing an active interest in Vedic texts and culture fall into four main groups:

- The curious and inquisitive. They realize Western knowledge banks have given them absolutely no intellectual framework to handle the rapid dawn of non-reductionist consciousness studies, contrary accounts of human antiquity, paranormal research, UFO investigations, and documented alien-abduction accounts. Western religions, by their inherent constitution, also share the inability to provide the people with the appropriate theological or doctrinal tools for grappling with this phenomenal boom in "new, alternative knowledge."

- The classic followers of major Vedic schools of thought. These academies, existing for hundreds and thousands of years, are constructed not of bricks but of particular Vedic emphases, and they are headed by a great patriarch. Known in Sanskrit as *sampradayas,* these prime vortexes of Vedic conclusion all take for granted the existence of a supreme controller; the eternal soul; the temporary astral body; transmigration of the soul from body to body; extraterrestrial life; the spiritual realm beyond time and space; and the nonmaterial entities who inhabit that spiritual realm. Furthermore, all the *sampradayas* accept the Vedic historical and cosmological treatises. Minor differences arise concerning topics far beyond the purview of matter. One *sampradaya* may stress specific aspects of the Supreme Godhead more than another, but all of the schools accept the Vedas as the ultimate authority, enunciated in a direct meaning of the texts.

- The accommodationists, desiring to keep a foot in both Vedic and modernist paradigms. Their technique is to make room for the Vedic literature as a corpus of genuine knowledge and truth regarding the perennial themes in human existence. Simultaneously, the accommodationists—in deference to their modern education—see these themes as thickly embellished with symbolism, imagery, and poetic license. Many contemporary Indians choose this response to the Vedas, so as to hold on to remnants of what they feel is valuable religious belief. The elasticity also allows them to remain faithful to Western science, by overlooking—as traditional esoterica and folklore—whatever Vedic themes contradict Western empiricism.

- The benign mythologists. Most Western scholars of Indology, history, anthropology, and comparative religion see the Vedic texts as an interesting but sometimes tedious potpourri of ancient fantasies, accumulated by highly creative but primitive poets. The spirited imagination of these ancient visionaries is seen as their valiant attempt to compensate for a total failure in the modern advantages of critical thinking and scientific analysis.

THE CLASSIC VIEW OF THE VEDAS

Approaching the Vedas in a classic way does not imply fanatical literalism. While creative interpreters sport about in a gymnasium of indirect and obscure meanings, extreme literalists assume they can fully discern the meaning of the literature merely by wielding a dictionary. They assure themselves that the sum total of dictionary definitions equals the meaning of the passage under examination.

A proper, direct reading, however, entails taking the text head-on, so to speak, without assuming immediate and complete understanding. The reader's cultural conditioning and lack of spiritual attainment may intervene, to force words out of the context intended by the author. Consequently, humility, patience, and sense control are required, to achieve the goal of comprehending the Vedic texts according to the meaning intended by the author.

The ability to translate the script of ancient texts is one thing; comprehension, another. For example, in the field of Egyptology a few notables have expressed their inability to actually get a hand on ancient Egypt. The distinguished translator of the Pyramid Texts, R. O. Faulkner, admits: "[The Pyramid Texts] provide problems and difficulties. . . . They include very ancient texts . . . imposing on the modern reader problems of grammar and vocabulary . . . and there are many mythological and other allusions of which the purport is obscure to the translator of today." [21]

Rather than pretend "the case is closed" and all the mysteries are solved—or dismissed as myth—it is best to admit that ancient texts have many surprises in store for us. The appraisal of Egyptologist Faulkner dates to 1969. But in 1997 another Egyptologist, Dimitri Meeks, confessed that little progress had been made: "The work of establishing the basic facts . . . has in reality barely begun. The moment has come, then, to read or reread the texts, not to bring them into line with our own fantasies, as in the past, but to try to understand what they really mean."[22]

Our approach to the ancient texts of India would benefit from such candor. Without a doubt we run smack into conceptual barriers, especially when we consult the Vedic texts about their own origin. First, our science doesn't accept a universe composed of anything other than matter. Second, our scientists tell us that human beings—especially intelligent ones—are a recent development in the history of Earth. Hence, without any further Vedic surprises, we Westerners already have hit a brick wall, in terms of what modernist paradigms will comfortably allow us to contemplate.

The Vedas assert that, along with matter, spiritual energy always exists. Furthermore, from the same source responsible for matter and spirit also emanates knowledge of both. In other words, perfect knowledge is a built-in ingredient of existence, just like matter and spirit. Thus, from the Vedic perspective, just as our normal intellectual capacity cannot trace the origin of matter and consciousness, so also it cannot trace when Vedic knowledge began. When we recall that Western science and religion are very weak on "origin questions," when we remember that no one can say what existed and how before the Big Bang, then a few of us may be patient with the Vedic description of itself as timeless.

WHY WRITING?

Readers may recall that Chapter 3 featured the section "Writing when?" which provided a quick overview of scholars' perplexity about the origin and development of writing. This present section, however, is not a summary. It is fuel for provocation: "Why writing?" A Vedic theme is that advanced human beings do not need to write things down.

Even in the more recent culture of ancient Greece, the reciters knew their Homer and other poets by heart. Their memories were trained to retain hundreds of thousands of lines, and in this way classics like the *Iliad* and *Odyssey* were originally passed down. The Vedic tradition tells us that up until approximately 5,000 years ago the memory of the Vedic intellectuals, brahmins, was so sharp that just by hearing knowledge once, they could retain it perfectly. In complete turnabout from our current notions, the Vedas assert that recording knowledge in books indicates not human progress, but human decline!

The incumbent Western assumption has been that the practice of writing is a decisive development in what is taken as the linear ascent of human culture. One the one side of the great divide are the preliterates—clever, but not smart enough. On the other, the writers—the ones who really take civilization to another level. Without showing traces of writing, a civilization, even though perhaps highly artistic, is always classified as substandard.

We have quite a difficult time conceiving of an advanced society that lacked writing. Is writing indeed a prerequisite for advanced intellectual expression and invention? A professor of brain and cognitive sciences at MIT has shown that many scientific breakthroughs do not depend at all on "thought-in-words," or written language. The scientist Steven Pinker, in his book *The Language Instinct*, explains that the actual method is often mind visualization:

> The most famous self-described visual thinker is Albert Einstein, who arrived at some of his insights by imagining himself riding a beam of light and looking back at a clock, or dropping a coin while standing in a plummeting elevator. He wrote that . . . "conventional words or other signs [e.g. writing] have to be sought for laboriously only in the secondary state, when the mentioned associative play is sufficiently established and can be reproduced at will."[23]

The same method turns up in the work of other major innovators of Western science: "ideas came to them in images."[24] James

Maxwell, Michael Faraday, Friedrich Kekule, Ernest Lawrence, Watson and Crick all attest to this mental visualization. Pinker's research reminds us that Faraday, the discoverer of electromagnetic induction, did not even have a formal education in mathematics. He "arrived at his insights by visualizing lines of force as narrow tubes curving through space."[25]

Why should our historians insist that the ancients needed to write in order to demonstrate advanced intellects? Ample research in cognitive science has revealed that humans think in symbols rather than in words.[26] Hence there is no need to draw a judgmental line between history and "prehistory"—between the supposed advanced writing cultures and substandard oral cultures. Better we start to consider other possibilities for encoding and transmitting knowledge.

The lost Vedic civilization may not be the only culture that minimizes the value of writing. Socrates relayed to Plato a legend indicating that the ancient Egyptians may not have been so impressed with writing:

> At Naukratis in Egypt it is said that there dwelt one of the old gods. . . . This god Thoth gave writing to the pharaohs of those times, with the words "This art, O King, will make the Egyptians wiser and of better memory; for it has been invented to aid remembrance and understanding." The pharaoh did not agree, and contradicted the god Thoth: "This invention will make striving souls more forgetful. . . . They will come to rely upon the outward signs of this writing; therefore they will no longer have inner and direct remembrance. Only outer memory will be aided by your invention, not inner remembrance."[27]

The oral nature of Vedic knowledge has made its genesis extremely difficult to pin down. The effort to erect a chronology for Vedic knowledge is like trying to catch a fugitive by apprehending the clothes he's left in various places. That is to say, *even if the obstacles in dating Vedic texts are overcome, still there is the impasse of catching the actual knowledge itself.* The texts are just a medium; when did the actual knowledge in the books originate?

The classic account of Vedic antiquity considers timespans of millions and even billions of years. We learn that originally there was one oral body of knowledge, called the Veda. Then, as human intelligence declined, this corpus of oral knowledge divided into four written texts: the *Rig-, Atharva-, Yajur-,* and *Sama-veda.* Concurrently these four Vedas were elaborated upon in Puranas, Vedic cosmological treatises. The term *purana* means "ancient history"; another meaning is "supplement." The Puranas are said to amplify the concise knowledge of the Veda in a supplementary way, through references culled from history. These texts, especially, highlight the lives of great sages and kings.

The original body of knowledge is traced billions of years back to the beginning of the cosmos. Here, the Vedas say, their oral tradition began, at the first appearance of matter and spiritual energy. This declaration goes hand in hand with the Vedic presentation that the first living beings in the cosmos are the most intelligent. These primeval geniuses received the knowledge from a source outside the cosmos—transcendental to time, space, and material limitation.

Next, the classic account of the Vedas' origin zooms us up to just 5,000 years back, at the start of what the Vedas call the Kali millennium. This point in time is said to mark human civilization's slide into enfeeblement. The extraordinary sage Vyasadeva—heeding the degeneration—codified and amplified the Veda so that the less intelligent moderns, soon to populate Earth, could benefit from Vedic knowledge.

According to Vedic standards, this consummate seer Vyasadeva was a living entity especially surcharged for the task by the Supreme Consciousness. Therefore, in Vedic eyes, Vyasadeva is known as a special type of avatar—not the Complete Whole, but a part who has become an empowered agent of the Complete Whole. Once again, our Western noses are pushed up against the empiric wall, as we confront the superhuman authorship of the Vedas' written version. Needless to say, only special intellects will press ahead.

The work of Vyasadeva is chronicled in the *Bhagavata Purana* (1.4.15–25). The text refers to the Sarasvati River, whose dried bed has now been verified by satellite.

15. As the sun rose, Vyasadeva took his morning ablution in the waters of the Sarasvati [near the Himalayas] and sat alone to concentrate.

16. The great sage Vyasadeva saw abnormalities in the duties of the millennium [Vedic guidelines for particular expanses of time]. This happens on the Earth in different eras, due to unseen forces in the course of time.

17–18. Full in knowledge, the great sage could see—by his transcendental vision—the deterioration of all aspects of material nature, due to the influence of the impending epoch. He could also see that the materialistic people would suffer reduced lifespans and that because they had no good qualities, impatience would agitate them. Therefore he pondered the welfare of human beings in all statuses of society.

19. He knew that the sacrifices mentioned in the Vedas were the means by which the people's social duties and interactions could be purified. And to simplify the process of rectification for them, he divided the one Veda into four, thus amplifying it.

20. The four Vedas, the four divisions of the original sources of knowledge, were established as separate components. The historical facts and authentic accounts mentioned in the Puranas are called the fifth Veda.

21. After the Vedas were divided into four divisions, Paila Rishi became the professor of the *Rig-veda,* Jaimini the professor of the *Sama-veda,* and Vaisampayana became glorified by the *Yajur-veda.*

22. Angira Rishi was entrusted with the *Atharva-veda.* And Roma-harsana was entrusted with the Puranas and historical records.

23. All these learned scholars, in their turn, passed on their entrusted Vedas to their many disciples, granddisciples and great-granddisciples, and in this way the various branches and schools of the Vedas developed.

24. Thus the great sage Vyasadeva, out of great compassion for the ignorant masses, edited the Vedas so they might be assimilated by less intellectual men.

25. Out of compassion, the great sage thought it wise that this would enable men to achieve the ultimate goal of life. Thus he compiled the great historical narration called the *Mahabharata* for women, laborers and unqualified relatives of brahmins [spiritual intellectuals].

Here we have the Vedic literature's own account of its development into related treatises. The schools specializing in a particular branch apparently carried on their work much like the modern university system—each department chaired by a preeminent scholar. The verse mentioning that the Mahabharata was especially written for woman, laborers, and unqualified members of intellectual clans is not to be taken as a sexist or social sneer. Human beings engaged in the traditional occupations of child-raising and manual skills were not expected to have the time to specialize in metaphysical studies. Furthermore, birth into a brahmin family—in the intellectual, priestly sector of Vedic society—did not guarantee intellectual qualities and performance.

The *Bhagavata Purana* reveals that Vyasadeva foresaw the

breakdown of the traditional intellectual dynasties. Besides show-ing consideration for persons busy in household affairs and physical labor, the sage also wanted to show compassion for unqualified members of brahmin families—knowing this social inconsistency would become the trend. Contemporary Vedic teachers like to tease that, although the *Mahabharata,* of which *Bhagavad-gita* is a chapter, was compiled specifically for persons too busy in daily affairs to be philosophers, today the greatest pro-fessors seem unable to understand *Bhagavad-gita.* Their attempted renditions and commentaries generally go in every direction except to the correct conclusion.

THE BIRTH OF THE VEDAS: THE MODERN VIEW

Quite different from the Vedic literature's own delineation of its origins is the modern vision. Some scholars will frankly admit to the insurmountable difficulties in establishing an academically acceptable Vedic chronology. Others plunge ahead with laborious hunches and guesses. A professor of religion and Indian studies at the University of Chicago, Wendy D. O'Flaherty, sketches this picture of the predicament:

> The early history of Hinduism resembles an Impressionist paint-ing rather than the sharp etching that historians generally aspire to: the coloring is strong and unmistakable, but the outlines are hopelessly blurred. There is no difficulty in telling what is *there,* but every difficulty in telling *where* it is in space or time. What emerges from a study of the ancient texts and archaeological re-mains is a personality. We can know it with far more intensity and intimacy than there is in our reconstructions of civilizations far closer to us in time or space, but we cannot begin to know precisely where or when such a personality existed.[28]

Predictably, whether the academic establishment opts for the bafflement approach to Vedic origins or the brash, self-assured approach, almost all see the Vedas as a mythic extravaganza. Nomads from the North poured into the Indian subcontinent and superimposed their creative visions upon the simple indigenous people. Though Sanskrit is easily recognizable as immeasurably more sophisticated than even modern languages, it was the legacy of these wandering barbarians. They brought it with them over the Khyber Pass, along with their cattle, goats, and dogs.

Anyone can see there is no correlation between the level of brilliance evidenced in the language and the supposed level of the people who created it. Commonsense would seem to dictate that there must have been an equally advanced civilization—to match the uncommonly advanced language. Nevertheless, based on scholars' speculations of crude but poetic marauders, the public has been handed a fable. Here is a typical presentation for the people, found in a popular Time-Life rendition entitled *Barbarian Tides:*

> The Aryan nomads who trekked over the Hindu Kush mountains and settled on the plains of northern India during the second millennium B.C. were given to musing about the origins of the universe. . . . People who could so eloquently ponder the riddle of how the universe was born. . . . were obviously a sophisticated breed of invader.
>
> They were, it is true, a race of warriors. . . . It is also true that for many years after arriving in India they built neither cities nor national political structures; instead they enjoyed a pastoral life and developed an elaborate system of spiritual ideas that would suffuse the character of the subcontinent and reverberate throughout the world for thousands of years to come. And although at first they had no writing, they demonstrated impressive intellectual powers by producing and preserving, through

the spoken word alone, a stunningly rich body of poetry that served as a repository for their religious ideas. Moreover, these illiterate immigrants introduced the language, Sanskrit.

They called themselves *aryans*, which meant "noble of birth and race" [*sic*]. These proud, tall, fair-skinned people, with their great herds of lowing cattle and high-spirited chestnut horses, their flocks of sheep and goats and packs of yapping, frisky dogs . . . came in tribal groups of varying sizes over hundreds of years. At night on the trail, they dressed in wool and hides to protect themselves against the bitter high-country cold, eating beef and drinking a beer-like beverage called *sura* round their fires.[29]

Obviously scholars will shy away from the lurid details that embellish this saga meant for a popular audience. But most Western Indologists accredit the core of it. And why not? The essence is born of them. Consequently, minus the technicolor imagery, the above drama has become the modern, acceptable version of Vedic origins. And certainly it repulses transcendentally attuned persons who have developed the necessary attributes for studying the Vedic texts with an open, peaceful mind.

Notes

1 See Michael A. Cremo and Richard L. Thompson, *The Hidden History of the Human Race* (Badger, CA.: Govardhan Hill Publishing, 1994), Chapter 1.

2 Giorgio de Santillana and Hertha von Dechend, *Hamlet's Mill* (Boston: David R. Godine, 1992), p. 345.

3 Ibid., pp. 4–5, 348.

4 Interview in *The Search for Lost Origins* (Livingston, Mo.: Atlantis Rising Books, 1996), p. 128.

5 C. C. Lamberg-Karlovsky and J. A. Sabloff, *Ancient Civilizations: The Near East and Mesoamerica* (Menlo Park, CA.: The Benjamin/Cummings Publishing Co., 1979), p. 160.

6 John Horgan, *The End of Science* (New York: Broadway Books, 1996).

7 "Microbes Inside the Earth," in *Scientific American* [online journal] (October 1996; available from http//www.sciam.com)

8 Reported by the Associated Press, 14 February 1997.

9 Article by Steve Farrar, science correspondent, *Sunday Times* (London), 22 November 1998.

10 Poll conducted by the Marist Institute for Public Opinion, as reported by the Associated Press, 16 December 1997.

11 Lynn Margulis and Dorian Sagan, *What Is Life?* (New York: Simon & Schuster, 1995).

12 Gustav Theodor Fechner, *Nanna, oder über das Seelenleben der Pflanzen* (Leipzig: Verlag von Leopold Voss, 1921).

13 Peter Tompkins and Christopher Bird, *The Secret Life of Plants* (New York: Avon Books, 1974).

14 Cleve Backster, "Evidence of primary perception in plant life," *International Journal of Parapsychology* 10, no. 4 (1968): 329–48.

15 Andrew Greely, "Beyond Death and Dying," *Omni*, Autumn 1995.

16 L. Poliakov, *The Aryan Myth* (New York: Basic Books, 1974), p. 188.

17 As quoted in J. P. Mallory, *In Search of the Indo-Europeans* (New York: Thames and Hudson, 1989), p. 222.

18 Ibid., p. 266.

19 Ibid., p. 143.

20 Thomas J. Hopkins, in his foreword to Satsvarupa das Goswami, *Readings in Vedic Literature* (Los Angeles: The Bhaktivedanta Book Trust, 1977), p. ix.

21 R. O. Faulkner, trans., *The Ancient Egyptian Pyramid Texts* (Oxford: Oxford University Press, 1969).

22 D. Meeks and C. Favard Meeks, *Daily Life of the Egyptian Gods* (London: John Murray, 1997), p. 4.

23 Steven Pinker, *The Language Instinct* (London: Penguin Books, 1995),
    p. 71.
24 Ibid., pp. 70-71.
25 Ibid.
26 Ibid., pp. 73, 81–2.
27 Plato, *Phaedrus* (London: Penguin, 1973).
28 Arthur Cotterell, ed., *The Penguin Encyclopedia of Classical Civilizations*
    (London: Penguin Books, 1995), p. 192.
29 *Barbarian Tides* (Amsterdam: Time-Life Books, 1987), pp. 127–28.

CHAPTER 8

UNIVERSAL LAW AND ORDER

~

A t a war crimes trial in 1998, a former head of the United Nations peacekeeping operation in Rwanda wept as he recalled the horror of the genocide in the Central African country. The Canadian general, Romeo Dallaire, testified that the UN Assistance Mission for Rwanda had to stand by, stymied by lack of resources. In three months 800,000 persons were slaughtered. Describing the UN's failure to stop the storm of death enveloping Rwanda, the military general almost completely broke down. Why must humans exterminate one another like this? Can it happen in developed Western nations—other than the Balkan states?

Sometime in the 1990s, a small American city in Connecticut staged its annual fair. From the city and nearby towns, families crowded the city center, its specially closed streets jammed with stalls, amusements, and sightseers. Two mothers, Joan Mason and Susan Ricci, brought their children to join the festivities. Just a short distance away from where the two families stood were the pony rides. Joan's youngest daughter, six-year-old Christine, wanted to see the ponies. Joan—leaving her older daughter,

Katie, with the other mother and her kids—walked little Christine across the street, to the amusement site.

Suddenly Joan heard a commotion behind her—and a piercing scream. Dropping Christine's hand she turned and found herself walking toward the sound. People were fleeing—immediately Joan saw why. A burly, hobo-like man stood over a prone little girl, his right arm flailing at her. As if in a trance, Joan moved closer. In the madman's hand was a knife. At his feet lay her beautiful nine-year-old daughter, Katie.

Now the street was silent and empty—motionless, except for the attacker's relentless slashing. The fairgoers, terrified for their lives, hid themselves inside shops and behind cars. They watched as the crazed man squatted beside his victim on the blood-reddened sidewalk. Oblivious to the world, he continued his mechanical chopping at her face and neck. Only the mother, Joan, stood in the street, eighteen feet away, transfixed by shock.

As to be expected, a few moments seemed like eternity. Then two men and a policeman appeared and struggled to subdue the assailant. Ignoring their combined force, the attacker—as if on automatic pilot—would not give up his relentless hacking. At last the men disarmed him. Joan rushed forward to pick up her child. Katie, by this time, was vomiting huge quantities of blood. Joan looked into her daughter's eyes and knew the child was about to die.

When Katie's butchered body arrived at the hospital emergency room, it was already too late. Staggered by the bizarre tragedy, the doctors and nurses tried every technique possible to reclaim her life, though they knew there was no hope. Finally they gave up. The atmosphere in the emergency room shifted from utter disbelief to rage. Why would someone do this to such a beautiful young girl? What kind of world is this?

Young Katie's killer was a paranoid schizophrenic. On the very morning of the attack he had been released by a nearby mental hospital, from its unit for the criminally insane. Immediately he caught a bus to the city center, purchased a hunting knife from a hardware store, and then happened upon the street fair. There he saw two cute young girls of the same age, wearing identical dresses. He saw Katie, the daughter of Joan, and Laura, the child of Joan's friend. Why did the madman choose one girl and not the other? He first shoved Laura aside. Then, grabbing Katie by the hair, the psychopath threw her to the ground. It was Laura, not Katie, whose shrill scream had announced the onset of the horror.[1]

Certainly the murder of one young girl, though heart-wrenching, cannot compare to the genocide of more than 800,000 men, women, and children. Yet in countless tragedies like these, which we hear about almost daily, the same questions haunt us: Why do these atrocities happen to certain people and not to others? Is there any sense of justice in life, or are we completely at the mercy of cosmic chance?

The Web of Karma

By now, the Sanskrit term *karma* has gained almost mainstream usage in the West. While it's chic to toss the word into conversations, the actual acceptance of karma as a cosmic reality entails massive consequences. Indeed, the stuff of karma *is* consequences. That means reactions to every action—not just the ones we casually choose to weigh and consider. The Vedic universal law of karma regulates all the actions and reactions of fully conscious entities.

Our present understanding of action and reaction allows for causality in the structure and processes of matter. Any scientist or layperson will accept action and reaction in matter. It appears to our modern vision as self-evident. The Vedic view of causality, however, includes consciousness. To the Vedic seer, the cause and effect of consciousness is self-evident. The Vedic sage knows that full consciousness—the special gift to humanity—spawns reactions. Since plants, animals, and other entities with little display of consciousness are analyzed as having no free will, in the Vedic system they do not accrue karma.

Why are some people born with a silver spoon in their mouth and others born into squalor and rags? Why do two persons grow up in the same circumstances, work equally hard for success, and still achieve completely different results? Why is one person born ugly or with low intelligence and another beautiful or with ingenuity? The Vedas explain that these routine inequities—an inherent feature of the cosmos—are effects of the law of karma. This universal regulator awards the appropriate reactions to human activity. Pious, virtuous deeds bring pleasing, desirable effects. Impious, selfish deeds bring troublesome, unwanted effects. Between the two poles of good and bad actions and reactions, a human can experience innumerable mixtures.

Basically, so-called good karma results in pleasurable material circumstances. Birth in a wealthy family, high education, personal beauty, luxury, and so forth are accepted as the usual outcomes of a virtuous past life. So-called bad karma translates into a next life of distresses such as poverty, disease, or legal problems. The application of the law of karma is described as complex, because human activities are generally neither all good nor all bad. For example, the Vedas would say that pious activities in the past life allowed Lady Diana to marry into the British royal family and enjoy worldwide fame and glamor. But then past impious activities overtook her, in the form of a marriage breakdown and a sudden early death. In the future someone else, propelled upward in material life by virtues from her past, may wed the prince and actually enjoy his company in Buckingham Palace.

The Vedic universal law of karma allows us to mold our destiny as we want. But once we act we must undergo the corresponding reactions. In this way predestination exists side by side with free will. The human being can always choose new actions while simultaneously suffering or enjoying circumstances brought about by the past. The Vedas would say that, owing to mistakes in the previous birth, a person is born with a clubfoot in North Korea. Certainly his or her material possibilities would be severely restricted, due to the birth defect and the oppressive regime. But the person can and will choose to act according to the options available. Perhaps the *karmi*—Sanskrit for "participant in the web of karma"—will volunteer to deliver relief supplies of grain during a famine.

A precise definition of karma is given the *Bhagavad-gita* (8.3): "Action resulting in the development of material bodies is known as karma, reactive work." Whenever there is karmic activity—whether good or bad—there is a resultant material body—whether superior or inferior. Explicit in the Vedic science of karma is the impossibility of our fundamentally altering the present quota of achievement and disaster through social, political, or economic measures. The correct allotment of happiness and distress is packaged with the body at the time of conception. As the body traverses its stages of growth and decline, the fitting karmic reactions transpire.

Tinkering with the nuts and bolts in our life may be possible, but the basic chassis remains unaffected. We will reap what we have sown. The future, however, is still in our hands. Karma can be changed or even dissipated—but not through ordinary material measures.

The Vedas reveal the soul as eternally and irrevocably active. In both its pure state and its material, embodied life, the living entity is always performing action. The Vedic texts do not proffer inactivity as a permanent solution to karmic entanglement. Be our shackles heavenly or hellish, the ultimate goal is to avoid all the bondage of karma by performing non-reactive work. Especially in the third chapter of *Bhagavad-gita*, Krishna explains this art: non-reactive activity by dedicating all results to the Supreme. This process is called karma-yoga. In a nutshell, karma-yoga means using our senses to serve the Lord of the senses. A person totally immersed in the non-karmic life style is classified as a transcendentalist, even though dwelling within the material world.

The Vedic view presents that the conditions we are born into stem from activities performed in a previous life. If we dismiss karma and its corollary, reincarnation, what are we left with to explain life's rampant inequities?

Take this sad case: little Ben de Knegt made medical history, in the small nation of New Zealand, as the first patient to receive a bone marrow transplant. In 1998, after several unexpected recoveries from near-death, Ben died in his mother's arms—two weeks before his third birthday. His body was incinerated in a bright yellow casket with his favorite dinosaur toy. The mother said, "We're glad he isn't hurting any more, but we will miss him so much." An only child, while battling the intense pain and anguish that cancer forced upon his short life, Ben had often lamented, "It's not fair."

Semitic religions can seem to demand of their followers a sense of helpless fate. How do we answer the "little Bens" of this world? Why do bad things happen to persons we consider good people? Submit we must, to the unfathomable powerplays of an omnipotent God? Though no true believer will ever say so—until he or she loses faith—the Almighty's dispensations in human affairs can appear almost monstrously insensitive and arbitrary.

Opposed to the Vedic system of karmic actions and appropriate reactions after death, Christians put forth the resurrection of the righteous. The belief says that all souls come into being only at birth, and only in humans. Then, after their short stint of life— only on Earth—these souls are branded as either good or bad. At the grand finale of the world, when the resurrection comes, only the good will rise for the eternal victory over bad.

In addition to tolerating the utterly inscrutable will of Providence, Christians have to adjust themselves to the doctrine of everlasting torture in hell—unmitigated punishment for wasting one short life. In churches catering to the more learned and intellectual, the hellfire and brimstone has been played down, or even tactfully retired. Nevertheless, whether the church is fundamentalist or liberal, the central problem remains: on the one hand Christianity stresses the hope of an afterlife as an essential tenet of Christian faith; on the other hand, though, the nature of this afterlife is undefined. Despite popular longings for it, nowhere is it explained. The glory of Christ's life and example notwithstanding, anyone dutifully thinking that either the Catholic or the Protestant church offers clear instruction on immortality and the resurrection is in for an unpleasant surprise. Sincere attempts to erect and contemplate heaven, hell, and purgatory foster so much confusion that smart theologians tactfully avoid discussing them.

Rather than condemning the twin tenets of reincarnation and karma, a few broad-minded Christian thinkers recommend careful consideration of these Vedic precepts. Certainly Christianity has never officially sanctioned these Vedic fundamentals, and has often frowned upon them. Yet, is it possible to weld reincarnation and karma to the Christian faith, without betraying devotion to Lord Jesus Christ? The early Church fathers utilized Greek philosophy as a vehicle to convey their doctrines. Perhaps Vedic metaphysics would serve modern Christian thinkers better. The Christian scholar of philosophy, Geddes McGregor, after researching the history of reincarnation in Christianity, gave this opinion:

> Surely, too, even countless rebirths as a beggar lying in misery and filth on the streets of Calcutta would be infinitely more reconcilable to the Christian concept of God than is the traditional

doctrine of everlasting torture in hell. The appeal of reincarnationism to anyone nurtured on hell-fire sermons and tracts is by
no means difficult to understand. Indeed, even apart from the
notion of everlasting punishment, traditional Christian doctrine
about "last things" (the destiny of humankind) is so notoriously
confused that vast numbers of people, even habitual churchgo-
ers, have given up believing anything about the subject at all.
Christian eschatology (as that branch of theology is called) is by
any reckoning the most unsatisfactory area of the Church's concern. A sitting duck for the Church's adversaries, it is also an embarrassment to thoughtful Christians. No wonder, indeed, that
the wisest of Christian theologians have discouraged "idle speculation" on the nature of the afterlife.[2]

Hand in hand with karma and reincarnation goes the ancient
Vedic science of astrology. Because the application of Vedic astrology is said to require sages of a caliber rarely found today, orthodox Vedic preceptors say its practice has rightfully fallen into
disrepute. Stellar affectations on our life can be calculated, but
few astrologers today exist—even in India—with the necessary
spiritual qualifications and training to interpret the data. Hence,
although currently Vedic astrology is used to reveal marriage
compatibility, character analysis, and hunches about world
events, its full glory, depth, and accuracy has not been revived yet.

The Vedas accept planetary influences on living beings as a
plain fact of nature. Every aspect of our body, mind, and intelligence is seen to be predominated by a particular planet. We take
birth at the time of an appropriate configuration in the skies, according to our karma from the past life. The correlation between
our moment of birth, the position of the stars, and our karma is
arranged by subtle laws of nature. Just as laws of a nation control
the citizens, similarly, these subtle laws of the universe bind all
living entities—the members of the universe.

CONSCIOUSNESS:
CAUSAL AND ACCOUNTABLE

The exactitude of physical arrangements in the universe awes contemporary thinkers. To uneducated eyes, the properties of the universe and their interactions may appear arbitrary. But scientists know that the constants of the cosmos reveal an eerie precision that is quite startling. What we take as incidental conditions just happen to be minutely right for life. Just consider what are deemed the four fundamental forces of nature: electromagnetism, gravity, and the strong and weak forces in the atom. Scientists are sure that any slight variance in them would render the universe—as we know it—impossible. A few examples of uncanny coincidences:

- If electromagnetism had been only 1033 times stronger than gravity instead of 1039, stars would have a mass one billion times less and would burn one billion times faster.
- If the weak force in the atom had been slightly less than 1028 times gravity, all the hydrogen in the universe would turn to helium. That means no water in the universe.
- Raise the strong force in that atom by as little as 2 percent and no protons would form. That means a universe without atoms. Decrease that same force by 5 percent, and the universe is starless.
- Alter even slightly the difference in mass between a proton and neutron, and no chemistry or life (as currently known) is possible.[3]

Besides deliberating the astounding "rightness" of how matter is arranged in the cosmos, we should also ponder the Vedic cosmic principle that every aspect of existence is 100 percent equitable. For living entities, cosmic justice prevails with an accuracy our best systems of law enforcement could never approach.

In the Vedic universe, just as variables of matter are micro-adjusted to a wondrous precision, so the reactions to consciousness are also minutely calibrated. The Vedic vision acknowledges a universal law of justice, exactly balancing the actions of consciousness with their consequences. Hence we should not anguish over why bad things happen to good people, or good things happen to the bad. The sages of the Vedas urge wise persons to verse themselves in what is appropriate and inappropriate action—not according to their own intuition, but in line with the authorized texts of universal law. Consciousness is both causal and accountable.

Settling into the Vedic universe means observing a reality where matter and consciousness coexist. We have already discussed the root of any discomfort we may feel in adapting to the Vedic cosmos. The main barrier to entry is a surprisingly unempirical belief in the primacy of matter and the universality of physical laws. This apparent faith can severely impede our attempts to plumb the Vedic mysteries of the self and the universe.

Closer to home, let's analyze a typical Western approach to solving ecological problems. We will see the underlying assumptions and premises of matter-ism at work. In Sweden, Dr. Karl-Henrik Robert is famous for "The Natural Step," an ecological educational program for inspiring corporations and households to recognize environmental realities and voluntarily submit to them. Endorsed by the king of Sweden as well as leaders in business and science, the precepts of "The Natural Step" have been distributed to every home and school in the country. Dr. Robert explains:

> Health, life, and economy rest on the same fundamental principles, which are constituted by ordered matter. . . . If matter on Earth is systematically concentrated and structured, that is the fundamental principle of prosperity and health. So, continued prosperity and health rest on the fact that we must not dissolve more matter into dispersed waste than is reconstituted back into

the ordered forms again. This is the overall cyclic principle of the whole biosphere we live in.[4]

With physicists and other scientists, Robert has made a flow diagram of our environment, to demonstrate four overarching principles for sustainability that are absolute and nonnegotiable. These rules apply regardless of the size of the system processing matter.

- Nature cannot withstand the systematic, intensive withdrawal of matter from Earth's crust. Whatever the petroleum and mining industries take out, it has to go somewhere. Since matter cannot vanish after we remove it from Earth and use it, a problematic buildup of garbage, originating from Earth's crust, then afflicts our habitat. Recycling is never perfectly complete; therefore, whatever matter we pull out of the Earth that we cannot put back eventually disperses into our environment and harasses us. A few of the consequences are heavy-metal poisons, greenhouse gases, and acid rain.

- Nature cannot tolerate our manufacture of more synthetic compounds than it can break down and assimilate. The thousands of manmade substances like DDT, PCB, and Freon will boomerang on us.

- Nature cannot function properly when, beyond what it can normally compensate for, its resources are exploited and its processes impeded. Spreading asphalt and concrete over Earth's surface, denuding the forests, and exhausting the soil all cause critical damage that prevents nature from rebalancing itself.

- To practice the mindful use of matter in the first three principles, we need to establish the kind of global economy that handles matter appropriately, that burns up resources efficiently and prudently. The input of resources needed to produce our products must be decreased.

Dr. Robert's legitimate anxiety is that long before humans run out of energy resources, they will have enthusiastically poisoned themselves, by bringing out of the Earth cadmium, lead, and other heavy metals. In 1989 "The Natural Step" program sent a booklet and audiocassette to every home in Sweden, and produced more than forty thousand copies of a board game for families, schools, and corporations. Playing it trained them in the governing bylaws of the ecosystem.

Obviously, few will deny the relative truth of the four "absolute, nonnegotiable" axioms. Yet, from the Vedic perspective, programs with a scope like "The Natural Step" are quite limited and incomplete. Therefore they are deemed ineffectual. The typical style of response to the real threat of ecological catastrophe might be called "matter matters."

We might consider: If the movements of matter in the environment cause such precise reactions, what about the movements of the most crucial ingredient in the ecosystem—consciousness? What are the natural reactions to the proper and improper use of consciousness? Who are the scholars who have catalogued the consequences of consciousness in its affairs with matter? Where is the knowledge system to inform and guide us about the whole of existence, not merely the inert, insignificant energy of matter?

The Vedas hold that consciousness indicates the presence of the superior, spiritual energy. Therefore, without denying the implications brought on by the reactions of the inferior, material energy, the Vedic vision sees the actions and reactions of consciousness as paramount. The Vedas certainly do not deny the field of material reaction; rather, they simply urge us to concentrate our major attention on the spiritual energy. Without contact with spirit, matter is inactive. Therefore, spirit matters most, and the pollution of consciousness is recognized as the deadliest environmental problem.

Naysayers may object that in the Vedic seers' attempt to understand the workings of the cosmos, they seem to have deftly transferred the problem of inconceivability from matter to spirit. Modern skeptics sometimes admit that materialists are always culpable for their glaring inability to account for conscious experience. Materialists, past or present, cannot explain how the subjective experience of consciousness—having no mass and occupying no space—emerges from inanimate matter. But the modern skeptics can also criticize the Vedic standpoint. It seems, some say, to have merely reversed the riddle. One the one hand, we have the miracle of matter producing consciousness; on the other, the miracle of consciousness—symptomatic of a spiritual energy—producing matter. What makes one miracle more justified than the other?

From the Vedic perspective, just the concession that modern brains have endowed matter with inconceivable mystic potencies is a great step forward. The world can only benefit from a fair comparison between the two metaphysical views: modern materialistic science and the ancient spiritualistic science of the Vedas. Then we would probably want to consider: Where's the best bet? Should we passionately throw all our support behind inanimate matter, or should we calmly investigate a hunch that consciousness—completely resistant to material dissection—may signal the reality of a spiritual energy, with its own appropriate laws of nature?

The Vedic advantage would seem to lie in its voluminous elucidation of a spiritual reality and a material derivative. Moreover, the venturesome among us can take advantage of clear-cut methodologies for verifying and experiencing the Vedic tenets.

Western science has given us neither understanding of how life or consciousness emerges from matter nor any empirical corroboration. Therefore how can we actually cope with the environment? Since we do not know all the substances that compose the environment, how can we know all the nonnegotiable laws that rule it? Consciousness is part of life, so what are the laws that govern consciousness?

A geological reality in California illustrates how major forces, beyond what we normally contemplate, initiate massive effects. As average Californians scurry about, executing daily affairs, they rarely consider two immense plates deep within Earth. These two underground tectonic plates—one holding up North America and the other, the Pacific Ocean—are constantly grinding at each other in opposite directions. If their inexorable dance suddenly lurches just an inch, then an unimaginable mass of earth jumps. The event is an earthquake that changes the lives, properties, and geography of the USA's West Coast. Some scientists say that "in a million years" San Francisco will be where Los Angeles is—350 miles to the south.

The Vedic literature reminds us of the havoc we bring down upon ourselves by not seeing the whole picture of the cosmos. This cosmic entirety includes consciousness and its laws. Without our knowing the Complete Whole, all our best efforts at compassion, love, and humanitarianism are rendered utterly inadequate. The Vedic literature says we need knowledge—full comprehension of the complete scene we call life and the universe. Otherwise, our response—based on limited and incomplete knowledge of the cosmos—will actually harm, not help. Real human life is described as a quest for all-inclusive knowledge, a ready acquaintance with all the factors at work in the biosphere or the cosmos. Like the grand movements of underlying tectonic plates, the consciousness laws of nature—though we are oblivious to them—produce monumental effects.

Ironically, ample incentive to look beyond the confines of matter-ism comes from some of the best scientists. Their wit and eloquence seems to bring us right to the Vedic doorstep, though certainly they have not directly undertaken the Vedic experience.

Two Dutch scholars at Princeton University, Piet Hut and Bas van Fraassen, have a delightful time poking at the clay feet of our present paradigms. In a published academic dialogue entitled "Elements of Reality," van Fraassen, a professor of philosophy, and Hut, an astrophysicist, advanced these pointers:

> When we start with a scientific view of the world, we are at loss when we try to deal with notions such as value, beauty, or meaning—or more down to earth: anger, fear, joy, color, smell, and other "secondary" qualities whose putative reduction seems today as difficult as ever. Do these qualities then have to be put in by hand, so to speak? Or could it mean that the scientific view itself fails to capture aspects of reality at least as fundamental as basic physical notions such as space, time, energy?
>
> Just imagine living for one minute in a world without beauty, value, or consciousness for that matter. Yes, conscious experience correlates with brain activity, but by measuring and mapping those correlations, have we come any closer to an understanding of what many scientists would like us to believe, that somehow consciousness emerges out of (oozes out of?) nerve cells? If I've ever seen an incompatible pair of concepts, it's a configuration of molecules and a conscious experience!
>
> Life "emerging" out of lots of molecules; consciousness "emerging" out of lots of nerve cells. Well, why not consider time as "emerging" out of clocks? Without clocks, no accurate time measurements. And a good clock provides excellent correlations with the flow of time. But time surely does not "emerge" out of a clock.[5]

In acclimatizing ourselves to the Vedic cosmic order, we may do well to remember a precept any present-day scientist accepts: *Where there is a fundamental property there are fundamental laws.* The hesitant may recall that in the nineteenth century, the phenomenon of electromagnetism would not submit to any previously recognized laws of nature. To remedy the situation, scientists certified electromagnetic charge as one of the basic components of the universe, and ascribed to it appropriate fundamental laws. Since it is quite obvious that consciousness refuses to bow to scientific explanations of structure and process, perhaps we should heed the Vedic call and look at the possibility of another set of universal laws—specific governances for consciousness and its interaction with matter.

Today's pundits put forth "laws of nature." In this way they acquiesce to the reality of something ultimate ordering cosmic phenomena. But if we moderns cannot vault over the chasm between physical process and consciousness, we will find that same insurmountable gap frustrating our versions of "the laws of nature." Eluding our attempts to discern overarching laws regulating everything in the universe, consciousness roams on its own—unexplained and unaccounted for.

The Vedas firmly tie consciousness to a spiritual energy, emanating from the Supreme. Tracking consciousness to its source in this way opens up an exciting realm of transcendental knowledge and experience. The ultimate causative principle that underlies reality is presented as a singular yet infinite self-conscious being, Krishna. Full of limitless knowledge, pleasure, and potency, Krishna emanates matter, as well as minuscule subjective selves. These tiny, finite selves—in minute quantity—possess the same self-conscious, spiritual nature as the unlimited Krishna.

Decades ago, the Nobel Laureate and patriarch of modern physics Niels Bohr concluded:

> We can admittedly find nothing in physics or chemistry that has even a remote bearing on consciousness. Yet all of us know that there is such a thing as consciousness. Simply because we have it ourselves. Hence consciousness must be part of nature or, more

generally, of reality, which means that, quite apart from the laws of physics and chemistry as laid down in quantum theory, we must also consider laws of quite a different kind.

To that fine summation, we might add, "We must also consider an ultimate source of quite a different kind."

THE THREE MODES OF NATURE

Entwined with the workings of the universal law of karma are the Vedic modes of material nature. Though pop notions of karma are common today, the Vedic three modes are still an untrendy tenet of the ancient knowledge. Known in Sanskrit as *gunas*—literally "ropes"—the three modes affect all interactions between matter and consciousness. Because the *gunas* are said to bind all conditioned living entities like strong ropes, the material cosmos—the realm of *maya*—is sometimes called *tri-guna-mayi*: the illusory environs of the three modes.

The law of the *gunas* operates congruently with the law of karma. According to the main mode of nature cultivated in the past life, a person gets a new body predominated by that particular mode. The three *gunas* are goodness (*sattva*), passion (*rajas*), and ignorance (*tamas*). By drawing upon the precise psychophysical information in the Vedic texts, we can easily picture the lives of persons under each mode. Let's see if we can recognize anyone we know.

Goodness

The symptoms of the mode of goodness are a penchant for virtue, integrity, self-discipline, abstinence, cleanliness, and, most importantly, peacefulness and a delight in profound knowledge. We can visualize a man or woman in this mode, *sattva-guna*, though nowadays such types are a rare breed. Fond of residing in a quiet locale— the mountains, forest, seashore, or countryside— the mode-of-goodness person lives simply, completely free from sensual hankerings and consumer urges. Known for fresh, clean clothes and a spotlessly tidy house, our candidate seems to exude bodily and mental purity. Certainly a vegetarian, he or she loves philosophy, poetry, art, music, and science that focuses upon the ultimate issues of life. Sound like anyone we know?

> The effects of the mode of goodness are experienced when knowledge illuminates all the gates of the body.

To teach us about the mode of goodness, this verse from the *Gita* (14.11) employs the Vedic analogy of the body as a city with nine gates: two eyes, two ears, two nostrils, the mouth, the genitals, and the anus. Through each of the gateways, we take in experiences of sense objects and pass things out. When the symptoms of goodness illuminate every gate, then the proprietor of the body is understood to have developed *sattva-guna*. In this mode of goodness, we can see things in the right perspective, hear the things we should hear, and our tastebuds function properly. Cleansed inside and out, our life radiates inner contentment.

Passion

The next *guna*, the mode of passion, puts us moderns on more familiar turf. The symptoms of *rajo-guna* are feverish endeavors to get ahead, pride in abilities and possessions, a hearty diet of physical indulgence—yet dissatisfaction even in gain and sensualism. In short, a life style of work, buy, consume, die.

Our quintessential mode-of-passion person loves to live where the action is. The closer to shops, malls, cinemas, and sports, the better. A veteran urbanite or suburban commuter, he or she is willing to work hard in offices or factories to earn money for the latest conveniences and entertainment. Prestige and social standing is eagerly appreciated. The main reward, however, is sex.

Besides keeping on top of new opportunities for more money or libido, our mode-of-passion hero also aims to keep abreast with knowledge of anything *except* the ultimate questions. The dedicated karmic achiever has neither time nor inclination to ask, "Who am I, what is the source of everything, what is my duty to that Source?"

Tour their home and check out the books, periodicals, videos, CDs, and art. You'll find that they all concern mainly the body and its intimate or social affairs. At best, you'll be able to peruse the latest speculations in reductionist science—or tufts of New Age cotton wool.

Go to the center of any city and you can feel the gale force of *rajo-guna*. Its influence, though, pervades all of modern society: knowledge, religion, and culture. According to the Vedic analysis, the progress of all materialistic civilizations and empires expands from this mode of passion. Religion in *rajo-guna* is also a passionate affair. Devotional platitudes accompany the pursuit of material enjoyment, much as background music at a department store or mall lightens the mood of shoppers.

Ignorance

The third mode, *tamo-guna*, the mode of ignorance, is considered the most perverse and lethal. Its devotees wallow in sloth, excessive sleep, dejection, and intoxication. The finale is deadly anger, pointless violence, and mental derangement.

Unfortunately we may have to agree that this mode plays a significant role in society today. The *tamo-guna* man or woman abhors work. Leaden and lethargic, this person lacks even materialistic ambitions or goals. Content to live as a parasite, he or she passes the days and nights in a cloudland of drugs, alcohol, dreaminess, and the blues.

The mode of ignorance favors any dirty habitat, as well as unwashed bodies and clothes. Its bastions are the nocturnal temples of delusion: pubs, casinos, brothels, drug dens, and entertainment clubs—the later into the night the better.

Contemporary Vedic teachers often point out that modern society specializes in the modes of passion and ignorance. Many of us who seem to evidence the Vedic mode of passion also may dabble in *tamo-guna*. And then there are the growing urban legions who, unemployed and dysfunctional, take full shelter in *tamas*.

THE CULTURE OF CONTAMINATION

We should remember that *guna* means "rope." All three *gunas* bind—even the mode of goodness. The Vedas describe that the mode of goodness conditions its subjects to a sense of very refined material happiness. The *sattva-guna* person feels an elevated state of material self-contentment and knowingness—far from the maddening crowd. The mode of passion conditions its adherents to the pursuit of material success—the rat race, as moderns refer to it. The mode of ignorance binds its fans to madness and depravity.

Real ecology, in the Vedic view, considers not only pollution of the air, water, or soil, but also pollution of consciousness. Nature is not a bizarre arrangement in which the mysterious property consciousness hangs loose—"it just is, whatever it is"—while inanimate matter undergoes processes of astonishingly precise action and reaction.

As a traveller passing through regions afflicted with an epidemic becomes duly contaminated, similarly the consciousness of the living entity—on an excursion through material existence—picks up contagions from the modes. We can understand *sattva-guna* as the lightest of the infections—a bad cold; *rajo-guna* as middling—hepatitis; and *tamo-guna* as the most virulent—anthrax.

The Vedas say that innumerable blends of the three modes manifest as all the innumerable varieties of phenomena in material existence. Not simply physical matter, but also entities of meaning and value—happiness, distress, war, peace, love, hate, progress, decline, and so forth—are presented as ingredients of the three modes. In the same way that changes in wind direction bring about changes in weather, the fluctuations of the modes foster various kinds of civilizations, cultures, ideas, art, music, and behavioral norms. Hence, the Vedic explanation for *zeitgeist*:

> Therefore material substance, place, result of activity, time, knowledge, work, the performer of work, faith, state of consciousness, species of life, and destination after death are all based on the three modes of material nature.
>
> O best of human beings, all states of material being are related to the interaction of the enjoying soul and material nature. Whether seen, heard of, or only conceived within the mind, they are without exception constituted of the modes of nature. (*Shrimad-Bhagavatam* 11.25.30–31)

Besides affecting the individual, the three modes bind universal affairs as a whole. That means Vedic sages discern *tri-guna-mayi* in the course of history. Like seasonal changes, the three *gunas* alternate in predominance, saturating all of existence with their respective characteristics. The Vedas describe that sometimes passion has the upper hand, sometimes goodness, or ignorance.

Just as the arrival of summer brings heat, a universal increment of the mode of passion brings an upsurge in economic development and sensuality. During the winter of the mode of ignorance, the inevitable frustrations of *rajo-guna* degenerate into the crazed wrath of *tamo-guna*. Then senseless wars break out, and millions die. Under the sway of the mode of ignorance, war crimes and mass atrocities permanently scar human civilization.

Then, years later, reflecting under the calming, clearing influence of *sattva-guna*, humanists and philosophers scratch their head, wondering, "Why did the whole world rush into destruction, for such petty, irrational reasons?"

Though one mode of nature is always particularly prominent, the effects of the others still manifest in a minor way. Therefore, while the wrath of ignorance horribly expends itself in world war, many persons flock to religious retreats, to embrace a contemplative *sattva-guna* life style.

The Vedas present the universe as an ocean tossing with the waves of the three modes of nature. How does the living entity, though actually spiritual, come under the sway of the modes? The texts describe that, through our mistaken identification with the body and mind, the spirit soul becomes immersed in material nature, buffeted by the modes. The three influences dominate all interactions in the cosmos. Everything in material existence can be analyzed through the *gunas*, for example, the type of food we eat, the way we give to charity, the quality of our determination, and even the nature of our convictions, theories, and worldview.

The following series of verses from the *Shrimad-Bhagavatam* (11.25.12–19) give us a deeper insight into the modes and their effects. Let us see where we fit, according to the Vedic standard.

12. The three modes of material nature—goodness, passion, and ignorance—influence the living entity, but not Me. Manifesting within his mind, the modes induce the living entity to become attached to material bodies and other material objects. In this way he becomes bound.

13. When the mode of goodness—luminous, pure, and auspicious—prevails over passion and ignorance, a person becomes endowed with happiness, virtue, knowledge, and other good qualities.

14. When the mode of passion—bringing attachment to matter,

separatism, and activity—surpasses ignorance and goodness, then a man begins to work hard to acquire prestige and fortune. In this mode of passion he experiences anxiety and struggle.

15. When the mode of ignorance overcomes passion and goodness, it covers a person's consciousness and makes him foolish and dull. Falling into lamentation and illusion, a person in this mode of darkness sleeps excessively, indulges in false hopes, and displays violence toward others.

16. When consciousness becomes clear and the senses are detached from matter, a person experiences fearlessness within his body and detachment from the material mind. You should understand that this situation reveals the predominance of the mode of goodness. In this state a person has the opportunity to realize Me.

17. You should recognize the mode of passion by its symptoms— the distortion of the intelligence because of too much activity, and the inability of the faculties of perception to disentangle themselves from mundane sense objects. Further basic symptoms are unhealthy physical organs that the body uses for work, and the unsteady perplexity of the mind.

18. When a person's higher awareness fails and then completely disappears, he is therefore unable to concentrate his attention. In this state his mind is ruined, manifesting ignorance and depression. You should understand that this situation reveals the predominance of the mode of ignorance.

19. When the mode of goodness increases, the strength of the virtuous similarly grows. When passion increases, the gross materialists become strong. And when ignorance rises, the strength of the utterly depraved expands.

The method of civilization outlined in the Vedas offers a progressive staircase up from the baser modes of nature to the mode of goodness. Those in *tamo-guna* are induced to rise to *rajo-guna*, and so on. Capacity for real spiritual understanding and realization is said to begin only in *sattva-guna*, goodness. From the position of goodness, a candidate for liberation can properly contemplate freedom from the modes altogether—by becoming a full-fledged transcendentalist.

The ancient seers emphasized that it is not enough that someone simply has a heartfelt desire to be a better person: "I *really* want to be good!" The perspective of the Vedas holds that appropriate purificatory processes and life style changes are essential—the best intentions alone will not stand up to the polluting winds of passion and ignorance.

At the dawn of the new millennium, some Western psychologists have newly discovered that the long overlooked system of Vedic psychology, the three modes, has untapped benefit for modern humanity. The prestigious academic journal *Psychological Reports* presented "A Psychometric Analysis of the Three Gunas."[6] In this article, the author and researcher, David B. Wolf, presented data that substantiates *tri-guna* as a valid framework for understanding human psychology.

State-Specific Knowledge

The Vedic law of the three modes seems to parallel the crest of the biggest wave in modern knowledge. The most accurate predictive tool known today is quantum mechanics, in short, a brilliant schema for charting subatomic activity without ever understanding the whys of that activity. A cardinal precept of this physics is that the observer is bound up with what he observes. The two are inseparable. How you look determines what you will see.

The father of the quantum uncertainty principle, the German Nobel laureate Werner Heisenberg, said, "What we observe is not nature in itself but nature exposed to our method of question-ing."[7] A careful consideration of the Vedic law of *tri-guna* will show that the Vedas, in their own way, had already accepted this fundamental—in its most pregnant application. That is, the de-pendence of the observation upon the observer applies not only to the microworld of subatomic physics, but also to the macroworld of human affairs. Rather than just declaring this gen-eral axiom, the Vedas also delineated the specific characteristics of all the basic standpoints possible in material existence. According to our situation in goodness, passion, or ignorance, we see both the micro and macro world accordingly. All attempts at ideas, knowledge, beliefs, moralities, ethics—any system of thought—derive from permutations of these basic modalities.

In the hands of the ancient Vedas, the axiom, "How you look determines what you see," becomes a full-fledged holistic prin-ciple: "Who you are determines what you see." Because all living beings are said to be tricolored by the three modes, therefore, "What you see is what you get," and "What you get is what you see." The knowledge of the world available to you depends on who you are—the seer, the knower. And your material identity springs from your situation in *tri-guna*.

In other words, the Vedas challenge: all knowledge is *state spe-cific*. A person's status in the three modes determines what that person can know and perceive. We are instructed that we should not expect a person immersed in passion or ignorance to perceive and comprehend the realities available to someone in the mode of goodness. Hence, in the contamination of our private world of perceptions and conceptions, we can detect the most sinister con-sequences of the modes. According to our infection, we will, in fact, see and think accordingly. The *state specificness* of knowledge reveals the full meaning of *guna*: the cord that binds. The Vedas exhort: adjust your health. That is, change your life style. Then you will see and know differently.

Often scholastic attempts at penetrating the Vedas make light of "antiquated taboos"—warnings that only those in suitable consciousness and life style can understand the content of the texts. For example, the *Gita* warns that its themes are a mystery grasped only by those who have harmonized their consciousness with Krishna. Yet everywhere, both in modern India and abroad in Europe and America, you'll find *Gita* commentaries attempted by non-adepts.

Hopefully, an understanding of *tri-guna* will dispel the notion that "irrational superstitions foolishly bar entry to the Hindu realm of saga and legend." In fairness to the Vedic perspective, we should note that every field of inquiry has its entry requirements and its learning curve. As pointed out earlier in this book, professors of quantum physics say it takes at least eight years to train students to adjust their thinking, so they can begin to grasp the strange world of subatomic paradoxes. We might say that the Vedic equivalent is the injunction, "If a person wants to understand *Brahman*, the inconceivable spiritual energy, he must become a brahmin." In the correct Vedic application, becoming a brahmin means by qualification, not by birth. A brahmin is completely fixed in the mode of goodness.

Albert Einstein noted: "The universe of ideas is just as little independent of the nature of our experience as clothes are of the form of the human body."[8] The common assumption, lurking deep in our social enculturation, is that we can pull off our rose-colored glasses anytime we want, and talk sensibly about the world as it really is. The triumph of Archimedes, perhaps the best of the ancient Greek scientists, provides an amusing reminder. Heartened by his uncovering the mathematical concept of the lever, he is said to have exclaimed, "Give me a place to stand and I will move the Earth."

To reach beyond the limitations of classical physics, scientists had to abandon the concept of a detached observer and an independent reality. The idea of a neutral standpoint outside the world, from which as detached spectators we may clearly view and comment on phenomena, is a myth—both from the current and Vedic scientific view.

> Deluded by the three modes, the whole world does not know Me, who am above the modes and inexhaustible. (*Bhagavad-gita* 7.13)

The mode of goodness can bring into distant focus the outer, impersonal precincts of the Supreme Absolute. Passion and ignorance allow only the shadows of substance. Ultimately, though, the Vedas do not deny an independent reality. They reserve transcendence, however, for the transcendentalists. Those who have entered the laboratory of pure consciousness and mastered the techniques can reach beyond the clutches of *tri-guna*. They are entitled to research and experience the three transcendental phases, *Brahman*, *Paramatma*, and *Bhagavan*, described in the next chapter.

GRAND THEORIES OF EVERYTHING

Theoretical physicist John Wheeler is renowned for constructing the basis of much of modern gravitational theory. Also famous, among his colleagues, for one-liners, he once quipped, "Never run after a bus or woman or cosmological theory, because there'll always be another one in a few minutes."[9] Decreasingly, the general public believes that between the physicists and the astrophysicists, all the fundamental features and laws of the universe are catalogued and explained. Cosmology had its heady days back in the 1980s, when marquee names such as Stephen Hawking and Steven Weinberg thrilled the world with bold expectations. The prophets foretold the birth of the Christchild, known as GUT, the grand unified theory. The Messiah is also called TOE, the theory of everything.

In the minds of talented science writers, the auspicious nativity scene had already taken its shape. All the known universal laws were ready to coalesce into a single primordial presumption, a solitary mathematical statement that would cover everything in the cosmos. Stephen Hawking, upon his accepting the chair of mathematics at Cambridge University, concluded his inaugural address suggesting that computers might soon overtake their human creators and attain the almighty theory on their own. A few years later Hawking dictated the celebrated finale to his fabulously successful book *A Brief History of Time*:

> If we do discover a complete theory, it should in time be understandable in broad principle by everyone, not just a few scientists. Then we shall all, philosophers, scientists, and just ordinary people, be able to take part in the discussion of why it is that we and the universe exist. If we find the answer to that, it would be the ultimate triumph of human reason—for then we would truly know the mind of God.

The biggest selling science books rarely break 100,000 copies. *A Brief History of Time*, however, turned out to be the Big Bang. By the turn of the millennium, it had sold more than 2.5 million copies. Make no mistake—the "mind of God" in the book's last sentence was a sneaky jab. Hawking, known to be an atheist, anticipated that the advent of the ultimate theory would finally rid the world of theism and mystery, once and for all.

Nobel Laureate Steven Weinberg entered the 1980s with a best-selling *The First Three Minutes*. There, while chronicling the initial moments of the universe, he propounded his well-publicized judgment: "The more the universe seems comprehensible, the more it seems pointless." He gave the 1990s an encyclical titled *Dreams of a Final Theory*, spotlighting the drive for GUT—the grand theory of everything. In the same book, the erudite physicist took a rough shot at providence—however conceived. "What kind of divine plan allows the Holocaust and other mass human sufferings?" he protested. What brand of overseer permits this misery?

But Weinberg did admit scientists have their own sticky problem: consciousness. How can there ever be a complete, all-inclusive theory of everything, he conceded, when the existence of consciousness continues to mock the power of physical laws and the omnipotence of physical derivation? At the close of the twentieth century Weinberg observed that dense clouds of GUT and TOE pessimism had set in: "As we make progress understanding the expanding universe, the problem itself expands, so that the solution always seems to recede from us."[10]

Even the upbeat Stephen Hawking, at the start of the new millennium, is tempering his zeal. Back in the 1980s he had predicted a 50:50 chance for TOE to appear before 1999. Now, like Weinberg, he admits to much treading of water: "Although we made great progress in the past 20 years, we don't seem much nearer to our goal."[11] It seems that TOE, the Theory of Everything, has become TON, the Theory of Nothing.

Dare we think that metaphysical investigators may exceed material scientists in commitment to a genuinely inclusive explanation of everything in the cosmos? Vedic adepts would agree. A philosopher at Rutgers University, René Weber, raises the possibility:

> It is mysticism, not science, which pursues the Grand Unified Theory with ruthless logic—the one that includes the questioner within its answer. Although the scientist wants to unify everything in one ultimate equation, he does not want to unify consistently, since he wants to leave himself outside that equation. Of course, with the advent of quantum mechanics, that is far less possible than it was in classical physics. Now observer and

observed are admitted to constitute a unit. But the full meaning of this has not yet caught up with most of the community of scientists who, despite quantum mechanics, believe they can stand aloof from what they work on.[12]

Vedic knowledge is a timely reminder from the inscrutable past that we would do well to put first things first. The Vedic process is to begin by examining what is most near and dear to us: the reality of consciousness. Next, while attempting to discern the laws that govern matter, we might profit by admitting consciousness as an irreducible feature of the universe. That concession should put us hot on the trail of unique laws of nature that regulate consciousness. Then we may become inquisitive of a supreme consciousness and the processes of verification.

The explanatory power of the universal law of karma quite elegantly handles the temporal glories and horrors of life. According to the Vedic version, the eminence of a particular scientist is a reaction to past good karma. Lacking the necessary past actions for present success, another scientist—equally as clever—may struggle in obscurity, and may have to endure others getting the credit for his lifelong work. Or he may even marry a brilliant scientist, and they both receive bounteous funding and facility. Then husband and wife become implicated in handing over nuclear knowledge to the enemy. The couple die in the electric chair, leaving their children bereft. Years later the former enemy nation becomes a friend.

Consciousness is causal and accountable: that is the secret mantra for beginning our Vedic quest. Just as matter has its actions and reactions, so does consciousness. As the main characteristic that distinguishes life from matter, consciousness leads us straight to the *atma*, the fundamental spiritual particle also known as the soul. The Vedas see life as the presence of the *atma*—nonphysical and nonchemical. Therefore the ancient sages would not be surprised that the mathematical laws modern scientists say govern matter fail to extend to life. Consequently, wouldn't it be reasonable to put forth the existence of higher-order natural laws that do govern the phenomenon of life? Since life effectively eludes the chemistry and physics of the living cell, wouldn't its laws also transcend the reach of our existing scientific paradigms and conceptual tools?

The Vedic law of the three modes amply describes the interactions between the symptom of the soul—consciousness—and matter. Certainly it may be revolutionary to posit a direct correlation between our life style and our powers of comprehension. "Do as I say, not as I do," has no place in Vedic culture. The best brains are the best behaved, and vice versa. Though the effects of our behavior on acquiring knowledge of technology may be inapparent, as soon as you crown consciousness the first step in real knowledge, then the relation of life style becomes clearer.

Vedic knowledge of the three modes is indeed humbling. Embarrassed by the shackles of passion and ignorance, we are advised to at least qualify our consciousness in the mode of goodness. Then we may dare begin talk of "the mind of God."

Notes

1   This true incident is taken from Sherwin B. Nuland, *How We Die: Reflections on Life's Final Chapter* (New York: Vintage Books, 1995).

2   Geddes MacGregor, *Reincarnation and Christianity* (Illinois: Quest Books, 1978), p. 12.

3   A full list of cosmic coincidences is available in John Leslie, *Universes* (London: Routledge, 1989), pp. 37–38.

4   Transcript of interview on New Dimensions Radio, available from World Wide Web at http://www.newdimensions.org

5   Piet Hut and Bas van Fraassen, "Elements of Reality: A Dialogue," in *Journal of Consciousness Studies* 4, no. 2 (1997): 167–80.

6   David B. Wolf, *Psychological Reports* 84 (June 1999): 1379–90. The abstract of the article states: "The Vedic Personality Inventory was devised to assess the validity of the Vedic concept of the three *gunas,* or modes of nature, as a psychological categorization system. The sample of 619 subjects consisted of persons of varying ages and occupations from a mid-sized city in the Southeastern United States, and also of subscribers to a magazine focusing on Eastern-style spirituality. The original 90-item VPI was shortened to 56 items on the basis of reliability and validity analyses. Cronbach's alpha for the three subscales ranged from .93 to .94, and the corrected item-total correlation of every item on the VPI with its subscale was greater than .50. Three measures of convergent validity and four measures of discriminant validity provide evidence for the construct validity of the instrument. The loading of every item on the scale was stronger for the intended subscale than for any other subscale. Though each subscale contains congeneric items, the factors are not independent. This non-orthogonality is consistent with Vedic theory. This instrument needs to be tested cross-culturally, and to be experimentally implemented in group research and individual assessment."

7   Werner Heisenberg, *Physics and Philosophy: The Revelation in Modern Science* (New York: Harper and Row, 1958), p. 58.

8   Albert Einstein, *The Meaning of Relativity*, 4th ed. (Princeton: Princeton University Press, 1953), p. 2.

9   John Horgan, *The End of Science* (New York: Broadway Books, 1997), p. 79.

10 Steven Weinberg, "Before the Big Bang," *The New York Review of Books*, 12 June 1997, p. 20.

11 Burt Herman, "Hawking Awaits Unified Theory Proof," Associated Press, 21 July 1999.

12 René Weber, *Dialogues with Scientists and Sages: The Search for Unity* (New York: Routledge, 1986), p. 10.

CHAPTER 9

DEEP COSMOLOGY: MATTER AND BEYOND

You place matter before life and you decide that matter has existed for all eternity. How do you know that the incessant progress of science will not compel scientists to consider that life has existed during eternity, and not matter? You pass from matter to life because your intelligence of today cannot conceive things otherwise. How do you know that in ten thousand years one will not consider it more likely that matter has emerged from life? Louis Pasteur (1822–95)[1]

The Vedic universe swarms with life and intelligence. What a relief to hear a cosmology that does not isolate the planet Earth and its residents from the rest of the cosmos. Naturally, we want to hear about the interrelationships between the various planets and peoples. In this way, we earthlings stop being aliens—strange creatures who have alienated ourselves from universal life.

Because Vedic cosmology is inextricably bound up with the spiritual, it transcends what we know as science. Those choosing to participate in special procedures for acquiring and experiencing spiritual knowledge gain entrance to the depths of Vedic science. Needless to say, our own type of science is not free from steep entry barriers. It imposes insurmountable physical limitations. For instance, the Big Bang Theory obviously forces us into deep water, far over our heads. How will we ever know why the so-called "Big Bang" happened, and what preceded it? With our limited intelligence and senses, we will never know, because the origin of the universe is too far from us in time and space.

Even within this universe, how will we understand life on distant planets and stars? To try and visit life on the nearest star, Alpha Centauri, would take a spacecraft ten times more powerful than what we have now. It would have to go one million miles an hour to get there in three thousand years.

How will we know whether there are other dimensions in space and time besides ours? Do other universes exist? The sixteenth-century Italian philosopher Giordano Bruno, among others before him, speculated that a countless number of isolated universes might exist, each with its own laws. Today it is fashionable to posit a plurality of universes. A stylish Western cosmological saying is that a universe is something that happens now and then. The Vedic view, however, goes far beyond that rate of occurrence. Universes are cheap and plentiful—like grains of sand at the beach. Here is a summary of Vedic extraterrestrial themes:

- Intelligent life abounds on other planets, many of which have civilizations far more advanced than anything Earth ever had.
- The sun is indeed the center of the universe—amidst many planets that cannot be detected by human eyes or instruments.
- Interplanetary communication and travelling is as routine as calling from a street payphone or cycling to a neighborhood shop. Previous civilizations on Earth were in constant contact with other planets.
- Not all extraterrestrials are benign. Some regions or dimensions

of the universe are the domain of negative entities—dedicated enemies of spiritual truth.

- The first living entities in the universe are the most intelligent, and their life spans and habitats far exceed our paltry understanding. These superior entities have the immediate responsibility for arranging and maintaining life throughout the universe. They do not, however, bear the ultimate responsibility. They are only agents of an ultimate conscious source. Life comes from life.

- Countless universes exist, like bubbles in sea foam. They vary in size, and are walled off from one another by immense layers of gross and subtle matter.

Though Vedic narrations of interplanetary and interspecies affairs are unrivalled in descriptive power, actually they are just the doorsteps of the full cosmology. For the trusting adherent, the voyage to the ultimate conscious source is the greatest thrill in store. Beyond planets of gross and astral matter, outside the innumerable universes of time and space, lies the final stop in the journey—a realm of pure spiritual consciousness, where no matter exists. The Vedas say only there, where we attain the full transcendental perspective, can we accurately perceive why and how universes of matter arise in the first place.

Consciousness Makes Things Happen

We live in a reality where matter and consciousness coexist. How is this possible? Resolving the apparent matter–spirit duality lies at the heart of Vedic cosmology. The Western paradigm, stressing the primacy of matter, is breaking down under stress. It commands, "Begin with matter!" On the other hand, the Vedic texts have always instructed that we begin with consciousness.

Let's say you've lived in darkness all your life. Chances are that when you finally encounter some light, you'll think it a product of darkness. But the person with superior understanding knows that darkness sets in after the original light dims or is blocked.

Similarly, the hard-core materialist, absorbed in matter, thinks it logical that everything comes from matter. The Vedic-trained person, however, asserts that consciousness is a fundamental feature of reality—not a by-product of inert, unconscious elements. Matter is viewed as the shadow energy of the supreme consciousness. When ignorance of the supreme consciousness sets in, matter appears to be the all-in-all.

Westerners cannot deny that, especially in the past two centuries, zealous faith in the primacy of matter is the hallmark of their attempt at knowledge. The conviction is that when we completely comprehend materialism—space-time-matter-energy—then we will understand everything in the universe. This *a priori* assumption reigns as the grand paradigm: the worldview that underlies all other worldviews.

Though fabulously successful within a narrow spectrum of technological prediction and control, the "matter-first-and-only" paradigm has little to say about consciousness. The reality of consciousness is apparent to us all; yet actually nothing in physicalist science says that living organisms should be conscious, or why. The way the current grand paradigm sees it, consciousness is a vexing anomaly—a major misfit in a cosmic puzzle we hoped our best scientists had almost solved.

The ancient Vedic standpoint reverses the modern position. Consciousness—the energy of the nonmaterial soul, and the symptom of the soul's existence—is considered primary. Matter is deemed secondary. Said another way, what the Western outlook holds to be fundamental—inanimate matter, physicality—the Vedas relegate to the status of a derivative, almost an extenuating, circumstance. In Sanskrit matter is referred to as *dvitiya*—"the second."

The preliminary Vedic methodology presented in Chapter 4

helps illuminate the Vedic interplay between the body and the conscious, nonmaterial, immeasurably minute soul. To understand the cosmos, Vedic-directed logic encourages us to use our intelligence in the same way. The Upanishads give us a strong hint: *anor aniyan mahato mahiyan*. "The Supreme Absolute Truth is present as the tiny living entity as well as the immense universe."[2] The direct implication is that first we can try to understand ourselves, the tiny living entity. We can analyze what are the components of our existence, what is the active principle. To successfully investigate ourselves as minute units will lead directly to our understanding the universe, as an immense whole. That genuine holistic comprehension will entail knowing what are the basic components of the universe, and what is its active principle—what makes the laws of nature produce effects.

Modern astrophysicists, from their materialistic perspective, often assert roughly the same proposition. We cannot understand the universe, the macrocosmic, they tell us, unless we understand the microcosmic, the subatomic realm. But their reductionism has left consciousness completely out of the picture. And of those who do consider it, most have faith that it is physical—though they lack evidence.

We know that consciousness is the only thing we *directly* experience; it is the utter necessity for knowledge of anything, whether subatomic or universal. Scientific reductionism proposes that by our understanding parts, we will understand the whole. But leaving consciousness out of an analysis of the micro engenders monumental problems. Certainly at least the same enormity of problems will render futile any attempts to comprehend the macro.

Vedic-directed logic proposes that we can parlay genuine cognizance of the living entity into knowledge of the entire universe. What you find in the living entity indicates what exists in the cosmos as a whole. The classic verse from the *Katha Upanishad*, *anor aniyan mahato mahiyan*, tries to nudge us in the right direction: since you find consciousness in the tiny living entity, you should also look for consciousness on a grand cosmic scale.

The Vedic science presents that our bodies are like small universes. Just as the bodies of the living entities are instruments of consciousness, similarly the universe is also the instrument of consciousness. That means the principle of the soul is essential not only for our existence on the microcosmic scale, but also for universal functions on the macrocosmic scale.

Why wince at suggestions that nature adheres to conscious direction? From the Vedic perspective, the body is an amazing physiological device, and the universe is an amazing cosmological device. The obvious difference is that one is miniature, the other immense. If we can understand that the miracle of consciousness directs our minuscule physical system, the body, then why is it fantasy to contemplate how that same miracle—materially inexplicable—may activate and direct planets, natural functions, and the entire universe?

In other words, to grasp the Vedic view, we should consider that consciousness is causative. Whether on the micro or macro scale, it makes things happen. This concept, though elementary in the Vedas, is on some scholars' shortlist for the next major revolution in Western knowledge. True, the majority of scientists rarely think about this issue. Nevertheless, some of the greatest brains on the cutting edge of science are calling into question Western assumptions about basic reality held almost blindly for several centuries. Stressing the primacy of consciousness, these scientists are considering the likelihood that the mysterious substance consciousness indeed "makes things happen."

Contemplating consciousness as causal draws the Western *avant-garde* quite near to Vedic civilization. For example, neuroscientist Roger Sperry, awarded a Nobel Prize in 1981 for split-brain research, published a ground-breaking paper in 1987 entitled "The Structure and Significance of the Conscious Revolution in

Science."[3] He presented the observation that the world of every-day affairs involves two kinds of causation. One he calls "upward causation." It is the usual concept we have all imbibed from Western education. The billiard balls of cosmic minutia—whether particles, waves, atoms, or molecules—bump into one another and interact. The subsequent microcosmic reactions—hidden to nonscientists—all add up to something happening on the macro-cosmic level—visible to everyone.

For instance, inside the cylinder of a car, molecular interaction causes combustion. The gas molecules expand, forcing the piston to move. The crankshaft revolves and ultimately the car backs out of the driveway and travels to the nearest motorway. This scientific mode of analysis, always championed in the West, is quite familiar to us. Ingrained in the Western belief system is the fundamental notion that the physical interaction of minutia causes all larger realities.

The second concept of causality, "downward causation," has been long neglected by scientists—though championed by the ancient Vedas. In brief, Sperry explains that my car's engine turns over and then the vehicle moves out onto the street because I decide to visit relatives for the day. In other words, *my consciousness* caused a complex chain of actions and interactions—on both the micro and macro scales. Consciousness, the Nobel Laureate states, is a "causal reality." He goes on to say not only that causality involves consciousness, but also that consciousness is qualitatively different from matter.

To those fixed in the physicalist grand paradigm, Sperry's contemporary proposal and the ancient Vedic axioms are odd—just like the notion of a solar system four hundred years ago.

Brahman and Beyond

Complete confidence that matter is all that matters leads to the conviction that the Vedic sages and their texts are irrelevant. The hardened materialist dismisses Vedic scientific information, wondering: "What are these aborigines talking about? Who needs it!" The most prolific author in the twentieth century, science writer Isaac Asimov, sarcastically shared that view. Author of over two hundred books, he charged that sentimentalists will always glorify ancient sages as the original knowers of theories that modern scientists have constructed only through painstaking trial and error. The dreamy ancient mystics, as Asimov sees them—"with their eyes closed and their intuitions working"—deserve scant credit.

> Whatever conclusions scientists arrive at concerning anything, it remains always possible to quote some item in Eastern speculation or Celtic mythology or African folklore or Greek philosophy, that sounds the same.
>
> The implication, on making the comparison, is that scientists are foolishly wasting a lot of money and effort in finding out what those clever Eastern (Celtic, African, Greek) sages knew all along. For instance, there are exactly three things that might be happening to the universe in the long run:
> - The universe may be unchanging on the whole and therefore have neither a beginning nor an end.
> - The universe may be changing progressively, that is, in one direction only and therefore have a distinct beginning and a different end.
> - The universe may be changing cyclically, back and forth, and therefore ends at the beginning and starts over.
>
> All the sages who have speculated on the universe intuitively must come up with one of these three alternatives. . . . At present, scientists are inclined to accept the second alternative. . . . What characterizes the value of science, however, is not the particular conclusions it comes to. They are sharply limited in

number, and guesswork will get you the "right" answer with better odds than you'll find at the racetrack. What characterizes the value of science is its methodology, the system it uses to arrive at those conclusions. A hundred sages, though speaking ever so wisely, can never offer anything more persuasive than an imperative "Believe!"[4]

A materialist never acknowledges the Vedic transcendental methodology, the techniques employed to experience the Vedic conclusions. Though the devotees of matter, of course, have passionate faith in matter, they imagine that they alone rely upon procedural verification—they think the sages depend only on luck and belief. Meanwhile, whether based on faith in matter or empiricism in matter, no scientist can adequately even begin to explain the presence of consciousness in the cosmos.

The Vedas teach that conscious energy pervades the universe. The literature asserts that from the subatomic level to the cosmic level and even beyond, you'll find it everywhere. The Chandogya Upanishad says, *Sarvam khalv idam brahma*, or "Consciousness, indicative of the spiritual energy, is limitless in its presence."[5] That all-pervading spiritual energy is known in the Vedas as *Brahman*, a term now found in many dictionaries—though rarely defined correctly. The Vedas tell us that because *Brahman* is not subject to material analysis, therefore its telltale evidence, consciousness, cannot be dissected.

The Vedic presentation of *Brahman* enchanted some of the twentieth century's most influential physicists. Austrian Nobel Laureate Erwin Schrödinger was a great fan of the Vedas, especially the Upanishads. He found in *Brahman* clear affirmation for his conceptions of "One Mind." David Bohm used *Brahman* to formulate his idea of the "explicate order and implicate order." Bohm's implicate order is the undifferentiated source of all the temporary, explicit varieties of the cosmic manifestation.

Brahman, according to the Vedas, exists beyond the perception of the senses. It has no material qualities or characteristics. Thus it is incapable of material description. Lying beyond the cause and effect of the material cosmos, it is eternal, limitless, beginningless, immutable, and unchanging. Matter, once again, is *dvitiya*, "the second." The energy of matter is temporary and inferior—a shadowy manifestation of *Brahman*. Matter depends on *Brahman* just as shadows in daytime depend on the sunlight.

According to the Vedic texts, the entire material universe and its material ingredients are but a temporary emanation of the Supreme Truth. The variegated material manifestations of the cosmos—subatomic phenomena, atoms, bodies, planets, space—are not ultimate causes in themselves, nor are they eternal. All of them are said to emanate from the eternal *Brahman*. The *Mundaka Upanishad* (1.1.7) says:

> As a web is expanded and withdrawn by a spider, as plants grow from the Earth, and as hair grows from a living person's head and body, so this universe is generated from the inexhaustible Supreme Absolute Truth.

Another Upanishad, the *Taittiriya* (3.1), states:

> Brahman, the Absolute Truth, is the original source of the material cosmos and of the living entities also—the nonmaterial souls. Everything is created by Brahman; after creation, maintained by Brahman; and after annihilation, conserved in Brahman.

For the sake of those whose spiritual understanding is only gradually awakening, the Vedas, especially the Upanishads, sometimes speak in general terms about an omnipresent spiritual consciousness and the *Brahman* it indicates. Sometimes there seems to be no distinguishing between the purely spiritual living entity and the Supreme—between the finite consciousness and the infinite consciousness. Hence, people hear these preliminary Vedic verses about *Brahman* and think they've heard the deepest knowledge the Vedas can reveal. They love to recite catchy fragments, ripped out of their proper context in the Upanishads: "Thou art That, I am That, and all this is That." Many swoon when they read the famous Vedic subordinate mantra *tat tvam asi*—"You are that *Brahman*."[6] They rejoice, "Just see! We are all the Supreme!"

Westerners have a standard misunderstanding of religious and metaphysical systems originating east of the Arabian Sea. We think they all stress monism. Supposedly everything Eastern pushes us to merge into nondistinction—the "ultimate attainment." Kenneth Kramer, a well-published American professor of comparative religion, says, "The afterlife traveler seeks to relinquish the will, to become unattached from the idea of the individual." Like so many other misreaders of Vedic philosophy, Kramer believes that a common aim of "fusion with higher consciousness" is present in all Eastern spiritual knowledge. "The goal of the journey is to let go of everything that keeps us separate from everything else."[7]

Inexperienced readers like to interpret that "since we are all *Brahman*, spiritual, that means we are all the One." "We are the limitless," they think. "We are the all-pervading, the infinite." Some even say that, as pure consciousness, we are the ultimate movers of the sun, the moon, the universe, and so forth.

Yes, the Vedas agree, consciousness, the soul's radiance, is extraordinarily causal. But the living entities—whether pure or illusioned—are eternally limited. Even in their pure state, they don't have the potency the Supreme possesses. On the other hand, the Supreme Consciousness, their controller and maintainer, is eternally in another category: omnipotent—limitless potential.

Vedic sages point out that the Vedas seem to promulgate the *Brahman* vision of nondistinction just to attract us away from matter-ism. Our hang-up has been our dogmatic acceptance of matter as inconceivable, as causal. Through *Brahman*, at least—if nothing else—we will accept the existence of a conscious, causative spiritual reality that is eternally beyond all material inertia. The Upanishads, as pointed out in Chapter 4, specialize in this task of metaphysical introduction. Western savants find the Upanishads' descriptions of inconceivable, qualityless *Brahman* so intriguing that many times they have no appetite to look further. But, in every Upanishad describing an impersonal spiritual dimension, somewhere the fuller understanding is clearly explained.

To accurately appreciate the Vedic tenet of consciousness as causal, our exploration into the Vedic world should not miss the complete presentation. An analogy of golden jewelry and a gold mine will help this discussion of *Brahman*. If we just talk about the gold that jewelry wearers and mine owners possess, all the owners of gold are equal, they all share in gold. Certainly it's nice to be alerted to this commonality. But as soon as we start talking quantity, that sameness immediately disappears. And the Upanishads do talk quantity. The *Katha Upanishad* (2.2.13) proclaims:

> Among all the eternal beings there is one supreme eternal. Of all conscious beings, there is one supreme consciousness. This supreme entity supplies the needs of everyone else. Wise souls who worship Him in His abode attain everlasting peace. Others cannot.

Among the causal conscious entities, qualitative equality is certain. Therefore the Sanskrit word *atma*, spirit self, can refer to both the Supreme and the living entities. Both are eternally conscious individuals—free from material deterioration, destruction, and contamination. Both are the causal consciousness of external bodies—whether a human body, a planet, or a universe.

The Supreme Self is infinite, and the living entities are finite, extremely small. Clearly, the Upanishads are telling us that one soul is predominant and the others are dependent, subordinate. There is oneness in quality but separateness in quantity.

SUPERCONSCIOUSNESS

What is the nature of the Ultimate Consciousness, the Supreme Causal Agent? The Vedic literatures declare that the one and same Supreme Absolute Truth is known according to three different levels of spiritual understanding. Knowing about these three tiers helps to clear away the misperception that the Vedas are a grab bag of assorted doctrines. Unskilled readers, even professors, often think that each text presents its own god, gods, or ultimate. When the literature is seen through the zoom lens of its own three perspectives, then the internal beauty of its unity and cohesiveness unfolds before our eyes.

The first level is the impersonal spiritual oneness, *Brahman*. The second level is *Paramatma*—the Supersoul in every microcosmic or macrocosmic structural unit. The last level is the all-attractive Supreme Infinite Person. These views of the same Supreme are known in Sanskrit as *Brahman*, *Paramatma*, and *Bhagavan*.

To help us fathom this three-tiered experience of the ultimate activating consciousness, Vedic teachers like to give the example of a mountain seen three different ways. From far off, we see the mountain as a hazy, indistinct object. As we draw nearer, we see that the mountain has a distinct shape and form. Finally, upon arriving at the mountain itself, we experience its full diversity. We see houses and roads, as well as vegetation, people, and animals.

Seeing Transcendence from far off means that through self-discipline, sense control, and rigorous metaphysical inquiry, a rare person can become totally aware of a universal spiritual energy. The Vedic texts explain that the temporary appearances of the cosmos are founded upon this inconceivably dazzling, impersonal spiritual potency. Experiencing it is called *Brahman* realization.

The Vedas rate this attainment as very preliminary and incomplete. They say that *Brahman* is as far as we can get without divine help. For that reason many ascetics and metaphysicians—as well as their Western admirers—do not go further. They do not penetrate through the indistinction to distinction. In fact, they misconstrue the all-pervasive haze of spiritual energy as all there is: "We are It and It is us." Further progress, however, is necessary.

The next stage, drawing nearer, is *Paramatma* realization. In this second stage, the spiritual seeker starts to see differentiation in the light of *Brahman*. Awareness of the difference between the two selves, the two *atmas*, begins to dawn. The individual soul, known as the *jivatma*, is seen as minute in comparison to the Supreme Soul, known as the *Paramatma*. The word *parama* means "supreme, over and above." From the Vedic view, the *Paramatma*—the Supersoul—is the presence of the Supreme, the Complete Whole, within the finite. Everything microcosmic or macrocosmic—even the universe itself—is said to contain the Supreme as Supersoul. The Vedas point out that if the unlimited cannot dwell within the limited, then obviously there would be incompleteness, a deficiency in the Supreme. The following verse appears in several Upanishads:

> The one Supreme Lord lives hidden inside all created things. He pervades all matter and sits within the hearts of all living beings. As the indwelling Supersoul, He supervises their material activities. Thus, while having no material qualities Himself, He is the unique witness and giver of consciousness.[8]

The source of consciousness can only be consciousness. Matter, the shadow, has no potency of its own, the Vedas declare. Though Lord *Paramatma*, the Supersoul, resides in everything—from atomic entities to the universe as a whole—material conditions do not affect Him. This Vedic reality of Lord *Paramatma* is easier to comprehend when we first learn to consider Him as the companion to the soul in our body. The *Bhagavad-gita* (13.28) states:

> One who sees the Supersoul accompanying the individual soul in all bodies, and who understands that neither the soul nor the Supersoul within the destructible body is ever destroyed, actually sees.

The minute being, the *jivatma*, lives in its particular body. The Supersoul, the *Paramatma*, however, is all-pervading. Because the Vedas present the two as one in spirit, confusion may arise in our understanding them. Therefore the simultaneous nondual and dual relationship cannot be overstated.

A common misconception holds that the Vedic references to soul and Supersoul merely describe two aspects of our own self. Supposedly the soul refers to the lower self, and the Supersoul to the higher self. Both are mistaken to be the same entity. Again, we must keep in mind that the Vedas do clearly point out the individuality of the two knowers in the body.

Again, while lauding the qualitative oneness of causal consciousness, the Upanishads openly distinguish between the superior and inferior agents of consciousness, the *Paramatma* and *jivatma*. Often enough, the literature describes this duality in unequivocal terms:

> Two companion birds sit together in the shelter of the same tree. One of them is relishing the taste of the tree's berries, while the other refrains from eating and instead watches over His friend.[9]

In this analogy the two birds are the soul and the Supersoul. The tree is the body, and the tastes of the berries are the varieties of sense pleasure available to the living entity in the material cosmos. *Paramatma* is the watching bird, guiding the embodied souls, witnessing their activities in material existence, arranging everyone's just desserts—the reactions to their actions.

According to the Vedas, erudition in metaphysical studies will not gain for us a vision of the Supersoul, the undivided that is present in all the divided. Awareness of the Supersoul in the core of every living entity is the goal of mystic yoga, *ashtanga-yoga*. Very dedicated practitioners of this mystic yoga—laced with a devotional attitude—attain this higher level. They can see the inconceivably beautiful transcendental form of the Supersoul in their heart and meditate upon Him. They know that owing to the presence of the Lord in the heart, the living entity can exercise cognizance and discrimination.

Furthermore, knowing that the Supersoul accompanies the minute soul in every kind of material body allows the accomplished yogi to see all living beings equally, regardless of species. This oneness of vision, the Vedas say, is the mark of a truly wise person.

> One who sees the Supersoul equally present everywhere, in every living being, does not degrade himself by his mind. Thus he approaches the transcendental destination. (*Bhagavad-gita* 13.29)

THE SUPREME ENJOYER

A civilization based on the Vedic literature would never accept matter as independently potent. The Vedas know the energy of soul as the power behind all structures and functions in the cosmos—and the cosmos itself. What activates the body to grow also activates the universe to expand. Grasping the crucial difference in conscious potency between the finite soul and the infinite soul paves the way for our hearing about the summit of Vedic knowledge: the personal attributes of *Bhagavan*, the Supreme Opulent One.

Vedic culture esteemed most highly those persons who attained this third stage of spiritual advancement, *Bhagavan* realization. Among strict followers of the Vedic tradition, this special recognition continues to this day. *Bhagavan* realization is the theistic experience of the Supreme Truth as the Supreme Infinite Person—possessed of inconceivable qualities, attributes, and activities. The Vedic literature asserts that *Bhagavan* realization is the most complete understanding of the Supreme—the last stop in our spiritual evolution.

When the progressive searcher realizes *Bhagavan*, he simultaneously realizes *Brahman* and *Paramatma*. These other two aspects are said to be not separate from *Bhagavan*; they culminate in *Bhagavan* and are present within. *Bhaga* means opulences and *van* means possessor. In correct Vedic usage, the full sense of the word can apply only to the Godhead, the Supreme Entity, the Conscious Cause of all causes.

The Vedic texts *Vedanta-sutra* and *Bhagavata Purana* both echo each other in enunciating that the Absolute is the source of everything. We should note that when the Vedas say everything emanates from Supreme Truth, these scriptures indeed mean *everything*: intelligence, consciousness, personality, form, qualities, activities, and so forth. How can the finite living entities possess something the Infinite lacks? The crucial difference, however, is that the Supreme displays pure and infinite personal existence— free from the limitations of mundane individuality and mundane qualities.

At a cursory glance, the Vedic personal understanding of the Absolute Truth may seem naively simple: "Oh, yes—someone like me, just much bigger." We should know, however, that because the attributes of *Bhagavan* have nothing to do with the material cosmos, *Bhagavan* realization can be very difficult to master.

The Vedas prescribe a thorough education, to prepare the ground for comprehending nonmaterial personality and form.

Immature minds have the habit of trespassing. Therefore, to fresh recruits, the Vedic texts offer *Brahman*—the Absolute Truth devoid of material attributes or qualities. Neophytes can find negativistic relief in the absence of all features of material existence. In *Bhagavan* realization, though, the most advanced transcendentalists relish the pure spiritual personal attributes of *Bhagavan*. As the *Taittereya Upanishad* states, *Raso vai sah*, or "The Supreme Absolute Truth, in all its fullness, is the reservoir of all spiritual personal tastes."[10]

The highest Vedic vision reveals the supreme consciousness as the active source of absolute pleasure. More than the prime mover of the cosmos, greater than the witness of the living entities, *Bhagavan* is the prime conscious initiator of eternal spiritual relationships. Self-sufficiently existing for His own enjoyment, *Bhagavan* is said to enliven His parts and parcels, the living entities, through dynamic, eternal spiritual bliss: *ananda*. Nevertheless, we should keep in mind that the other two aspects—*Brahman* and *Paramatma*—are also found in *Bhagavan*. The one Transcendental Entity is seen from different angles of vision and—most importantly—different degrees of completeness.

References to all three visions will be found throughout all Vedic texts, but some texts have their speciality. The Upanishads can seem to focus on *Brahman*. The literature on mystic yoga, the *yoga-sutras*, highlights *Paramatma*. The *Bhagavad-gita* and *Bhagavata Purana* soar to *Bhagavan*. Only those properly introduced to the *Bhagavan* pinnacle can begin to understand Krishna. Especially the *Bhagavad-gita* and the *Bhagavata Purana* award knowledge of Krishna. In Sanskrit *Krishna* means "the all-attractive reservoir of transcendental pleasure." An expert Vedic guide can demonstrate how Krishna, the Supreme Absolute Truth, is found throughout all the Vedas.

Krishna, who is also known as Govinda [He who delights the spiritual senses], is the supreme controller. He has an eternal, blissful, spiritual body. He is the origin of all. He has no other origin, for He is the prime cause of all causes. (*Brahma-samhita* 5.1)

We have seen that the Vedic literature gives us a spellbinding and profound vision of consciousness as causative—the true active agent. Both the soul and Supreme Soul energize inert matter, although the Supreme Soul is always the predominator. As we learned from the Upanishads, *Anor aniyam mahato mahiyan*, or "The Supreme Absolute Truth can be found throughout the whole range of existence, from the minuscule part to the cosmic whole."

Inert matter is accepted as an energy of the Supreme, and so is consciousness. It is not that they come into being as the result of some kind of timebound sequence. The Vedic picture is that, as energies, matter and spirit always exist. Because the material world imposes limitations upon our perception, we are prone to think of energy "coming into being."

The Vedas instruct us that when spiritual consciousness energizes matter, then matter has the potential to display its innumerable actions and reactions. The Vedas are firm that matter has no initiative of its own. The literature never accepts material nature as the ultimate cause of the cosmic manifestation. Nowhere do the Vedas allow us to think of material nature and its components as independent or self-activating. The Supreme is always the predominator of spirit and matter.

Whether micro or macro, everything is sustained and activated by spirit soul. Both the living entity and the Supersoul are fully conscious. We are conscious of our bodily existence, and the Supersoul is conscious of the gigantic cosmic manifestation. Because of the soul's presence within the body, the life processes work; similarly, because of the Supersoul's presence within the universe, the laws of nature have effect.

The material world is the shadow facsimile of the spiritual world. The Vedas assert that proper procedure will allow us to verify and attain the spiritual world. Many Vedic literatures introduce this pure realm of infinity and variety. The *Bhagavata Purana*, also known as the *Shrimad-Bhagavatam*, elaborately describes the spiritual world. There is no inanimate matter in this realm— everything is composed of pure personal consciousness.

Notes

1 Quoted in Robert Keith Wallace, *The Neurophysiology of Enlightenment* (Maharishi International University of Management, 1991), p. 24.

2 *Katha Upanishad* 1.2.20.

3 Roger Sperry, "Structure and Significance of the Consciousness Revolution in Science," *Journal of Mind and Behavior* 8 , no. 1 (Winter 1987): 37–66.

4 Asimov, Isaac, "Scientists and Sages," *New York Times Book Review*, 27 July 1978.

5 *Chandogya Upanishad* 3.14.1.

6 *Chandogya Upanishad* 6.8.7.

7 "Beyond Death and Dying," *Omni*, Autumn 1995, p. 65.

8 *Shvetashvatara* (6.11), *Gopala-tapani* (Uttara 97), and *Brahma* (4.1) *Upanishads.*

9 *Shvetashvatara Upanishad* (4.6), *Mundaka Upanishad* (3.1.1–2).

10 *Taittiriya Upanishad* 2.7.1.

CHAPTER 10

VEDIC TIME

~

U nlike time in both the Judeo-Christian religious tradition and the current view of modern science, Vedic time is cyclic. What goes around comes around. What goes up must come down, and vice versa. The Vedic universe passes through repetitive cycles. Moreover, the entire cosmos itself undergoes recurring cycles of creation and destruction. During the annihilation of the universe, energy is conserved, to manifest again in the next creation.

Our contemporary knowledge embraces a version of change and progress that is linear. The saga of the universe proceeds in a straight line, beginning at unique point A and ending at unique point B. Obviously, because this modern conception of time differs so markedly from the Vedic vision, we would expect to find two significantly different approaches to life.

Our scene for gaining admittance to the world of Vedic time is a great gathering of sages near the Himalayas, in a forest still known today as Naimisharanya. From the modern Indian city Lucknow, you can take a train to a station called Nimsar. In the vicinity is the forest of Naimisharanya. The approximate date of the meeting there is five thousand years ago, at the onset of what the Vedas refer to as Kali-yuga, or the Age of Quarrel—the worst age of the cycle of four Vedic ages.

Looking into the future, the assembled sages, as relayed in the *Shrimad-Bhagavatam*, knew what was nearing. Based on their knowledge of cosmic cycles, they wanted to prepare themselves and humanity, so they convened in the forest for a meeting of marathon duration. How can the population best survive the coming Iron Age, with its notorious focus on machines, machine-like people, and mechanistic thinking? At Naimisharanya the best brains deliberated on this crisis, for the welfare of society.

In accord with Vedic methodology, the assembled sages recognized the most advanced transcendental scholar and yogi among them and deferred their judgment to him. Publicly avowing the qualifications of this chief sage, Suta Goswami, they noted his complete freedom from vice and erudition in the Vedic texts. In addition to his status as the eldest sadhu, he had been duly certified by his own preceptor in disciplic succession. That blessing meant Suta Goswami was *Bhagavan* realized—he knew what lay beyond impersonal *Brahman* and the Supersoul. The sages, confident that their choice was a genuine master of spiritual science, prompted him for a pronouncement:

O learned one, in this iron age of Kali men have but short lives. They are quarrelsome, lazy, misguided, unlucky and, above all, always disturbed. (*Shrimad-Bhagavatam* 1.1.10)

The Vedic cycle of *yugas* entails civilization beginning in an enlightened, advanced state and then gradually sinking to the pits of chaos and ignorance. Once the bottom of the cycle is reached, the cycle starts anew. Then Earth becomes populated with people in an original state of purity and astounding knowledge, as the same progression repeats.

The preceding ages, *yugas*, were known sequentially as Satya-yuga, Treta-yuga, and Dvapara-yuga—or the Golden, Silver, and Bronze Ages. As the darkness of Kali-yuga began to fall, the sages braced themselves for what would inevitably ensue: the rapid demise of all the finer qualities of humanity.

Organized spiritual development, the bulwark of previous *yugas*, would die a quick death—hastened by social institutions that militate against self-realization. Colossal wars, at the slightest misunderstanding, would become routine events. As economic development and sensuality became the heart and soul of society, the people's intellect and physical strength would shrink—and their life span too.

The eventual collapse of family structure and social harmony would lay bare the battered individual to face the hailstorms of confusion alone. The mystic and psychic powers commonplace in previous *yugas* would become extinct. Higher beings, who frequented Earth in other ages, would cease their visits. All Vedic knowledge of subtle, astral technology would almost disappear. Worst of all, the transcendental conclusions of the Vedas would become obscured. In short, both individually and collectively, constant disturbance and anxiety would be the standard of the day.

The chief sage Suta Goswami had become preeminently qualified by submitting to his preceptor. Therefore the sages at Naimisharanya knew they would only benefit by submitting to him. In this way, they in turn became preeminently qualified to teach.

We think that we have met Your Goodness by the will of providence, just so that we may accept you as captain of the ship for those who desire to cross the difficult ocean of Kali, which deteriorates all the good qualities of a human being. (*Shrimad-Bhagavatam* 1.1.22)

Here is the Vedic process of acquiring knowledge through disciplic succession, a chain that traces itself beyond the cosmos, to *Bhagavan* Himself. The Vedic injunction is *acintya khalu te bhava*: no need to waste time arguing or speculating about things beyond the range of the senses and intellect. Just find a qualified authority and, through hearing, learn what is beyond the limited. Then adjust your life style according to what you hear, and you will experience what you hear. By this process today's student becomes tomorrow's master, and in this way Vedic knowledge perpetuates itself.

THE FOUR SEASONS OF THE UNIVERSE

Understanding the *yuga*-cycle takes us once again to the three modes of nature. The four Vedic millennia are manifestations of these modes. In the best period, Satya-yuga, also known as the Age of Truth, the mode of goodness predominates: vice is almost unknown. The worst era, Kali-yuga, is the antithesis: virtue is almost unknown. In that Age of Quarrel, the mode of ignorance reigns. In the intervening two *yugas*, either passion is dominant (Treta), or a blend of passion and ignorance (Dvapara). Vice enters in the second *yuga*, spreads in the third, and saturates the fourth.

Satya-yuga

The Age of Truth is the crown of material existence, the best of times. Today we would think it heavenly—a paradise lost. The Vedic view, however, holds that although pristine and sublime, Satya-yuga still is within the purview of material existence. In this first age, the minds of all the people are described as self-effulgent—brilliant in clarity and spiritual perception. Humanity delights in spiritual knowledge and austerity. "The people of Satya-yuga are for the most part self-satisfied, merciful, friendly to all, peaceful, sober, and tolerant. They take their pleasure from within, see all things equally, and always endeavor diligently for spiritual perfection." (*Shrimad-Bhagavatam* 12.3.19) Generally everyone's mind, intelligence, and senses are solidly fixed in the mode of goodness—at the very least. Most of the population, though, are *paramahamsas*, transcendentalists beyond even the mode of goodness.

At that time, because of the extremely exalted intelligence of humanity, the Vedic information was said to be available compressed into one Veda, rather than a proliferation of many texts. According to Vedic tradition, as the *yuga* cycle progressed, the same compacted Vedic information became expanded into many explanatory branches. We should note, however, that from the Vedic viewpoint this pragmatic expansion does not imply the assimilation or creation of new doctrines. The waning intellectual powers of humanity required an expansive elucidation. Hence the same concise Vedic codes were elaborated upon at length, making their comprehension easier for lesser brains.

Treta-yuga

The second age fosters devotion to what we would consider colossal rituals of sacrifice and extraordinary austerities. In Treta-yuga, the transcendentalists are no longer the numerical majority, though their effect still predominates. Most of the population are brahmins, religious intellectuals. The mode of passion, however, begins to gain the upper hand. Therefore, to accommodate a humanity that generally lives under the influence of the three modes, the complete Vedic social system for progressive development unfolds, and the Vedas themselves begin to unfurl into branches. People diligently execute the Vedic formulas for religiosity, economic growth, and disciplined gratification of their senses. On this gradual path of advancement, however, their performance is marred by ulterior motives, especially by the desire for prestige. Nevertheless, they are free from excesses of lust and anger.

Dvapara-yuga

The third age brings about glory and nobility, with all the accompanying excesses of passion. In addition to religious intellectuals, the population also contains large numbers of the Vedic martial and administrative class. The people devote themselves to Vedic study as well as extraordinary wealth, fame, and power. Large families are common, and humanity enjoys life with gusto and zest—while clinging to Vedic guidelines. Because the mode of ignorance has begun to seep in, Dvapara-yuga has the qualities of passion tinged with some ignorance. Greed, selfishness, dissatisfaction, false pride, hypocrisy, and envy become more prevalent.

Kali-yuga: The Age of Quarrel

We get the most descriptions for this age because it is so far from what the Vedas deem the standard. Seen from the Vedic perspective, the Age of Kali is the most perverse—the diametric opposite of the Golden Age of Truth. According to Vedic chronology, we are 5,000 years into the total 432,000 years of Kali-yuga, which thoroughly destroys any remaining good qualities in humanity. "Religion, truthfulness, cleanliness, tolerance, mercy, duration of life, physical strength, and memory will all diminish day by day because of the powerful influence of the Age of Kali." (*Shrimad-Bhagavatam* 12.2.1) Whereas in previous ages, either transcendentalists or religious intellectuals or noble statesmen predominated, in the Iron Age, what the Vedas consider the mentality of crude laborers and barbarians becomes the norm.

Because the descriptions of Kali-yuga are much more than for the other *yugas*, what follows is a twofold approach to discussing life in the Iron Age of Darkness. First is a series of verses from one of the chapters in *Shrimad-Bhagavatam* (12.3.30–32, 37, 39–40, 42) describing Kali-yuga. Then this is broken down into categories, using verses from other chapters. Significantly, the Vedas hold that these descriptions are all predictions, forecasts compiled before the onset of Kali-yuga, approximately 5,000 years ago. The Vedic projection for personal and social behavior in Kali-yuga is indeed quite foreboding:

30. When there is a predominance of cheating, lying, sloth, sleepiness, violence, depression, lamentation, bewilderment, fear, and poverty, that age is Kali, the age of the mode of ignorance.

31. Because of the bad qualities of the Age of Kali, human beings will become shortsighted, unfortunate, gluttonous, lustful, and poverty-stricken. The women, becoming unchaste, will freely wander from one man to the next.

32. Cities will be dominated by thieves, the Vedas will be contaminated by speculative interpretations of atheists, political leaders will virtually consume the citizens, and the so-called priests and intellectuals will be devotees of their bellies and genitals.

37. In Kali-yuga men will be wretched and controlled by women. They will reject their fathers, brothers, other relatives, and friends and will instead associate with the sisters and brothers of their wives. Thus their conception of friendship will be based exclusively on sexual ties.

39–40. In the Age of Kali, people's minds will always be agitated. They will become emaciated by famine and taxation, and will always be disturbed by fear of drought. They will lack adequate clothing, food, and drink; will be unable to properly rest, have sex, or bathe themselves; and will have no ornaments to decorate their bodies. In fact, the people of Kali-yuga will gradually come to appear like ghostly, haunted creatures.

42. Men will no longer protect their elderly parents, their children, or their respectable wives. Thoroughly degraded, they will care only to satisfy their own bellies and genitals.

Society

The prognosis for government in the Age of Kali is gloomy—judged according to the Vedic standard. Instead of governmental administrators organizing and protecting the citizens' spiritual development, they will simply exploit their positions while duly mouthing slogans like "Of the people, by the people, for the people."

> Unpurified, neglecting prescribed human duties, and covered by the modes of passion and ignorance, the lowest degenerates, in the guise of government members, will virtually devour the citizens.
>
> The citizens governed by these low-class kings will imitate the character, behavior and speech of their rulers. Harassed by their leaders and by each other, they will all suffer ruination. (*Shrimad-Bhagavatam* 12.1.40–41)

In the Iron Age, gross habits and lifestyles will warp whatever meager human abilities remain. Malefic social institutions will expand this destruction on a mass scale. No longer will austere sages—spiritual intellectuals—guide the government leaders. Clever jugglers of words and theories will become the only scholars. The second chapter of the twelfth canto goes on to predict that might will certainly become the only right.

> Law and justice will be applied only on the basis of power, and whoever can accumulate the most power will control society. Eventually the citizens will feel so harassed that they will abandon their land and home. Fleeing to remote areas, they will live in constant fear of government officials who are no better than merciless, dedicated plunderers. (12.2.7–8)

Money

The economy will become the deity of society—all else will

fade far into the background. Human progress and decline will be measured by economic indicators.

> Wealth alone will be considered the sign of a man's good birth, proper behavior, and fine qualities. Success in business will depend on deceit. A person's propriety will be seriously questioned if he does not earn a good living. Those lacking money will even be judged unholy. Merely filling the belly will become acceptable as a proper goal in life, and society will regard any man who can adequately maintain his family as an expert. (12.2.2–6)

Family Life

Sex will become the essential expression of selfhood. Disconnected from its reproductive function, intercourse as recreation will be the juice of life.

> Men and women will live together merely because of superficial attraction, and womanliness and manliness will be judged according to sexual expertise. They will arrange their marriages simply by verbal agreement, and will think their beauty depends on their hairstyle. (12.2.3,5,6)

> Women will have more children than they can properly take care of, and lose all shyness. (12.3.34)

Nature

In Vedic science, consciousness is connected to the processes of nature. Therefore as the decline of humanity worsens, the cosmic ecosphere responds accordingly. Besides the diminution of human strengths and abilities, the functions of nature decline in effectiveness also. The rains, sunlight, soil, and air are predicted to become comparatively impotent. Their deficiency profoundly affects the supply of food, minerals, precious stones, and other natural resources—all the more reason for the health, memory, and mental clarity of humanity to wane.

In reaction to the disastrous caliber of human society, the seasons become irregular and natural disasters regular.

> Harassed by famine and excessive taxes, people will resort to eating leaves, roots, flesh, wild honey, fruits, flowers, and seeds. Struck by drought, they will become completely ruined. The citizens will suffer greatly from cold, wind, heat, rain, and snow. They will be further tormented by quarrels, hunger, thirst, disease, and severe anxiety. The maximum duration of life will be fifty years. Most plants and herbs will be tiny, and all trees will appear like dwarfs. Clouds will be full of lightning, homes will be devoid of piety, and all human beings will have become like asses. (12.2.9–16)

YUGA SOLUTIONS

The cycle of the four ages revolves throughout the duration of the universe. In this way, the same general patterns of environmental, political, social, familial, and individual conditions repeat themselves. A further elaboration is that each of the four ages appears as a small sub-period in the other ages. That means, for example, even within the holocaust of the Kali-yuga there is a mini–Golden Age—for those who take advantage of special lifelines given in the Vedas. Or in Satya-yuga, a powerful demonic person may temporarily wreak some havoc.

By the time the present Age of Kali is said to wind down—approximately 427,000 years from now—the Vedic texts describe that humans will be short-lived midgets, and all plants and trees will be tiny. The Vedas will be completely forgotten, and even religiosity for material gain will be extinct. Ruled by plunderers, the outright savage people of this time will have as their occupational choices only lying, stealing, or violence.

Upon the close of the Age of Darkness, the bestial population will die out, and the few remaining citizens of goodness will re-populate Earth with extraordinary children, to inaugurate the Satya-yuga. Vedic knowledge and civilization will then fully re-turn, as the cycle begins from the top again.

Taking into account the qualities and conditions of the times, each age has its own prescription for spiritual liberation. We should always bear in mind that the Vedas are not theoretical and dogmatic, but methodological and prescriptive. For each *yuga*, the Vedic texts recommend a main technique for spiritual liberation, known as the *yuga-dharma*—the most appropriate, practical spiritual method of the particular time. Hence the Vedas always stress the need for a proper Vedic guide—to trum-pet the appropriate spiritual pathway enunciated in the Vedas for each age. Also the genuine Vedic guide demonstrates how to apply that pathway.

For the Golden Age, Satya-yuga, the *yuga-dharma* is medita-tion. The people are said to have the long life span and sanctified atmosphere necessary for meditation to produce its ultimate benefits. Vedic histories describe persons spending the first 60,000 years of their life at home and then the last 40,000 alone in the Himalayas, where they mastered the yoga system of meditation on *Brahman*, *Paramatma*, and *Bhagavan*. In the Treta-yuga, monu-mental sacrifices are the main means of spiritual deliverance. These gargantuan efforts required exceptionally virtuous and powerful executive heads of government. Only leaders of this caliber could marshal all the immense resources necessary. Fur-thermore, unusually qualified priests—religious intellectuals—were needed to perfectly conduct the rituals. Just one ingredient lacking or one procedural flaw would render the whole grand event useless.

Dvapara-yuga, the Bronze Age, stresses magnificent temples, where authorized Deity forms of *Bhagavan* receive opulent service from the people. In Kali-yuga, however, owing to the nonexistence of longevity, good government, qualified priests, and ample natural resources, only the congregational glorification of the Supreme *Bhagavan* through sound is prescribed.

> Whatever result was obtained in Satya-yuga by meditating on Visnu, in Treta-yuga by performing sacrifices, and in Dvapara-yuga by serving the Lord's lotus feet can be obtained in Kali-yuga simply by chanting the Hare Krishna *maha-mantra*. (*Shrimad-Bhagavatam* 12.3.52)

DATING KALI-YUGA

The time is midnight. The date is 18 February—3102 B.C. Your location is the Indian subcontinent. The seven planets, including the sun and moon, are invisible, because they are lined up in one direction on the other side of Earth. According to the Vedic supplementary astronomical texts, known as *jyotisha-shastras*, this rare planetary alignment and the specified date of its occurrence marked the beginning of Kali-yuga. The Vedic scriptures record that in the years immediately preceding this crucial turning point, Bhagavan Krishna ended His earthly appearance, and soon after this date worldwide Vedic culture disappeared. Consequently, any contemporary research to verify this planetary alignment would shed much light on the Vedic version of ancient history. The *Shrimad-Bhagavatam* harkens to that lost time:

> This *Bhagavata Purana* [*Shrimad-Bhagavatam*] is as brilliant as the sun, and it has arisen just after the departure of Lord Krishna to His own abode, accompanied by religion, knowledge, and so forth. Persons who have lost their vision due to the dense darkness of ignorance in the Age of Kali shall get light from this Purana. (*Shrimad-Bhagavatam* 1.3.43)

Naturally the mainstream view of Western scholars is that the date for Kali-yuga and its forecast symptoms are figments of the immense Vedic mythic and poetic imagination. Computers and software, however, are coming to the rescue of Vedic integrity. Astronomical software takes the coordinates and dates we enter and then displays approximations of the sky as our remote ancestors saw it. Today calculations are underway that strongly support the Vedic picture of the skies in 3102 B.C.

An American mathematician, Dr. Richard Thompson, specializing in probability theory and statistical mechanics, has devoted himself to analyzing ancient Vedic cosmology. Part of his investigation has centered upon the dating of Kali-yuga, according to Vedic astronomy. Since the first days of the British Empire in India, Vedic traditionalists have been pained at how modern Indologists sweep this date away, along with the antiquity of the *Gita* and Puranas. The scientist Thompson, who studied at Cornell University and did work at Cambridge, wrote in his book *Vedic Cosmography and Astronomy:*

> We would suggest that the dating of the start of Kali-yuga at 3102 B.C. is based on actual historical accounts, and that the tradition of an unusual alignment of the planets at this time is also a matter of historical fact. The opinion of the modern scholars is that the epoch of Kali-yuga was concocted during the early medieval period. According to this hypothesis, Indian astronomers used borrowed Greek astronomy to determine that a near planetary alignment occurred in 3102 B.C. After performing the laborious calculations needed to discover this, they then invented the fictitious era of Kali-yuga and convinced the entire subcontinent of India that this era had been going on for some three thousand years. Subsequently, many different *Puranas* were written in accordance with this chronology, and people all over India became convinced that these works . . . were really thousands of years old.

One might ask why anyone would even think of searching for astronomical alignments over a period of thousands of years into the past and then redefining the history of an entire civilization on the basis of a particular discovered alignment. It seems more plausible to suppose that the story of Kali-yuga is genuine, that the alignment occurring at its start is a matter of historical recollection, and that the *Puranas* really were written prior to the beginning of this era.[1]

Vedic sympathizers have been saddened to observe that many contemporary scholars indirectly accuse their culture of fraud. Traditional Western education asserts that knowledge of Kali-yuga was cooked up during the early centuries of the Christian era, then buttressed with astronomy appropriated from the Greeks, and finally projected back into time several thousand years before. In this way the Western world gets the impression that the Vedic Puranas are fable on the scale of mass delusion. More open-minded moderns scrutinize the quality of the actual predictions themselves, noting that their breadth, content, and accuracy far surpass the visions of both our medieval and modern soothsayers—Nostradamus, Edgar Caycee, and the like.

The twenty-year research of A. Seidenberg, mathematician and historian of science, may cheer the heart of modern Vedic partisans. In the next chapter we will review his research. Seidenberg's work seeks to demonstrate how Vedic mathematics preceded even Egyptian and Babylonian mathematics—not to speak of later Greek developments. The Egyptian mathematical texts are stated to go back before 2000 B.C., thereby pushing the dates for their Vedic antecedents, the *sulba-sutras*, back even further. Now that scientifically trained scholars are beginning to take all departments of Vedic science seriously, we can expect to know soon whether Vedic astronomy lagged far behind, waiting for the Greeks, while its mathematics soared ahead long before the era of Pythagoras.

More than a few times Vedic literatures mention astronomical sightings of equinoxes and solstices apparently corresponding to eras many millennia ago. More research is needed, however, to satisfy critical scholarship. The problem is not astronomical computation but interpretation of the Sanskrit context. Generally, until very recently, academics have ignored these irksome references as "anomalies" or worse still, "fabrications."

VEDIC TIME SCALES

The Vedic system of the four *yugas* presents the lengths of the ages as 4,3,2, and 1 times an interval of 432,000 years. That means the first age, Satya-yuga, lasts 1.728 million years; the second, Treta-yuga, lasts 1.296 million years; the third, Dvapara-yuga, lasts 864,000 years; and the present Iron Age, Kali-yuga, lasts 432,000 years. Obviously this system has little resonance with our current theories of human history.

The Vedic version contradicts our present conceptions about not only human antiquity but also human longevity. At the height of the *yuga*-cycle, in Satya-yuga, the life span is listed as 100,000 years. Then it decreases through each of the successive ages by a factor of 10. Thus, in the next age life spans reduce to 10,000 years; then 1000; until in the present Kali-yuga, the maximum is stated as 100 years, shrinking to 50 at the end.

A good background for delving into Vedic time is a general awareness of ancient time conceptions and also of an apparent correlation between Judeo-Christianity and modern science. When we examine the conceptions of the Mediterranean societies preceding the rise of European civilization, we see that evidently the people of the ancient Mediterranean world had a markedly different view of the human past. They believed human history extended far beyond what we moderns are now willing to acknowledge.

For example, the Babylonian historian Berosus (ca. 290 B.C.) presented knowledge of a remote antiquity. His chronicle, though surviving only in fragments, passed on the history and culture of Babylonia to the ancient Greeks. Berosus assigned 432,000 years as the period ruled by the Babylonian kings before the Flood.[2]

Readers conversant with the Bible may note that although it allows for a comparatively very brief span of human history, it does chronicle life spans near 1,000 years. Among ten of the most long-lived before the Flood, you'll find an average duration of 912 years. After the Flood, longevity gradually reduces to Joshua's 110 years.

The Jewish historian Flavius Josephus (first century A.D.) cited many historical works to support his contention that life spans of 1,000 years were an ancient fact. That almost none of the works he cites are still extant may indicate that our knowledge of the ancient past is still quite spotty. We can probably safely conclude that there's much we don't know.

> Now I have for witnesses to what I have said all those that have written Antiquities, both among the Greeks and barbarians, for even Manetho, who wrote the Egyptian history, and Berosus, who collected the Chaldean monuments, and Mochus, and Hestiaeus, and beside these, Hiernonymous the Egyptian, and those who composed the Phoenician history, agree with what I here say: Hesiod also, and Hecataeus, Hellanicaus, and Acuzilaus, and besides Ephorus and Nicolaus relate that the ancients lived a thousand years: but as to these matters, let everyone look upon them as he sees fit.[3]

The ancient Egyptians, Babylonians, and Assyrians all have fingers of time pointing to a distant, hidden past. More references will be given in the next chapter, on ancient astronomy. Nevertheless, Vedic chronology is much more expansive and sophisticated. It exceeds even the total cycle of four *yugas*, lasting 4.32 million years. The texts state that 1,000 rotations of the *yuga*-cycle form what is called a day of Brahma. Known in Sanskrit as a *kalpa*, each day of Brahma has a matching night of the same duration—4.32 million years. When the curtain of Brahma's night falls, the contents of almost the entire universe shut down—almost all the planets are devastated. Then, at the dawn of another day of Brahma, the devastated planets manifest again, with their appropriate life forms.

Each day of Brahma can be divided into 14 periods called *manvantaras*. A *manvantara* lasts 71 *yuga* cycles. Before and after each of the *manvantaras* is a junction known as a *sandhya*, lasting 1,728,000 years. Each of these *sandhyas*, connecting seams, has its own partial devastation and reappearance of life.

Let's do a quick rehash: a *yuga* cycle of 4.32 billion years combines in a set of 71 to compose a *manvantara*. Each *manvantara*, lasting 306.72 million years, combines in a set of 14 to form a *kalpa*, one day of Brahma. That day equals 4.32 billion years. The night is of the same duration.

Amazingly, the Vedic time scale does not stop there. You take 36,000 *kalpas*, days of Brahma, and 36,000 nights—each day and each night lasting 4.32 billion years—and you have what is called the life of Brahma. This complete period of Brahma, comprising many partial devastations and replenishments, is the actual Vedic measurement of the cosmic duration. The staggering total is 311.04 trillion years.

Where are we now, according to this colossal duration? Even amid such an unfathomable span, the Vedic timeframe allows us a glimpse. At least within a *kalpa*—a 4.32 billion-year day of Brahma—we can pinpoint our location. We are 5,000 years into the Age of Kali, within the twenty-eighth *yuga*-cycle, during the seventh *manvantara* period of the current day of Brahma—about high noon. That means according to Vedic cosmology, the appearance of life on the present Earth has an age of 2.3 billion years. Curiously, paleontologists today hold that the oldest undisputed organisms they've found are approximately that old. Algae fossils, such as those from the Gunflint formation in Canada, are said to be that age.

Cyclic time is not peculiar to the Vedic culture. As discussed in Chapter 2, the ancient Greeks saw the cosmos this way, though they did entertain other concepts also. We can safely say that several of their most prominent thinkers put forth cycles of time quite similar to that described in the Vedas. For instance, Hesiod's *Works and Days* presents a series of epochs comparable to the Vedic *yugas*. He lists ages of gold, silver, bronze, heroic, and iron that progressively worsen. Empedocles, in *On Nature*, refers to cosmic time cycles, Plato's dialogues describe revolving time and recurring catastrophic destruction of human civilization, and the works of Aristotle in many places state that the arts and sciences have manifested many times in the past.

But when Judeo-Christian culture enveloped Europe, another vision of time took over. A sharp break from the ancient Vedic and Greek cosmology, the newly prominent concept featured a unique progression of the universe from beginning to end. Creation, the appearance of humans, salvation, and the finale—Judgment Day—only occur once. Just as the cosmic drama only happens once, so the individual only lives once. The early Church fathers, though maintaining their general appreciation of Greek thinking, denounced the cyclic view of the world as pagan.

Upon the fall and pillage of Rome in the fifth century A.D., non-Christians attributed the calamity to the people's abandoning of their pagan gods. St. Augustine, writing between A.D. 413 and 426, produced ten volumes to maneuver the fall of Rome into a more appropriate light. His magisterial treatise, *The City of God*, announced that history had deliberately brought about Rome's collapse—to bring about a new Christian civilization.

In Augustine's hands, time was always going somewhere. It followed a linear path, in a specific direction fixed by God's will. The process was irreversible, and the course was preset. Each civilization surpassed its predecessors, as humanity moved ever onwards and upwards. The pious researcher would observe that through this linear march of progress unfolded the divine plan for Christian redemption.

Augustine's march of time toward a predetermined goal has influenced Western thought for more than fifteen hundred years. His vision of time—escaping serious challenge for thirteen hundred years—even today remains an often-unconscious pillar of our Western cultural inheritance. Modern ideas of purposive history and progress—whether Marxian or empirical—owe their birth to Augustine's early labor.

Scholars share other predominant Judeo-Christian assumptions. Mainline anthropologists and archaeologists believe that human civilization is a very recent phenomenon and that its earliest appearance was in the Middle East. A modern dean of Indology, D. D. Kosambi, while slashing the Vedic testimony of an advanced civilization, brandishes the familiar linear notion:

> Nowhere is any evidence found of a lost golden age, a state of pristine glory. Man did not progress uniformly or steadily; but he did progress on the whole, from a fairly inefficient animal to a toolmaking and tool-using creature who dominated the whole planet by his numbers and by the varied forms of his activity, and has now only to learn to control himself.[4]

Keeping the cosmological legacy of the Judeo-Christian outlook in mind, it is indeed tantalizing to see the same concepts in modern mainstream science—quantum exotica excepted. Secularized, stripped of any divine hand, the same vision seems to prevail: our universe is a unique occurrence, humans have arisen once, on this planet only, and the future evolution of the human species is so unique that it is unpredictable—though greater heights are guaranteed. Despite the best efforts of scientists to abandon the constraints of Judeo-Christian religion, have the same notions unconsciously seeped into their theories?

FATALISM AND THE VEDAS

A popular misconception is that inevitability and predetermination stifle Vedic culture, suppressing the human capacity for creative initiative and opportunism. Many think the Vedic cycles share the fatalism associated with Babylonian, Egyptian, and Mayan cosmologies. Stanley Jaki, a Benedictine priest who holds doctorates in both physics and theology, has made an extensive study of time in ancient cosmology. He compares the Vedic cycles to an inescapable treadmill, which transfixes the people in a stupor of resignation and powerlessness. Therefore, he opines, the hallmark of Vedic culture is despair and despondency.[5]

Jaki tells the story of a Mayan people, the Itza, whose leaders informed two Spanish missionaries that on a particular date eighty years in the future, an age of calamities would beset the tribe. The missionaries devotedly informed the conquistadors. Right on schedule—eighty years later—a small contingent of Spanish soldiers appeared. The Itza, though well armed and numerically superior, immediately surrendered without a fight. This docility in the face of predetermined adversity is said to hamper all cyclic cultures.

Nothing could be further from the Vedic truth. The Vedas emphasize our executing prescribed social, familial, and occupational duties in all circumstances—whether the tide is with you or not. By this resolute determination, in the face of the shifting fortunes of life, strong character and moral backbone is expected to develop. Consequently, society will become a highly principled unit that eventually can rise to the platform of transcendental knowledge.

> The nonpermanent appearance of happiness and distress, and their disappearance in due course, are like the appearance and disappearance of winter and summer seasons. They arise from sense perception, and one must learn to tolerate them without being disturbed.
>
> The person who is not disturbed by happiness and distress and is steady in both is certainly eligible for liberation. (*Bhagavad-gita* 2.14–15)

As for the so-called mesmerizing effect of Vedic time on the human spirit, we might want to be a little more charitable and admit there's no harm in getting a good weather report. The Vedic presentation of Kali-yuga purports to be just that. A modest, re-strained approach to the world of the *yuga* cycles would be to see how much the predictions of Kali-yuga are actually visible in today's world.

When people hear that rain is forecast, they carry an umbrella. But still they energetically go about their affairs. Foreknowledge of impending circumstances would most likely increase their effectiveness, not decrease it. The Vedas blatantly state that our happiness and distress for this life are already prepackaged at birth. Regardless of that destiny, though, we are required to execute the duties prescribed by the Vedic texts. The crux of this metaphysic is that the next life is not prepackaged. As explained in the preceding chapter on karma, we are said to bear the burden of the past into an uncharted future. The next life is molded according to our present choices.

The most intelligent persons are advised to completely tran-scend the law of action and reaction, piety and impiety, heaven and hell. Here lies the greatest wealth of the Vedas. In other words, Vedic culture does not bind us to an inescapable treadmill of despair and despondency. Instead, it offers the joyous key to something immeasurably superior. Vedic seers want us to grasp that material existence as a whole is deadening—whether cyclic or linear, heavenly or miserable. The entirety of material existence is the dreary treadmill. But perhaps because we know nothing better, we do protest when material existence is devalued.

At the least, newcomers to the Vedic world should glimpse the profound opportunities that abound in Vedic culture: an industrious person can transcend material existence, even in the present body. And the less diligent among us are enrolled in a gradual course of elevation, spanning a few or even many births—if necessary for achieving the ultimate goal. The most advanced brains of society are advised to work ceaselessly for that summit, far beyond the temporary appearances of happiness and distress.

> Persons who are actually intelligent and philosophically inclined should endeavor only for that rare transcendental position that cannot be attained by wandering up and down from the topmost planet to the lowest planet in the universe. Whatever material happiness is available we can attain by the force of time, just as we attain distress though not desiring it. Since these are not attained by spiritual consciousness, we should not try for them. (*Shrimad-Bhagavatam* 1.5.18)

If we only agree to physicalism, the world of matter and its reactions, then the Vedic message may seem bleak to us—it's debasing the only experience we know. Upon considering the Vedic perspective, though, we then view a life of struggling with material happiness and distress as bleak—and binding too. Since real exhilaration and freedom is available only on the spiritual plane, we are urged to work vigorously—for achieving the supreme objective.

Notes

1 Richard Thompson, *Vedic Cosmography and Astronomy* (Los Angeles: The Bhaktivedanta Book Trust, 1990), p. 21.

2 J. D. North, "Chronology and the Age of the World," in *Cosmology, History and Theology*, ed. Wolfgang Yourgrau and A. D. Breck (New York: Plenum Press, 1977), p. 315.

3 D. W. Patten and P. A. Patten, "A Comprehensive Theory on Aging, Gigantism and Longevity," in *Catastrophism and Ancient History*, vol. 2, part 1 (August 1979), p. 29.

4 D. D. Kosambi, *The Culture and Civilization of Ancient India* (London: Routledge and Kegan Paul, 1965), p. 28.

5 Stanley Jaki, "The History of Science and the Idea of an Oscillating Universe," in *Cosmology, History and Theology*.

CHAPTER 11

MYSTERIES OF THE
EARTH AND SKY

~

We like to credit ancient humans with scant factual knowledge of the cosmos. "Their myths were many, but their facts were few," is the established view. Yet how much of the universe do the biggest modern brains understand? We stand on ever-shifting sands. What is known as scientific knowledge today will certainly not be the same as what we consider acceptable knowledge tomorrow. Since our knowledge of the solar system is in a constant state of flux, how can we unilaterally kick at every thought the ancients had about the cosmos?

Current cosmology admits that most of the matter in the universe is completely unknown to us. "Dark matter," the mysterious stuff is called. Undetectable by direct observation, dark matter is said to be cosmic substance that refuses to interact with our senses and instruments. Our only clue comes from indirect inference. Gravitational effects imply that invisible matter is present.

How much matter is missing—imperceptible to our senses and instruments? The predominance of dark matter in the universe is staggering. American astronomer Vera Rubin, a winner of the

National Medal of Science, explains the immensity of our cosmic bafflement:

> Based on 50 years of accumulated observations of the motions of galaxies and the expansion of the universe, most astronomers believe that as much as 90 percent of the stuff composing the universe may be objects or particles that cannot be seen. . . . Nowadays we prefer to call the missing mass "dark matter," for it is the light, not the matter, that is missing. . . . So important is this dark matter to our understanding of the size, shape, and ultimate fate of the universe that the search for it will very likely dominate astronomy for the next few decades. . . . Perhaps in the coming century, another—as yet unborn—big brain will put her eye to a clever new instrument and definitively answer, What is dark matter?[1]

Though estimates of dark matter in the universe generally hover at around 90 percent, sometimes the calculations shoot as high as 99 percent. We are forced to accept that the kind of matter we know about makes up only a minuscule 1–10 percent of the total cosmos—very humbling knowledge indeed. Chances are, totally dark stars, systems, and galaxies are completely eluding us.

Meanwhile, extra-solar planet-hunting is the latest astronomical game to hit town. The push to detect planets orbiting distant stars has aroused both specialists and laypersons alike. In this way the search for extraterrestrial life has extended to realms outside our solar system. Astronomers speculate that as many as 10 percent of all the stars in our galaxy have planets orbiting them. That would mean, they say, the existence of 10 billion planets in just the Milky Way galaxy alone.[2] It seems that "alien worlds," normally the mainstays of science fiction—and the Vedic literature— are knocking on the doors of scientific fact. By the end of the year 2000, more than 40 official candidates for planet status had emerged, but none by direct perception.

Since no one could directly observe these new planets outside our solar system, their confirmation depended on inference only, by observing the behavior of the parent star. The theory is that minute shifts in the color of light emanated by a star are the result of gravitational effects exerted by an orbiting planet. A technique known as Doppler spectroscopy allowed scientists to infer the orbit and minimum mass of the candidate planet—but nothing of its constitution. Though the existence of the planets is posited only through inference, the majority of astronomers feel persuaded.

For the future, new instruments like the Terrestrial Planet Finder (TPF)—a space-based set of telescopes and other sensors—are in the works, to go after the smaller, Earth-like planets that the Doppler technique is unable to catch. "Life on Earth is by no means the only kind of life that can exist," explained Nick Woolf, an astronomer from the University of Arizona. He described the Terrestrial Planet Finder as "a device we are developing that will pick up a particular subset of life."[3] The TPF, slated for operation in the year 2010, will go after conventional assumptions of life indicators, such as the presence of oxygen, ozone, and methane in an atmosphere. Ten years later, in 2020, the Life Finder spacecraft, planned by the Jet Propulsion Laboratory in California, would further the quest.

What has set off the biggest stir at the onset of the new century is the first discovery of multiple planets orbiting stars. An American astronomer, Geoff Marcy, found a family of three large planets—two of them much larger than Jupiter—orbiting the star Upsilon Andromedae. Scrambling to adapt to this first detected ensemble of extrasolar planets, scientists christened the birth of a new academic field: the comparative study of planetary systems.[4]

Surprisingly, the ancient texts also shared in planetary mystery. What we now call *archaeoastronomy* is the research of the celestial observations and cosmic lore of ancient cultures. Archaeoastronomy, strictly understood as the anthropology of astronomy, seeks the social origins and cultural development of astronomy. It has expanded to include the interrelated studies of ancient calendar systems, concepts of time and space, mathematics, counting systems, geometry, and navigational methods.

Throughout the world, an unknown advanced intellect seems to have left its fingerprints, in the form of mysterious ancient accounts. We can wonder how the Sumerians, who were just learning how to write, seemed to evidence knowledge of the distant planets of the universe. They seemed to know of celestial bodies that cannot be seen with the naked eye. In what modern scholars of Mesopotamia call the Atra-Hasis text, the non-mainstream researcher Zecharia Sitchin sees an account of alien contact. Although we may not accept Sitchin's extraterrestrial rendition of Sumerian history, he may deserve immediate credit for using the ancient Sumerian texts to point out that Neptune is watery. He had written about the Sumerian knowledge of the waters of Neptune years before the unmanned satellite *Voyager 2* sent back pictures. The satellite's probing revealed Neptune as watery—not just gaseous, as scientists had previously thought.[5]

Sitchin enthusiasts derive even more elation from the newly announced possibility of a huge planet beyond Pluto. At the turn of the millennium, astronomers from two separate teams presented evidence that seems to confirm the presence of a huge planetlike body far beyond the orbit of Pluto. Many readers of Sitchin are convinced the discovery fits a theory he advanced regarding a huge, distant planet known to the ancient Sumerians as Nibiru.

THE DOGON

More puzzling is the astronomical knowledge possessed by a primitive tribe in Africa, the Dogon. In 1931 French anthropologist Marcel Griaule visited the Dogon in what was then French West Africa. After World War II, in 1946, he returned there, accompanied by ethnologist Germaine Dieterlen, now General Secretary of the Societé des Africanistes at the Museé de l'Homme in Paris. What fascinated the two scholars was their discovery that the tribe had specific knowledge of invisible stars. In 1951 they published an ethnological account, presenting the results of their four-year study. The news of their research, however, never penetrated beyond a small circle of specialist colleagues. Then, in the last quarter of the century, independent researchers such as Robert Temple broadcast the mystery of the Dogon's knowledge to the general public.

The esoteric part of Dogon culture is their oral tradition that thousands of years ago beings from the stellar vicinity of Sirius visited their ancestors. For what scholars have determined to be incalculable centuries, the Dogon, located in what is now Mali, have worshipped these beings, who they say tried to teach them divine knowledge.

The exoteric part of Dogon lore is nothing short of amazing. Long before modern astronomers knew that Sirius is a double star, the Dogon apparently had this information. Furthermore they knew that the planets revolve around the sun, that Saturn has rings and that Jupiter has moons. Their knowledge of Sirius, also known as the Dog Star, is hardest to explain away. The brightest star in the night sky, Sirius is 8.5 light years away from Earth (one light year = 5.9 billion miles). Sirius actually is two stars. The main entity, Sirius A, gives off light 23 times that of the sun. This Sirius A is visible to the naked eye. The other entity, Sirius B, is a dwarf star orbiting its sister. Sirius B is completely invisible, except through modern telescopes. Also, the unaided eye cannot see the rings of Saturn.

Modern suspicion that Sirius is a binary system began in 1834, when the German astronomer Friedrich Wilhem Bessel inferred the existence of a double. Then, in 1862, the American optician Alvan Clarke built a telescope that enabled him to actually see Sirius B. The peculiar knowledge of the double was shared only within a small circle of astronomers until 1928, when Sir Arthur Eddington put forth his theory of "white dwarfs" as a comprehensive explanation.

Did some unknown eccentric astronomer venture into the jungle to teach the Dogon such intricate astronomical knowledge? Hard-core mainstreamers immediately reach for this option. For example, the late Carl Sagan proposed that in the 1920s French missionaries felt the need to teach the Dogon about Sirius B. An obvious problem with this convenient hunch is that the Dogon have been performing their Sirius rituals for more than a few centuries—long before Eddington's theory alerted the Western world to Sirius B.

Additionally, our judgment should include a striking testimony by Griaule. In true anthropological style, the Frenchman won the Dogon's confidence enough to be admitted into their inner secrets. The tribe assigned a series of elders to teach him. Upon the death of one aged tutor, another would take his place. After passing through four levels of initiations, Griaule was astonished to receive instruction in a theology he declared as complex and expansive as the Summa theologica of Thomas Aquinas—the "Angelic Doctor" of the Catholic Church.

The Dogon's special ceremony can be repeated only once every fifty years, after which they store the masks and ritualistic beer vessels they use. Through this paraphernalia they pass their heritage down to succeeding generations. Did the tribe know that Sirius B takes fifty years to orbit Sirius A? If so, from where did the Dogon get this high-quality technical information?

The tribe's chief advocate in the Western world is Robert Temple, who penned *The Sirius Mystery*, a popular work of alternative research. Through exhaustive analysis and detail, Temple has secured a wide audience. Naturally he has his critics. In their face he has heightened his challenge. The first edition of his book, in 1976, asserted that the Dogon know Sirius to have yet another component—a third star. At the time of the book's first release, no Western astronomer had posited the existence of this Sirius C. Now, astronomers are speculating about it. Temple chuckles:

> I made a daring prediction 20 years ago, based upon tribal information I analyzed. I suggested that astronomers would eventually confirm the existence, in the system of the star Sirius, of a third star . . . and that the third star would be a red dwarf. . . . I'm delighted to point out that in 1995, two French astronomers, Benest and Duvent, published an article in *Astronomy and Astrophysics*, saying that they'd completed eight years of analysis of the perturbations in the Sirius system and they could confirm the existence of a third star, and that it was a red dwarf. . . . In which case, I would suggest that everybody ought to sit down and read *The Sirius Mystery* and really think about what this means. Because I've passed the scientific test: I made a prediction that's been verified.[6]

The Dogon today number about 350,000. They say their knowledge goes back thousands of years—to their alien mentors. Many of us would probably choose to attribute the Dogon's information to unknown Egyptians. But that hypothesis just pushes the hot potato onto someone else's lap. The same basic problem remains: a lost, prescientific people possess advanced knowledge of celestial phenomena that is invisible to the human eye.

STONEHENGE

Sophisticated archaeoastronomical alignments have been discerned at ancient sites all over the world. Stonehenge is a prime example—not just because of its structure, but also because of its dating. In just 800 years, its official date has gradually receded into the past by more than 3,000 years. First, in the days of knights and nobles, Stonehenge was considered a monument erected by Merlin the Magician, honoring British leaders slain by Saxon invaders around A.D. 450. Next, learned authorities of the 1500s and 1600s looked to Stonehenge as the work of Druid priests around A.D. 50, during Roman times. The established view in the mid-1800s was different still. By then the megaliths had become the handiwork of one of Israel's lost tribes, who built it around 1200 B.C. Now, at the onset of the twenty-first century, the earliest structures of Stonehenge are dated at 3100 B.C.

Tourists concentrate upon the great stone circles and horseshoe arrangements that make Stonehenge famous. These constructs, however, though perfect for picture postcards, are later additions—mostly Stonehenge III. They are not essential for lunar and solar calculations.

Sightseers generally overlook Stonehenge I. How did its builders—at least 5,000 years ago—incorporate into the design a system for predicting eclipses? Around the beginning of the twentieth century, the astronomer Sir Norman Lockyer posited that Stonehenge might be some kind of astronomical calculator, indicating the positions of the sun and moon. His fellow scientists thought the idea ludicrous. After all, weren't the builders of Stonehenge crude barbarians? But Lockyer was able to demonstrate what is scientifically accepted fact today: the northeast axis of the megalith aligns with the summer-solstice sunrise.

Later, around 1933, a Scot named Alexander Thom began to study stone-circle megaliths throughout the UK and concluded the builders were master geometricians, sophisticated in knowledge. For most of his life, experts on ancient Britain considered him a foolish eccentric. The American astronomer Gerald Hawkins, while at Harvard, sought to confirm Thom's main contentions by running data from monuments like Stonehenge through his computer, to prove the megaliths were calculators for predicting lunar and solar eclipses.

Mainline Stonehenge experts ridicule Hawkins' presentation and any proposals like it. The latest contender is Duncan Steele, a leading British authority on comets. His research tells him that Stonehenge was an early warning system for meteor storms. R.J.C. Atkinson, archaeologist from University College, Cardiff, insists: "Most of what has been written about Stonehenge is nonsense or speculation. No one will ever have a clue what its significance was."[7] The debate over Stonehenge's meaning—or lack of one—continues.

The Egyptians

The main interest in archaeoastronomy focuses upon Egypt. How deeply the Egyptians were immersed in mathematics and astronomy is just starting to become understood. Other peoples of the Mediterranean area did not hide their awe of the Egyptian knowledge of the skies. The Greek historian Herodotus (490–409 B.C.), the earliest traveller on record, said the Egyptians were the first to discover the solar year, by observing the stars.[8] Plato (429–347 B.C.) stated that the Egyptian priests had observed the stars for "ten thousand years or, so to speak, for an infinite time."[9]

Then in the first century B.C. the Greek historian Diodorus Siculus left more information. A contemporary of Julius Caesar and Augustus, Diodorus makes it clear in his statements that he traveled in Egypt during 60–57 B.C. He wrote: "The positions and arrangements of the stars as well as their motions have always been the subject of careful observation among the Egyptians. . . . From ancient times to this day they have preserved the records concerning each of these stars over an incredible number of years.[10]

Herodotus, if he is to be believed, left us a startling note in his "Canon of the Kings of Egypt." Writing of Egypt's remote past, he says that "during this time they affirm that the sun has twice risen in parts different from what is his customary place, that is to say, has twice risen where he now sets, and has also twice set where he now rises."[11] Can these words refer to anything other than the complete transit of the stellar background? The 360-degree revolution of the heavens takes a precessional cycle of 25,920 years. Herodotus may be handing us shocking implications that ancient civilization in Egypt had seen one and a half precessional cycles. That means a span of 38,880 years.[12]

Sooner or later, exploring Egyptian archaeoastronomy means confronting the Great Pyramid at Giza. Hundreds of books have sought to unravel its mysteries. Generally, these books, overloading readers with occult reflections, skimp on the facts. Amid the dubious esoteria, however, hard evidence does stand out. Data indicates that the ancient Egyptians possessed strangely accurate knowledge.

We now have realized the accurate cardinal orientation of the Great Pyramid. Its four sides, averaging 230.6 meters, are aligned to the four cardinal points with an accuracy at which modern engineers can marvel. The recognized modern metrologist Livio Stecchini has pointed out another curiosity: the perimeter of the Great Pyramid—921.453 meters—precisely equals half a minute of latitude at the equator. The measurement is exactly 1/43,200 of Earth's circumference.[13] That means the perimeter is an exact rendition of Earth's equator, to a scale of 1:43,200.

The correlations don't end there. The height of the pyramid, 146.59 meters, when multiplied by 43,200 gives us a number just shy of Earth's polar radius—that is, the distance from the Earth's center to the North Pole.[14] How close is the match? If you divide Earths' polar radius by 43,200, you get 147.15 meters—compared to the Pyramid's height of 146.59 (this is a difference in the scale model of less than 0.5 percent). Furthermore, the Great Pyramid sits at the exact center of Earth's biggest mass of land.

The metrologist Stecchini is able to demonstrate that when the first Pharaoh is said to have appeared, around 3100 B.C., the Egyptians had already plotted the location of their land in relation to the longitude and latitude of the Earth.[15] Stecchini summarizes the whole picture:

> The basic idea of the Great Pyramid was that it should be a representation of the northern hemisphere, a hemisphere projected on flat surfaces, as is done in map-making. . . . The Great Pyramid was a projection on four triangular surfaces. The apex represented the pole and the perimeter represented the equator. . . . The Great Pyramid represents the northern hemisphere in a scale of 1:43,200; this scale was chosen because there are 86,400 seconds in 24 hours.[16]

Any of the several current books on Egypt's lost legacy can present many more of these surprising geodetic correlations. Of course, mimicking conventional Egyptologists, we can always dismiss these strange facts as coincidental. Yet, even if we do accept the Great Pyramid's obvious relation to the Earth—a 1:43,200 scale model of the northern hemisphere—still we may have grasped just a mere piece of a huge puzzle. For example, until 1994, no one saw what archaeoastronomer Robert Bauval finally pointed out: the three stars in the constellation Orion's Belt became the celestial model for arranging the three Giza pyramids on the ground.

Still in the realm of theory, however, is his contention that the pattern of almost 15 million tons of perfectly laid stone on the ground, while generally corresponding to Orion's Belt in all eras, precisely and exactly matches a pattern in the sky in 10450 B.C.

Bauval asserts that this faultless, spot-on correlation is no acci-
dent. "It can't be a coincidence," said Bauval, "that such a perfect
alignment of the terrestrial and the celestial occurs at around
10,450 B.C. . . . The real question is *why?* Why was it done?"[17]

We should note that his explanation is not that the Giza pyramids were constructed in 10450 B.C., but that they were planned
way back then. For some extraordinary reason, now unknown,
could the Egyptians have chosen to make a monumental statement about the eleventh millennium B.C.? Predictably, mainstream Egyptologists threw up a united front against the full scope
of the Orion implications.[18] It is true that Bauval and his cohorts,
Graham Hancock and Adrian Gilbert, are known for their eager-
ness to magnify intriguing insights into revolutionary discoveries.
Also, even their sympathizers note that the precision of calculations pointing to a distant millennium is not as exact as they
would have us believe. Still, many do accept that the sky references at Giza certainly indicate a general timeframe well before current conventions allow. More research—not dogma—is
needed to confirm or reject the controversial part of the Orion
correlation.[19]

In 1998 came the discovery in southern Egypt of megalithic
alignments and stone circles dated at 4800 B.C. The stones resemble Stonehenge and other megalithic sites in Europe, but they
predate Stonehenge by 1000 years. The standing stones at Nabta
are now the oldest astronomical alignment accepted by the academic establishment. This ceremonial complex, near the Nubian
Desert, is arranged according to the zenith sun at the summer
solstice. University of Colorado astronomy professor J. McKim
Malville and his team used a global positioning satellite to verify
the stones' alignment to the summer-solstice sun as it would have
appeared 6800 years ago. Malville, specializing in archaeoastronomy, says the Nabta culture suggests the early development
of a complex society.[20]

THE BABYLONIANS

Ancient historical records reveal the statements of Porphyry (ca. 234–ca. 305), a Neoplatonist Greek philosopher. Porphyry is important to us as both an editor and a biographer of the philosopher Plotinus, as well as for his commentary on Aristotle's Categories. He recorded that a companion of Alexander in the Persian War named Callisthenes dispatched to Aristotle many Babylonian records of eclipses. Porphyry stated that these records spanned 31,000 years.

Also, Iamblichus (ca. 250–ca. 350), another major figure in Neoplatonism and the founder of its Syrian branch, left some surprises for us. He quoted Hipparchus (ca. second century B.C.), the ancient Greek astronomer and mathematician who discovered the precession of the equinoxes and calculated the length of the year to within six and a half minutes. Iamblichus stated on the authority of Hipparchus that the Assyrians had made astronomical observations for 270,000 years and had recorded the return of all seven planets to the same position.

THE MAYA AND OTHER EARLY AMERICANS

The Maya mysteries of archaeoastronomy begin with their unbelievably accurate series of calendars. Their precision, superior to our modern Gregorian calendar, begs the question: Why would anyone want such precise calendars, spanning thousands of years? Mesoamerican experts claim these astonishing calendars were needed for agricultural planning. But why the accuracy covering hundreds and thousands of years? Long-range gardening strategies?

The Maya, who inherited their calendar from the Olmecs a thousand years before them, produced a mathematics with at least two outstanding developments. Their use of positional numeration—a place-value system—and their use of a zero are deemed preeminently brilliant achievements. The Maya Palace of the Governor at Uxmal in Yucatan is aligned with Venus—a planet very important to them. Maya astronomy finely calculated both the duration of the solar year and the synodical revolution of Venus. The Dresden Codex, one of the few important texts to survive the Spanish, contains incredibly accurate tables for predicting solar eclipses as well as lunar and Venusian cycles.

The Maya ancients somehow calculated that 149 lunar cycles last 4,400 days. Modern astronomers say 4400.0575 days. The Maya also established that Venus takes 584 days to orbit the sun. Modern scientists say 583.92 days. How did the ancient Maya come so close?

Mainly because of these exceptional calculations, the fame of the Maya as astronomers is well established; yet independent researchers are now scrutinizing Maya texts and traditions for much deeper revelations, which are still in the controversial stage. And always there are the questions of how much the Maya inherited—from whom, and how far back in time.

The Andes Mountains, in what is now Bolivia, contain the ruined city Tiahuanaco. There, a large enclosure known as Kalasasaya, or "Place of the Standing Stones," is the focus of a dating controversy. The late Professor Arthur Posnansky, a German-Bolivian scholar, studied all the ruins of Tiahuanaco for almost 50 years. Kalasasaya is a 500 square foot area surrounded by stone slabs over twelve feet high. Posnansky discovered that the stones indicate astronomical positions. The accepted date for Kalasasaya had been A.D. 500. Posnansky, however, used archaeoastronomy to put forth the revolutionary date of 15000 B.C.

The German-Bolivian scholar had put in almost a half century of work on the ruins of Tiahuanaco. Yet his calculation for Kalasasaya promptly earned him fame as a crackpot—until a special German astronomical commission pored over his work. From

1927 to 1930 the commission critiqued his research and eventually confirmed that the site was indeed an ancient celestial observatory aligned according to archaeoastronomy. The commission, with Hans Ludendorff of the Potsdam Astronomical Observatory at the helm, decided to proffer what it thought was a more digestible date of 9300 B.C. Still the negative uproar continued. Therefore one of the commission, Rolf Müller, a professor of astronomy at the University of Potsdam, convinced Posnansky that, if his calculations were "reworked," he could make peace with orthodox academia, by saying the correct date could either be 4500 or 10500 B.C.[21]

In 1997 the archaeologist Neil Steede pursued Posnansky's angle for dating Kalasasaya. Steede confirmed the late scholar's method, but used state-of-the-art methods to refine his date. Whereas, during Posnansky's time, conventions dictated a date of A.D. 500, our current sensibilities had permitted 200 B.C. The archaeologist Steede modernized Posnansky's calculation to 10000 B.C.[22]

Like the Kalasasaya ruins at Tiahuanaco, the site Machu Picchu in Peru is also a dating dispute. Orthodox scholastic opinion assigns a date of around A.D. 1500. Respected but lone-wolf scholars have disagreed. One eminent dissenter was the same Rolf Müller. Citing evidence that Machu Picchu was aligned astronomically, Müller used mathematical calculations of star positions to conclude that the original layout of the site dated between 4000 and 2000 B.C.[23]

ICE AGE STAR MAPS

From seventeen thousand years ago comes evidence that the ancients in Europe possessed knowledge resembling what we now consider as science. In central France, the cave paintings of Lascaux, discovered in 1940, have been known for their dramatic demonstration of prehistoric artistry. Dated to circa 15000 B.C., these friezes decorating the walls establish that the Paleolithic people of that time were aesthetically sensitive. Scholars established a consensus that the Lascaux network of caves served as a temple. The animal paintings of bulls and strange creatures were meant to guarantee success in hunting.

Lascaux was in the grip of an ice age seventeen thousand years ago. The people mainly hunted reindeer, not bulls. For hunting success, why would they adorn their temple with paintings of bulls and apparently shamanist creatures? After sixty years, that scholarly consensus has very recently vanished. Now we know that the pictures provided a map of the summer sky circa 15000 B.C.

German researcher Dr. Michael Rappenglueck, of the University of Munich, has discovered that the fresco of a bull, birdman, and bird on a stick depicts three bright stars—Vega, Deneb, and Altair—known to us as the Summer Triangle. These are among the most prominent objects overhead during the midst of the northern summer.

The prehistoric planetarium at Lascaux presents other indications of ancient astronomical intelligence. Near the entrance of the cave is a painting of a bull. Above its shoulder is what turns out to be a map of the Pleiades, the cluster of stars sometimes called the Seven Sisters. Looking inside the bull painting, an observer can see indications of spots that most likely represent other stars found in that region of sky—what we consider as part of the constellation of Taurus the bull.

The scholar Rappenglueck's victory did not end at Lascaux. In Spain, in the mountains of Pico del Castillo, he also identified a star map on the walls of a cave. Dated circa 12000 B.C., the painting known as the Frieze of Hands can demonstrate correlation to the constellation we call the Northern Crown.

So far, Rappenglueck's research has survived peer review. Archaeologists checking his conclusions have agreed that he has uncovered the earliest evidence of human interest in the stars.[24]

Portolans: How Did They Do It?

In Chapter 5 we discussed portolans. Whether these ancient maps revealed the Earth before ice covered Antarctica is now a well established controversy. That these incredible maps incorporated spherical trigonometry and sophisticated projections is known to many. The identity of the brilliant cartographers is not known to anyone. The mathematical and geographical knowledge necessary to put together just one of the many portolans cannot be treated with full justice in this book. How upending it is to find these maps giving latitudes and longitudes with modern precision!

For the European intelligence, calculating latitude was not a big problem. But the inescapable fact of Western civilization is that until around 1720, calculating longitude was impossible. At that time, the English clockmaker John Harris's invention of an appropriate chronometer became widely available. Until then, longitude—for anyone in recorded history—was a dream only.

A contemporary authority on global mapping puts the situation this way: "The search for longitude overshadowed the life of every man afloat, and the safety of every ship and cargo. Accurate measurement seemed an impossible dream, and 'discovering the longitude' had become a stock phrase in the press like 'pigs might fly'."[25]

Now how do we explain the portolans, the ancient maps of unknown origin? Even if we just forget about the originals, and consider only the reproductions available to us, we have a huge problem. European mapmakers living before the advent of Harris's technology drew the later renditions. For example, Piri Reis wrote on his map that it derived from far earlier sources. Yet his map has South America and Africa in the exact relative longitudes. The Coronets Fines map depicts the coasts of Antarctica in proper latitude and relative longitude, with a generally accurate area for the entire continent. Humans of recorded history would not match such a geographical feat until the twentieth century. What people had the technological ability to pull this off? Charles Hapgood, the ostracized portolan researcher, requested a professor at the Massachusetts Institute of Technology, Richard Strachan, to evaluate his collection of ancient maps. Strachan confirmed that complex mathematics—including projection techniques and spherical trigonometry—were needed to make the portolans. Additionally, he pointed out that the unknown ancient cartographers required geographical knowledge of Earth's sphericity. Consequently, Strachan too began to wonder about the mysteriously advanced people of antiquity responsible for the maps.

United States Air Force expert Lorenzo Burroughs, as chief of the Cartographic Section at Westover Air Base, labored over the Oronteus Finaeus map. He sent his conclusion to Hapgood: "We are convinced that the findings made by you and your associates are valid, and that they raise extremely important questions affecting geology and ancient history."[26]

VEDIC SCIENCE REVIVAL

Turning to the Vedic archaeoastronomy of ancient India, we need to understand that here we are plunging into deep water, beyond our present empirical corroboration. Though some of the information can be grasped and put into a Western context, much of the Vedic science seems, literally, to be of other dimensions.

A less sympathetic way to refer to the incomprehensibility would be to stick on Vedic science the easy label "mythology." The *Encyclopaedia Britannica*, avoiding that outright dismissal, skirts the issue quite diplomatically: "Far less is known about science in India, largely because few scholars have investigated it. . . . Indian thought, however, was primarily philosophical and otherworldly and was concerned more with escaping this world than with understanding it."[27]

Few Western scholars have investigated Vedic science because, until very recently, none of them took it seriously. But now an increasing flock of both Indian and Western scientists are painstakingly researching the waves and currents of Vedic science within their reach. They can glimpse that the Vedic vision indeed concerned understanding the world—besides, of course, how to escape its temporariness. The problem is, however, that Vedic understanding is not immediately understandable to moderns.

Until the 1920s it was commonly supposed that mathematics had its birth among the ancient Greeks. At that time, Egypt seemed to clearly offer little mathematical precedent, and India was out of the question. Later, success in deciphering and interpreting the technical materials from ancient Mesopotamia passed the math crown from ancient Greece to Old Babylonia. Only in the last quarter of the twentieth century did something else emerge—a Vedic origin. A professor of mathematics at the University of California, A. Seidenberg, after a twenty-year study, traced the origin of mathematics to Vedic commentaries called the *Shulbasutras*. These works are primarily technical manuals delineating the mathematics needed for designing sacrificial altars.

The *Shulbasutras* highlight a religious origin of mathematics. Moreover, they enable us to date Vedic intellectual elements through the precision of mathematics—rather than linguistic theory. In doing so, Seidenberg pushed far back past the mathematics of both Egypt and Babylonia. He observed two distinct lines of development in ancient mathematics: the arithmetic and the geometric. If both traditions could be traced to the same source, then the unique origin of mathematics had been found.

In a series of ground-breaking studies, now found in the Archive for History of Exact Science, Seidenberg examined the mathematical connections between Babylonia, Egypt, Greece, and India. He established that they all shared the same origin. In cautious scholarly expression he identified the common source: "Hence we do not hesitate to place the Vedic altar rituals, or, more exactly, rituals exactly like them, far back of 1700 B.C. To summarize the argument: the elements of ancient geometry found in Egypt and Babylonia stem from a ritual system of the kind described in the *Shulbasutras*."[28]

Seidenberg had to carefully select appropriate language to present the results of his research. Although his tracing of Egyptian and Babylonian mathematics to Vedic knowledge took him "far back of 1700 B.C.," the Sanskrit scholars he consulted would not grant him linguistic confirmation of the Vedic texts for such a remote date. Certainly, the philological barrier they had erected had nothing to do with the exactitudes of mathematical history. Sanskritists rule on the basis of linguistic conjecture—frequently the ultimate arbiter in Indology.

To circumvent the linguistic logjam, Seidenberg rather obviously sheathed his pointed conclusion in rhetoric of "an earlier source exactly *like* the *Shulbasutras*," or he would say, "an unnamed source prior to Babylonia." Clearly, in this way he could push ahead with his scientific demonstration of the mathematics of these Vedic commentaries without incurring the wrath of his Indological brethren. He explained:

> Sanskrit scholars do not give me a date so far back as 1700 B.C. Therefore I *postulate* a pre-Babylonian ... source for the kind of geometric rituals we see preserved in the *Shulbasutras*, or at least for the *mathematics* involved in these rituals.[29]
>
> A common source for the Pythagorean and Vedic mathematics is to be sought either in the Vedic mathematics or in an older mathematics very much like it. The view that Vedic mathematics is a derivative of Old Babylonia having been rejected, a common

source for these mathematics, different from Old Babylonia of 1700 B.C., was indicated. Thus what are regarded as the two main sources of Western mathematics, namely Pythagorean mathematics and Old-Babylonian mathematics, both flow from a still older source.[30]

Dethroning both the Greeks and the Old Babylonians to establish a Vedic origin is very risky business. Even such a distinguished Western scholar of mathematics and the history of science as Seidenberg had to tread carefully. There had been at least a century of efforts to take anything acceptable as scientific in the Vedic past and attribute it to Hellenistic Greece. When Sumerian and Babylonian mathematics began to intrigue modern scholars, India still did not arouse primary interest.

Indian mathematics was credited with only a comparatively recent and subordinate role. It was seen to have assisted Islamic mathematics, by contributing the decimal system. Also, some distinction was granted to India for developing the zero and the trigonometric function "sin."[31] But Seidenberg dug deeper. For both wings of ancient mathematical development, he exposed the root sunk beyond both Greece and Babylonia.

He traced the arithmetical or computational tradition in Egypt and Babylonia to a source "exactly like the *Shulbasutras*" and demonstrated that geometric constructions, geometric algebra, and the concept of proof in Greece arose from the same "twin" of the *Shulbasutras*. He reproduced a proof on the area of a trapezoid to dissipate previous notions of scholars that no proofs preceded Euclid: "Many writers who refer to the *Shulbasutras* say that there are no proofs there. We can only suppose that these writers have not bothered to examine the work."[32]

Disagreement is a normal part of critical scholarship, and Seidenberg certainly has his polite detractors. For example, Carl Boyer in his *History of Mathematics* chooses not to support

Seidenberg's conclusions.[33] Vedic mathematics, however, is a relatively unexplored frontier. Much more work is needed—not peremptory dismissal of a possible Vedic origin for Babylonian and Greek maths.

Modern mathematicians, astronomers, and other scientists are the last to show up at the Indology party. Because linguists were the first to show, their theories overspread the future of Indic studies like an ice cap enveloping a continent. Archaeology, a latecomer, was easily glaciated, as prominent archaeologists now frankly attest. Western Sanskritists and Indo-European language specialists sometimes seem to react to the scientific latecomers as if the linguistic scholars were being shoved into the back seat, while the scientifically trained scholars took over the driving. Often an attitude rears its head that Indology is a field of "humanities," and that therefore scientists are ill-prepared to stick their noses into it. After all, how does a background in physics and mathematics help one to sort out what many scholars perceive as the tangled web of Vedic myth?

We might consider: If a scientific book happens to be written in the German language, does that make an expert in German grammar automatically the ruling authority on the scientific information the book conveys? If we apply the same standards of linguistic domination that have bound Indic studies, we would probably have to answer yes. This academic hegemony often seems to impede the new wave of Vedic scientific researchers— once they have warded off the old specter of Hellenistic Greece as the source of all rationalistic thinking.

ASTRONOMY IN THE VEDAS

New initiatives in the long-overlooked field of Vedic astronomy promise to be as illuminating as Hapgood's study of portolans. More than two hundred years ago, in 1790, a Scottish mathematician, John Playfair, championed a starting date of 4300 B.C. for Vedic astronomical observations recorded in tables still used in India.[34]

During Playfair's time, a French astronomer, Jean-Sylvain Bailly, also supported a remote antiquity for Vedic astronomical lore. He asserted: "The motions of the stars calculated by the Hindus before some 4,500 years vary not even a single minute from the [modern] tables of Cassini and Meyer. The Indian tables give the same annual variation of the moon as that discovered by Tycho Brahe—a variation unknown to the school of Alexandria and also the Arabs."[35]

Amazingly, since the bygone days of Playfair and Bailly, little scientific work has been done to either reject or support the antiquity of Indian astronomical tables. Indeed, the reigning Sanskritist and Indologist at Harvard University, Michael Witzel, affirms: "The Vedic night sky has remained somewhat of a neglected stepchild of cosmological and cosmographical studies. . . . Even now, after some 150 years of the study of Vedic texts, our understanding of the Vedic night sky still is in its infancy."[36]

Although more than two hundred years have passed since Playfair and Bailley's bold declaration, fresh winds are finally blowing. At last scientific-minded scholars are seriously poring over Vedic astronomical data and texts. We will have to be patient, however, in spite of the excitement the new research is generating. Academia requires a slow process of deliberation. For the informed public, the latest studies are just shy of the point that allow nonspecialists a settled overview of the gems emerging. Otherwise, a survey of Vedic astronomy, to do it justice, should be a lengthy section of this book, instead of just an appetizer.

Contemporary voices that argue for a revision in Indology often cite the apparently potent references to ancient astronomical sightings in the Vedas. The *Rig-*, *Yajur-*, and *Atharva-vedas* especially have been milked in this way. The Puranas and

Mahabharata are waiting their turn. These texts mention equinoxes and solstices that may indicate distant millennia.

Mental barriers over two hundred years of Indological studies have made rare the Western scholar who gave serious credence to these planetary alignments. The ancient Indians were dismissed as unscientific—hence, no research necessary. Furthermore, any hint of brilliance in the Vedas was always ascribed to foreign influence at a later date, and the Vedic texts themselves, of course, were attributed to a later date.

In the minds of revisionist scholars, a way not to go is the well-known route of the established scholar David Pingree. Looked upon as an authority on Indian archaeoastronomy, he refuses to allow the ancient Indians basic astronomical techniques. His reasoning? The Vedic texts do not specifically delineate these skills. Therefore, Pingree chooses to conclude, any potentially radical references can be immediately dismissed.

Scholars of Pingree's ilk argue: where, outside the Vedic texts themselves, are there any possible indicators of a genuine observational astronomy in ancient India? So far, archaeologists have not dug up any images of ancient stargazers at work. No instruments, charts, daily notes, or symbols revealing observational techniques have emerged from the ground.

Scholars keen on an overhaul disagree, of course. They point out the obvious: the very existence of the references means the skills necessary to formulate them also existed. Somehow, the Indians of antiquity were able to analyze the skies and heavens.

A major quest is to understand whether the Vedic literature—more precisely, Vedic knowledge in written form—existed far earlier than conventionally thought. New breakthroughs from astronomy, indicating an earlier Vedic origin, may not suffice to satisfy everyone. Even if the astronomical references are accepted as actual data from remote antiquity, naysayers can always object that these sightings were traditions passed down over the millennia, to a more recent time when the texts were assembled. For example, in the case of the *Rig-veda*, prominent Indologist Romila Thapar admits, "References to what have been interpreted as configurations of stars have been used to suggest dates of about 4000 B.C. for these hymns." But she objects that "planetary positions could have been observed in earlier times and such observations have been handed down as part of an oral tradition." Thus, she concludes, these astronomical observations, even if genuine, "do not constitute proof of the chronology of the Vedic hymns."[37]

Because the boom in Vedic archaeoastronomy is new, we need to tread carefully. For example, however shockingly ancient appear the Vedic passages that allude to astronomical phenomena, their textual contexts, and the interpretation of these contexts, have been open to intense debate. The incumbent Dean of Indology, Witzel, for one, immediately sallies forth to deflect any readings that may foster radical conclusions: "Too much emphasis seems to have been laid on taking the Vedic statements literally, as if they were made from a modern observatory."[38]

Dr. Koenraad Elst, considered a gadfly in the eyes of his conservative colleagues, takes the antiquity of Vedic astronomical references very seriously. Still, for the sake of objectivity, he provides us with a brief example of "the ambiguity battle," in regards to precessional phases.

To say that a constellation "never swerves from the East" (as is said of Pleiades in the *Shatapatha Brahmana* 2.1.2.3) seems to mean that it contains the spring equinox, implying that it is on the equator, which intersects the horizon due east. But this might seem insufficiently explicit for the modern reader, who is used to a precise and separate technical terminology for such matters. But then, the modern reader will have to accept that technical terminology in Vedic days mostly consisted of fixed metaphorical uses of common terms.[39]

Research of the Vedic sky has become easier because of the latest planetarium software. With the click of a mouse, programs such as SkyMap Pro and PancAng2 can display millions of stars and other celestial bodies as seen from any location on Earth, at any date. Although a personal computer can generate, with remarkable reliability, the Vedic night sky as the Vedic people saw it, still the crucial problem remains: interpreting Vedic passages according to current understandings of Vedic language and culture. Hence, linguistic scholars are apt to resoundingly protest any ancient astronomy theory that is apparently built upon just one isolated sentence from a Vedic text.

The appropriate academic restraint and conservatism serve their purpose, of course, in the careful pursuit of knowledge. Nevertheless, some scholars have already conceded that Vedic archaeoastronomy is an awakening bull, with the potential for shattering all the old china in the closet. The new breed of scientifically trained Vedic researchers say they are taking sufficient time to present their final conclusions, in a way that will satisfy reasonable, unbiased scholars.

Some of the potential finds do suspiciously point to distant millennia. They entail references to the precession of the equinoxes, as well as summer solstices and solar eclipses. There are still loose ends, however. Western scholars have ignored these potential references for so long, and the present focus upon exact sciences in the Vedas is so fresh. Certainly the best results will come from a joint effort by scientific and linguistic experts—not domination by one over the other.

Revisionist scholars do more than just debate the meaning of individual passages in the Vedas. They are quick to alert us to the surprising overall picture of chronology that is emerging. So far, all potential astro-chronological references in Vedic literature—whether indirect or direct, obscure or explicit—consistently point to a much earlier chronology than what scholars have allowed.

The nonconforming researchers assert: just show even one astro-chronological hint in the Vedic texts that confirms a late chronology. Furthermore, these dissenting scholars delineate the answer that habitually trots out of the old barn to meet their challenge.

Invariably the astro-chronological content of a passage is denied in one of two ways. Denial-response number one: mainstream academia does not allow that a particular passage under investigation has anything whatsoever to do with astronomy. Non-mainstreamers do agree that sometimes this is possible. As explained earlier in this section, Vedic astronomical terminology is constructed out of ordinary, nontechnical words that, in a passage, have been endowed with a technical meaning, to convey astronomical information. Sometimes renegade scholars, in their quest for an upset, can read too much into a passage, just as the establishment scholars can refuse to see what is there.

Denial-response number two: luminaries such as Witzel and Thapar agree to recognize the astronomical content of a passage but refuse its connection to the date when the text was composed. In other words, they say that, however antiquated references to the Vedic night sky appear, actually they have somehow or other become embedded into a text that is of unarguably recent composition.

The new Vedic archaeoastronomers counter that this tactic, when repeatedly employed, implies the Vedas suffer a strange preoccupation. When conservative scholars continually resort to this maneuver, in grappling with one astro-chronological reference after another, they thereby, inadvertently, accuse that the whole mass of Vedic literature has a perverse hang-up—it likes to predate itself. The implication is that—just to fool modern Indologists, or to impress the people of that time—the Vedic sages consistently ignored the stellar patterns visible in the sky above them. Instead they took delight in strewing, systematically, all the Vedic texts with references to ancient configurations of distant millennia. This bizarre conspiracy plot has never been proved.

In any case, another agenda is becoming more crucial than the latest debates over dating the Vedic texts through astronomy. Innovative eyes are watching the mission to demonstrate advanced intelligence in the India of remote antiquity. Here the new probes can certainly score mightily. Explorers of the ancient astronomy of India can help confirm that intelligent people existed in the far distant past—a civilization advanced enough to make precise astronomical observations and pass them along accurately, in an oral Vedic system of knowledge.

Spearheading the new research into Vedic archaeoastronomy is Cornell University Ph.D. and Cambridge researcher Dr. Richard Thompson, mentioned in the previous chapter. Sensitive to the traditions of both Vedic and Western epistemology, his work indicates advanced knowledge of astronomy and geography in the *Bhagavata Purana.*

Recently Thompson and his colleagues have intensified their formidable revision on the dating of Kali-yuga. First, they allow our sticking to Indological convention, by attributing the Vedic astronomical texts, the *jyotisha-shastras,* to A.D. 500. Next, they watch amusedly as we reach for the skies. Our credulity must stretch past the breaking point, they now point out, because we are burdened to explain how the people of that period, amazingly—in this limited case only—conjured up the advanced astronomical knowledge necessary for calculating a planetary alignment several thousand years before.

Back-calculating planetary positions is a highly sophisticated and complex task. Certainly, modern scholars can attribute no such scientific skills to ca. A.D. 500. Yet, the Indians of that time, to justify their myths and dogmas, pulled the job off. They deviously but correctly calculated a planetary alignment thousands of years prior. We must allow that amazingly—in this case only—the Indians demonstrated consummate knowledge.[40]

Thompson and his research associates urge us to opt for the obvious: the planetary alignment signifying Kali-yuga was observed as a historical fact in 3102 B.C., and was passed down in the Vedic histories, which date to that time. Later people, in ca. A.D. 500, knew about it not from a miraculous contrivance—far beyond the expertise of their time—but from their accurate ancient histories.

Thompson's work has been published in the *Journal of Scientific Exploration*, the most rigorous forum for critical, peer-reviewed research into unexplained phenomena. The quarterly journal is the organ of the Society for Scientific Exploration (SSE), an international academic organization run by scientists from Stanford and Princeton universities. Its mission statement explains:

> The primary goal of the SSE is to provide a professional forum for presentations, criticism, and debate concerning topics which are for various reasons ignored or studied inadequately within mainstream science. A secondary goal is to promote improved understanding of those factors that unnecessarily limit the scope of scientific inquiry, such as sociological constraints, restrictive worldviews, hidden theoretical assumptions, and the temptation to convert prevailing theory into dogma.[41]

In the Society's journal, Thompson presented his work on the ancient Vedic astronomical text *Surya-siddhanta:*

> This paper discusses a rule given in the Indian astronomical text *Surya-siddhanta* for computing the angular diameters of the planets. By combining these angular diameters with the circumferences of the planetary orbits listed in this text, it is possible to compute the diameters of the planets. When these computations

are carried out, the results agree surprisingly well with modern astronomical data. Several possible explanations for this are discussed, and it is hypothesized that the angular diameter rule in the *Surya-siddhanta* may be based on advanced astronomical knowledge that was developed in ancient times but has now been largely forgotten.[42]

The cosmological information contained in the *Bhagavata Purana* has occupied most of Thompson's attention. During his nearly three decades of scrutiny, he has uncovered remarkable parallels. For example, the Vedic universe can provide an amazingly accurate map of our solar system. When seen from a certain perspective, the cosmos described in the *Bhagavata Purana* can present distances between celestial bodies that strikingly approximate the distances scientists have calculated between the major planets. How could the ancient Vedic sages have come so close—without our technology?

Significant for the revival of Vedic astronomy, Thompson is advising a unique project in West Bengal, on the bank of the Ganges River. An enormous "Temple of the Vedic Planetarium" is scheduled for completion around 2015. Under the auspices of the International Society for Krishna Consciousness and partially funded by the grandson of automobile titan Henry Ford, the awesome temple will include a two-hundred-seat planetarium with state-of-the-art projection.

High-tech displays are also planned. Employing 3D computerized graphics, on high-definition screens, these exhibits will offer "tours" through the Vedic cosmos of higher and lower realms and beings. The Krishna devotees, practitioners of the Vedic Vaishnava tradition, say the purpose of the unparalleled task is to demonstrate to pilgrims the worthiness of Vedic cosmology and astronomy. The late founder of the international Krishna organization, A. C. Bhaktivedanta Swami Prabhupada, instructed his followers: "We will show the Vedic conception of the planetary system within this material world and above the material world. We want to exhibit Vedic culture throughout the whole world." [43]

As consultant for the project, Dr. Thompson says his mission is to render the ancient Vedic knowledge of astronomy into visual experiences an international audience will not forget. Obviously, someone is taking the Vedic sciences very seriously.

Notes

1 Vera Rubin, *Magnificent Cosmos*, Scientific American Presents 9, no.1 (Spring 1998): 107, 110.
2 Ibid., p.15.
3 Reuters, 21 May 1999.
4 John Wilford, "A Discovery Provides Grist for Planetary Comparisons," *New York Times*, 20 April 1999.
5 Z. Sitchin, *Genesis Revisited: Is Modern Science Catching Up with Ancient Knowledge?* (Santa Fe, New Mexico: Bear and Company Publishing, 1991), pp. 5–9.
6 Interview on talk radio "The Zoh Show," WCBM (AM 680) in Baltimore, Maryland, on 9 October 1998; published in Hieronimus & Co. Newsletter, nos. 15–16.
7 "Stonehenge," Britannica CD-ROM, Encyclopaedia Britannica Inc., 1997.
8 Herodotus, *The History*, trans. David Grene (Chicago: University of Chicago Press, 1987), 2:4.
9 E. M. Antoniadi, *L'Astronomie Egyptienne* (Paris: Imprimerie Gauthier-Villars, 1934), pp. 3–4.
10 Diodorus Siculus, Book l, trans. C. H. Oldfather (London: Loeb Classical Library, 1989), pp. 279–80.
11 Herodotus, "Canon of the Kings of Egypt," in I. C. Cory, *Ancient Fragments*, orig. ed. 1832 (Minneapolis: Wizards Bookshelf, 1975), p.171.
12 Andrew Collins, *Gods of Eden* (London: Headline Book Publishing, 1998), p. 316.

13 See Livio Stecchini, "Notes on the Relation of Ancient Mysteries to the Great Pyramid," in Peter Tompkins, *Secrets of the Great Pyramid* (London: Allen Lane, 1996), pp. 287–382.

14 See William Fix, *Pyramid Odyssey* (Toronto: Jonathan-James Books, 1978), pp. 30–31.

15 See Stecchini, in Tompkins, pp. 287–382.

16 Ibid., p. 373.

17 In Graham Hancock, *Fingerprints of the Gods* (London: Mandarin Paperbacks, 1996), p. 484.

18 For the full presentation of Bauval's research, see Robert Bauval and Adrian Gilbert, *The Orion Mystery* (London: Heinemann, 1994). Also see Robert Bauval and Graham Hancock, *Message of the Sphinx: A Quest for the Hidden Legacy of Mankind* (New York: Three Rivers Press, 1996).

19 Mainstream Egyptologists often fret that maverick researchers and their paradigm-challenging conclusions receive unwarranted attention from the public and the media. Meanwhile, they feel, establishment scholars receive no such limelight. Readers looking for a mainstream response to alternative theories on the pyramids may consult *Giza the Truth*, by Ian Lawton and Chris Ogilvie-Herald, Virgin Publishing Ltd, 2000.

20 Letters to *Nature* from J. M. Malville, F. Wendorf, A. A. Mazar, R. Schild, *Nature*, 2 April 1998.

21 See Arthur Posnansky, *Tiahuanacu: The Cradle of American Man*, 4 volumes (New York: J. J. Augustin, 1945).

22 See Neil Steede's presentation in the Discovery TV documentary "Myths of Mankind," first broadcast in Europe in August 1997.

23 J. Alden Mason, *The Ancient Civilizations of Peru* (London: Penguin Books, 1991), p. 237.

24 David Whitehouse, BBC News Online science editor, BBC News, 9 August 2000. Dr. Micheal Rappenglueck presents his research at http://www.infis.org/contents.htm. 11 September 2000.

25 Simon Bethon and Andrew Robinson, *The Shape of the World: The Mapping and Discovery of Earth* (London: Guild Publishing, 1991), p.117.

26 Charles H. Hapgood, *Maps of the Ancient Sea Kings* (Philadelphia: Chilton Books, 1966), pp. 244–45.

27 "History of Science/India," Britannica CD-ROM, Encyclopaedia Britannica Inc., 1997.

28 A. Seidenberg, "The Ritual Origin of Geometry," *Archive for the History of Exact Sciences* 1 (1962): 515.

29 A. Seidenberg, "The Origin of Mathematics", *Archive for the History of Exact Sciences* 18 (1978): 324. Emphasis in original.

30 Ibid., p. 329.

31 See Johannes Bronkhorst, "A Note on Zero and the Numerical Place-

value System in Ancient India," in *Asiatische Studien/Etudes Asiatiques*, 48, no. 4 (1994): 1039–42.

32 Seidenberg, "Ritual Origin of Geometry", p. 519.

33 Carl B. Boyer, *A History of Mathematics* (New York: Wiley, 1968).

34 Playfair's argumentation, "Remarks on the astronomy of the Brahmins," Edinburgh 1790, is reproduced in Dharampal, *Indian Science and Technology in the Eighteenth Century* (Hyderabad: Academy of Gandhian Studies, 1983; Delhi: Impex India, 1971), pp. 69, 124.

35 Quoted in S. Sathe, *In Search for the Year of the Bharata War* (Hyderabad: Navabharati, 1982), p. 32.

36 Michael Witzel, "Looking for the Heavenly Casket," *Electronic Journal of Vedic Studies* (vol. 1.2, 1995 [cited 15 June 1998]); available from http://nautilus.shore.net/~india/ejvs/

37 Romila Thapar, "The Perennial Aryans," Seminar, December 1992.

38 Michael Witzel, editor's notes, Electronic Journal of Vedic Studies (vol. 5.2, December 1999 [cited 29 December 1999]); available from http://nautilus.shore.net/~india/ejvs/

39 Koenraad Elst, "Astronomical data and the Aryan question" (Leuven, Belgium, 21 December 1998 [cited 29 December 1999]); available from http://members.xoom.com/KoenraadElst/

40 Dr. Koenraad Elst presents this elaboration on the planetary conjunction that the Vedic literature claims began the Kali-yuga: "True, the conjunction was not spectacularly exact, having an orb of 37° between the two most extreme planetary positions. But that exactly supports the hypothesis of an actual observation as opposed to a back-calculation. Indeed, if the Hindu astronomers were able to calculate this position after a lapse of many centuries (when the *Jyotisha-shastra* was written), it is unclear what reason they would have had for picking out that particular conjunction. Surely, such conjunctions are spectacular to those who witness one, and hence worth recording if observed. But they are not that exceptional when considered over millennia: even closer conjunctions of all visible planets do occur. . . . If the Hindu astronomers had simply been going over their astronomical tables looking for an exceptional conjunction, they could have found more spectacular ones than the one on 18 February 3102 B.C." See Koenraad Elst, "Astronomical data and the Aryan question."

41 Society for Scientific Exploration Homepage [cited 15 June 1998]; available from http://www.scientificexploration.org/jse.html

42 Richard Thompson, *Journal of Scientific Exploration*, vol. 11, no. 2, p. 193.

43 A. C. Bhaktivedanta Swami Prabhupada, 27 February 1976. See http://www.iskcon.org.uk/mayapur_design

CHAPTER 12

THE DEVAS:
CONSCIOUSNESS
CONTROLS NATURE

~

T
he theory that nomadic invaders or migrants known as
the Aryan race carried the seeds of Vedic civilization
into India is now under attack. Examining this old
surety in the light of new criticism is happening at the
post-doctorate level of Indic studies. Yet, judging from the information available to the general educated public, we would never
know of the call for revision. Libraries continue to disseminate
confident declarations of the so-called Aryan race and its entrance
into India.

Here is a lucid rendition from the mainstream, still fed to
university students and the general public:

> The classical civilization of India developed from the earlier Vedic
> literature, and the Vedic civilization was the creation of the
> Aryans, an invading people, whose first arrival in the subconti-
> nent is probably to be dated about 1500 B.C. Perhaps some 200
> years after this estimated date there had begun to come into being
> a collection of religious hymns which were eventually organized
> as the *Rig-veda*. . . . The culture which we find in the *Rig-veda* was

not developed in India, but, in most essentials, imported, already formed, from outside.[1]

Thus stated T. Burrow, the occupant of the Boden Chair of Sanskrit at Oxford University from 1944 to 1976—hardly a pedigree to sneeze at. The pronouncements of contemporary authorities such as Burrow certainly cannot be explained away as "the past excesses of the colonial era in academia." Nor can the effects of this scholarship be made to disappear overnight, though the new challenges are intensifying.

The massive misunderstanding of the Sanskrit term *arya* was discussed in Chapter 7. From *arya* the anglicized "Aryan" was derived. Needless to say, no Vedic texts use this anglicized form. Western scholars created "Aryan" to refer to a certain class of languages, as well as an ethnic group they thought they saw in the Vedas.

The text *Rig-veda*, especially, has often been cast almost entirely in terms of ethnic battles in northwestern India. A clear snapshot supposedly arises there, of many nomadic Aryan tribes fighting with aborigines known as *Dasas* and *Dasyus*. Eventually, through military and/or cultural conquest, the Aryan intruders are said to have triumphed and imposed their Vedic ways.

If the Indo-Aryans indeed entered India from without, perhaps skeletal remains would establish this foreign origin. Brian Hemphill of Vanderbilt University has compared ancient human remains from Central Asia and the Indus Valley and found no skeletal traces of intruders from the outside.[2] Are the Aryans a distinct Indian race? The scholar Kenneth A. R. Kennedy confirms that physical anthropologists find no skeletal remains identifiable as different from the standard old population of North India. In his article "Have Aryans Been Identified in the Prehistoric Skeletal Record from South Asia?" Kennedy firmly declares, "All prehistoric human remains recovered from the Indian subcontinent are phenotypically identifiable as South Asians. Furthermore, their biological continuity with living peoples of India, Pakistan, Sri Lanka, and the border regions is well established across time and space."[3] Certainly, the attempt to see the Rig-vedic Aryans as a physically distinguishable race is a mistake.

The *Rig-veda* is clearly neither a historical document nor a geographic handbook. Yet, although no one—Vedic adherent or academic—sees the *Rig-veda* as history or geography, modern scholars naturally feel the pressure to glean as much non-esoteric information out of the text as possible. Its language, rich in metaphor, is notoriously problematic for scholars. They like to refer to the *Rig-veda* as complicated Indo-Aryan and Indo-European poetry. Understandably, they expect that their educational qualifications will allow them to "read between the lines," to gain a vision into the times.

Both Vedic adepts and scholars agree that in the *Rig-veda* are references to two oceans, eastern and western, and an area of seven rivers that is obviously northwestern India. Seen through the traditional geocentric vision of Western scholarship, these few earthly details have been seized upon to lock the *aryas* into northwestern India—after they immigrated, of course.

Vedic sympathizers, however, see something much greater. Who would dare think to follow the *arya* trail "off planet"? Yet, an extraterrestrial scope is clearly where the Vedas lead.

Many verses in the *Rig-veda* refer to Indra as the head of the *aryas*. But no Vedic literature ever treats Indra as the mere chieftain of an earthly tribe. Whether we accept the actual existence of a powerful extraterrestrial entity known as Indra or deem him mythological, readers cannot make sense out of the *Rig-veda* unless they see Indra as a prime *arya* mover on the universal scene. Living in the Vedic higher planets, Indra sometimes involved himself directly with residents of Earth—before the onset of Kali-yuga ended celestial visitations.

What is true for Indra also holds for other prime *arya* cosmic movers in the *Rig-veda*, such as Varuna and Agni. Like Indra, their portfolio is clearly interplanetary. Based in celestial planets said to feature material amenities, life spans, and powers far beyond what Earth offers, these universal managers—*devas*, or demigods—are neither terrestrial mortals nor spiritual immortals. Vishnu, however, is always in a unique status—eternally beyond even the heavenly realms of the material cosmos.

DASAS AND DASYUS: PRE-VEDIC ABORIGINES?

The main Vedic sense of *arya* denotes practitioners of Vedic spiritually based life styles and metaphysics. The Vedas show that sometimes certain people can possess *arya* qualifications, and sometimes they can fall away. When they degenerate they become classified as inimical. Thus *aryas* can appear to be whimsically fighting other genuine *aryas*, when the actual situation is that one group, deviating from the high *arya* standard, has debased into condemnable behavior.

An earthbound and ethnocentric reading of the *Rig-veda* puts *arya* tribes in permanent ethnic conflict with indigenous tribes known as *dasas* and *dasyus*. The *aryas* triumphed, militarily and/or culturally. They are said to have erected the Vedic social ladder and forced the luckless predominated tribes to the bottom of it.

When Indologists turn to Monier-Williams' Sanskrit dictionary, they find that the perennial classic translates the root of both *dasa* and *dasyu* as "to suffer want, become exhausted," and so forth. Lacking proper qualities, the *dasas* and *dasyus* are deemed inferior. Vedic preceptors have always said that it is degraded behavior that puts the *dasas* and *dasyus* in conflict with the *aryas*. The following two passages from the *Rig-veda* illustrate this cause of the clashes:

[To Indra:] Distinguish between the *aryas* and the *dasyus*. Make the *dasyus* submit to those who are worshipers. Correct them, who have no law. (*Rig-veda* 1.51.8)

[To Indra:] The *dasyu* is against us. He is without good deeds and devoid of good thoughts. He follows other laws, and is not human. Indra, O killer of unfriendly people, outwit the *dasas'* weapon. (*Rig-veda* 10.22.8)

In the *Rig-veda* the two appellations *dasa* and *dasyu* both refer to people of hostile and unintelligible speech, and people who may be either human or extraterrestrial. Bearing in mind that the prime criterion for classification as an *arya* or *arya* foe is behavior—spiritual acumen—we should also know that language and family line are used as secondary indicators.

All the Vedic literatures generally describe ancient history based on a preponderance of *arya* or non-*arya* qualities in particular peoples and dynasties. Often the ethical and the ethnic do coincide—owing to families, peoples, and even whole regions of the universe perpetuating certain standards. But the relationship between ethnicity—whether terrestrial or extraterrestrial—and spirituality should never be taken as *quid pro quo*. Many a scholar, unaided by Vedic guidance, trips over this perhaps subtle point.

Moving from the *Rig-veda* to the *Mahabharata*, the same behavioral criteria between *arya* and non-*arya* accompany us, though the Sanskrit used in the two texts clearly differs. The language of the *Rig-veda* has been labeled Vedic and that of the *Mahabharata* has been designated epic. The two are like parallel dialects—one cannot be shown to proceed out of the other.

In the two texts the generic names for non-*aryas* can differ. Although in the *Mahabharata*, *dasyu* denotes thieves and plunderers, the term *dasa* refers to domestic servants. The *Mahabharata* refers to degraded peoples with a term not found in the *Rig-veda*:

mleccha. A person seen from the Vedic perspective to be unclean and barbaric is called a *mleccha.* A subordinate characteristic is that he does not speak Sanskrit. When viewed from the perspective of a spiritual culture that transmits its knowledge and techniques through spoken or recorded Sanskrit, not knowing that language is obviously a severe disadvantage.

Mlecchas can arise even in families and regions where *arya* quality predominates. Though the deviants' external characteristics, such as language and family line, seem to indicate they are *arya,* their disconnection from Vedic guidelines lowers them to the *mleccha* category.

Both the *Rig-veda* and *Mahabharata* frequently refer to *Brahman,* the Vedic generic term denoting the eternal spiritual reality. *Brahman* is the ultimate principle and basis of the world. The *Rig-veda* poets frequently mention "our *Brahman,*" and describe persons having an affectionate relationship with *Brahman.*[4] They also often speak of other people who despise *Brahman.*[5] In the *Mahabharata,* the Pandava brothers fight specifically against those who are anti-*Brahman.*[6] The chapter of the *Mahabharata* known as the *Bhagavad-gita* presents Krishna's personal statement that *Brahman* rests on Him:

> I am the basis of Brahman, of that which is immortal, undecaying, and endless, of that upon which ultimate happiness is founded.[7]

A popular misconception today holds that the *Rig-veda* and *Mahabharata* are completely different works, which cannot be grouped together under the banner of Vedic literature. Sometimes specialists in the *Rig-, Sama-, Yajur-,* and *Atharva-veda* protest loudly when an erudite Vedic teacher's quotations easily jump to and fro between the *Rig-veda* and a Vedic history like the *Mahabharata.* Though certainly the *Rig-veda* and the *Mahabharata* each has its uniqueness, their continuity and commonality are readily discerned. They share terms, personalities, and, most importantly, they share in *dharma*—the Vedic metaphysic and universal outlook. Both texts present confrontations between *aryas* and non-*aryas*—those for and against the Vedic standard of civilization.

The stage of the *Rig-veda* is predominantly cosmic. The battles are both on-planet and off. In the *Mahabharata*, the action is much more Earth-based, but the extraterrestrial scope is still there. In the *Rig-veda*, humans on Earth do not fight against the non-*aryas*; the celestial heavyweight Indra does. Previous academic attempts to make Indra into a Eurasia-originated "Aryan invader," who around 1500 B.C. destroyed a few cities in the Indus Valley civilization, are ludicrous.

An equally ridiculous mistake was to misread references to the conflicts between light and darkness as biological indicators of battles between light-skinned (European) and dark-skinned (Indian) races. These blunders obliterated the actual scenario: a battle of *consciousness*, between *arya* and non-*arya* states of awareness. Instead of this clear reading, we still hear that the Vedas advocate racism and race wars.

Recently, established Western Indologists have finally risen up to oust the old racial interpretation of the *Rig-veda* from academic discussion. But as usual, their efforts will not manifest in books the general public reads for another ten or so years. The University of Michigan, in October 1996, hosted a conference, "Aryan and Non-Aryan in South Asia." The Harvard Oriental Series published its proceedings and papers in the volume *Aryan and Non-Aryan in South Asia. Evidence, Interpretation and Ideology*. Thomas R. Trautmann, in his paper, "Constructing the Racial Theory of Indian Civilization," traces the blame to race theories of the nineteenth century. Laying bare the historical roots of Indology, he shows how predominant notions of race forced contorted interpretations of text fragments that have persisted almost until the twenty-first century.[8]

Hans Heinrich Hock contributed "Through a glass darkly: Modern 'racial' interpretations vs. textual and general prehistoric evidence on *arya* and *dasa/dasyu* in Vedic society." He too traces the genesis of scholars' racial interpretations of the Vedas to the "scramble of the European powers to divide up the non-European world."[9] For example, the light-skinned British could read into the ancient *Rig-veda* their colonial designs on the darker-skinned subcontinent. In this way, "the British takeover of India seemed to provide a perfect parallel to the assumed takeover of prehistoric India by the invading 'Aryans'."[10] Hock demonstrates that the race notions invented by European colonialism and imperialism have nothing to do with remote antiquity and its clashes between *arya* and *dasa/dasyu*.[11]

Another popular misconception Indologists have distributed to the public is that the *Rig-veda* describes a nomadic culture. This mistake is another instance of the strain to see in the *Rig-veda* text a mass influx of Aryan nomads. Looking for nomads, a priori, furnishes us with a nomadic reading of the *Rig-veda*. Consequently we shut our eyes to anything contrary.

For example, the prominent Sanskritist Michael Witzel feels that the *Rig-veda* people "do not know of cities or towns but speak, instead, of ruined places where one might collect potsherds for ritualistic purposes."[12] The archaeologist Greg Possehl countered, "The *Rig-veda* does refer to places as *pur*, 'walled', a 'fort', or a 'stronghold'. There is a reference to places of this sort as being of metal, or *ayas*."[13]

An open-minded analysis of references to material culture in the text reveals a people fully aware of both urban and rural life. Somehow many scholars like to overlook the references to thousand-pillared houses, thousand-doored houses, and pillars of copper covered with gold. They also overlook boats with one hundred oars, and many references to ships and maritime trade. Are these vivid descriptions the stuff of pastoral nomads who never knew the sea?

The *Mahabharata* chronicles the personal struggle of the Pandava brothers and their allies against two types of foe. One group consisted of fallen *aryas* who, though speaking the same language and belonging to the same dynasty, had deviated from the proper standard of Vedic spiritual integrity. The other group entailed *mlecchas*, persons whose external traits as well as consciousness were completely outside the Vedic purview. Deeper acquaintance with the *Mahabharata* reveals that some of the Pandava brothers were seeded by *devas* coupling with humans. Particularly, Arjuna, a main hero in the epic, is known as the son of Indra, the *deva* who punishes the non-*aryas* in the *Rg-veda*.

THE *DEVAS* RECONSIDERED: A POST-MODERN VIEW

Navigating the Vedic ocean of knowledge, we have encountered consciousness as an island of nonmaterial reality. The substance consciousness, we have seen, is accepted as signaling the presence of the spirit soul. The Vedas hold consciousness to be causal as well as accountable. To give the *devas* a fair hearing, we need to look at the ancient Vedic hierarchy of consciousness as an active controlling agent. Also, our appraisal of the *devas* can benefit from a brief look at some startling trends in current science.

Our current science of consciousness has only recently emerged out of academic exile, into the light. At last, on the cutting edge of contemporary science, we will find consciousness investigated—instead of ignored. The provocative mysteries of consciousness now consume our best researchers.

Nobel Laureate Roger Sperry's paper, discussed in Chapter 9, put forth the radical concept of "downward causation." Sperry's argument, "The Structure and Significance of the Conscious Revolution in Science," attributed causal activity not merely to the traditional reductionism of molecular interplay but, more fundamentally, to the holistic phenomenon of consciousness.

A famous international conference, now held biannually at the University of Arizona, showcases the theme "Toward a Scientific Basis for Consciousness." At its inaugural assembly in 1994, David Chalmers—an Australian scholar equally qualified in mathematics, cognitive science, and philosophy—proposed that scientists consider information as essential a property of reality as matter and energy.

A surprised journalist from *Scientific American* observed that this bold concept actually resonated with the erudite audience of scientists and philosophers. Thronging around Chalmers—now a major defining voice in the current world debate—the illustrious brains offered their hearty appreciation. One notable exception, the journalist observed, was Christof Koch, a German neuroscientist who collaborates closely with the famed Nobel Laureate Francis Crick. As the spirited discussion wound its way from the auditorium to the hotel bar, the reductionist-minded Koch, bristling at Chalmers' contention, shot back, "Why don't you just say that when you have a brain the Holy Ghost comes down and makes you conscious!"[14]

In Chapter 8 we discussed the rather startling thought-work of Piet Hut, an astrophysicist, and Bas van Fraassen, a philosopher—both at Princeton University. Going deeper into their dialogues, we will find they propose considering meaning equally fundamental to the universe as time and space—that means meaning as a third essential dimension:

Van Fraassen: So we will stress that anything at all is *in* space, is *in* time, and always *has* some form of meaning.

Hut: Yes, anything whatsoever partakes *in* meaning, not only through its own specific meaning, but also by being embedded in a meaningful context.

Van Fraassen: Just like any event with a specific location in space and time is embedded in space and embedded in time. The fact that we consider meaning as thus being on a similar footing with space and time contrasts starkly with the view that meaning is something that has to be somehow *added* in the end, plunked into the arena of space and time from we don't know where (or when).[15]

Calling forth information to play a fundamental role in the universe, along with matter and energy, is a backhanded, ingenious way of saying that life and consciousness are fundamental to the universe from its very beginning. Clearly, to exalt information to the rank of a cosmic essence makes no sense unless there is an information processor. There would have to be some kind of conscious creature—whether a microbe or a physicist—that acquires the information and acts on it.

The same consequences apply when we invite meaning to share the cosmic stage equally with time and space. If everything partakes of its own specific meaning and also is embedded in an overall meaningful context, then you must have consciousness—life—as fundamental to the universe. What you are indirectly but unmistakably saying is that consciousness is both a local and omnipresent reality. Inanimate matter does not let loose with meaning—only conscious entities emanate the stuff.

The Vedic vision organizes all meaning and information in the universe into a hierarchy of consciousness and control. Living entities known as *devas*, or demigods, direct all the activities of material nature. Far more advanced than human beings, these *devas*—33 million of them, the Vedas say—reside on their own planets in the universe, with facilities, life spans, and pleasures far exceeding what a human can conceive of. Among the demigod group there are gradations of power and control. Some *devas* control relatively minute functions of nature, and some have massive portfolios. Inferior to the *devas* are sub-demigods known as *upa-devas* (nearly *devas*). They are classified as in between *devas* and human beings.

The radical upshot: human life is embedded in increasingly larger nested fields of cosmic intelligence. These superior fields of organization are more powerful than us because their consciousness is more inclusive. Furthermore, the consciousness of these superior fields of organization can cope with more complexity than our consciousness can handle. Moreover, these superior fields of consciousness can generate more creative options. Therefore, their meanings and information are much more significant and consequential than ours.

The Vedic texts give us a picture of a cosmos that features intelligence at every level of process and activity. Just as consciousness organizes the wee affairs of humans, so it also organizes solar systems and galaxies and the functions of nature. The Vedas prompt us to see the controlling potency of consciousness on all levels of the universe.

The latest trends in science announce a boom in consciousness studies. Finally, the rush is on to acknowledge consciousness—and attribute some potency to it. The Vedas, however, have long been way down that road. In Sperry's revolutionary "downward causation," rather than saying the physical interaction of minutia causes larger realities, instead we can pronounce that consciousness has caused a complex chain of actions and reactions. This chain of events caused by consciousness is both microcosmic and macrocosmic. The Vedas take things one step further. "Consciousness is causal" means consciousness controls. That consciousness controls means the interactions of the cosmos depend on consciousness.

Brilliant scientists and philosophers such as Chalmers, Hut, and van Fraassen dare to posit information and meaning as an inherent, basic dimension of the universe. But the ancient Vedas have already pushed this vision to its completion: there are lower and higher fields of information and meaning, possessed in a hierarchy of less advanced and more advanced conscious beings.

Once we are clearer on consciousness and its role in the universe, then, if we so desire, we can steer our way through notions that obscure the Vedic world of the *devas* and their hierarchy in the universal government. Different levels of consciousness have access to different levels of meaning and information. The Vedic vision is that certain levels of consciousness are so powerful that they can control aspects of material nature. This supervision of matter by consciousness is the full conclusion of the current trend to admit consciousness as primary and causal in the universe. The buzz phrase of the next decade may well be *consciousness controls nature.*

RIG-VEDA: POLYTHEISM CONFUSION

The population of *devas*, with their supernatural wielding of information and control, confuses even scholars trying to find their way in Vedic literature. Perhaps overwhelmed by the grand cosmic scale of Vedic consciousness and its interaction with nature, more than a few academics and writers of popular literature on ancient India mistakenly interpret Vedic civilization as polytheistic.

Particularly, they flock to the *Rig-veda,* where diverse incantations to various prominent *devas* abound. Indeed, there may seem no unanimity in identifying a *summum bonum.* Amidst the 10,589 verses of the *Rig-veda,* 1028 are hymns dedicated to 33 different *devas.* For example, some mantras celebrate Indra as the chief of all moving and nonmoving beings; others pay homage to Agni as the master of the heavens—the higher planets in the universe where the *devas* are said to reside.

Another popular misinterpretation is that the Vedic cultural system never excluded anything. In the course of time it simply assimilated new gods and new creeds, much the way today's computer software continuously adds newer features, gradually becoming bloated and complex. Hence, some say there are more religions within the Vedic camp then outside it. This notion works hand in hand with the conjecture that the total mass of Vedic knowledge evolved over thousands of years, and that consequently there is clearly early knowledge (B.C.) and later knowledge (medieval). Adherents of this view have allowed themselves to point to a seemingly gradual eclipse of certain "classical deities of the *Rig-veda* period" by what they consider the "popular deities of more recent, Puranic times."

Still another conception is that all the *devas* are freely interchangeable and identifiable with one another. This idea holds that since all is actually one, the *devas* are a fascinating potpourri of conceptual tags that—for the sake of convenience and artistry—are affixed to the "undifferentiated oneness." Supposedly, you choose whatever metaphorical doorway you fancy—whatever variety of the monistic oneness that inspires you. No matter what, you get the same result.

The patriarchs who have guided India's Vedic culture judge all these pet theories as far from the mark. The problem, they say, arises both from the profundity of the Vedas and the inabilities of current human intelligence. Put simply, they say the Vedas are just too voluminous and deep for the mechanistic, anxiety-ridden brains of today. Moreover, when major portions and essential directives are overlooked or rejected, Vedic literature can appear chaotic, incoherent, and inconclusive. Therefore, unaided by purified intelligence, we get lost. Like babes in the woods, we can't see the forest for the trees. Once again we may remember that

Vedic knowledge and culture is avowedly state-specific. According to your level of consciousness, you have access to appropriate levels of meaning and information.

In the hands of advanced Vedic adepts, the Vedic texts reveal a symphonic harmony that thrills any unbiased, submissive listener. The splendor of the Vedic texts as a single, integrated, comprehensive whole is a banquet not to be missed. Hence, the Vedic tradition prompts a prospective student to learn the literature at the feet of one who exemplifies the literature in word, thought, and action. What follows is a concise orthodox presentation of the world of the *devas*, as acknowledged by all the main schools of Vedic teachers.

Brahma — Shiva — Vishnu

Misconceptions abound about the grossly misnamed "Hindu trinity." Formerly, Christian missionaries and scholars attempted to bend the Vedas nearer to Christian theology. Therefore they strained to see in Brahma, Shiva, and Vishnu a familiar Christian landmark. Lately the misnomer "trinity" has begun yielding to "triad"—regretfully with scant improvement in understanding.

Brahma, Vishnu, and Shiva are the most powerful *devas*. Their superiority is implicit in their Vedic classification as *guna-avataras*, controllers of the *gunas*—the modes of nature. Chapter 10, "Vedic Time," presented the day, night, and lifetime of Brahma. The Vedas document Brahma as an actual person. Known as *adi-kavi*, the original scholar in the universe, Brahma is the first living entity to manifest in the cosmos. Contrasting starkly with current theories of human evolution, the Vedic version is that the first living being to appear in the cosmos is the most intelligent, and that things go downhill from there. Brahma's life span is the duration of the universe—311 trillion years—and his death marks the cosmic annihilation.

The unique consciousness of Brahma, inconceivable to humans, allows him access to information for designing and constructing the whole universe. Nevertheless, the Vedic texts refer to Brahma as a jewel whose brilliance reflects the light of the sun. Based on resources, empowerment, inspiration, and direction from *Bhagavan*, the Supreme Personality of Godhead, the *guna-avatara* Brahma is the secondary agent of universal creation. Besides arranging the production of the material cosmos, Brahma also supervises how *rajo-guna*, the mode of passion, effects the universe.

Shiva convenes the annihilation of the cosmos at the end of Brahma's life. Though Shiva is also in charge of *tamo-guna*, the mode of ignorance, we are instructed not to conclude that Shiva is affected by ignorance. In fact, the *Shrimad-Bhagavatam* (12.13.16) states, "Shiva is the greatest Vaishnava [devotee of Vishnu]." In the *Padma Purana*, Shiva himself asserts:

> Beyond the Vedic recommendations to worship the demigods, the worship of Vishnu is topmost. However, above even the worship of Lord Vishnu is the rendering of service to Vaishnavas, the servitors of Lord Vishnu.

Vishnu conducts the maintenance of the universe, after its manifestation and before its annihilation. Vishnu also controls *sattva-guna*, the mode of goodness. Actually, though, Vishnu is not a *deva*, a demigod. Certified in the Vedic texts as one of the many expansions of Bhagavan Krishna, the *guna-avatara* Vishnu ultimately arranges the affairs of even the demigods. Vishnu is Bhagavan Krishna in an official, "institutional" capacity—as universal maintainer. The immeasurable difference between Brahma and Shiva on one hand, and Vishnu on the other, is that Vishnu is a plenary manifestation of the Complete Whole. Brahma, Shiva, and the *devas* are not in that category.

Sometimes Vedic culture and philosophy are correctly described as Vishnu-centered or Vishnu-predominated. Frequently, though, the central focus is either missed or ignored. Heavenly accounts of the *devas* and their activities can captivate a reader's mind. The *Rig-veda*, however, while extolling the glories of various *devas*, clearly relativizes their positions. In the *Rig-veda* (3.54.5) we find this mantra:

> Who in this world actually knows, and who can explain, whence this creation has come? The *devas*, the demigods, after all, are younger than the creation. Who, then, can tell whence this world has come into being?

It can be said that the *Rig-veda* mentions several *devas* many times and Vishnu only a few. The *devas* Indra, Agni, and Soma seem to garner most of the laurels. For instance, more than two hundred hymns are for Agni. On the other hand, Vishnu apparently appears directly by name only five times. This statistical analysis would seem to indicate no special position for Vishnu in the *Rig-veda*, and leaves the door open for ideas that the supremacy of Vishnu is a later accretion to primeval Vedic culture.

Suppose we overhear our family members discussing themselves with one another. As they animatedly exchange experiences, a few times they refer to a distant relative who happens to be the Prime Minister. Shall we conclude that our immediate family members have more governmental authority than the Prime Minister does—just because their names were mentioned much more frequently in the conversation?

The *Rig-veda* is definitive in its pronouncement:

> The supreme objective of the *devas* is Vishnu, and they always look towards His supreme abode. (1.22.20)

Though the *Rig-veda* is a favorite Vedic text among interpreters seeking to dodge the monotheistic, personal *Bhagavan*, we see that it indeed clearly pays deference to Vishnu's omnipotence. The Sanskrit in this verse—*paramam padam*, or supreme abode—is inarguable in its exclusiveness and is repeated for emphasis. It refers to the supreme spiritual destination. Beyond even the *devas'* heavenly world, the supreme realm thrives outside of the material cosmos of time and space.[16] Some Western Indologists, such as Howard Resnick and F.B.J. Kuiper, do accept Vishnu's supremacy in the *Rig-veda*.[17]

A properly qualified Vedic explicator can show how all the texts of the Vedas coordinate and crosscheck with one another. Truly a wondrous experience it is to catch a glimpse of the unity spanning the entire vast Vedic library. Though rarely found, an erudite Vedic teacher can demonstrate that there are no disharmonious or incongruous elements. For example, we will find that the *Shvetashvatara Upanishad* (4.7–8) refers to the *Rig-veda* by both conclusion and name:

> The Supreme Controller is He who is referred to by the mantras of the *Rig-veda*, who resides in the topmost, eternal sky, and who elevates His saintly devotees to share that same position. One who has developed pure love for Him and realizes His uniqueness then appreciates His glories and is freed from sorrow. What further good can the Rig mantras bestow on one who knows that Supreme Person? All who come to know Him achieve the supreme destination.

Universal Utilities: Heat, Light, Water, Air

Upon brief acquaintance, the Vedic world of the *devas* may seem like any routine ancient pantheon of mythological personalities. The myth master, Joseph Campbell, spent most of a life-time cataloguing leitmotifs—recurring major themes he found in the ancient world's myths and legends. India was indeed a rich treasure for him.

The Greco-Roman and other attempts to posit personal con-trol of nature may tickle our intellectual curiosity. But the Vedic cosmic hierarchy assigns these toys to the sandbox, because com-paratively they are child's play. The universal government pre-sented in the Vedas is inexplicably brilliant in both scope and detail. One objective reason for the superiority is that the Vedic cosmic hierarchy is firmly tied to knowledge of consciousness and its dimensions of information and meaning. Furthermore, the planets, time scales, culture, abilities, and habits of the *devas* are fully described—even their celestial vacation spots are listed.

We should not confuse the *devas* with the primitive animism found throughout the non-Westernized world. For example, Patrice Malidoma Somé writes of his immersion into the native ways of his ancestors. After years of Jesuit education, culminating in a distinguished university career, Somé returned to his tribe in Burkina Faso, West Africa, and attempted to reintegrate himself with the animism practiced there. After undergoing the trauma and power of traditional initiation, his tribal coaches told him to pick a tree. They instructed him to observe it continuously, until he could actually "see it." After many hours of watching his cho-sen tree, Somé finally met the "green lady" of the tree. At last he understood what the elders had meant: the tree was much more than what Somé's Western education had taught him to see. The green lady, he described, was an energy form overflowing with strength and power. Never before, he said, had anyone bestowed upon him such love and care.[18]

Somé's dilemma was his straddling of the African tribal world and the Euro-American developed world. Since that time of his reemersion into the old ways, however, he has become a popular attraction in the West. The people of the post-industrial world are said to be reenchanting nature. Fascinated with the shamanism of the undeveloped world, increasing numbers of Westerners seek the old-world ecological magic. They yearn to dwell in an ecosphere alive with spirits, powers, and mystical experiences.

Besides the native shamanism of Africa and South America, the pre-medieval Celtic culture also appeals to moderns. When Saint Patrick arrived in Ireland in the fifth century A.D., he encountered the vivid nature worship of the Celts. Instead of worshiping a monotheistic God, they found their religion in the environment: the animals, hills, rivers, sea, and sky.

Celtic heritage is now becoming a major player in Anglo-America, as alternative-minded people attempt to recapture their creative imagination and connection with nature. Lessons in shamanistic interaction with trees, animals, and stones are no longer an oddity in Western metropolitan areas. Seers of forest fairies, elves, and assorted other "etheric nature-entities" now can receive respect and some fame—especially if they are known to teach their skills to others.

At the forefront, though, are the so-called New-Age gardeners, who seek communion with their plants and crops as a means for higher yields. Back in the 1960s, a family living in the small village of Findhorn, Scotland began to grow amazing flowers and vegetables on barren, sandy soil. When cabbages and broccoli almost too heavy to lift started coming out of the ground, people wanted to know why.

The family explained their gardening secret: cooperation with the nature spirits and "*devas*" in charge. Dorothy MacLean said she could communicate telepathically with what she called the *deva* responsible for each plant type. She said she could also contact the overall *deva* of the Findhorn garden. The family head, Peter Caddy, the actual gardener, exactly followed the instructions MacLean received. For example, before plants were moved, the family informed "the *devas*," so the plants had time to withdraw their energies from their roots. Soon Findhorn attracted many visitors, coming from all over the world to see the miraculous abundance. Some stayed, and the Findhorn community began.[19]

Another famous garden is Perelandra, in Virginia, USA. Its gardener, Machaelle Small Wright, inspired by Findhorn, began her work in 1976. Since then she has written several books explaining that partnership with the nature spirits is the key to her wondrous results. She calls the method "co-creative gardening": her joint effort with "the garden *devas*."

Maurice Shapiro, in *Awakening to the Plant Kingdom*, describes his agricultural tutelage under "the corn *deva*." These days, any trendy urban bookshop can supply at least a few "*deva* gardening manuals." You'll find titles such as *The Deva Handbook: How to Work with Nature's Subtle Energies*; or *Plant Spirit Medicine*; and also *Garden Notes from the Nature Devas (helpful hints that enable you to communicate and learn on the devic level to heal the Earth)*.

Mistakenly, well-intentioned nature-lovers apply the Sanskrit term *deva* to the entities they may encounter. Vedic culture, however, judges worship of tree, garden, or forest spirits as low-class. These entities are considered the preoccupation of primitive, dull minds. The *Bhagavad-gita* (17.4) states, "Those in the mode of ignorance worship ghosts and spirits." We must be clear that the *devas* of the Vedas are something else altogether.

"Who has seen the *devas*?" That's the modern challenge. The Vedic reply would be "Who today has the qualifications to see?" Uniformity of observational capacity is never assumed in the Vedas. Knowledge, information, is state-specific; hence, the necessity of both acquiring the correct training and living the prescribed life style. Then, according to the Vedic stance, higher, seemingly esoteric truths can be experienced.

The texts tell us that in the present age, known as Kali-yuga, the *devas* are not visible, owing to the decadence of earthlings. Interplanetary and intergalactic space travel between the higher realms of the *devas* and Earth are said to be a norm in previous ages. But in Kali-yuga the visitations cease. The residents of the superior civilizations on *deva* planets keep themselves outside the spectrum of human perception.

Surprisingly, in a 1993 poll conducted for *Time* magazine and the CNN Network, 69 percent of adult Americans said they believe in angels. Moreover, 46 percent said they had their own guardian angel. Still, whatever angelic presence they believe in is not what the Vedas mean by *deva*.

How do the real *devas* affect everyday human life? Today's citizen is indebted to public utilities. We have to pay money to the water, electric, or gas departments of a city. The Vedas say that human beings are similarly indebted to the *devas*. In a cosmos controlled by consciousness, when the *devas* are ignored, that means the bills haven't been paid. Consequently the orderly supply of natural resources and necessities becomes erratic, reduces, or even shuts off completely.

In the science magazine *Nature*, researchers from the University of Maryland presented the world with a bill for $16 trillion to $54 trillion US dollars per annum. This is the amount they calculated humanity owes nature annually, for global services. Included in their analysis are the obvious natural resources and raw materials: food, water, air, lumber, rocks, metals, jewels, oil, and so forth. But also they tabulated charges for replenishing soil, treating waste, and containing soil erosion. They even included wages for employing bees and other creatures to pollinate plants.[20]

Obviously a dramatic gesture by ecologically concerned scientists, "the bill from nature" had no intent other than reminding us how much we are dependent on nature's graces. Vedic civilization, however, takes the bill for real.

The *Bhagavad-gita,* third chapter, gives us a good synopsis of how the Vedas say the universal system responds when we pay for the services of cosmic-conscious government.

> 11. The *devas,* the demigods, being pleased by your sacrifices, will in turn please you. Through this systematic reciprocation between humans and *devas,* prosperity will reign.
>
> 12. When the *devas,* administering the resources of nature, are satisfied by the performance of sacrifice, they will supply all natural requirements to you. Anyone who attempts to enjoy the products of nature without offering them in sacrifice to the demigods is certainly guilty of theft.

Here we should remember that the *devas* are authorized agents of supply, who work on behalf of Vishnu. The Vedas take for granted that it is more scientific to say we depend on our satisfying the conscious managers of nature than to say we depend on the sterile functions of a mechanistic cosmos—a cosmos unable to account for consciousness and its fundamentals of information and meaning.

Sacrifices to the *devas* mean that a quota of what nature supplies humanity is committed to precise rituals, detailed in the Vedas. Aimed at the appropriate departmental heads of nature, these sacrifices indirectly worship Vishnu as the chief beneficiary. Many of these elaborate rituals require execution by special priests, who the Vedas say can vibrate the Sanskrit mantras so perfectly that even if an animal is put into the sacrificial fire, it will emerge with a new life. Because the present *yuga* lacks this expertise and the required natural resources, all Vedic sacrifices repose in sonic glorification of the Supreme Godhead.

> 13. The devotees of Lord Vishnu eat only food offered first in sacrifice directly to Vishnu; therefore they incur no karma.

> Others, who prepare food for their own sense enjoyment,
> actually eat sinful reactions.

Because Vishnu is the root and support of the *devas*, the most intelligent persons—going right to the Source—directly apply their sacrifices there. Vedic civilization accommodated both levels of intelligence: pursuing the innumerable *devas* through the multifarious techniques of propitiation, or singularly concentrating on Vishnu. As the root of all matter and spirit, Vishnu automatically includes every *deva*.

Worship of the *devas* brings good karma, but Visnu worship is transcendental to both bad and good karma. The perfect culmination of Vishnu sacrifice is freedom from material existence—whether heavenly or hellish. Then the celebrant can enter into the supreme transcendental abode, the *paramam padam*. Therefore the third chapter of the Gita, while explaining the reciprocation between humans and *devas*, advocates work and sacrifice performed directly for Vishnu.

14. All human bodies require food grains. These grains require rains. The rains come from the performance of sacrifice, and the sacrifices derive from Vedic prescribed duties.

15. Systematic activities of civilization are prescribed in the Vedas. From the Supreme *Brahman*, *Bhagavan*, the Vedas directly manifest. In this way the all-pervading Transcendence is eternally situated in acts of Vedic sacrifice.

16. Humans who do not adhere to the Vedic cycle of sacrifice certainly lead a life full of sin. Such persons, living only to gratify their senses, live uselessly.

A foundational principle of Vedic culture is that human beings cannot manufacture even one of their essential requirements. The Vedas underline our dependency on the production of the

Earth and skies—not factories and offices. Needless to say, human endeavor cannot overcome disturbances in sunlight, rainfall, and the orderly cycles of nature. History does show us the displacement or dispersal of entire civilizations because of extreme weather changes, massive natural disasters, epidemics, and—less dramatic but equally ruinous—soil infertility.

Humanity, in its daily affairs, works under the direction of the sovereign state. According to the Vedas, however, above our civic duties, we have our cosmic duties—we are indebted to the universal government.

The Vedic texts present the cosmic codes of work. Activity outside these Vedic directives brings bad karma; within those sanctions, activity accrues good karma. Those who know the actual conclusion of the Vedas avoid karma altogether and transcend the material world.

As we all know, human beings are eager for material enjoyment. The Vedas deal with this desire in a systematic, remedial way. By working according to the formulas prescribed by the universal government, gradually the human being becomes purified of the desire to enjoy matter. Ultimately, the life style of a transcendentalist becomes attractive.

Unbridled expansion of wealth and sensuality has no place in Vedic life. Simply to receive supplies from the *devas* and use them for becoming more deeply illusioned is considered criminal—a major violation of cosmic purpose. Our lesson to learn, we are informed, is that, if we fail to honor the directives of the cosmic-conscious government, then we will receive only short feverish spurts of apparent economic growth—followed by miserable demise or traumatic crashes. From the Vedic standpoint, attempts to establish peace on Earth while ignoring the *devas* and the ultimate authority behind them are foolhardy and futile—just like the attempts of Mafiosos to establish honorable dealings within the underworld.

PERSONALITY AND
THE LAWS OF NATURE

Just four hundred years ago, Western humans saw the universe much differently than they do today. We know that in the seventeenth century an educated fellow had no doubt the Earth was the center of the universe—the exclusive stage for the once-only drama of Christian redemption. But what is of direct relevance for our discussion of *devas* is that any educated person then—certainly a Christian—saw the planets and stars controlled by intelligent, divine spirits.

The universe then was teleological—alive and endowed with divine purpose and meaning. Human beings were ranked between the lower animals and celestial beings known as angels. Furthermore, the planets, by their locations and aspects, were readily accepted as influencers of human events.

When we move up in history just one hundred years, to the eighteenth century, we find that the educated descendants of the previous generation or two still were Christians. But now—unless they lived in a Vatican-dominated country—they had no doubt that Earth was just one of many orbs rotating around the sun. God was still in ultimate control, but now the universe itself was dead. After being set into motion by the Creator, the universe was now seen to proceed according to cold mechanical forces and laws.

Whereas the seventeenth-century learned man would easily acknowledge heaps of popular evidence for miracles, enchantments, witches, and paranormal beings, his eighteenth-century, educated grandson scorned it all. By that time the power of the priesthood had waned. With it had faded the traditional system of intellectual authority, known as scholasticism.

In the heyday of the medieval scholastics, the universe had been a world alive and guided in every aspect. God, then, was directly in control, for human benefit. Philosophical and scriptural authority had provided the key for entering this world. The goal of education was the harmonizing of sense experience with religion. In the eighteenth century, however, the scientific revolution had become the dominant reality. Final authority switched from tradition to observation and experiment. Sensory inputs mediated by open inquiry became the standard—not official Church dogma.[21]

Modern times were upon us. Soon Providence as the foreman of the cosmic factory was made redundant. Though He was still doing something somewhere up in heaven, His job down on the floor, running the assembly line of nature, was taken over by mechanical laws. Almighty God, in the mind of the new scientists, had retired behind the cosmic clouds. By the mid-twentieth century, He completely disappeared off the company roster. The mechanical laws of nature still had employment. But they ran on their own.

Primitives and medievals, we moderns believe, did succeed in observing some regularities in nature. But because they lacked the knowledge we have today, they invented personalities to explain patterns of natural phenomena. Our modern paradigm tells us that, owing to ignorance, previous peoples understood nature to be controlled by a crew of powerful superior beings. Consequently, out leapt the sun god, moon god, river god, and so forth. The traces of personal purposefulness in nature still linger in our speech today: "Water seeks its own level," and "Planets obey Newton's laws."

To save the day from such unintellectual anthropomorphism, as well as outmoded theism, our present-day science likes to advocate that the universe can create itself—first given the laws of nature. The foundation of reality originates from these laws. They are eternal precepts; the universe is built upon them. The laws are here—free-floating, so to speak. That is enough to know.

In spite of the profound mystery of this explanation, few modern scientists chose to go further. Rare are the courageous brains who try to shine their brilliance on the nature of the laws themselves. It seems that amid the rush to discover ultimate cosmic laws, until recently few had time to question their origin. What is the composition of these laws? Where do they come from? How do the laws exist in relationship to the universe? Moreover, are they independently existing without, or packaged within?

Scientists assume that the regularities they observe in nature are real. The patterns are truly "out there." These designated regularities are accepted as more than mere projections of consciousness (whatever that is), in its vain attempt to make sense of the world. Scientists are confident that they are not just looking for faces in the flames of a campfire—or worse yet, seeing celestial gods in the firmament. Research requires that scientists possess firm faith that whatever patterns they observe are dependable. For example, the sun *will* rise every morning. Without this conviction of cosmic dependability, they cannot push on in their enterprise.

A truly mighty law of science ties into other dependable phenomena, beyond what its discoverer foresaw. Newton's law of gravity, to take one, accurately portrays the motion of all the planets that we have encountered. But it also accounts for ocean tides, the motion of spacecraft, and much more. The majesty of full-blown ultimate laws is said to be their ability to continually reveal more relationships among the various aspects of the physical universe, and to generate unexpected discoveries.

Award-winning science writer Paul Davies has noted that what we now call the laws of nature have been surcharged with many of the attributes formerly ascribed to a personal control of nature. As we have seen, just four hundred years ago—to say nothing of in Vedic times—people saw these personal attributes in personality, not in mechanical laws. The divine qualities that

Davies and other shrewd analysts discern in the contemporary materialistic doctrine of scientific law are as follows:

- Laws are now seen as universal. We are sure they apply throughout the cosmos, in all times and in all places. They will never fail us. They are perfect.
- Laws are absolute. Self-sufficient and primeval, they do not depend on anyone or anything. To echo a verse in the Bible, "They are that they are." The laws affect the physical states of nature, but no states counteraffect them. In this way, the laws are aloof and always liberated from all their consequences— they are simultaneously "in the cosmos but not of the cosmos." Various states of nature may change in time, but the laws that describe the changes never undergo change.
- The laws are eternal. Their timelessness is borne out by the mathematical structures scientists use as models of the universe.
- The laws are omnipotent. Nothing is said to exist outside their grasp. Loosely speaking, they are also omniscient, in that the physical systems they govern do not have to inform the laws about themselves. The laws, without "hearing from the subordinate physical states," can regulate them precisely.[22]

How do we get in touch with these laws? If they only appear to us through the physical functions of the cosmos, how will we ever attain them? We can never get our hands behind the phenomena of the cosmic systems to grab them.

Only the physicists, with their mathematics, are said to really understand the laws, because all their fundamental laws of nature are mathematical in essence. Thus our modern "spiritual" quest becomes how to contact these subtle, abstract entities of mathematics, which most physicists believe enjoy a transcendental status. Yet in spite of the laws' divinelike empowerment, somehow they have to be matter, and originate from matter because, for a materialist, matter—physical states—is all that exists.

Molecular biochemist T. D. Singh, alert to the inescapable trap matter-ism has dug for itself, explains:

> Now, if nature were simply an array of particles moving according to mathematical equations, it would be possible to predict events such as birth, death, accidents, and wars with the help of these equations. Indeed, it should be possible to understand all the intricacies of life—past, present, and future—in terms of mathematical equations. However, all careful thinkers, especially the scientists, know that this is impossible—that a purely mathematical approach to the understanding of life is too restrictive and very unsatisfying."[23]

Something seems to be missing? Yes—awareness and meaning and information. More precisely, our consciousness. The biggest brains apparently have erected this intricate mechanistic edifice just to replace the personal supervision of nature. But, in so doing, they also replace ourselves—conscious entities. The whole scam collapses when consciousness and its unassailable properties of awareness, meaning, and information are addressed.

A science buried in materialism has to demonstrate how consciousness—"something" that has subjectivity, a personal sense of selfhood—emerges from objectivity, inert matter. Precisely how does such a crucial "thing"—possessing no mass and occupying no space—evolve from matter, which is massive and spatial?

Upon finally confronting the irrefutable reality of consciousness, Western materialists have as their only hope the impossibility of tracing consciousness to a material substance. It's got to fit under those "omnipotent, absolute, universal, and eternal" mathematical laws of physicality. Otherwise . . .

Since consciousness is nonphysical and nonchemical, the

mathematical laws that govern the activities of inert matter do not apply. Nevertheless, it is reasonable to suppose that there must be *some* laws and governance for consciousness and its affairs.

The Vedic literature beckons to us, with its age-old knowledge that consciousness is the irreducible basis of cosmic functions. This irreducibility of conscious personality can only be effectively explained when we accept consciousness as the energy of a nonmaterial, subjective particle, the spirit soul.

The consciousness of the *devas* is described as much more powerful than ours. Therefore their scope for control and management of matter is far beyond our human capacity. The Vedas present that, in the planetary system of the *devas*, the laws of nature these celestial entities supervise there are incomprehensible to the puny brains of humans on Earth.

THE ULTIMATE INFORMATION STANDARD

The Vedic hierarchy of conscious order enmeshes living entities in an interrelated cosmic network of controller and controlled. Besides the departments of nature, our bodily senses—including the mind and intelligence—are understood to be under the *devas'* control. Each of our sensory faculties depends on natural conditions to function. For example, sight depends on light, taste on water, and so forth. In this way the Vedas interlink the cosmos, its departmental supervisors, and our organs of perception.

Like us, the *devas* are living entities in material bodies. The difference is that they are empowered to administrate nature, and we are dependent on their control of nature. All the positions in the Vedic hierarchy of consciousness are graded according to karma. That means the living entity receives its station in the network of controller and controlled according to past activities. A high grade of pious karma allows any living being to become a *deva*, a controller—even a Brahma. Likewise a low grade embeds the living entity deeply into the system of the *devas'* control.

The distinction between the *devas* and those they control is bodily. Both groups have bodies made of matter, but the *deva* bodies are far more powerful in strength, intelligence, enjoyment, mystic potencies, and duration. The hierarchy is supervised by the Supersoul, who collates, so to speak, all the living entities into their correct interrelated slots. Actually, the Vedas say, all the power and control manifest by any entity in the cosmos reflects the original power of the Supersoul, who enters into each universe. Within the cosmos, that original potency of the Supersoul refracts into gradations of control.

Despite material differences in bodily ability, both controllers and the controlled are equal as spirit souls. All living entities belong to the Supreme Soul, the source of all interdependency and interrelationship. Ultimately the Vedic system for both material and spiritual reality traces back to *Bhagavan*, the source and shelter of all. Even *Brahman* and Supersoul, or *Paramatma*, are subordinate to Bhagavan Krishna, who speaks in the *Gita:*

> Neither the hosts of *devas*, demigods, nor the greatest sages on the
> highest planets of the universe know My origin or opulences, for,
> in every respect, I am the source of the demigods and sages.
> (*Bhagavad-gita* 10.2)

The Vedic texts describe that all the variegated entities of the universe—whether Brahma, Shiva, the major and minor *devas*, the lowly forest spirits and ghosts, humans, beasts, birds, insects, aquatics, and vegetation—demonstrate only a fragment of the immeasurable potency of the Supreme. Many persons are astonished by the potencies imbued in various aspects of the cosmos, but they lack factual knowledge of the source of all potency. The Vedic texts label them *shaktas*. This tag classifies them as devotees of potency, *shakti*. The Vedas recognize different levels of this adoration of power—energy worship.

The Vedic lens observes that different societies worship particular potent manifestations of the Supreme. Unenlightened societies are seen to mistake the powerful exhibitions of energy for the ultimate. On the lowest level of *shakti*-worship, or potency adoration, are the primitive tribes. Transfixed by nature and its wonders, they celebrate an exceptional thunderbolt, a gigantic tree, a mighty waterfall, or a huge mountain. From the Vedic perspective, these persons are classified as crude because merely a slight display of supreme potency captivates them. They then venerate these phenomena as their deity. Other primitive *shaktas* worship their clan, ancestors, race, nationality, or gender; also animals, forest spirits, ghosts, and channeled beings.

The more advanced *shakti* worshipers are said to be pundits like our modern scientists. Though also captivated by the power of nature, they can often possess a deeper and broader understanding of grosser cosmic functions and processes. Certainly they can apply more meticulousness in their scrutiny than a nonscientist can.

The most developed *shakti* intellects are those who acknowledge the *devas* and seek to satisfy them. Vedic sacrifices to the *devas* are a sort of inducement for humanity to realize the existence of higher authorities in the universe. Upon acknowledging their jurisdiction, we can then assume the appropriate obligations.

By the arrangement of the Supreme, the demigods take their places as controllers of material affairs. Hence, according to the Vedas, when a demigod is worshiped, the process is accepted as indirect worship of the Supreme. The most advanced intellects, however, go straight to the ultimate source of all potency and control. They apply their concerted efforts there.

The whole Vedic process of civilization is to transform the *shaktas*—potency worshipers of all levels—into *bhaktas*, direct servants of the Supreme Transcendence. The paramount Vedic injunction overrides offering sacrificial compensation to the demigods—if we engage in the direct service of the Supreme.

When *sattva-guna*, the mode of goodness, dawns in the consciousness of the Vedic follower, a natural question then arises: what is the wellspring of the whole conscious system? From where expands the animate mesh that encompasses all living entities and all inanimate matter? A major Upanishad dealing primarily with universal proprietorship and control states:

> The Personality of Godhead is perfect and complete, and because He is completely perfect, all emanations from Him, such as this phenomenal world, are perfectly equipped as complete wholes. Whatever is produced of the Complete Whole is also complete in itself. Because He is the Complete Whole, even though so many complete units emanate from Him, He remains the complete balance. (*Ishopanishad,* invocation)

Conscious control in the Vedic cosmic hierarchy is truly a fascinating read. Yet even more alluring is knowledge that reveals the source of the entire conscious system of interrelation. Human life is embedded in the vast conscious fields of *deva* organization. Nevertheless, the *devas* themselves are embedded. The Vedas describe that the origin of all the relationships of interdependence in power and control must also be conscious—but completely self-sufficient. This ultimate, absolute source of all interdependence is the Supreme Truth, the Complete Whole—independent of all, dependant on none.

Vedic texts such as the Upanishads describe that, although everything, all potencies, emanate from the Supreme, still this ultimate source undergoes no reduction in completeness. Depletion is a feature of matter and material existence.

Both the spiritual energy and the Complete Whole, the source of all matter and spirit, are unaffected by the subordinate, inferior laws that govern the material energy. As the fountainhead of everything, the Complete Whole—changeless and inexhaustible—maintains the fullness of infinity. The most advanced Vedic adepts focus their efforts here, to the *ultimate conscious standard* for all meaning and information.

Notes

1   T. Burrow, "The Early Aryans," in *A Cultural History of India* (Oxford: Oxford University Press, 1975), pp. 20, 24.

2   Jonathan Mark Kenoyer, "Birth of a Civilization," in *Archaeology*, January/February 1998, p. 61.

3   Kenneth A. R. Kennedy, "Have Aryans Been Identified in the Prehistoric Skeletal Record from South Asia," in Georg Erdosy, *The Indo-Aryans of Ancient South Asia: Language, Material Culture, and Ethnicity* (Berlin: Walter de Gruyter, 1995), p. 60.

4   *Rig-veda* 1.152.6–7, 5.85.1, 8.1.3.

5   *Rig-veda* 2.23.4, 5.42.9, 6.53.2–3, 7.104.2, 10.125.6.

6   *Mahabharata* 9.16.45.

7   *Mahabharata* 6.36.27, or *Bhagavad-gita* 14.27.

8   *Aryan and Non-Aryan in South Asia. Evidence, Interpretation and Ideology,* Harvard Oriental Series Opera Minora, 3 (1999): 287–88.

9   Ibid., p. 168.

10 Ibid.

11 Ibid., p. 159.

12 Michael Witzel, "Early Indian History: Linguistic and Textual Parametres," in Georg Erdosy, *The Indo-Aryans of Ancient South Asia: Language, Material Culture, and Ethnicity* (Berlin: Walter de Gruyter, 1995), p. 98.

13 Greg Possehl, book review of *The Indo-Aryans of Ancient South Asia: Language, Material Culture, and Ethnicity*, in the *Journal of the American Oriental Society* 118.1 (1998): 120–21.

14   John Horgan, *The End of Science* (New York: Broadway Books, 1997), pp. 181–82.

15 Piet Hut and Bas van Fraassen, "Elements of Reality," *Journal of Consciousness Studies* 4, no. 2, (1997): 182.

16 The *Aitareya Brahmana*, thought by scholars to be the earliest "commentary" on the *Rig-veda*, declares in its first statement that Vishnu is supreme among the *devas*. Other "early" Vedic texts such as the *Satapatha Brahmana* and the *Yajur-veda* itself state that Vishnu is the goal of all the sacrifices in the Vedas.

17 See, for example, F. B. J. Kuiper, "The Three Strides of Visnu," *Indological Studies in Honor of W. Norman Brown,* ed. Ernest Beader, AOS, 1962; and Kuiper, "The Basic Concepts of Vedic Religion," *History of Religions,* August 1975, 15:2, pp. 107–20.

18 See Patrice Somé, *Of Water and the Spirit* (New York: Bantam Books, 1994).

19 See Paul Hawken, *The Magic of Findhorn* (New York: Harper and Row, 1975), and Peter Tompkins and Christopher Bird, *The Secret Life of Plants* (New York: Avon Books, 1974), pp. 372–83.

20 *Nature*, 15 May 1997.

21 This elucidation of the seventeenth and eighteenth century owes much to Willis Harmon, *Global Mind Change* (California: Institute of Noetic Sciences, 1998).

22 See Paul Davies, *The Mind of God* (Touchstone Books, 1993), chap. 3, "What Are the Laws of Nature?"

23 T. D. Singh, "The Principle of Reincarnation," in *Consciousness: the Missing Link* (Los Angeles: Bhaktivedanta Book Trust, 1982), p. 61.

CHAPTER 13

VEDIC TECHNOLOGY
AND MYSTIC POWER

~

Our present knowledge of ancient India provides an insightful contrast with what we know of the Mesoamerican civilizations. Scant literary evidence exists from the days of the Mayas and Aztecs, not to speak of their predecessors. These people had no complete writing system, but neither had they a precise oral tradition for transmitting structured knowledge. Almost none of their textual records, known as codices, survived the Spanish conquest.

The ancients of Mesoamerica did leave us a vast treasure of archaeological remains. Newfound cities and tombs continue to emerge from the distant past. Therefore archaeological information predominates our modern understanding of pre-Columbian America. Meanwhile, the linguistic study of the pre-Columbian family of languages, lagging far behind, has contributed little to what is accepted knowledge today.

In marked contrast, the study of ancient India, from the start, has been a linguistic specialty. Only recently has archaeology moved into the spotlight. A massive collection of textual evidence—whether originating in sound or writing—has pre-occupied scholars since the Europeans first arrived in India.

Mesoamerica left behind an abundance of archaeological delights; ancient India very little yet discovered. India of remote antiquity preserved for us an immense wealth of textual knowledge; pre-Columbian America a poverty. Studies based on archaeology have long soared in Mesoamerica. On the Indian subcontinent, they assumed importance only recently. The Mayas, Aztecs, and other peoples of Mesoamerica have escaped analysis by linguistic scholars. For instance, the Mayan glyphs have just been deciphered. On the other hand, the languages of the Indian subcontinent have long been under the microscope, though linguistic scholars say much more work is necessary.

Exotic archaeological finds of pyramids, temples, and tombs in tropical rainforests make for exciting visual presentations. Especially in the television age, "seeing is believing." Ancient India, however, has bequeathed to us knowledge, handed down in words. What we moderns think of this knowledge—our current assumptions and cultural lenses—would seem to profoundly influence our ability to benefit from that inheritance.

Generally, our academic leaders have not encouraged us to take Vedic knowledge seriously. That is to say, outside of "mytho-religious import," we are not led to consider the Vedas a source of "objective knowledge," as the sciences of today may be esteemed. Here is a typically gracious and well-intentioned judgment on Vedic thought and culture:

> Without being one-sidedly intellectual, it gives free scope to the emotional and imaginative sides of human nature . . . our distinction between the subjective and the objective, our contrast between reality and appearance are almost meaningless . . . thought often appears wrapped in imagination; logical reasoning is by no means lacking but blended with affective and irrational tendencies.

A more than superficial study of many chapters of this literature requires of the reader, to some degree, familiarization with a non-modern 'mentality' . . . with mythical formulations of thought which, though products of imagination, are far from being mere fantasy; with various forms of speculation that, as a rule unrestricted by disciplined confrontation with the results of objective and analytical investigation, found unlimited possibilities of development. He will be impressed by a luxuriant imagination and a great narrative power.[1]

In so many words, this contemporary Indologist is equipping us with the almost universal academic window on the Vedas: "Just see! How spirited the Vedas are in creative expression— though they utterly lack the precise discipline and scientific analysis of our advanced, modern society." Owing to this ingrained attitude, few academics take the Vedic technology seriously, though the textual evidence is there before our eyes.

In the Vedic literature we will find:

- many references to aircraft and flight;
- vivid descriptions of advanced military technology;
- Earth wars and star wars;
- mystic or psychic powers far superior to what contemporary humans now toy with;
- planets inhabited by beings with varying levels of ability and purity;
- interplanetary travel via aircraft;
- interplanetary travel via personal yogic power.

REMOTE VIEWING: ANCIENT AND MODERN

Spiritual circles throughout the world revere the Vedic text *Bhagavad-gita* as a preeminent spiritual classic. Well-read persons who are not spiritually inclined at least recognize it as one of the world's greatest literatures. How many readers, whether spiritual enthusiasts or not, realize that the narrator of the *Gita* says he has given a firsthand account without being physically present? Though not at the scene, nevertheless he said he could see all the events.

The *Gita* is a battlefield dialogue between Krishna, the Supreme Absolute Truth incarnating on Earth, and Arjuna, a dear devotee. In the midst of two huge armies ready to collide, Krishna imparts knowledge of self-realization to Arjuna. The events on the battlefield, including the dialogue, are relayed by Sanjaya, a royal secretary, to his lord, Dhritarashtra.

War as described in the Vedas meant that all the royalty and their vassals would go off to battle. The ordinary citizenry was never enlisted to fight. Dhritarashtra, though a member of the Vedic martial and administrative order, was exempted from combat. He was blind. But he marshaled his chief assets, his one hundred sons. They and their allies sought to eradicate Krishna's devotee Arjuna and his associates. The battle began at a traditional Vedic place of pilgrimage, Kurukshetra. Even the *devas* were said to visit this special area, still existing on the map today. Owing to the sacredness of Kurukshetra, the blind Dhritarashtra felt uneasy.

He knew his sons were cheaters, hellbent on aggression. On the other side, the sons of Pandu—Arjuna's brothers—were paragons of virtue. They had done everything to resolve the conflict nonviolently. The blind old monarch worried that the atmosphere of the sacred place, favoring piety, would influence his devious sons to mend their crooked ways. The last thing he wanted was a last-minute peace.

In the first verse of the *Gita*, the worried king asks his trusted royal secretary: "O Sanjaya, my sons and the other side, the sons of Pandu, have all assembled at Kurukshetra, the sacred pilgrimage ground. They are ready to fight. What is happening now?" Then

Sanjaya describes the scene to him, as it unfolds. Both the royal secretary and the blind monarch are far removed from the battle-field. Yet Sanjaya sees all, and tells everything that transpires.

We are proud of our advancements in communications tech-nology, but Sanjaya in the *Gita* displays the natural ability to wit-ness an entire scene without normal physical presence. This gift is considered a secondary Vedic mystic power: *dura-shravana-darshana*, the power to see and hear despite physical barriers and distances. Even today in modern India, a nationwide television network is called Doordarshan, a derivative of the original San-skrit *dura-darshana*, with the same meaning: "seeing in spite of physical separation from the event."

Most scholars of Indic studies politely mock what they think are hoary Vedic fables. Unable to lift their noses from the aca-demic grindstone, few of them realize that the CIA and their Rus-sian counterparts paid many millions of dollars to produce just a sliver of the skill Sanjaya demonstrated in the *Gita*.

Western scientists call what Sanjaya was doing "remote view-ing." Another term is "non-local awareness." The terms refer to the psychic ability to describe far-off situations and activities. In-formation on the other side of the globe can be accessed as easily as if it were in the next room. When the Soviet psychic researcher Dr. Abraham Shiffrin arranged his exodus to Israel in the mid-1980s, he revealed that he had worked for the Moscow Institute for Information Transmission. The scientific institute was experi-menting with Central Asian psychics who could meticulously describe details of Soviet missile sites far away.[2]

The CIA was not asleep at the wheel. Somehow the American media did not catch on when, in 1977, the then CIA director Stansfield Turner told a press conference that he had a man who could see through walls. When the CIA declassified some of its reports in July 1995, the public finally took notice.[3] "CIA con-firms US used 'psychic spies'," announced the Associated Press news wire. "Project Stargate employed psychics to hunt down Libyan leader Muammar al-Qaddafi, find plutonium in North Korea and help drug enforcement agencies."[4]

In September, 1995, the international news agency Reuters quoted former President Jimmy Carter telling college students in Atlanta that during his administration the CIA used remote viewing to locate a downed plane in Zaire, Africa. When spy satellites failed to find the plane's wreckage, Carter said the CIA chief Turner put a psychic searcher on the case. "While she was in trance," Carter described, "she gave some latitude and longitude figures. We focused our satellite cameras on that point, and the plane was there."[5]

Pressed by the race to keep up with the Soviets, in the early 1970s the CIA turned to the nation's second biggest think tank, Stanford Research Institute (SRI) in California. There it bankrolled two physicists, Russell Targ and Hal Puthoff. When Puthoff left in 1985, another physicist, Edwin May, took over. Then in 1990 the entire program moved from SRI to a major defense contractor, Science Applications International Corporation (SAIC).

Targ conducted experiments with a man called Pat Price, a former police commissioner. He was the person whom the CIA chief, in 1977, had referred to in his press conference; he was "the man who could see through walls." The psychic viewer, we now know, had used his prowess to spy on a Soviet weapons laboratory in Siberia. "Price immediately described and sketched the plant with incredible precision," the SRI physicist Targ writes. "Not only did his drawings show previously unknown external structures that later were confirmed by satellite photography, but he also described in remarkable detail a complicated assembly process being conducted indoors, inside a secure building. The existence of this completely secret process was verified by satellite photography several years later."[6]

Edwin May described a test conducted for the benefit of government clients who desired a live demonstration of how productive remote viewing might be for intelligence operations. If precious data could be obtained without sending espionage agents into the field—at great expense and risk of life—then military intelligence, of course, was highly interested. Moreover, since remote viewing was known to penetrate even shielded or hidden structures, the technique seemed especially attractive.

May relates that the live test involved giving a remote viewer no prior information of the target other than that it was "a technical device somewhere in the United States." The target, in the southwest, was a high-energy microwave generator. Though kept totally in the dark, the remote viewer was able to draw a device amazingly similar to the actual target. Accurately describing its size and function, as well as the structure that housed it, the viewer even correctly "observed" that it had "a beam divergence angle of thirty degrees."[7]

The CIA told the American people that, during twenty-four years, they had spent 20 million dollars on the project, before shutting it down in 1994. The spy agency said they got an accuracy rate of 15 percent. Not so, asserts remote viewer David Morehouse, in his exposé *Psychic Warrior: Inside the CIA's Stargate Program*. He says he inspired 17 out of the then 18 remote viewers on the CIA's payroll to leave the program and dedicate their skills for peaceful purposes. He reveals the CIA's project to have had a viewing accuracy of 85 percent, and the budget to have been far more than admitted to the public. Furthermore, he is adamant the work is still going on—under much deeper secrecy. "My whole point in sacrificing my career," states Morehouse, "was because of my belief in what remote viewing under controlled conditions can do for humanity."[8]

The three chief American scientists who researched remote viewing—Targ, Puthoff, and May—all agree that the program provided astonishing accuracy in a fraction of the trials. Thanks to their efforts, and the work of the Russians, some of us may be inspired to take the ancient *Bhagavad-gita* at its word. In the finale of the *Gita* (18.76–78), the royal secretary and counselor, Sanjaya, gives his blind master the official conclusion of his full-fledged remote viewing: no hope. Observing the future as well as the present, Sanjaya foresaw that the crooked sons of the blind king would suffer complete defeat—they would not return home alive.

> O King, as I repeatedly recall this wondrous and holy dialogue between Krishna and Arjuna, I take pleasure—I am thrilled at every moment.
>
> As I remember the wonderful form of Lord Krishna, I am struck with wonder more and more, and I rejoice again and again.
>
> Wherever there is Krishna, the supreme master of all mystics, and wherever there is Arjuna, the greatest archer, you should know there will always be extraordinary power, opulence, morality, and victory.

Ordinary scientists shut their eyes to the ESP research done at special institutes, because it violates physicality. Remote viewing, for example, has nothing to do with modern human conceptions of time and space. If we look at the whole list of Vedic mystic powers, we may wonder how much of the cosmos does have any relation with modern notions of space-time.

UNSOLVED ANCIENT MYSTERIES

Certainly, we would hope that progress in Western attitudes toward the Vedic texts has come a long way since the days of colonialism. Barriers, however, still exist. The main blockade to the Vedic world of subtle technology is the confidence or dogma of present-day science. Contemporary intellectuals sympathetic to the Vedic vision still have a difficult time escaping the modern mold of physicalism and reductionism. These are the blinders we have forced upon our eyes because of our exclusive absorption in gross matter. Therefore, almost to this very day, Vedic descriptions of advanced technology and abilities have generally been ignored.

It is now known that the Germans under Hitler secretly scoured India for texts giving knowledge of Vedic aeronautics. They hoped hints from the ancient Vedas would give them a scientific edge in World War II. But this clandestine academic work is the exclusive exception. Almost always, mainstream academia follows the golden rule: no superior technology existed in remote antiquity; modern humanity has no peers in advancement; contemporary humans are the crown of creation.

Before we sample more of the stunning world of ancient Vedic technology, we should be aware that major unsolved mysteries of technology exist right before our eyes. We might consider that for the past thirty or so years, miners in South Africa, in the Western Transvaal region, have brought to the surface strange metallic grooved spheres that indicate metallurgy billions of years back in time. To date, over two hundred of these perfectly round spheres have been discovered, in deep rock dated over two billion years old. Especially bizarre are the spheres with three parallel grooves around their middle. The artifacts fall into two categories: solid bluish metal with white flecks, and hollow objects with a strange, white, spongy material inside.

The curator of the Klerksdorp Museum in South Africa, where some of the spheres are stored, testifies that they cannot be scratched even with a metal point. "The spheres are a complete mystery," the curator, Roelf Marx, describes. Nevertheless, holding tight to the traditional notion of human antiquity, he affirmed, "They look man-made, yet at the time in Earth's history when they came to rest in this rock, no intelligent life existed."[9]

Mainstream scientists struggle to explain the spheres away. They hotly retort that, rather than the obvious product of human intelligence two billion years ago, the spheres—grooves and all—are "common natural concretions." Yet when alternative researchers challenge their establishment counterparts to please present evidence of nature forming metallic spheres—with parallel grooves around their equator—the establishment falls silent.

The mysterious spheres of South Africa are small yet troublesome signs that something is wrong with our version of history. Colossal contradictions, however, loom right before our eyes:

- The Great Pyramid of Egypt weighs over six million tons and contains more stonemasonry than the combined total of all the churches, chapels, and cathedrals built in medieval Europe. Do we really accept the official explanation that the Egyptians moved all that stone up the side of the Pyramid, into mathematically precise settings, by employing ramps and a huge army of workers?

- Astoundingly sophisticated craftsmanship—enviable even by modern standards—is evidenced in the King's Chamber of the Pyramid. Also, the Serapeum at Saqqara, where sacred bulls were entombed, as well as the swan-neck vases of Saqqara all defy our conceptions of what the ancients could do.

- One of the pyramids at Cholula, near Mexico City, is three times the size of the Great Pyramid of Giza. How was the stone transported from distant quarries, and how did the Aztecs carve their huge stone statues and raise them to the top of pyramids?

- In the Andes Mountains of Bolivia, the ruins of Tiahuanaco present their own riddles of construction. One building block there is more than double the weight of the biggest blocks of the Sphinx temple at Giza.

- Near Cuzco, Peru, miraculous construction is the hallmark of both the citadel of Sacsayhuaman and the fortress at Machu Picchu.

Egyptian Enigmas of Construction

The Great Pyramid of Egypt has blocks weighing between 10 and 15 tons on its upper levels, above smaller blocks of a mere 6 tons. The whole structure consists of 2.5 million limestone blocks, forming 203 levels of limestone and granite masonry. Why and how did the builders put the smaller blocks on the ground and the particularly huge blocks up high? Normally, of course, we would think and do the reverse.

Forced to come up with a construction theory based on crude sweat and blood, most scholars favor the ramp and slave-gang approach. For example, Professor I. E. S. Edwards, a past curator of Egyptian antiquities at the British Museum, asserted, "Only one method of lifting heavy weights was open to the ancient Egyptians, namely by means of ramps composed of brick and earth which sloped upwards from the level of the ground to whatever height was desired."[10]

John Baines, professor of Egyptology at Oxford University, helps the general public digest this predominant notion. In a Time-Life book he elaborates: "As the pyramid grew in height, the length of the ramp and the width of its base were increased in order to maintain a constant gradient (about 1 in 10) and to prevent the ramp from collapsing. Several ramps approaching the pyramid from different sides were probably used."[11]

Coming down from the clouds, when you call for construction experts, you get a different angle: bewilderment. Nimble engineering brains, determined to show the travesty of Egyptologists' rationalizations, have pointed out that the envisioned ramp would have to have been almost a mile long. In addition, it would have to be built of three times the amount of material used to make the pyramid itself. To bear the extraordinary load, the mile-long ramp would have to consist of huge blocks, just like the pyramid itself.

Besides a ramp, we could imagine some kind of crane. It would have to be made of wood, since the ancients knew nothing else, we are sure. But the pyramid is 500 feet high. For the Egyptians to hoist heavy blocks that high in the air, they would have required a lifting device made of several super trees. Only the special giants growing in California would do. And remember that the pyramid is composed of about 2.3 million blocks in 203 levels. Also remember that some of the ledges are only 6 inches wide.

Chapter 5 discussed the controversy in dating the Sphinx. We should also know that, whenever the ancient builders did actually build the Sphinx, they chose blocks weighing 200 tons each—far exceeding those forming the Great Pyramid. Across from the Sphinx, the Valley Temple of Khafre has main walls of blocks often weighing 100 and sometimes even 200 tons each. The sizes of the stones are incredulous. Many are as much as 16 feet long, 10 feet wide, and 7 feet high. Some stone blocks are even 27 feet long, 10 feet wide, and 10 feet high. These dimensions are stupendous enough to suggest giants, not humans, as builders. Of course, we know better than to entertain thoughts like that.

Picture a modern freight container or diesel locomotive. Some of the stones forming the Valley Temple are larger and heavier. Yet the mysterious Egyptian builders could cut these colossal blocks out of the bedrock surrounding the Sphinx, transport them as far as 225 feet to the site of the Valley Temple, and then position them. Why did the builders choose such immense blocks when smaller ones would suffice? The walls of the Great Pyramid have blocks averaging 2 tons—they get the job done just as well, at 100 times less weight.

More pressing is the "how" of the astonishing endeavor. Ask some construction specialists in huge structures, and you'll find they refuse to venture a speculation. Before 1970, no crane could lift more than 100 tons. Since then a few monsters, with enormous counterweights, can lift up to 250 tons, and most recently, an exceptional crane can hoist 1,000-ton payloads.[12] Therefore we can only wonder how the builders of the Valley Temple assembled their blocks into walls 35 feet high.

The Great Pyramid, as we now know it, weighs more than the combined weight of all the buildings in the famous Square Mile section of London. But formerly it weighed even more. At one time its four faces were covered with mirrorlike stone—each one of the estimated 115,000 polished cladding stones given a weight of 16 tons. Most of them shook loose during an earthquake in A.D. 1301. They were then hauled off to construct the present city of Cairo.[13]

Near the end of the nineteenth century, enough cladding remained in place for the renowned archaeologist W. M. Flinders Petrie to examine the fittings. Though each casing stone weighed 16 tons and occupied an area of 10.5 square feet, Petrie was astounded to observe that the average thickness of the joints between them was one-fiftieth of an inch. Moreover, the massive stones had been joined and cemented so accurately that he could not insert even a fine-bladed pocketknife in them. Petrie had to conclude, "To merely place such stones in exact contact at the sides would be careful work; but to do so with cement in the joint seems almost impossible."[14]

Petrie had set sail from England to Egypt in 1880, on a personal quest to conduct the most thorough, accurate study ever undertaken of the temples and monuments. He brought to light the baffling stonecutting prowess necessary to construct the Giza pyramids, their temples, and the sarcophagi inside them.

Inside the Great Pyramid, the King's Chamber features 43 huge beams of granite, each weighing between 45 and 70 tons. How were they cut? The red granite sarcophagus found in the King's Chamber was cut out of stone so precisely that its external volume is exactly twice its internal volume. What tools were used to cut it out of granite? Next, once cut out, what tools were used to hollow the granite sarcophagus so accurately? Petrie saw no answer to these riddles except straight and circular bronze saws set with sapphires or rubies, and also jewel-tipped tubular drills. And how did the tools spin, in order to hollow out the inside?

Furthermore, let us consider artifacts found beneath the Step Pyramid of Zoser at Saqqara. Archaeologists discovered more than 30,000 vases made of diorite, basalt, and quartz. With slender, swanlike necks and elegantly flared insides, the vases often had fully hollowed shoulders. The necks are so thin, a child's hand cannot fit down them. Some are too narrow for even a little finger to enter. Modern engineers have noted the artifacts are beyond the abilities of today's stone carvers armed with tungsten-carbide drills.

Without any signs of evolutionary stages of development, the ancient Egyptians demonstrated skills in manufacturing stone vessels that completely baffle modern scholars. Some major Egyptologists have refused to ignore the mystery:

> The really finest stone vessels appear in the First Dynasty: for technical skill and sheer mastery of form their work is unparalleled. (Michael Rice)[15]

> The ancient Eygptian stone statues, particularly those in such hard materials as diorite, granite, quartzite . . . have long been a source of . . . wonder and speculation as to the nature of the tools used. (A. Lucas)[16]

> Nowhere in the world have there ever been more skilful stoneworkers than the Egyptians, and the perfection of the innumerable vases, jars, plates and so forth found in the Step Pyramid . . . is as much a wonder as the Great Pyramid itself. (Sir Alan Gardiner)[17]

> No country then or since has achieved such perfection . . . unfortunately we have no really satisfactory evidence of the method of manufacture of these stone vessels. (Walter Emery)[18]

Though the ancient Egyptians' astonishing stonework is undeniable, efforts to give them the right tools for getting the job done
meet with indifference or, worse, stiff resistance. True, archaeologists have not found any sophisticated tools. Simple copper tools
abound. Nevertheless, the stone artifacts themselves bear witness
to advanced implements. It is quite obvious that the tools on display in museums could not have produced the very artifacts that
the same museums also display.

Petrie's study took several decades. He published the results of
his research in his book *The Pyramids and Temples of Gizeh*. The ex-
tensiveness and thoroughness of his research has never been
equalled. After his death in 1942, he was deemed worthy enough
for London's University College to establish the Petrie Chair of
Egyptology. Current scholars certainly respect Petrie's pioneering
work. For example, although Petrie's book now dates back over a
century, a current pillar in mainstream Egyptology, Z. Hawass,
confirms that it is still considered "an accurate and important archaeological investigation and a basic reference for the site."[19] But
when most of these same Egyptologists encounter Petrie's proposals for advanced technology in ancient Egypt, they generally look
the other way.

An American tool specialist, Christopher Dunn, has upset the
establishment with a startling solution to the stonecutting mystery. Rather than relying upon the usual nontechnical approach
for researching the ancients, Dunn invaded mainstream Egyptology with his engineering knowledge. In 1983 he took to investigating Petrie's assertions of jewel-tipped technology. Scrutinizing blocks in the Valley Temple, the tooling specialist observed
that they had been hollowed out with some kind of drill. He examined the incisions and calculated that whatever drill had done
the job, it had chewed into the rock at the rate of 0.09 of an inch
per revolution of the drill. Impossible by hand, but what about by
modern machines?

An American firm in Ohio that specializes in drilling granite explained to Dunn that, although their drills spin at 900 revolutions per minute, they only bite into the rock at 0.00021 of an inch per revolution.[20] How can we attribute to the ancient Egyptians a drill 500 times faster than what our best technology offers today? Dunn felt forced to a daring conclusion: the Egyptians employed a process known today as ultrasonic drilling.

Though inconceivable to orthodox Egyptologists, no other drilling technique accounts for the telltale symptoms in the granite cores and boreholes. Cutting into hard rock by using ultrasound to assist drills is a process perfected only in the last fifty years. How could the ancient Egyptians have been so high-tech? The proposal is shocking, perhaps, only until we hear whispers from the past indicating the Egyptians used sound to build walls.

Loud Hints of Sonic Construction

Around the tenth century A.D., inquisitive Arabs often traveled to Egypt in search of hidden esoteric knowledge. Thirsty for secrets of the pyramids, they particularly sought out elderly Coptic Christian priests in Old Cairo. The wandering Arab historian al-Mas'udi, noting down anything of interest, is known to have visited Armenia, Sri Lanka, India, Madagascar, and Zanzibar. Later in his life he resided in Egypt. Almost all the many books he compiled are now lost. One that survived is *Kitah Muruj al-Dhahah wa Ma'adin al-Jawhar*, "The Meadows of Gold and Mines of Gems." In it al-Mas'udi relates witnessing a meeting between Ahmad ibn Tulun, who ruled Egypt between A.D. 868 and 877, and an unnamed Coptic priest.

The Arab itinerant historian recorded the esoteric Coptic explanation of how the Egyptians built the pyramids: "In carrying out the work, leaves of papyrus, or paper, inscribed with certain characters, were placed under the stones prepared in the quarries; and upon being struck, the blocks were moved at each time the distance of a bowshot (about 150 cubits), and so by degrees arrived at the Pyramids."[21]

What the account of al-Mas'udi suggests is that the Egyptians moved their immense blocks of granite by sound levitation. According to his description, first papyri inscribed with magical characters were placed beneath the stones. Then each block was struck with some kind of rod. Next the block rose in the air and traveled the equivalent of 260 feet, before the process would be repeated again. The implication is that by the ancient Egyptians' striking the blocks, they established a sound vibration that allowed the blocks to defy gravity and move.[22]

Obviously rare is the academic who will accept al-Mas'udi's account as factual. Most of our scholars will tell us that the old Coptic Christians, like all ancients, were just manufacturing fables to ennoble their ancestors.[23] But can we afford to be so certain? Other distant cultures also whisper these hints of sonic construction.

Mesoamerican Mysteries

Upon crossing the Atlantic Ocean, from Egypt to Mesoamerica, mystery also accompanies us. Near what is now Mexico City, the great pyramid at Cholula, three times the size of its Egyptian rival, is an obvious construction enigma. Then, deep in the jungles of Mexico's Yucatán Peninsula is Uxmal, a temple complex of the Maya. Legends claim the structure was established by a race of dwarfs—a notion we can easily discard as fantasy. The fables of old attribute abnormal building techniques to these dwarfs: "Construction work was easy for them, all they had to do was whistle and heavy rocks would move into place."[24] Amid these perhaps confusing tales of antiquity, are we getting hidden insights into the forgotten power of sound? The dwarfs, though they "needed only to whistle to bring together stones in their correct positions in buildings," were said to have perished in a great flood.[25]

Further south, in the Andes Mountains of Bolivia, are lesser known but equally problematic structures. On the bank of the world's largest freshwater lake, 137 miles long and sometimes 70 miles wide, are the ruins of Tiahuanaco, once a port. Why did its people choose to work with blocks of stone 30 feet long and 15 feet wide? One of the blocks is 440 tons—twice the weight of the huge blocks forming the Sphinx Temple.

Intriguing folk-memories of sonic power haunt us here also. Shortly after the Spanish conquest, some Aymara Indians of the area told a Spanish traveller that the city Tiahuanaco was constructed long before the time of the Incas. The founders, they said, were able to levitate stones off the ground and then dispatch them from quarries in the mountains to the construction site. The stones "were carried through the air to the sound of a trumpet."[26]

In the ruins at Tiahuanaco is an immense archway, built with approximately 10 tons of stone. Called the Gateway of the Sun, its face is carved with a male figure said to be Ticci Viracocha, the legendary founder of the city. According to folklore, after establishing Tiahuanaco, he and his associates, together known as the "Viracocha," moved north to spread civilization. The first Spanish travelers heard from the Aymara Indians of Bolivia and Peru that Viracocha was a master of many arts and technologies. Said to have been a scientist, sculptor, agronomist, and engineer, Viracocha "caused terraces and fields to be formed on the steep sides of ravines, and sustaining walls to rise up and support them."[27] The great civilizer could empower stones in such a way that "large blocks could be lifted by hand as if they were corks."[28]

Turning our gaze to Peru, near Cuzco, we find the ancient fortress of Sacsayhuaman, composed of perfectly balanced and connected blocks that weigh more than 100 tons. Amid the aesthetic arrangement of precisely hewn and placed stones is one particularly gigantic block, 26 feet high. It is calculated to weigh 361 tons (approximately equal to 500 large cars).

On top of a mountain, the breathtaking fortress of Machu Picchu also demands an answer. Some ancient people built this citadel on a mountaintop by so perfectly joining gigantic blocks of stone that often even a sheet of paper cannot enter between them. In this jigsaw-puzzle arrangement, one of the blocks perfectly interlocks with other blocks in at least 33 different angles. Another stone there weighs at least 200 tons. The combined miracle of transporting, lifting, and then perfectly fitting huge stone blocks together *on a mountaintop* begs a rational analysis.

Greek Myth?

Today some of the official chronology we've devised for the ancients is moving back in time. This pushing of dates a mere one or two thousand years further into the past seems the maximum revision of history most mainstream scholars can accommodate. Who can dare think our remote ancestors knew how to manipulate stone blocks with sound? Understandably, rare is the academic ready to entertain that possibility. Even some alternative researchers halt at the hurdle. Nevertheless, clues have arisen on both sides of the Atlantic Ocean—Egypt, Mesoamerica, and also Greece.

Classical Greek writers say that the ancient city Thebes, a rival of Athens, was built by a legendary person named Amphion. Interestingly, Amphion was to have erected the walls of Thebes by using sounds from a harp to move large stones.[29] Pausanias, a Greek historian and geographer during the second century A.D., mentioned this phenomenon in his lengthy *Description of Greece*— a work still lauded today for its accuracy. The celebrated anthropologist and classical scholar Sir James Frazier gave Pausanias this rating: "Without him the ruins of Greece would be for the most part a labyrinth without a clue, a riddle without an answer."[30] The ten-volumed *Description* noted that Amphion built the walls of Thebes "to the music of his harp."[31]

A third-century B.C. poet Apollonius gave some information in his *The Argonautica*, a four-volumed epic. The poet, also a chief librarian at Alexandria, described that Amphion would play "loud and clear on his golden lyre" and consequently "a rock twice as large followed his footsteps."[32]

Undeniably, references to sonic technology are a global mystery. Different peoples, cultures, and continents have left behind faint traces of the concept. But is sonic power just myth and superstition? Or do we have some hope of historical fact, perhaps embedded within legends of godlike ancestors? Amazingly, uncommon knowledge from the twentieth century echoes the loud hints of antiquity. Our own modern times may be capable of shaking the stonelike rigidity of dominant mainstream notions.

Tibetan Secrets

In the 1950s, Swedish engineer Henry Kjellson recorded two separate accounts of sonic technology in Tibet. Two Western travelers, unrelated, provided testimony. We get not a murky, perhaps myth-wrapped picture from the remote past. Rather, we have in our hands modern eyewitness reports from the first half of the twentieth century.[33]

Kjellson relays the observations of a Swedish doctor visiting a Tibetan friend at a monastery southwest of the capital Lhasa. The doctor told him he saw stone blocks—4 feet long and 3 feet high and wide—being raised into the air by sonic technology.

In a meadow facing cliffs, a group of monks established a construction site. Their goal: constructing a wall in a cave of the cliffs. The distance from the meadow up to the cave: 750 feet. The doctor's testimony is extensive and meticulously detailed. In brief, he describes an orchestra of yellow-robed monks with trumpets and drums. Chanting and playing rhythmically, the formation of monks aimed their sounds at a stone block before them. After four minutes, the stone block first wobbled on the ground and then rose into the air. In an arc-like pattern the stone traveled up to the ledge at the cave's entrance—750 feet above. There the stones abruptly crashed to a halt, sending dust and gravel flying in all directions. Just as abruptly, the sonic-technology orchestra silenced. Then the musician-builders readied another stone on the ground and repeated the same process.

In this way they hoisted up to the mouth of the cave between five and six blocks per hour. Occasionally a stone block would land on the ledge with too much force and consequently shatter. Then the monks working above would clear the rubble from the cave's entrance by pushing the pieces out and over the edge, down to the meadow far below.

Kjellson withheld the doctor's name. Also, the date of the event—attributed to the 1920s or 1930s—is not given. Still, the meticulousness of the testimony is quite persuasive. The elaborate detail of the doctor's account makes for an exciting read. Those familiar with Tibetan Buddhism, however, will not be surprised. They will recognize certain esoteric Tibetan meditation practices of combined sonic and mental power. The actual abilities are almost lost now, though knowledge of their existence still lingers in the memories of monks today.

Next, Kjellson relays his conversation in 1939 with an Austrian filmmaker named Linauer. The man declared to Kjellson that during his travels in Tibet during the 1930s, monks showed him a special gong and stringed instrument. He watched as the two musical devices were used to render stones weightless through sound. Their combined sonic effect enabled a monk to lift one of the stones with just one hand. The monks informed Linauer that their little demonstration was a glimpse into the way their ancestors constructed defensive walls throughout Tibet. Moreover, they told him (though not showing him) that their sonic techniques could dissolve or disintegrate matter.

Normally, the monks explained, they would never allow a

foreigner to witness any of their prowess. They feared that if their ancient technology ever reached the West, it would be abused for negative purposes. Hand in hand with their mystic knowledge was the solemn responsibility to guard its secrets from destructive societies.

Turning to the Vedic presentations of mystic powers, we will find a security measure of a different sort. The Vedic accounts clearly delineate mystic powers far surpassing the lost wonders of Tibet. Simultaneously, the Vedic texts clearly explain that the deprived and depraved humans of today lack the longevity, intelligence, and austerity necessary to develop these techniques. Therefore, no need to hide the information—humans today can neither use it nor abuse it.

Sonic Knowledge, Not Stone and Bone

Monuments, temples, and cities of stone are a delight for the educated eye. The ancient edifices—still standing or in ruins—fill our eyes. What's more, we can kick stone, and handle it with our fingers. When we turn to understanding the Vedic age, however, we have no huge stone structures to aid our speculations. Nor have archaeologists uncovered telltale bones that allow a reconstruction of Vedic history.

To the contrary, the Vedic treasure is knowledge. It is a colossal bank of information both terrestrial and extraterrestrial, both material and nonmaterial. The immense megaliths of knowledge are accessed through oral transmission and written texts. We might long for the day when the mystery of writing in ancient India becomes completely solved. But Vedic contemporary teachers do not hold their breath. They accept that the knowledge of the Vedas—whether as written symbols or spoken word—is a body of information with a sonic origin beyond what humans can trace.

The Vedic information-bank handles timespans of billions of years with casual aplomb. From its vast perspective, the affairs of modern humans are puny and stunted. The irritating yet pygmy-ish trends of recent millennia are but a speck of dust in the conscious eye of eternity.

Why not take the Vedic knowledge as it is, and try to enter it according to its own precepts and methodology? Perhaps if we moderns would treat the Vedic knowledge as a towering mo-nument of stone left for our benefit, we could derive immense advantages. Unfortunately, the majority is sure that the Vedic de-scriptions of paranormal technology are just vivid imagery. The word *imagery* currently reigns as our polite equivalent for *fantasy*. In this way, convinced that the Vedas contain scant definitive knowledge, many scholars devote their short lifetime to only mi-croscopic linguistic analysis of the texts. Could they be missing the forest for the trees?

Mystic Powers

Eight mystic perfections, or *siddhis*, are recognized as para-mount in the Vedic texts. Additionally, various other skills are considered secondary or less. When hearing of these mystic opulences, we should remember that the Vedic vision perceives a universe populated with living entities of differing abilities. What is astonishing on one planet, such as Earth, is routine on another planet. Not only do the Vedas list the mystic perfections, but also they fill our minds with rich accounts of mystic exper-tise in action. Ultimately, we learn that pride in the mystic or psychic arts impedes the development of pure, transcendental spirituality.

The first three primary powers concern radical transformations of the physical measurements of the material body:

(1) *Anima-siddhi*: the ability to reduce the body even to an atomic size without disrupting its structure, so that a yogi can enter into stone or pass through any barrier.

(2) *Mahima-siddhi*: the power to expand the size of the body

without disrupting its structure, even to the extent that a yogi can be seen to fill the land and sky.

(3) *Laghima-siddhi*: the skill of levitation, or antigravity, by which the weight of the body becomes so light that a yogi can float in the air or on the water, and even ride on the sun's ray into the sun.

The next two involve acquisition. By them, an expert yogi can ignore conventional physical, sensory limitations:

(4) *Prapti-siddhi*: the power to reach for whatever the heart desires and grab it—without having to traverse space to the place. For example, the yogi can touch another planet and then, extending the grasp, take anything from there. Also, such a master yogi can use the senses of other living entities to acquire anything.

(5) *Prakamya-siddhi*: the ability to directly experience any object of enjoyment—anywhere in the universe.

The last three primary mystic potencies concern wondrous manipulation and control of nature:

(6) *Ishita-siddhi*: the power to perform "miracles," by manipulating lesser forces of nature, in conjunction with the laws of nature. A yogi with the full measure of this expertise can even create or destroy a planet.

(7) *Vashita-siddhi*: the skill of long-distance psychic control. The adept can control the minds of others from far away. Also, the full development of this ability allows one to live uninfluenced by the three modes of material nature.

(8) *Kamavashayita-siddhi*: the utmost magnitude of material acquisition, control, and enjoyment possible in the cosmos, irrespective of nature's gross and subtle laws. In short, have whatever you like, do whatever you like, and enjoy whatever you like.

These eight primary arts accomplish their perfections without technology as we know it, or industrialization. The Vedic literature never mentions factories or research laboratories. The mystic powers are the natural, organic outcome of either birth, yoga practices, or the recitation of mantras.

Less important than the eight major abilities are ten secondary talents:

(1) The power to escape hunger, thirst, and other physical disturbances.
(2) The skill of hearing sounds no matter where they are vibrated.
(3) The skill of seeing events regardless of their location (remote viewing).
(4) The ability to move in the body at the speed of mind.
(5) The capacity to assume whatever physical form one desires.
(6) The power to enter the bodies of others and experience life therein.
(7) The ability to choose the moment of death.
(8) The power to visit the celestial pleasure gardens of the *devas*, accompanied by celestial women in airplanes.
(9) The capacity to thoroughly execute one's determination.
(10) The expertise to issue commands that are always fulfilled.

At the bottom of the pile are five arts considered quite inferior because they are said to represent rather ordinary adjustments of the body and mind:

(1) Knowing the past, present, and future.
(2) Tolerating extremes of heat and cold.
(3) Mental telepathy and mind reading.
(4) Checking the effects of fire, poison, weapons, curses, and so on.
(5) Invincibility in battle.

Mere smatterings of the ten secondary powers and the five inferior powers are now known in the West. We should note that our modern world has almost no knowledge of the eight prime perfections, or *siddhis*. In the present Vedic age of Kali, of degradation, these eight major powers are almost extinct in their full capacity.

The Vedas describe that living entities can receive mystic talents along with their body at birth, or the skills can be developed through yoga, mantras, herbs, or even the blessings of an empowered person. In the *Bhagavad-gita*, the impeccable remote viewer and hearer Sanjaya says he owes his talent to the graces of his spiritual master Vyasa.

The juice of the herb *soma* is often mentioned in the Vedas for its properties of celestial invigoration. Indologists like to speculate what type of vegetation produces this *soma-rasa*, heavenly beverage, and they propose various plants known today. Or else they say perhaps the plant is now extinct.[34] The Vedas are clear, however, that the *soma* plant is nonearthly—its habitat is the heavenly planets. In the remote past, highly advanced civilizations on Earth had access to the *soma*, courtesy of the *devas*. At that time, the *devas'* interactions with Earth were visible to humans. Our forcing the Vedas into a geocentric mold conveniently obliterates our serious consideration of the extraterrestrial references to *soma*.

In Vedic epochs, *yugas*, said to be more favorable for spiritual development, the eightfold yoga system, known as *ashtanga-yoga*, was a prime means for mystic attainment. Said to require a life span of 100,000 years to perfect, the mystic yoga system—practiced in complete solitude—has these eight limbs:

(1) *Yama*: refraining from negatives such as violence, stealing, lying, sex, and greed.

(2) *Niyama*: accepting favorables such as cleanliness, asceticism, solitude, serenity, and study of the Vedas.

(3) *Asana*: scientific yogic postures.

(4) *Pranayama*: systematic breath control.

(5) *Pratyahara*: completely withdrawing the senses from their objects.

(6) *Dharana*: unbroken concentration.

(7) *Dhyana*: fixed meditation on the Supreme.

(8) *Samadhi*: total absorption of the self in divine consciousness.

Knowledge of mystic yoga entails understanding that the subtle body has energy centers called *chakras*. These are connected by pathways called *nadis*, along which subtle energy, *prana*, flows. The *chakras* are situated vertically on the central axis of the body, from the base of the trunk to the top of the skull. They are especially important for travelling via mystic yoga to whatever destination the yogi chooses. Lifting the spirit soul from the heart to the chest, the yogi then raises it to the neck, the forehead, and then finally out through the top of the skull. Choosing the moment of death, the expert yogi aims himself to his next destination. The ultimate goal is to bypass the heavenly regions of the universe and immediately get out of the material cosmos completely. Nevertheless, an adept still attracted to mystic enjoyments within the universe can opt to dally in celestial material realms with enjoyments inconceivable to earthlings.

Besides *ashtanga-yoga*, the correct vibration of mantras also is said to generate mystic abilities. In the present Age of Kali, the Vedic literature recommends the *maha-mantra* (topmost mantra) as the only feasible means of spiritual elevation. Therefore this *maha-mantra*, the Hare Krishna mantra, is stressed for straightaway attaining the ultimate goal of mysticism: freedom from material existence and establishment in a pure spiritual relationship with *Bhagavan*, the Supreme Person.

After enumerating in the *Bhagavata Purana* the major, secondary, and inferior mystic powers, Bhagavan Krishna asserts:

Learned experts in devotional service (*bhakti-yoga*) state that the mystic perfections of yoga that I have mentioned are actually impediments and are a waste of time for one who is practicing the supreme yoga, by which one achieves all perfection in life directly from Me. (*Shrimad-Bhagavatam* 11.15.33)

In the *Gita*, after reviewing the different steps on the yoga ladder, Krishna says:

> And of all yogis, the one with great faith who always abides in Me, thinks of Me within himself, and renders transcendental loving service to Me—he is the most intimately united with Me in yoga and is the highest of all. That is My opinion. (*Bhagavad-gita* 6.47)

THE WEST GROPES FOR PSYCHIC POWERS

That Western civilization is spiritually blind has long been the charge broadcast by contemporary Eastern sages. Yet even in the matter of materialism, still the Vedic standard judges the West as far from the mark. The mind—more accurately the subtle body—is matter. Yet, for so long Western culture, while exploiting the gross resources of nature, has ignored the immense potencies of subtle materialism. Modern humanity is just beginning to realize its failure to understand the mind—subtle or astral matter—and its latent potential to dominate gross, physical matter.

The investigation of psychic phenomenon used to be the domain of scientists deemed crackpots and eccentrics by the mainstream. Now the most prestigious institutions in the world are quietly forging ahead into the psychic frontier. We have already discussed the remote viewing research started at Stanford Research Institute (SRI), when that scientific think tank was affiliated with Stanford University. Also in the USA, Princeton University has its Princeton Engineering Anomalies Research (PEAR) Laboratory. There Professor Robert Jahn, Dean Emeritus of the Princeton School of Engineering, and Brenda Dunne, also of Princeton, have published authoritative data showing that the human mind can influence physical matter in a way that a laboratory can statistically measure.

Based on almost half a million experimental trials, the tests by Jahn and Dunne unarguably reveal a minute yet definite and quantifiable ability for the mind to influence the output of electronic devices. The two frontier scientists demonstrated the mind's influence by using microchip devices that randomly generate thousands of computerized dice rolls per hour.

Brenda Dunne explained, "Gamblers throughout history have believed that they could affect the outcome of a random process like rolling dice or shuffling cards. The phenomenon we're measuring is a lot more subtle, but it's the same idea and we've measured it in the laboratory."[35]

Sitting calmly in a relaxed atmosphere, volunteers would declare their intent and then try to mentally "coax" the microchip into yielding numbers either higher than the average or lower.

Both the volunteers' intent and the random result that the electronic device generated were directly fed into a computer. The results of a half million tests demonstrated the unmistakable "footprints" of consciousness. Undeniably, the mind was able to prod the electronic dice in a desired direction.

The Western wonders went still further. The rigorous experiment at the PEAR lab revealed that the same slight nudging by the mind was statistically detected even when the volunteer was thousands of miles away, or, yet more startling, when gaps of time separated the experimenter's intent from the actual "throwing" of the electronic dice. A volunteer in Paris on Monday would mentally concentrate on a desired outcome; the actual electronic procedure, by prior agreement, would not happen until Friday, across the Atlantic Ocean at Princeton University's lab.

Professor Jahn commented, "All forces known to physics, like gravity for example, diminish with distance. And no forces in physics operate freely across time like this. It's as if consciousness is somehow able to direct its influence directly across space and time, an understanding that certainly poses a challenge for science. It's something science cannot afford to simply ignore any longer. And besides, it's such an exciting challenge to our whole way of thinking about the physical world."[36]

The other half of the prestigious team, Brenda Dunne, did not shrink from the inevitable conclusion: "This is similar to what the mystics have claimed through the ages, but now we have scientific evidence."[37]

Paranormal scientific exploration certainly has its share of fraud and mistakes. We might remember, though, that "normal science" does too. Sometimes phenomena thought to be paranormal turn out to have "rational explanations"—physical cause and effect. A century of psychic research, however, has shown that many phenomena that were ignored or else blindly trusted to "normal, physical causes" indeed do violate known physical concepts of nature.

For example, firewalking is now a popular anomalous experience in the West. Organized walks began in the USA and Europe during the early 1980s. Since then, many thousands have defied rationality by putting their flesh to the flame and emerging unscathed. The procedure calls for the participants first to mentally internalize the assurance that no harm will befall them. Then they tread over a bed of burning coals, 1200 to 1400 degrees Fahrenheit. Scientists, from their cavernous stable of normality, have trotted out valiant physical explanations, attempting to account for the lack of burnt feet. A layer of ashes insulates the feet; a layer of steam protects them; a layer of perspiration shields them; and so on. Meanwhile, indigenous shamans and their Western pupils casually demonstrate that, if the mind is situated one way, the feet are unharmed. To experiment, all the doubting Thomas has to do is change his belief and then experience how the burning coals inflict severe third-degree burns.

Here is a list of psychic phenomena currently acknowledged by bold scientists on the frontiers. Note the advent of suitable vocabulary, to "westernize" preliminary knowledge of rudimentary mystic phenomena.

Extrasensory perception (ESP)—information is obtained in ways that bypass normal sensory inputs and operations:

- Telepathy: mind-to-mind communication
- Retrocognition: knowledge or memory of the past unknowable by ordinary means
- Precognition: abnormal knowledge of the future events
- Clairvoyance: direct awareness of information that a physicalist would certify as inaccessible (such as via remote viewing).

Psychokinesis (PK)—the human mind directly alters the physical environment:

- Routine psychokinesis: psychic gymnastics like metal-spoon-bending with the mind
- Psychic medicine: healing, including psychic surgery
- Teleportation: causing an object to disappear from one location and appear in another
- Levitation: raising the body in the air by psychic power
- Thought photography: an image held in the mind resulting in a corresponding image on film.[38]

Probably the most famous practitioner of elementary psychokinesis in the West is Uri Geller. Throughout the 1980s Geller fascinated American TV audiences with PK spoon-bending. His favorite line: "Don't use the good silver!" In the early 1980s his psychic abilities were thoroughly tested at Stanford Research Institute. Preeminent scientists like Wernher von Braun certified his skills as genuine. Official interest in PK began to increase, and in 1976 Geller met US President Jimmy Carter. He pleaded with Carter that because the Soviets were making mighty strides in psychic warfare, America must match their research or forfeit the world to them. Later, Geller had meetings with Gorbachev and Bush to brief them on psychic affairs.[39] Now, if you surf Geller's website on the Internet, you might win one million US dollars. Geller can afford to award the prize—not by bending spoons. He's put his psychic talents into the employ of multinational conglomerates seeking to unearth new sources of gold and other minerals.

A lesser known but perhaps more competent practitioner of PK is Wolf Messing, who during World War II had his abilities personally tested by Stalin. A Polish Jew, before the war Messing held international stature. Luminaries like Einstein, Freud, and Gandhi had examined him. But when he publicly declared in 1937 that, if Hitler tried to expand eastward, he would die, the Führer, wary of the paranormal, put a 200,000 mark price on his head. Messing fled, taking his psychic expositions to theaters in Russia.

In 1940, amid a sellout performance in Belorussia, the secret police walked on stage and told the audience the show was over. Putting Messing into a car, they drove him straight to Stalin. Never a man to waste time, Stalin quickly got to the point. Messing was supposed to have paranormal abilities to telepathically broadcast his thoughts into another person's mind, and to control or cloud the mind. Stalin would see for himself. He ordered Messing to stage a psychic bank robbery.

Messing walked into the Moscow Gosbank, handed the cashier a blank piece of paper, and placed an open attaché case on the counter. The bank teller studied the blank paper, opened the safe, took out 100,000 rubles, and handed the banknotes to Messing. While Stalin's officers observed, the psychic stuffed the money into his case and departed.

Then Messing walked back into the bank, to the same teller, and returned the wad of cash. The cashier looked at Messing, the cash, and then the blank piece of paper on his desk. Immediately he fell to the floor in shock. Stalin's witnesses could understand that Messing had mentally willed the teller to accept a blank piece of paper as sufficient documentation for handing over the huge sum. When Messing returned, he allowed the cashier to realize his mistake. With an unclouded mind, the cashier immediately understood he had given the cash merely on the basis of a blank piece of paper torn from a notebook. The instant trauma sent him crashing to the floor, with a nonfatal heart attack.

Stalin's examination was not over. The dictator ordered that Messing be taken inside a high-security government building. Three sets of guards were specifically ordered not to let him out of the building—not even out of the room. Clouding their minds, Messing emerged onto the street with ease, waving to Stalin's aides watching from the windows.

Messing's exploits were not hidden by Stalin's regime. The Soviets published them in an official atheistic journal *Science and Religion*. The Russian Nobel laureate chemist Dr. Nikolai Semyonov, who was also vice-president of the Academy of Sciences in the USSR, commented in the journal, "It is very important to scientifically study the psychic phenomena of sensitives like Wolf Messing."[40]

Scientists who knew Messing say that the dictator also had him attempt to sneak into his private dacha. Friends of one of Stalin's granddaughters have confirmed this caper. A platoon of special guards surrounded the home; another platoon was stationed inside the residence. All staff members were trained secret police agents. Yet in walked Messing, past Stalin's expert bodyguards and meticulously trained domestic staff. The soldiers stood aside respectfully; the domestics cleared his way. Stalin, secure in his private room, looked up from his reading, astonished to see Messing peering at him. The psychic explained that he had mentally projected into the guards and staff that he was Lavrenti Beria, Stalin's infamous ace in charge of the secret police. Beria was a frequent visitor to the private compound. Messing, however, did not even slightly resemble him or his mannerisms. The whole charade was "in the mind."

As news of Stalin's personal examination of Messing spread, some upper-level Soviets began to fear Messing was a dangerous man for the state. Stalin obviously did not agree. During one of the most repressive regimes the world has ever seen, Messing toured the Soviet Union on behalf of the Ministry of Culture. Visiting almost every city in Communist Russia, Messing staged his roadshow, "Psychological Experiments," almost every night of the year. The sellout crowds were eager to see his telepathy and other psychic powers.[41]

In the early 1960s, the Soviets revealed decades of experiments with long-range hypnosis. It had become the quintessential Soviet venture into psychic powers. Scientific attention began in 1924, when at the All-Russian Congress of Psychoneurologists, in front of a packed hall of scientists, Dr. K. I. Platonov knocked out a woman telepathically. While a woman chatted onstage, Platonov hid from her, yet kept in view of the audience. He touched his brow to signal the audience he was going to put the woman to sleep, and suddenly she did so. Then he woke her up, and again put her back to sleep. Platonov could even, from an anteroom, suspend her in mid-step while she waltzed with a partner.[42]

Beginning in the 1930s, physiologist Dr. Leonid Vasiliev and his colleagues thoroughly experimented with telepathic hypnosis. Determined to prove that telepathy had a physical basis, they shut their knockout subjects inside iron Faraday cages—to bar electromagnetic waves. Then they built a lead capsule—to bar radiation. Nevertheless, the telepathic knockout sessions went on as usual. Finally, without telling the subject, Vasiliev's team sent the scientist performing the telepathic sleep–wake to a city 1,000 miles away. Still, from far off, he was able to do his job. For several decades, Vasiliev could not freely publish his research. He lived just long enough to see his book *Experimental Research of Mental Suggestion* finally printed in Russia in 1962. An English translation followed the next year.[43]

Chess masters playing representatives of the USSR accused the Soviets of beaming disruptive psychic energy at them from the audience during World Chess Championships. Defected Russian grand masters Boris Spassky and Victor Korchnoi, as well as Gary Kasparov attested to this harassment. Korchnoi registered the loudest complaint. Two years after his defection, in 1978, he faced the Soviet Anatoly Karpov for the world chess crown. Karpov arrived for the decisive match in the Philippines with a huge entourage of aides. The recently defected Korchnoi recognized the head of the contingent: Dr. Vladimir Zoukhar, a KGB expert in telepathic hypnosis. "Expel him immediately!" the enraged Korchnoi demanded, to no avail. The chess officials allowed Dr. Zoukhar to take a ringside seat.

Korchnoi and Karpov played the longest match in championship history, before the harassed Korchnoi finally conceded defeat. Afterwards he lamented to reporters that, although he had come to the Philippines ready to compete against one chess player, instead he had to battle the psychic powers of the Red Army. The narrowly defeated Korchnoi explained that, during the championship, he felt a constant stream of telepathic bombardment: "Stop playing. Stop playing. You are a traitor to the Soviet Union."[44]

A word of caution to trendy Western spiritual seekers: faint, watered-down traces of the Vedic mystic art *vashita-siddhi*—long-distance psychic control—are more common in modern India and the West than we like to believe.

> By this perfection one can bring anyone under his control. This is
> a kind of hypnotism which is almost irresistible. Sometimes it is

found that a yogi who may have attained a little perfection in this *vashita* mystic power comes out among the people and speaks all sorts of nonsense, controls their minds, exploits them, takes their money and then goes away.[45]

VEDIC MASTERY OF THE MYSTIC ARTS

Turning to the prolific accounts of Vedic mysticism, the level of accomplishment jumps extraordinarily. Those experiencing difficulty accepting the child's play of modern spoon-benders, gold-finders, and mind-clouders will certainly blanch at the Vedic standard of psychic power. Its level of expertise correlates with remote ages hidden from contemporary historians of humanity.

The Vedic history of the mystic yogi Saubhari Muni is instructive in more ways than one. As described in the ninth canto of the *Bhagavata Purana*, this yogi had the ability to submerge himself in the depths of the Yamuna River—without diving equipment. While practicing his regimen of austerities underwater, he happened to see a pair of fish copulating. His mind agitated by sexual desire, he surfaced, came ashore, and went to see the king. He seemed to feel that as a great yogi wanting to marry, he automatically qualified for the king's daughters. The king, however, brushed him off, conveniently replying that any of his daughters could marry whomever they wanted—in other words, no.

The yogi then undertook a realistic self-appraisal. "I am a feeble old man, with grey hair, slack skin, and an unsteady posture. Furthermore I look like what I indeed have been doing: practicing severe yogic austerities underwater. Therefore women are not attracted to me. The king has rejected my bid, but with my accumulated mystic power I'll change his tune. I will transform my body so that even celestial women will long for me, not to speak of the daughters of earthly kings."

Psychically shape-shifting his body into that of an uncommonly beautiful young man, Saubhari once again approached the throne. Immediately he was granted access to the private residence of the princesses. He had the green light.

Overwhelmed by Saubhari's stunning appearance, all fifty of the king's daughters rushed to claim him. Abandoning their bond of sisterhood, each one sought Saubhari at the expense of the others. They fought: "This wondrous man is perfect for me; but you should forget him—he's not compatible with you."

Saubhari took them all. Then, with his yogic power he constructed a palatial residence, replete with opulent garments, bodily ornaments, luxurious furniture, delightful gardens, elegant servants, and delicious food. Specifically by expertise in chanting mantras—sonic techniques—the yogi had materialized his own private estate of superb material enjoyment. Even the king was humbled by the opulence Saubhari created through yogic powers.

The former ascetic enthusiastically plunged into sense gratification. Yet as time passed he began to realize that satisfaction ever eluded him. In this connection, the Vedic text notes that, just as a blazing fire never diminishes when constantly supplied with drops of fat, similarly no amount of enjoyment would satiate Saubhari's desires. He was caught in the perennial dilemma of burning desire yet no peace even after feeding the flames.

Sitting in solitude, Saubhari, the renowned mantra chanter, began to reflect upon his fall from yogic austerities. Simply by contemplating the sexuality of fish, he had abandoned his ascetic life style. His lusty desires had forced his emergence from the watery depths. On land, his passions further aroused, Saubhari had tried his hand at mantra-produced sensuality.

"Everyone should learn from my downfall," he concluded. "I rigidly followed all the rules and regulations of mystic yoga—even secluding myself under water. Yet simply by observing the mating of fish, I threw away all my accumulated mystic potency—squandering my sonic psychism on constructing material enjoyment."

The incomparable translation of the *Bhagavata Purana* by A. C. Bhaktivedanta Swami Prabhupada accurately and eloquently presents the psychic's poignant lament:

> In the beginning I was alone and engaged in performing the austerities of mystic yoga, but later, because of the association of fish engaged in sex, I desired to marry. Then I became the husband of fifty wives, and in each of them I begot one hundred sons, and thus my family increased to five thousand members. By the influence of the modes of material nature, I became fallen and thought that I would be happy in material life. Thus there is no end to my material desires for enjoyment, in this life and the next. (*Shrimad Bhagavatam* 9.6.52)

At the final stage of his life, Saubhari, in accordance with the Vedic social system, left his opulent home for the forest, to resume a life of renunciation and austerity. His yogic concentration properly focused again, he achieved the supreme destination, the Supreme Soul.

Women also had mystic power. The Puranic history of the intense romance between Usha and Aniruddha also showcases the top-notch psychic talents of the female mystic yogi Chitralekha. We saw in the life of Saubhari the potential of psychic sound to construct a magnificent structure, replete with all amenities—seemingly out of thin air. In the yogic activities of Chitralekha, we get a splendid display of powers such as extra-sensory perception, mystic travel through space, and teleportation—moving physical objects through physical barriers as if the barriers did not exist.

In the ancient kingdom of Shonitapura, the *Bhagavata Purana* describes, a monarch named Banasura ruled. As was usual, his young unmarried daughter, Usha, lived in a protected inner section of the palace. According to the Vedic standard of civilization, unmarried women are not tossed about from one man to another, but are kept away from prying eyes until a happy marriage with a qualified husband is arranged. While sleeping in the special royal chambers of the palace, one night the young princess dreamed of a beautiful young man who became her lover. Suddenly the amorous encounter ended. Emerging from her vivid dream, Usha cried out, "My dear lover, where are you?"

Fully awakening, Usha remembered that royal girlfriends, who also lived in the female quarters of the palace, surrounded her. Therefore she was acutely embarrassed to have exposed her intimate longings so dramatically. At this point her trusted companion Chitralekha intervened with her highly developed psychic skills.

One of Usha's girlfriends was Chitralekha, who was the daughter of Banasura's prime minister. Chitralekha and Usha were intimate friends, and out of great curiosity Chitralekha asked, "My dear beautiful princess, as of yet you are not married to any young boy, nor have you seen any boys until now; so I am surprised that you are exclaiming like this. Who are you searching after? Who is your suitable match?"

On hearing Chitralekha's inquiries, Usha replied, "My dear friend, in my dream I saw a nice young man who is very, very beautiful. His complexion is swarthy, his eyes are just like lotus petals, and he is dressed in yellow garments. His arms are very long, and his general bodily features are so pleasing that any young girl would be attracted. I feel much pride in saying that this beautiful young man was kissing me, and I was very much enjoying the nectar of his kissing. But I am sorry to inform you that just after this he disappeared, and I have been thrown into the whirlpool of disappointment. My dear friend, I am very anxious to find this wonderful young man, the desired lord of my heart."

After hearing Usha's words, Chitralekha immediately replied, "I can understand your bereavement, and I assure you that if this boy is within these three worlds—the upper, middle and lower planetary systems—I must find him for your satisfaction. If you can identify him from your dream, I shall bring you peace of mind. Now, let me draw some pictures for you to inspect, and as soon as you find the picture of your desired husband, let me know. It doesn't matter where he is; I know the art of bringing him here. So, as soon as you identify him, I shall immediately arrange for it."[46]

The Sanskrit name Chitralekha signifies skills in drawing or painting. *Chitra* means "excellent," and *lekha* means "the art of sketching or painting." True to her name, the female mystic began to draw various possibilities, seeking to jog the memory of her girlfriend. But the psychic did not restrict her sketches to the best young men found on Earth. Though a young girl, she was aware of the different life forms on different planets and in different dimensions of the cosmos.

Based on this traditional Vedic knowledge of the universe, she drew pictures of humanoid and human persons among the *devas*, sub-*devas*, and earthlings. She knew that Usha's dream lover could come from a wide variety of terrestrial or extraterrestrial locales. Among the human species on Earth, Chitralekha drew pictures of the dynasty known as Vrishni, in which Krishna had advented. As the ESP search filtered through the Vrishni clan, Usha became increasingly bashful. Finally, when she saw the picture of Aniruddha, her head dropped in embarrassment: "He's the one who stole my heart," she happily confessed. Neither of the two girls had ever seen the young man before, but Chitralekha's extrasensory perception immediately homed in on his identity. It was the peerlessly fine Aniruddha.

Chitralekha, having deployed her talents in psychic drawing

and ESP to process all the eligible bachelors in the universe, next called upon another Vedic mystic ability. Known in Sanskrit as *vihayasa*, this yogic art allows travel through the subtle substance of cosmic space—unimpeded by gross matter. That very night, traveling through the astral spaceways, the female yogi quickly reached Krishna's capital city, Dvaraka.

Though the city was well protected, Chitralekha used her mystic power to penetrate Aniruddha's palatial residence. Once within his abode, she found him sleeping in his bedroom. She entered the palace and found Aniruddha sleeping in his bedroom on a very opulent bed. If Aniruddha had been awake he would have seen a woman appear out of nowhere, who then scooped him up and vanished—with him—from the bedroom. He would have understood that he was becoming the happy victim of a mystic courier and teleportation scheme. Undeterred by guards or physical barriers or what we consider the laws of time and space, Chitralekha transported the young man to a distant city and inserted him directly into the private female quarters of Banasura's palace.

This account resembles many modern alien abduction stories. They relate that exotic entities enter human bedrooms literally through the walls, grab their astonished target, and "float" the frightened abductee through gross matter to the intended destination—usually some kind of spacecraft for a bizarre medical examination. Chitralekha, however, was so expert that she transported Aniruddha in his sleep. The young man, still resting peacefully, was undisturbed by the flawless caper. And certainly, upon awakening at his final destination, he felt no trauma or surgical probes. Within Usha's private quarters, his eyes opened to her amorous charms.

Normally, a male could not even see the secure female sanctum, let alone enter it. With her advanced mystic arts, however, the yogi Chitralekha had easily accomplished the satisfaction of her dear girlfriend. Undetected for many days, Aniruddha exulted in the princess's affection. Eventually the palace guards and Usa's father found out. Their shocked discovery led to another phenomenal scene. Perhaps it should be noted that, although the relationship between Usha and Aniruddha seems to resemble ordinary passion, the Vedic text provides a profound, nonmundane explanation, for those who care to look deeper.

Romance was certainly not the only province of mystic power. The Vedas describe brahmins, spiritual intellectuals, so powerful that they could vibrate sound that would kill. They could also burn someone to ashes with their glance. Such events, however, were said to be exceptional. Though Vedic intellectuals had the psychic power to dispatch someone immediately to their next life, rarely would they ever become involved in law enforcement. Managing the order and stability of society was the affair of the martial, administrative sector.

The *Bhagavata Purana*, fourth canto, describes a ferocious king named Vena, installed by the sages in an emergency. The particular society had been rendered leaderless by the former king's sudden retirement to the forest. Immediately, lawless elements— always eager to pounce upon such opportunities—swarmed out of hiding to harass the people. Vena, the only son of the king, was a known problem child who never straightened out. In fact, his violently selfish tendencies were the cause of his father's premature embrace of solitary asceticism in the forest. The sages, however, felt they lacked any other suitable choice. They knew Vena would be no beacon of sanctity and spiritual prowess. They calculated, however, that at least his renowned viciousness would keep the criminals at bay. Moreover, they hoped they could influence Vena to accept their counsel.

Against the objections of the governmental ministers, the sages, as the ultimate brain-trust in society, installed Vena on the throne. The thieves and rogues did flee. But Vena's malignancies did not wait long to surface. He decided to use his royal power to ban Vedic sacrifices.

The saintly intellectuals understood, of course, the disastrous consequences of this official policy. The people would wallow in sinful activities, and nature would withhold its resources. The resulting burden of negative karma would crush the society. Yet the sages, as usual, were reluctant to intervene in political affairs. They had done so before only out of desperation. They considered, however, that unless they tried to dissuade Vena from his hell-bent ways, they would share part of the karmic blame for his ruinous activities.

The sages approached Vena, to lecture him on Vedic sociology and political science. They reminded him that, since everything emanated from the Supreme, society should dedicate itself, through sacrifice, for the pleasure of the Supreme. In this way all the *devas* would automatically be satisfied. The rogue Vena immediately condemned their good advice. Furthermore, he commanded the sages to worship him as the ultimate source of cosmic vitality and sustenance.

Shocked by such brazen, militant atheism, the sages in unison vibrated a special high-frequency sound. This joint exhibition of psychic, sonic power immediately terminated Vena's life.

High-Tech Vedic Culture

Like it or not, the Vedic cosmological treatises are loaded with references to aircraft and devastating weapons. There is no way to ignore the plain fact. Yet, most Indology experts have managed to do just that. How do you overlook or trivialize these innumerable descriptions? It is impossible to escape them unless your mind is already made up to reject them. Discard them you must, because mainstream academia will not consider that humans in remote antiquity could have been advanced—not to mention expert—in a technology far more subtle than the crudities we are proud of today. Remember, even a simple concept like intelligent life on other planets still raises eyebrows at the academy.

Vedic technology does not resemble our world of nuts and bolts, or even microchips. We might label Vedic technology *psychic-based*. Mystic power, especially manifest as sonic vibration, plays a major role. The right sound—vibrated as a mantra—can launch terrible weapons, directly kill, summon beings from other realms, or even create exotic aircraft.

Air *Vimana*

Aircraft in the Vedic literature are generally referred to as *vimanas*. Especially throughout the *Mahabharata, Bhagavata Purana,* and the *Ramayana,* these flying devices appear. Moreover, in the Vedic texts, different races of the universe pilot these crafts. Various beings on various planets have their particular type of airplane. The Vedic perspective is that, on gross planets such as Earth, the airplanes are gross machines; on subtle planets where more refined civilizations prevail, the airplanes are subtly powered by mantras.

Dare we admit that the ancient Vedic people regarded flight as an ordinary part of their life? To an open mind, the many references would seem to justify that conclusion. But even avant-garde thinkers run into turbulence when they realize that the flight patterns of the Vedas, unlike those today, were not just terrestrial. Apparently, in the lost Vedic culture, interplanetary travel was a norm.

Because recent years have seen a boom in books and Internet sites extolling the glories of Vedic *vimanas,* this book will not attempt to cover all the numerous references and accounts. Readers may consult the bibliography for more specialized sources. The *vimanas* described in the Vedas are generally of four types:

- Single or two-passenger aircraft;

- Huge airships for interplanetary pleasure tours;
- Huge military aircraft for warfare;
- Self-sufficient flying cities ("space stations") for indefinite stays in space.

The third canto of the *Bhagavata Purana* presents a lengthy account of the yogi Kardama Muni's aeronautical adventures. With his mystic power, he produced an aerial-mansion type of *vimana* and took his wife Devahuti on a pleasure tour of the universe. His airship was virtually a flying palace, replete with every possible luxury.

> He traveled in that way through the various planets, as the air passes uncontrolled in every direction. Coursing through the air in that great and splendid aerial mansion, which could fly at his will, he surpassed even the demigods. (*Shrimad-Bhagavatam* 3.23.41)

The demigods are considered the standard for luxury and prowess in cosmic flight. Kardama Muni, though an Earthling, had excelled the *devas* at their specialty. Together with his wife, he visited all the *devas'* choicest vacation spots in the universe.

Weddings and Vedic sacrifices were popular destinations for *deva* interplanetary flights. The *Mahabharata*, for example, describes a wedding feast where no less than six species of cosmic entities arrived via celestial vehicles. The fourth canto of the *Bhagavata Purana* describes the marital predicament of the *deva* Sati, the wife of Shiva. The father of Sati was staging a Vedic sacrificial ceremony on Earth. Knowing it would also be a wonderful family get-together, Sati wanted to attend. The problem was that her father had offended her husband, Shiva, who is also known as Mahadeva, "the great *deva*." Therefore Shiva did not share his wife's desire to go.

Lamenting, Sati saw that the sky above her planet was full of *deva* air traffic, coming from all parts of the cosmos. She knew they were all heading to Earth, to attend her father's sacrificial ceremony. As the *deva* couples flew overhead in their *vimanas*, Sati could even hear their enthusiastic chatter about the gala event.[47]

The Vedic epic *Ramayana* provides details of a majestic aerial-mansion *vimana* that a terrorist with cosmic prowess had hijacked from the *devas*. The huge craft flew according to its master's telepathic commands and was staffed with a crew of beings with round and deep eyes. Observed hovering over a capital city, it no longer bore celestial *devas* on their pleasure outings. Now it ferried the troops of a hideous, man-eating race.

> [Hanuman] saw in the middle of that residential quarter the great aerial-mansion vehicle called *Pushpaka-vimana*, decorated with pearls and diamonds, and featured with artistic windows made of refined gold.
>
> None could gauge its power nor effect its destruction. . . . It was poised in the atmosphere without support. It had the capacity to go anywhere. It stood in the sky like a milestone in the path of the sun.
>
> It was the final result of the great prowess gained by austerities. It could fly in any direction that one wanted. It had chambers of remarkable beauty. . . . Knowing the intentions of the master, it could go anywhere at high speed.[48]

In both the *Mahabharata* and the *Bhagavata Purana*, we get an account of a huge military aircraft belonging to a hostile entity named Shalva. The parallels with modern UFO reports are inescapable. Here is a summary of the Vedic version:

> It was a very big machine, almost like a big city, and it could fly so high and at such a great speed that it was almost impossible to

see; so there was no question of attacking it. It appeared to be almost covered with darkness, yet the pilot could fly it anywhere and everywhere. Having acquired such a wonderful airplane, Shalva flew it to the city of Dvaraka, because his main purpose in obtaining the airplane was to attack the city of the Yadus, toward whom he maintained a constant feeling of animosity.

The airplane occupied by Shalva was very mysterious. It was so extraordinary that sometimes many airplanes would appear to be in the sky, and sometimes there were apparently none. Sometimes the plane was visible and sometimes not visible, and the warriors of the Yadu dynasty were puzzled about the whereabouts of the peculiar airplane. Sometimes they would see the airplane on the ground, sometimes flying in the sky, sometimes resting on the peak of a hill, and sometimes floating on the water. The wonderful airplane flew in the sky like a whirling firebrand—it was not steady even for a moment.[49]

Page after page of modern UFO reports put forward the same characteristics: glowing luminescence, logic-defying movements, as well as sudden appearances and disappearances. Also, modern UFOs are often reported to hover over water or land on it, after which they abruptly shoot off into the sky. Dr. Richard Thompson, besides his explorations of Vedic astronomy, has published a thorough study comparing Vedic aeronautics and modern UFO incidents. To illustrate the uncanny parallels with Vedic descriptions of Shalva's craft, he cites a UFO observed by the US Air Force on 17 July 1957:

An Air Force RB-47, equipped with electronic countermeasure (ECM) gear and manned by six officers, was followed by an unidentified object for a distance of well over 700 miles and for a time period of 1.5 hours, as it flew from Mississippi, through Louisiana and Texas, and into Oklahoma. The object was, at various times, seen visually by the cockpit crew as an intensely luminous light, seen visually by the ground-radar and detected on ECM monitoring gear aboard the RB-47. Of special interest in this case are several instances of simultaneous appearances and disappearances on all three of these physically distinct "channels," and rapidity of maneuvers beyond the prior experience of the air crew.[50]

In the fascinating book *Alien Identities*, Thompson paraphrases more details of the Air Force report, so that we can fully grasp the resemblance to the Vedic report:

One of the apparent disappearances of the object occurred as the RB-47 was about to fly over it. The pilot remarked that it seemed to blink out visually and simultaneously disappear from the scope of ECM monitor #2 (an electronic surveillance device). At the same time it disappeared from radarscopes at AFC site Utah. Moments later the object blinked on again visually and simultaneously appeared on the ECM monitor and ground radar. The observers on the RB-47 also noted that the UFO sometimes generated two signals with different bearings on their electronic monitoring equipment. Although we don't really know what the UFO was doing, this is reminiscent of the statement that Shalva's *vimana* sometimes appeared to be in multiple forms.[51]

Thompson, in spite of his Ivy League pedigree, is seen by academia as a nonmainstream scholar. The unconventional projects that he scientifically pursues are not yet what the average university professor would risk a career on. Yet, even the venerated Sanskritist J.A.B. Van Buitenen also saw relevant parallels in the Shalva account. Renowned in academia for his scholarly notated rendition of the *Mahabharata*, Van Buitenen comments on the eventual destruction of Shalva's aircraft and its personnel by Krishna:

Here we have an account of a hero who took these visiting astronauts for what they were: intruders and enemies. The aerial city is nothing but an armed camp . . . no doubt a spaceship. The name of the demons is also revealing: they were Nivatakavacas, "clad in airtight armor," which can hardly be anything but spacesuits.[52]

The *Mahabharata* also challenges us with the exploits of self-sufficient cities stationed in outer space. Depending on no other planet or physical locale for support, these space stations, as we can call them, cruised in space indefinitely. Arjuna, the hero of the *Mahabharata*, attacked a space station named Hiranyapura, peopled by dangerous entities of the malefic Daitya races.

The Daityas easily held their celestial, divinely effulgent, airborne city, which could move about at will. Now it would go underground, then hover high in the sky, go diagonally with speed, or submerge in the ocean. I assaulted the mobile city . . . with many kinds of missiles.[53]

Eluding Arjuna's pursuit, the space city abandoned its position in outer space and took shelter of Earth. Resembling the reported behavior of modern UFOs, the besieged flying city attempted to escape underwater. It also fled underground. More than a few modern witnesses say they have seen UFOs enter or leave water. Some accounts trace the modern craft to terrestrial bases underground or undersea.

Arjuna was able to follow the Daitya space station wherever it tried to escape on Earth. Then, as the city took off for outer space again, he blasted it—breaking it apart. When debris and bodies fell to the Earth, the *Mahabharata* describes that Arjuna landed, to make sure no survivors were hiding amidst the wreckage.

MANTRA WEAPONRY AND WARFARE

The Vedic histories are full of military action in which warriors use bows and arrows. According to the information the texts reveal to us, these bows and arrows wrought a havoc no medieval bowmen could ever dream of. Relying not only on conventional swords, lances, and arrows, the Vedic warriors, when necessary, armed their arrows with mantras—precise sound vibration. The bow was a launching device. The arrows in the warrior's sonic arsenal could inflict troubles such as extreme heat or cold, firestorms, water problems, thunderbolts, hailstones, and severe hurricanes. Besides manipulating the effects of nature, the arrows of Vedic warriors could also affect the mind of opponents. They could produce psychic illusions to terrify their opponents, and the arrows could put their foes into deep sleep. For every one of these offensive weapons, an anti-weapon existed. Therefore in Vedic descriptions of battles, fantastic volleys of arrows and their countermeasures fill the air.

Some armaments were sound-seeking. Some even generated localized nuclearlike blasts that would search out and kill only predesignated persons. A section from the *Mahabharata* vividly chronicles the Vedic capacity for controlled nuclearlike destruction. At the end of the great Kurukshetra War, few warriors survived, on both sides. Seeing no hope for victory, one of the generals on the losing side, in desperation, launched "the last weapon." This terrible armament was almost never activated—no matter how bleak the circumstances. The besieged general touched water for ritualistic sanctification and chanted the appropriate mantras. The sonic procedure allowed him to set off a localizable kind of nuclear blast known as a *brahmastra*. It would hunt and destroy the remaining generals opposing him.

The *Mahabharata* describes that although the *brahmastra* would kill only its preassigned targets, the extreme heat it generated troubled all the planets of the universe and scorched the inhabitants. The most powerful warrior on the winning side was left with no choice. His enemy, though going down in defeat, had recklessly set off this terrible weapon. Therefore the winning general had to counteract the enemy's *brahmastra* with his own. After purifying himself by touching water, he reluctantly chanted the rarely used Vedic hymns for a *brahmastra*. His purpose was to neutralize the blast set off by an unethical opponent, who sought to unleash as much destruction as possible while losing.

Modern humans have discovered the atomic bomb, but they have not discovered a counterweapon that can negate an atomic blast. The Vedic literature describes a subtle science that can not only detonate nuclear-like blasts but also neutralize them. Whereas our nuclear weapons require an elaborate industrial process involving dangerous substances, the Vedic *brahmastras* needed only water and sound—mantras.

The *Mahabharata*, if it is to be believed, firmly establishes that chanting Vedic hymns can produce a weapon far more subtle than our military's gross armaments. Vedic histories say that the right sound activated a bomb made of subtle elements of matter, beyond the gross elements modern scientists explore. Contemporary Vedic teacher A. C. Bhaktivedanta Swami Prabhupada gives this background information to the ancient Vedic accounts:

> The *brahmastra* is similar to the modern nuclear weapon manipulated by atomic energy. The atomic energy works wholly on total combustibility, and so the *brahmastra* also acts. It creates an intolerable heat similar to atomic radiation, but the difference is that the atomic bomb is a gross type of nuclear weapon, whereas the *brahmastra* is a subtle type of weapon produced by chanting hymns. It is a different science, and in the days gone by such science was cultivated in the land of Bharata-varsha [ancient name for India]. The subtle science of chanting hymns is also material,

but it has yet to be known by the modern material scientists. Subtle material science is not spiritual, but it has a direct relationship with the spiritual method, which is still subtler. A chanter of hymns knew how to apply the weapon as well as how to retract it. That was perfect knowledge. But the son of Dronacharya [the losing general], who made use of this subtle science, did not know how to retract. He applied it, being afraid of his imminent death, and thus the practice was not only improper but also irreligious.[54]

As the fireballs of the two "last weapons" merged, thunder resounded, meteors fell, and the Earth trembled. Mutual neutralization was under way. But the *Mahabharata* describes that all is not well when two *brahmastras* cancel each other with their subtle energies. Severe consequences afflict the environment. As a result of the original launch being foiled, total drought afflicts the land for twelve years.

At the last possible minute, as the combined fireballs approached their peak intensity, the paramount sages Narada and Vyasa entered the battlefield. Acting quickly to prevent impending ecological havoc, the sages ordered that the combatants voluntarily retract their ultimate weapons of destruction. Recalling a *brahmastra*, however, requires abnormal purity of consciousness combined with exceptional military expertise.

Upon hearing the sages' command, the winning general immediately retracted his launching. Unlike the loser, his ultimate weapon had been fired just to counteract the danger—not to kill his opponent. Without concern for his own safety, the virtuous general complied, to save the environment. The loser, however, lacked the necessary consciousness for controlling his blast. He shamefully admitted to the sages that once launched, his weapon could not be recalled. In other words, he was incompetent and had acted rashly.

Now unopposed, the villain's weapon was still on the loose.

Locked on its target, it was ready to take out the generals on the magnanimous side. How these virtuous leaders were saved without harming the environment, how the last weapon of the ignoble general was thwarted, and how that villainous warrior was punished, all form an exciting chapter of military history in the *Shauptika-parva* section of the *Mahabharata*.

Mystic illusions were also called upon as weapons of last resort. Their effect, however, was "all in the mind." In this way mass destruction of the people and environment was averted. In the *Bhagavata Purana*, fourth canto, is the lengthy account of the king Dhruva Maharaja. He traveled northward to the Tibetan area to battle a people known as the Yakshas. Though outnumbered, Dhruva crushed them so mightily that even they, his opponents—in true Vedic martial spirit—glorified his prowess. The Yakshas mounted another counterattack, but this time Dhruva thrashed them so soundly that those warriors still alive fled the battlefield—reprehensible according to the Vedic martial code. Thinking to savor his victory, Dhruva desired to see the capital city of his defeated foes. Then he had second thoughts:

21. Dhruva Maharaja, the best of human beings, observed that in that great battlefield not one of the opposing soldiers was left standing with proper weapons. He then desired to see the city of Alakapuri, but he thought to himself, "No one knows the plans of the mystic Yakshas."

22. In the meantime, while Dhruva Maharaja, doubtful of his mystic enemies, was talking with his charioteer, they heard a tremendous sound, as if the whole ocean were there, and they found that from the sky a great dust storm was coming over them from all directions.

23. Within a moment the whole sky was overcast with dense clouds, and severe thundering was heard. There was glittering electric lightning and severe rainfall.

24. In that rainfall there was blood, mucus, pus, stool, urine, and marrow falling heavily before Dhruva Maharaja, and there were trunks of bodies falling from the sky.

25. Next, a great mountain was visible in the sky, and from all directions hailstones fell, along with lances, clubs, swords, iron bludgeons, and great pieces of stone.

26. Dhruva Maharaja also saw many big serpents with angry eyes, vomiting forth fire and coming to devour him, along with groups of mad elephants, lions, and tigers.

27. Then, as if it were the time of the dissolution of the whole world, the fierce sea with foaming waves and great roaring sounds came forward before him.

28. The demon Yakshas are by nature very heinous, and by their demoniac power of illusion they can create many strange phenomena to frighten one who is less intelligent.[55]

The *Bhagavata Purana* goes on to describe that, as the projected illusions filled the land and sky around Dhruva, he began to succumb. Even though he had correctly anticipated a paranormal attack from the almost defeated Yakshas, the colossal display of psychic warfare was so lifelike and terrifying that his mind and fighting resolve weakened. As an exemplary spiritual monarch, however, Dhruva relied upon the counsel and support of great sages—pure transcendentalists. Immediately they gathered to communicate spiritual encouragement and advice to the gallant head of state. The saints urged him to remember transcendental sound vibration. Dhruva should chant mantras with the name of *Bhagavan*, the Supreme, because that sound has all the potency of the Infinite Person it refers to.

His spiritual consciousness replenished, Dhruva reached for a special, transcendental weapon—far superior to the physical and psychic armaments of the Yakshas. Charging the arrow with sound, Dhruva launched it with his bow. The special arrow immediately dissipated the illusory atmosphere projected by the Yakshas. Simultaneously, from this one arrow a torrent of multiple arrows emanated. With a great hissing sound this barrage entered the bodies of the enemy—"just as peacocks enter a forest with tumultuous crowing." At this point the battle was practically over.

MODERN PARANORMAL WARFARE: THE NEW MENTAL BATTLEFIELD

Skeptics may find the Vedic presentations of psychic, sonic warfare farfetched until they hear snatches of what our modern superpowers have been up to. Previously, most reports came from the former Soviet Union, because of its breakup. Recently, however, the Internet abounds with documents revealing that during the Cold War, both the USSR and the USA were racing to develop electromagnetic weapons capable of modifying weather and human behavior.

After the fall of the iron curtain, a former KGB major-general, Oleg Kalugin, in charge of foreign counterintelligence, went on nationwide television in America to expose what he knew. In a 1992 documentary on the ABC network, he revealed that Yuri Andropov—KGB head from 1967 to 1982, and later premier of the USSR—issued personal orders to fast-track all research into psychic and electromagnetic warfare. His directive, Kalugin said, also urged scientists to abandon squeamish sentiments about hurting or killing research subjects—the ends justified the means. The hope was to produce new forms of deadly weapons that would catch the capitalist West, with their supposed scruples, off-guard. These exotic devices of warfare—unrestricted by any arms accords—would tip the balance of power in the Cold War. The Military-Industrial Commission and the KGB awarded funding estimated at 500 million rubles.[56]

The former KGB major-general stated that Soviet scientists

had indeed developed devices that could capture, store, and then release electromagnetic energy. Biologist Edward Naumov, one of the prime movers in Russian paranormal research, explained, "A psychic generator can influence an individual or a whole crowd of people. It can affect a person's psyche mentally and emotionally. It can affect memory and attention span. A psychotronic device can cause physical fatigue, disorientation, and alter a person's behavior."[57] Paranoia, depression, insomnia, and suicidal thoughts were other mental productions projected by these contraptions. Naumov, a critic of Soviet mind-control research, served one year at a labor camp, and then upon the end of the communist regime toured the USA and Canada, warning of what he knew.

Back in 1976, a defected KGB agent, Dr. Nikolai Khokhov, entered the employ of the CIA, with the specific portfolio of investigating Soviet psychic research. He documented twenty top-secret labs, run by hundreds of the best scientists. They would experiment with stopping the hearts of animals telepathically. Putting death-row prisoners to good use, they would use PK to paralyze sections of their spinal cords. Newborn rabbits were separated from their mothers, electrocuted, and then the mothers' subtle "brain waves" were charted. All this brought the Soviets to the conclusion that human brains are devices for receiving and transmitting.[58] The next phase of research would be how to program these human devices with desired behavior.

A particularly unsettling psychic breakthrough was the subtle transmission of disease: "sick waves." In 1974 a Soviet scientist, A. P. Dubrov, discovered that special radiation from living cells broadcast information from one group of cells to another—even over a distance. Diseased tissue transmits diseased messages, which healthy cells can pick up, though separated by distance. In the late 1970s, defecting scientists revealed that the Soviets had succeeded in transmitting disease at a distance to creatures such as flies and frogs. The US Army took note. Lt. Colonel

John Alexander, in the US Army's *Military Review* of December 1980, revealed how Russian researcher V. P. Kaznachayev infected chick embryos with toxic viruses broadcast as special radiations from diseased tissue. What next? "Virus waves" from afar, transmitted to humans?

Alexander's article, appropriately titled, "The New Mental Battlefield," elaborated upon weapons in the works for controlling enemy soldiers and unruly civilian populations: "Psychotronics may be described as the interaction of mind and matter. . . . The possibility for employment as weaponry has been explored. To be more specific, there are weapons systems that operate on the power of the mind and whose lethal capacity has already been demonstrated."[59] Certainly the American military, in spite of its humane self-image, was not exempt from nefarious research. Keeping pace with their Soviet foes, some clandestine agencies pursued the same agendas. In the book *The CIA and the Cult of Intelligence*, coauthor and former CIA agent John Marks revealed that mind control and amnesia were major secret aims. In a program known as MK-Ultra, the CIA bankrolled or directly conducted mind-control experiments at 180 prisons and mental hospitals. The unsuspecting human specimens received doses of LSD and other drugs, and underwent brainwashing, depatterning of the thinking process, sensory deprivation, radiation, and other bizarre laboratory analyses. The CIA scientists succeeded in what their official jargon called "Radio-Hypnotic Intra-Cerebral Control," and "Electronic Dissolution of Memory." That is to say, they are accused of discovering how to erase human hard drives and then install new software. Upon blanking someone's memory, they would then insert a multiple personality and control the person's actions by specific sounds. The US Senate conducted an investigation into the controversy. Regardless of how much the Senate was actually allowed to see, in 1976 it did order a halt to some of this research.[60]

Skeptics are now free to examine documents such as the recently declassified CIA memo "MKULTRA Subproject No. 83." Written on 18 April 1958 by Dr. Sidney Gottlieb, chief of the Chemical Division of the CIA's Technical Services Staff, the official directive reviewed CIA support for research studies of "controversial and misunderstood" areas of psychology such as psychic powers, subliminal perception, hypnosis, truth drugs, and subliminal persuasion. By the end of the twentieth century, the mind had fully emerged on the battlefield. References to the technology of mental combat were no longer rare. For example, in 1994 the US Army War College released a study "The Revolution in Military Affairs and Conflict Short of War." The authors declare: "Behavior modification is a key component of peace enforcement." Explaining that "the advantage of [using] directed energy systems is deniability," the authors ask, "Against whom is such deniability aimed?" They answer their own question: "the American people." The nature of mental warfare allows the military to easily hide its use from the citizens.

Tactfully presented as a projection for the year 2010, the study speaks of "perception molding" and "advanced psychotechnologies" to eradicate public protest. In typical military fashion, the authors identified the main obstacle to their tactics: "traditional American ethics [are] a major hindrance," and thus, "old-fashioned notions of personal privacy and national sovereignty [are to be] changed."

In the new world of mental control, troublemakers would have nowhere to run. The Army study calls for them to be "identified using comprehensive interagency integrated databases." Next, they would be "categorized" and then "sophisticated computerized personality simulations" would be employed "to develop, tailor and focus psychological campaigns for each."[61]

Remember that, in Vedic accounts of warfare, localized weather modification played a prominent role. While we may choose to brand Vedic weather weapons as pure myth, both the US and Russia are known to have developed weaponry for electromagnetically altering the environment. But as with nuclear armaments, the deadly secrets now seem to have drifted into the hands of "rogue regimes." US Defence Secretary Cohen was moved to publicly expresses government fears about eco-terrorists wielding scalar electromagnetic weapons: "Others [terrorists] are engaging even in an ecotype of terrorism whereby they can alter the climate, set off earthquakes, volcanoes remotely through the use of electromagnetic waves. . . . So there are plenty of ingenious minds out there that are at work finding ways in which they can wreak terror upon other nations. . . . It's real, and that's the reason why we have to intensify our [counterterrorism] efforts."[62] We have seen that the Vedic texts clearly describe civilizations conversant with warfare in space. Today the wealthier nations are also sizing up the advantages of space armaments. A US Air Force has released a study, "Air Force 2025," put out by its Air University. The report extends current military objectives and anxieties off the Earth, into the orbital space around our planet:

> Space superiority, like air superiority today, will be a vital core competency in the year 2025. US national security is already heavily leveraged in space—a trend which will increase in the future. Likewise, other countries and commercial interests will continue to seek the valuable "high ground" of space. Where space interests conflict, hostilities may soon follow. Protecting the use of space and controlling, when required, its advantage is the essence of counterspace.[63]

Just as the technology for nuclear weapons and electromagnetic warfare is no longer the exclusive property of the most powerful nations, similarly, the report forecasts, at least by 2025 the few wealthy nations and transnational corporations now exploiting space will lose their monopoly. Therefore the Air Force study calls for the development of manned and unmanned combat spacecraft—to safeguard friendly satellites, space stations, and shuttle-craft from attacks by hostile nations and high-tech terrorists.

Whether citizens of democracies or totalitarian regimes, people have long grown accustomed to receiving scant idea what military research their governments are actually pursuing. Anxious whistleblowers are particularly concerned with electromagnetic mind-altering on a mass scale. How far has paranormal warfare actually progressed? How much of the disclosure is inaccurate and how much turns out to be understatement? We'll have to wait for the next major conflict, to experience whatever advanced weaponry the biggest powers now keep under wraps. In the meantime we can study the Vedic literature to learn how Vedic sages curbed the extraordinary paranormal prowess of their culture.

Notes

1   Jan Gonda, *A History of Indian Literature 1.1—Vedic Literature* (Wiesbaden: O. Harrassowitz, 1975), pp. 1, 3.

2   Sheila Ostrander and Lynn Schroeder, *Psychic Discoveries* (New York: Marlowe and Company, 1970, 1997), p. 345.

3   As a result of Executive Order No. 1995–4–17, issued by President Clinton, entitled "Classified National Security Information." From opening paragraph: "In recent years, however, dramatic changes have altered, although not eliminated, the national security threats that we confront. These changes provide a greater opportunity to emphasize our commitment to open Government."

4   Associated Press release, 28 November 1995.

5   Jim Schnabel, *Remote Viewers: The Secret History of America's Psychic Spies* (New York: Dell Books, 1997), p. 215.

6   Russell Targ and Jane Katra, *Miracles of the Mind* (New World Library, 1998).

7   E. C. May, "AC Technical Trials: Inspiration for the Target Entropy Concept," in *Proceedings of Presented Papers,* 38th Annual Parapsychological Association Convention, ed. by N. L. Zingrone (Massachusetts: The Parapsychological Assoc., 1995), p. 204.

8   Ostrander and Schroeder, *Psychic Discoveries*, p. 352.

9   Michael Cremo, *Hidden History of the Human Race* (California: Govardhana Hill Publishing, 1994), p. 121.

10 I.E.S. Edwards, *The Pyramids of Egypt* (London: Penguin, 1949), p. 220.

11 John Baines and Jaromir Malek, *Atlas of Ancient Egypt* (Virginia: Time-Life Books, 1990), p. 139.

12 Crane information supplied by Liebherr of Welham Green, Hertfordshire; as quoted in Andrew Collins, *Gods of Eden*, (London: Headline Book Publishing, 1998), p. 25.

13 Peter Tompkins, *Secrets of the Great Pyramid* (New York: Harper and Row, 1978), pp. 17, 232, 244.

14 W. M. Flinders Petrie, *The Pyramids and Temples of Gizeh* (1893; reissued, London: Histories and Mysteries of Man, 1990), p. 13.

15 Michael Rice, *Egypt's Making* (London: Routledge, 1990), p. 41.

16 A. Lucas, *Ancient Egyptian Materials and Industries,* 4th ed. (Edward Arnold, 1962).

17 Sir A. Gardiner, *Egypt of the Pharaohs* (Oxford: 1961), p. 41.

18 Walter Emery, *Archaic Egypt* (Penguin Books, 1991), pp. 214–15.

19 Z. Hawass, in W. M. Flinders Petrie, *The Pyramids and Temples of Gizeh*, 1993 ed., p. 98.

20 As informed by Donald Rahn of the Rahn Granite Surface Plate Company, Dayton, Ohio; as stated in Christopher Dunn, "High-Tech Pharaohs?", in *Amateur Astronomy and Earth Sciences*, December 1995, pp. 38–42; January 1996, pp. 38–40.

21 al-Mas'udi, quoted as an appendix in Colonel R. W. Howard, *Operations Carried on at the Pyramids of Gizeh in 1837*, vol. 2 (London: James Fraser, 1840), p. 325.

22 For an amplified description, see Collins, *Gods of Eden*, pp. 35–37.

23 al-Mas'udi, no fool, is known by later historians as "the Herodotus of the Arabs"—a title considered "not unjust" by Arab scholar Reynold A. Nicholson, *A Literary History of the Arabs* (Cambridge: Cambridge University Press, 1956), p. 353.

24 John Bierhorst, *The Mythology of Mexico and Central America* (New York: William Morrow & Co., 1990), p. 8.

25 J. Eric Thompson, *Maya History and Religion* (Norman, Okla.: University of Oklahoma, 1970), pp. 340–41.

26 Harold Osborne, *Indians of the Andes: Aymaras and Quechuas* (London: Routledge and Keegan Paul, 1952), p. 64.

27 Francisco de Avila, "A Narrative of the Errors, False Gods, and Other Superstitions and Diabolical Rites in Which the Indians of the Province of Huarochiri Lived in Ancient Times," in *Narratives of the Rites and Laws of the Yucas*, vol. 48, trans. and ed. Clemens R. Markhem (London: Hakluyt Society, 1873), p. 124.

28 Harold Osborne, *South American Mythology* (London: Paul Hamlyn, 1968), p. 76.

29 Horace, *Odes and Epodes*, trans. C. E. Bennett, (London: William Heinemann, 1914), 3. ode 11. 2. 1–4; *Ars Poetica*, ed. Augustus S. Wilkins (London: Macmillan, 1971), 2: 394–96.

30 "Pausanias," *Encyclopaedia Britannica*, CD-ROM, 1998.

31 Pausanias, *Description of Greece: Boeotia*, trans. W.H.S. Jones, 5 vols. (London: William Heinemann, 1935), vols. 7–8.

32 Apollonius Rhodius, *The Argonautica*, trans. R. C. Seaton (London: William Heinemann, 1919), 1: 735–41.

33 Kjellson's book *Forsvunnen teknik* (1961) has not been translated from Swedish to English. The information presented derives from a Danish translation, published in 1974 by Nihil, Copenhagen. The Danish title is *Forsvunden Teknik*. For the Tibetan information in that edition, see pp.

49–56. For an English presentation of the relevant passages in the Danish edition, see Collins, *Gods of Eden*, pp. 66–72.

34 See Gavin Flood, *An Introduction to Hinduism* (Cambridge: Cambridge University Press, 1996), p. 43.

35 Press release from Society for Scientific Exploration (SSE), 15 December 1992. For full information see *Journal of Scientific Exploration* 6, no. 4.

36 Ibid.

37 Ibid.

38 Based on a list compiled by Willis Harmon, late president of the Institute for Noetic Studies, in *Global Mind Change*, 2nd edition (California: Institute of Noetic Sciences, 1998), pp. 50–51.

39 Sheila Ostrander and Lynn Schroeder, *Psychic Discoveries* (New York: Marlowe and Co., 1997), p. 347.

40 Ibid., p. 41.

41 Information about Messing can be found in Ostrander and Schroeder, *Psychic Discoveries*, chap. 4. Messing wrote an autobiography, *About Myself*. Sections of it were published by the Soviet government in their journal *Science and Religion* (Russian), nos. 7 and 8, 1965. To be published in such an influential journal, the sections had to pass through leading scientists as well as official censors of the regime—both with an overtly anti-metaphysical mandate. Thus the credibility of Messing's accounts is hard to deny.

42 Ostrander and Schroeder, *Psychic Discoveries*, pp. 89–91.

43 Leonid Vasiliev, *Experimental Research in Mental Suggestion* (Leningrad: Leningrad University Press, 1962); English edition, *Experiments in Distant Influence* (London: Wildwood House, 1963), p. 144.

44 Ibid., p. 333.

45 A. C. Bhaktivedanta Swami Prabhupada, *The Nectar of Devotion* (Los Angeles: The Bhaktivedanta Book Trust, 1982), p. 12.

46 A. C. Bhaktivedanta Swami Prabhupada, *Krishna, The Supreme Personality of Godhead*, vol. 2 (Los Angeles: The Bhaktivedanta Book Trust, 1996), p. 75. This work is a special summary of the tenth canto of the *Bhagavata Purana*.

47 *Shrimad-Bhagavatam*, fourth canto, Chap. 3.

48 Tapasyananda Swami, *Sundarakandam of Srimad Valmiki Ramayana* (Madras: Sree Ramakrishna Math), pp. 46–48.

49 A. C. Bhaktivedanta Swami Prabhupada, *Krishna*, p. 210.

50 James E. McDonald, "Air Force Observations of an Unidentified Object

in the South-Central U.S., July 17, 1957," in *Astronautics and Aeronautics*, July 1971, p. 66.

51 Richard Thompson, *Alien Identities* (San Diego: Govardhana Hill Publishing, 1993), pp. 225–26.

52 J.A.B. Van Buitenen, trans. 1975, *The Mahabharata*, Books 2 and 3 (Chicago: the University of Chicago Press), p. 202.

53 Ibid., p. 550.

54 A. C. Bhaktivedanta Swami Prabhupada, *Shrimad-Bhagavatam* (Los Angeles: The Bhaktivedanta Book Trust, 1972), first canto, commentary to Chap. 7, Text 28.

55 *Bhagavata Purana* (*Shrimad-Bhagavatam*), fourth canto, Chap. 10.

56 Ostrander and Schroeder, *Psychic Discoveries*, pp. 329–30.

57 Ibid., p. 330.

58 Ibid., pp. 330–31.

59 *Military Review*, December 1980.

60 For more (of varied quality) on CIA clandestine mind-control research, see Victor Marchetti and John D. Marks, *The CIA and the Cult of Intelligence*; Jim Keith, *Mind Control, World Control* ; and Alex Constantine, *Virtual Government: CIA Mind Control Operations in America*.

61 Steven Metz and James Kievit, *The Revolution in Military Affairs and Conflict Short of War* (US Army War College, 1994).
The US Air Force also has seen that the future belongs to mind control weapons. In 1996 the US Air Force Scientific Advisory Board published a massive fourteen-volume study of future developments in weapons, entitled "New World Vistas." Page 89 of a supplementary fifteenth volume provides more chilling insights into the future "coupling" of man and subtle mind weapons. Within a section dealing with "Biological Process Control," the study refers to an "explosion" of knowledge in the field of neuroscience. The ominous new vistas: "One can envision the development of electromagnetic energy sources, the output of which can be pulsed, shaped, and focused, that can couple with the human body in a fashion that will allow one to prevent voluntary muscular movements, control emotions (and thus actions), produce sleep, transmit suggestions, interfere with both short-term and long-term memory, produce an experience set, and delete an experience set."
(In everyday, nonmilitary English, to produce or delete an "experience set" means to erase your memory banks and substitute new, fictitious life-memories.)

62 Secretary of Defense William Cohen at the "Conference on Terrorism, Weapons of Mass Destruction, and U.S. Strategy," University of Georgia, Athens, 28 April 1997.

63 *Air Force 2025* full study available at http://www.au.af.mil/au/2025/. The report on CD-ROM can be ordered at this site.

CHAPTER 14

THE PURANAS: DOWN TO EARTH?

~

Throughout the world are signposts that point to monumental achievements buried deep in the sands of the remote past. Bold researchers yearn to see these puzzling clues fall into a striking pattern that will herald a new vision of antiquity. The Vedic accounts of lost millennia, when advanced human civilizations thrived, can set this agenda for completely rewriting human history. The Vedic reservoir of ancient wisdom, as we have seen in previous chapters, especially deserves our attention because it extends to knowledge of the extraterrestrial dimension. Consequently, when adventurous brains choose to reassess the Vedic accounts of history on Earth, their intellectual pleasure only begins.

The Vedic texts do reveal a people with extensive knowledge of oceans, forests, deserts, and mountains. The Vedic scope, however, does not end on the planet Earth. In no way does the literature see Earth in isolation from the rest of the cosmos. The Vedas consider Earth as just one station for the train of life—one stop in a universe teeming with life forms and intelligent species. We gain knowledge of material realms far more subtle and refined than earthly existence. Ours for the taking is a fascinating tour of a universe that offers planets of dense physical matter as well as realms of subtle celestial matter. Ultimately our journey of Vedic discovery leaves the material cosmos completely. The final destination is a nonmaterial realm of pure spiritual consciousness, beyond matter, time, and space.

The Vedic literature known as the Puranas particularly intrigues forward-thinking readers. The Puranic challenge leads straight to the heart of the cosmic mystery. Besides realizing that we are not alone in the universe, we also become acquainted with our duties and responsibilities as citizens of a universe packed with diversity. Earthly problems of gender and enthnicity seem quite infantile when compared to Puranic concerns of interplanetary and interspecies relationships.

Sadly, for so long, Western small-mindedness has banished the Puranas to the Siberia of preposterous myth. Typical academic appraisals of Puranic mysteries go something like this: "These texts of India are wishful descriptions of imaginary divine power. The people who generated them sincerely felt the need to endow their leaders and kings with a mystical, unearthly aura. Latter-day Indians certainly invented the incredible and invulnerable attributes of personalities mentioned in the Puranas, and then they projected them back into the remote, prehistoric past. The fanciful excesses of legend multiplied with each successive generation."

Life on other planets does have some precedence in the philosophical tradition of Western, Mediterranean-derived culture. Over two thousand years ago, the Greek philosophers known as atomists concluded that human beings cannot be unique in the cosmos. Based on their speculation that the universe is a void filled with indestructible particles, they reasoned that if atoms can combine to form life on Earth, the atoms might do so elsewhere too.

Until recent years, the prevailing minds of modernity assumed they were firmly on track in their endeavors to fathom the universe. They were proud of their progress from an Earth-centered universe to a planetary system revolving around the sun. In either case, though, whether living in a geocentric or heliocentric cosmos, they were alone. As the zenith of either God's creation in six days or Darwinian evolution over millions of years, humans on Earth were the sole recipients of intelligence in the universe. Therefore, with an erudite knee-jerk reaction, most scholars politely overlooked or vehemently rejected any references by the ancients that might indicate nonhuman intelligence on other planets.

Upon the dawn of the twenty-first century, a new intellectual pursuit has arisen. Outside of the academic establishment, non-mainstream thinkers and researchers ache to know: who are the extraterrestrials? Since nothing in a Western university education or religious upbringing prepares people for non-earthly life forms, naturally an entirely new sector of Western intelligentsia had to spring up, to cope with the steady flow of inexplicable clues and evidence.

Without a doubt, the failure of mainstream Western culture to handle extraterrestrial phenomena, combined with its basic inability to understand consciousness, will prove to be its Achilles heel. Said another way, the real Renaissance has been long overdue. And the Vedas are waiting for a serious call. Here, once again, is a summary of Vedic extraterrestrial themes, especially as presented in the Puranas:

- Intelligent life abounds on other planets, many of which have civilizations far more advanced than anything Earth ever had.
- The sun is indeed the center of the universe—amid many planets that cannot be detected by human eyes or instruments.
- Interplanetary communication and traveling is as routine as calling from a street payphone or cycling to a neighborhood shop. Previous civilizations on Earth were in constant contact with other planets.

- Not all extraterrestrials are benign. Some regions or dimensions of the universe are the domain of negative entities—dedicated enemies of spiritual truth.
- The first living entities in the universe are the most intelligent, and their life spans and habitats far exceed our paltry understanding. These superior entities have the immediate responsibility for arranging and maintaining life throughout the universe. They do not, however, bear the ultimate responsibility. They are only agents of an ultimate conscious source. Life comes from life.
- Countless universes exist, like bubbles in sea foam. They vary in size, and are walled off from one another by immense layers of gross and subtle matter.

ALONE IN THE UNIVERSE?

A Polish merchant's son named Nicolaus Copernicus incited a revolution in the sixteenth century that transformed the Western world. Fascinated by astronomy but dissatisfied with Ptolemy's accepted geocentric interpretation of the cosmos, Copernicus began to search for an alternative. An adequate scholar in Greek, he poured over ancient Greek texts and discovered that some of them advocated a heliocentric model of the planetary system. At first the concept that the Earth moved around the sun seemed absurd—the notion violated the ironclad doctrine of the day. But when Copernicus applied his data to the model, it worked more elegantly than Ptolemy's construct.

The Copernican revolution toppled the entire scientific, philosophical, and religious framework of the era. Now the Earth had to be seen as just one among other planets—no longer was it the crown of creation. The outmoded idea that the other planets revolved around the Earth had magnified the Earth's pride of place as the unique staging ground for Christian redemption. Therefore, upon the Earth's removal from the center of the universe, Western culture shook to its core. Whether scholar, priest, or layperson, everyone became by transformed by the new vision of the cosmos.

Today we stand on the brink of another revolution provoked by the cosmos. Even the everyday man and woman want to know more about the universe. For example, when in 1996 the American Astronomical Society announced the discovery of two new planets orbiting the stars 70 Virginis and 47 Ursae Majoris, the news made the front pages of daily newspapers. Topmost in the public's mind, though, is whether other planets can support life.

The flood of unofficial UFO and alien-abduction information has pushed many ordinary citizens to question both the abilities of their scientists and the honesty of their governments. Amid the deluge of strange sightings and contacts, the everyday man or woman gets no explanation from any of the traditional citadels protecting the status quo. Governmental, educational, and religious institutions offer no explanations or understanding. This unique predicament will certainly produce monumental social consequences.

A poll conducted in America by the Scripps Howard News Service and the University of Ohio exposed the coming crisis. Taken in 1997, the poll points to a dangerous future for the USA in the new millennium:

- Fifty-one percent of Americans believe either it is very likely or somewhat likely that their own government killed President John F. Kennedy.
- More than a third harbor degrees of suspicion that TWA Flight 800, bound from New York to Paris, was shot down accidentally or purposely by the US Navy.
- A majority believes, to varying degrees, that the CIA may have aided Central American drug kings to flood black ghettos with cocaine.

- Sixty percent believe the US government is withholding information about the chemical "Agent Orange" used in the war in Vietnam War. Forty-eight percent believe the government is concealing Iraqi use of nerve gas and germ warfare in the Persian Gulf wars.[1]

"This is not good," lamented Governor Frank Keating of Oklahoma. "When we believe that our free institutions can commonly be corrupted to dark and evil purposes, it is a statement of a feeling of helplessness. We are in for some turbulent years ahead as a nation."[2] A Gallup poll conducted in conjunction with the University of Virginia in 1996 underscores the point. It found that more than half of all Americans—61 percent—have either little or absolutely no confidence that their government tells them the truth.[3]

Roswell, New Mexico, in 1947, is a festering sore of government mistrust. It also currently reigns as the world's most famous UFO event. The fiftieth anniversary of the mystery made the front cover of the international newsweekly *Time*. The public has to cope with the alleged crash of a flying saucer, with dead aliens strewn around it. The military is accused of recovering the wreckage and having it secretly delivered to labs for "reverse engineering." Research "beyond top-secret" is suspected to have exploited the remains of the spacecraft, to accelerate development of advanced technology on Earth.

Despite countless personal testimonies, the alien abduction phenomenon is easily the most incredulous aspect of UFOism. But when a skeptical professor of psychiatry at Harvard University entered the controversy, the tide of belief dramatically changed. John Mack, in addition to his stellar academic profile, is also the winner of a Pulitzer Prize—America's top literary award. Initially he thought alien abductions were delusions born of mad minds. Then a nonmainstream expert in these strange encounters introduced him to hundreds of people who, though claiming abduction, all struck Mack as completely sane and reliable. The professor decided to conduct a thorough mainstream study of the eerie accounts—a rare move for such a distinguished academic.

After clinically interviewing and analyzing seventy-eight supposed abductees, the scholar of psychiatry emerged a changed man. Extraterrestrials are for real, he concluded. The abductees and their chilling testimonies of embryo extractions, sperm sampling, artificial insemination, and mysterious implants are factual events, he affirmed. He denied that the accounts were the stuff of psychological delusions or hallucinations.

Like most Westerners, Mack can offer no understanding of "the bigger picture." That is, he cannot clarify his alien findings within a full cosmological context. He did conclude, however, that humans are clearly "participants in a universe that is swarming with intelligent life forms, from whom we have cut ourselves off."[4]

Such a bold pronouncement would probably win Dr. Mack an audience with the ancient Vedic seers. The Vedic text *Brahma-samhita*, for example, describes our universe as comprising planetary systems with different environments, all inhabited by living beings that possess bodies suitable for their particular circumstances.[5] As discussed in Chapter 7, the Vedas advocate that a real Aryan knows how to relate to all living entities, irrespective of their body and their cosmic locale.

The sixth American astronaut of moon-walk fame, Edgar Mitchell, publicly declares his acceptance of UFOs. Mainly it is the press outside of America and the Internet that has let the world know. For example, headlines in the *Sunday Times* of London proclaimed "Edward Mitchell: US Covers Up Aliens for 50 Years."[6] "For me, with all the evidence, it's not a matter of believing," the astronaut and scientist said. "It's a matter of the preponderance of evidence, and the evidence keeps building."[7] Besides his heroic stature as an *Apollo 14* moon-trekker, Mitchell is loaded with the most cherished academic and governmental endorsements: Doctor of Science in Aeronautics and Astronautics from Massachusetts Institute of Technology; honorary doctorates from three other universities; the Presidential Medal of Freedom; the US Navy Distinguished Service Medal; and the NASA Distinguished Service Medal.

Dr. Mitchell goes on record to raise the issue of government secrecy and appropriated alien technology in the hands of a sinister cartel:

> In our briefing of the Joint Chiefs of Staff Intelligence Group, it became very clear to us that they were naive. They did not really know any more about this effort than we do, if as much. That is because . . . most of the people in government were not in government when I retired twenty-five years ago, they are younger people. The files going back fifty years just no longer exist. They've either been purged, compromised or whatever. They don't exist. So when we blame government for not being forthright, they really don't have anything to be forthright about, at least at that level.
>
> Now, somewhere there's knowledgeable people. . . . And in my own efforts in talking with these folks [those who know] and talking with government, the question often comes up as to how they could have kept this a secret for so long. And friends they haven't. It's been around us all the time, but it has been denied, and obscured.
>
> We are looking at likely reverse engineered technology in the hands of humans that are not under governmental control. I find that quite alarming. . . . I work with folks who do know what is in our technological database and what is available to modern armies. The so-called ET technology, the ability to have silent engines and flying machines that make no sound, flying machines

that have the characteristics that are consistent with reproduction of UFO sightings, are not in any nations arsenal, but they do exist. So if there are back engineered technologies existing, they are probably in the hands of this group of individuals, formerly government, formerly perhaps intelligence, formerly under private sector control with some sort of oversight by military or by government. But this [supervision] is likely no longer the case as a result of this access-denied category that is now operating.

I call it a clandestine group. The technology is not in our military arsenals anywhere in the world, but it does exist, and to me that's quite disconcerting.[8]

The former astronaut minces no words about the Roswell controversy: "Make no mistake, Roswell happened. I've seen secret government files which show the government knew about it—but decided not to tell the public."[9] Dr. Mitchell explains that his privileged status as an astronaut and NASA scientist granted him special access to persons in the military and intelligence. Their testimonies convinced him that the American government has hidden the truth about UFOs and aliens for fifty years.[10]

The military people I spoke to are tired of the secrecy surrounding Roswell and similar cases, particularly as the information is being leaked. I firmly believe that this documentation will have to be made public within the next three or four years. . . . Not all governments are anxious to keep their findings quiet. The Belgians have admitted that aliens may be out there. . . . There is a very simple reason why governments have been so secretive: fear. . . . The world would have panicked if we'd known aliens were visiting us.[11]

When a South American country like Chile chooses to officially acknowledge the UFO mystery, much of the world can easily opt to look the other way. The head of the Chilean Air Force, now retired, joined with civilian aviation specialists to investigate near-collisions of UFOs and commercial aircraft. Chile, of course, has little global influence. But what about France?

High-ranking French officials have begun the new century by breaking ranks with the unstated policy of UFO denial. A group including retired generals from the French Institute of Higher Studies for National Defense—a government-financed military think tank—undertook a three-year study into aeronautical sightings, radar contacts, and pilot reports from around the world. Their conclusion: "Numerous manifestations observed by reliable witnesses could be the work of craft of extraterrestrial origin," and that the most likely explanation is indeed "the extraterrestrial hypothesis," though it is not proven.

In the face of skeptics, the French committee presents impressive credentials. The originators of the study include four-star General Bernard Norlain—former commander of the French Tactical Air Force as well as military advisor to the prime minister; and André Lebeau— former head of the National Center for Space Studies, France's equivalent of NASA. In addition to four generals, also the national head of French police, a three-star admiral, and many scientists and engineers collaborated.

The French report dares to chastise the USA for an "impressive repressive arsenal" on the UFO issue, and it acknowledges the successful American policy of disinformation.[12]

Across the channel in England, the former head of the British Ministry of Defense, Admiral Lord Hill-Norton, has come to the same conclusion and is calling for the USA to sponsor open governmental hearings. The Admiral has combined with Edgar Mitchell to request the European Union to apply diplomatic pressure on the USA, "exerting useful pressure to clarify this crucial issue, which must fall within the scope of political and strategic alliances."[13]

Extraterrestrialism does more than break the last traces of faith in our governments; it does more than humiliate our scientists. Acknowledgment of intelligent life on other planets devastates the fundamentalism of our Semitic religions. Will the bulwarks of Christianity, Judaism, and Islam survive such an assault?

Premier science writer Paul Davies, a theoretical physicist, predicts, "Almost certainly, Christianity would not survive the discovery of advanced alien beings."[14] Often traditional Christians have recoiled at the possibility of non-earthly civilizations. Perhaps more than other religions, Christianity, as conventionally known, runs smack into severe doctrinal difficulties. Jesus Christ is accepted as the exclusive Redeemer of only Earth-domiciled humans. If life equally as intelligent or more exists elsewhere, how does it fit into the New Testament plan for salvation? A special new millennium edition of the *Wall Street Journal* neatly summarized the problem:

> The Christian creed that God so loved the world he gave it his only son simply assumes that this world alone received God's main attention. But what if a culture on a different planet harbors a similar belief—or doesn't? In a planet of little green men, would God have asked his Son to become one? How would it affect the Jewish faith to learn that a culture on a different planet believed itself to be God's chosen? How do we know God doesn't love these other creatures better than us?[15]

Times are swiftly changing. Some religious leaders indicate they are ready to walk onto the uncharted waters. Others hold their ground. In 1998 the London newspaper *Sunday Times* surveyed forty-two Anglican (Church of England) bishops and found that forty of them, or 95 percent, accept that alien life forms are possible. Thirty-one, or 74 percent, believe that some aliens may be intelligent. Since traditional church dogma says that man, created in the image of God, is unique in the cosmos, most of the bishops polled agreed that any solid evidence of alien life forms would necessitate an overhaul of Church doctrine.[16]

A Vatican insider, Monsignor Corrado Balducci, has proclaimed on Italian television that extraterrestrial contacts are real. Balducci, a member of the Vatican department, Congregation of the Evangelization of the Peoples, says that he also belongs to a Vatican commission researching alien encounters. He has shouldered the task of assuring the faithful that Catholicism does not conflict with belief in aliens. His first question to an alien? He would inquire about their concept of God.

Prodded to comment on Balducci's series of television interviews, a spokesperson for the Catholic Media Office in London ventured a theological judgment: "The fundamental creation message relates to humans here on Earth. If aliens were shown to exist, this would not cast doubt on the veracity of the Gospels. But we would have to ask whether the Christian atonement was applicable to them."[17]

One of the most powerful leaders of America's fundamentalist Protestants sounded a more ominous note. On a national broadcast, Pat Robertson advocated that, according to God's instructions in the Old Testament, UFO enthusiasts should be stoned. Denouncing extraterrestrialism, the televangelist charged, "It's a clear violation of God's word."[18]

At the turn of the millennium, the mountain of evidence for UFOs, abductions, and other kinds of alien contact towers high. Furthermore, some sources are so reputable that for us to unilaterally dismiss their reports would necessitate our blanket rejection of all knowledge and evidence based on human testimony. As the American comedian Jimmy Durante used to say, "My head's made up—don't try to confuse me with the facts." It is quite intimidating to contemplate that out of all the countless

UFO reports—many of which certainly are hoax or disinformation—all we require is just one true incident, and the predominant Western mindset lowers into the grave.

Certainly the prospect of alien intelligence thrusts at us a ponderous agenda for spirited discussion and research—enough to overwhelm a modern brain. When there is virtually nothing in Western religion, philosophy, and science to accommodate extra-terrestrialism, why reject a comprehensive, profound explanation ready at our fingertips—albeit from a vastly different culture and era?

THE PURANA PROBLEM

Though the Purana problem may not end on Earth, for us it begins there. Our first hurdle is the sheer size of the literature in the Purana category. To be sure, the Vaishnavas (devotees of Vishnu), who form the largest Vedic school, accept the *Bhagavata Purana* as the preeminent Puranic text—in a class by itself. Still, it must be said that the volume of literature going by the name Purana is overwhelming. Vedic practitioners generally accept eighteen Puranas as main. Yet there are scores of Puranas deemed either minor or less authoritative.

Bafflement at the sheer quantity of Puranic material goes back a long time. "To speak of this enormous literature with any authority requires a life's study; but nobody [no scholar] has as yet given his life to it," said the scholar Haraprasad Shastri in 1928.[19] Later, in 1953, V. Raghavan said, "The Puranas form the largest part of the writings in Sanskrit, a most voluminous and bewildering mass."[20] In surveying the huge expanse of major and minor texts, Raghavan concluded, "To take stock of them is an impossible task."[21]

Let us travel back farther, to the beginning of the nineteenth century, when Indian antiquity excited European scholars. At that time the Puranas basked in attention. The scholars Vans Kennedy and H. H. Wilson led the way. After mid-century, however, the Puranas faded from the academic limelight. One strong reason may be that Wilson, the Indologist who had done the most work on Puranic literature, ended his labors by judging Puranic research as not worth the effort. "It is not very probable that many of them will be published or translated," he announced, his negative verdict dictating the future.[22]

Wilson's ardor for Puranic research had waned, owing to his conjecture that the Puranas are latecomers to the Vedic scene. His contemporary, Vans Kennedy, holding to a Puranic origin in unknown antiquity, hotly disagreed:

> I am . . . well aware that the recent composition of Sanskrit works, and particularly of the Puranas, is a prevalent opinion; but as I have never met with it . . . under any other shape than that of bare assertion unsupported by the slightest argument or proof, I am completely at a loss to understand on what grounds it could have been formed.[23]

Though Kennedy was a heavyweight, Wilson sat on the imperial Boden Chair of Sanskrit at Oxford University. Furthermore, Wilson's verdict was certainly the much suppler one for subjugating barbaric India. Subtly the Crown had to root out of the Indians any pride in a glorious, lost past. British scholars lead the way.

Once again, we should remember that contemporary Indologists flinch at any suggestion that their founders, such as H. H. Wilson, set the academic agenda far into the twentieth century. Yet, Wilson's judgment on the Puranas did just that. Vans Kennedy, though a major player of the day, was lost to time, and Wilson's edict was enshrined. His branding the Puranas with a late date and pronouncing them unoriginal effectively dissuaded early Indologists from taking the Puranas seriously. After all, though

German-led Romanticism had sunk into the twilight and British colonial scholarship was on the rise, still the scholars could muster crucial enthusiasm only for things reputed to be ancient and original.[24]

The current industry standard in Puranic scholarship is the work of German Indologist Ludo Rocher. His overview, *The Puranas*, points out another reason for the early fade of Purana academics. The necessary investment of hard labor to crack the Puranas probably discouraged scholars. Without a doubt, Puranic research is quite a chore:

> One reason, in addition to the Puranas being "late" texts, for the lack of interest in these books during the early period may have been the inability of scholars to deal with the overwhelming mass of materials contained in them. It is characteristic of twentieth century Purana research that it starts looking for ways and methods to control this mass of materials.[25]

Hesitation owing to the unmanageable size of the Puranas combined with the "recent production" stigma affixed by Wilson. The result was the waning of Puranic research. Moreover, certainly the contents of the Puranas shocked many a scholar—whether European or modernized Indian. Theodore Goldstücker, a major player in his day, railed against the Puranas in his *Inspired Writings of Hinduism:* "When by priestcraft and ignorance, a nation has lost itself so far as to look upon writings like these as divinely inspired, there is but one conclusion to be drawn: it has arrived at the turning point of its destinies."[26] In the prestigious journal *Calcutta Review*, a contributor who chose to remain anonymous declared, "Of all false religions, that of the Puranas is perhaps the most monstrous in its absurdities—a stupendous memorial to the easy credulity of an imbecile race.[27]

Understandably, the plethora of exotica in the Puranas,

stretching and snapping the Western paradigm, did not bode well for Western acceptance—then or now. Though the days of the first Indologists have long passed, today the predominate Western mindset continues to recoil—politely though—upon sifting the contents of the Puranas.

Another factor contributing to Purana bashing has been negative campaigns waged by some Hindu thinkers near the start of the twentieth century. Hindu leaders such as Devendranath Tagore and Dayananda Sarasvati sought to turn their countrymen away from the Puranas, to focus exclusively upon the four Vedas and the Upanishads. They reasoned that what they construed as "the more sedate, generic Vedic texts" would prove a more effective basis for Hindu unity. The Puranas, with their apparently vast stock of diverse perplexities, were seen as a political and ecumenical barrier. Today the sect known as Arya Samaj is known for openly disclaiming the Puranas as authoritative texts. It also rejects the traditional authorship of Vyasa. The Western-originated Theosophical Society, founded on Madame Blavatsky's *The Secret Doctrine*, propagates a standoffish attitude to the Puranas, neither accepting nor rejecting them.

When we examine the relationships many Western scholars see between the Puranas, the four Vedas, and the Upanishads, we run smack into stormy seas. As touched upon early in this book, orthodox Vedic preceptors see all facets of the Vedic corpus of knowledge as existing together in a harmonious whole. The main Vedic schools do not attempt to oust the Puranas from the Vedic tradition. The most widely publicized attitude in Western academia, however, erects a stone wall between what are deemed "original Vedic works," and "later Puranic creations." Authors of nonspecialist books have broadcast this notion to the general public. Consequently, even at university libraries, this notion is all the student or teacher will find.

Unfortunately, once again we can trace a currently popular

idea to the founding fathers of Indology in the nineteenth century. After H. H. Wilson's dismissal of the Puranas, Max Müller followed, closing the door and sealing it tight. With self-assurety, he pronounced:

> If it be unsafe to use the epic poems [Mahabharata and Rama-yana] as authorities for the Vedic age, it will be readily admitted that the same objection applies with still greater force to the Puranas. Although only one of the eighteen Puranas has as yet been completely published, enough is known of their character, partly by Professor Burnouf's edition of the Bhagavat-purana, partly by extracts given from other Puranas by Professor Wilson, to justify our discarding their evidence with reference to the primitive period of Vedic literature.[28]

Goldstücker chose to be more proactive. He called for a massive campaign "to prove to the people that their real faith is neither founded upon the Brahmana portion of the Vedas, nor on the Puranas, but on the *Rig-veda* hymns."[29] He elaborated in his *Sanskrit and Culture*:

> Even a superficial comparison of the contents of the present Puranas with the ancient lore of Hindu religion, philosophy and science, must convince every one that the picture of religion and life unfolded by them is a caricature of that afforded by the Vedic works, and that it was drawn by a priestcraft, interested in submitting to its sway the popular mind, and unscrupulous in the use of the means which had to serve its end.[30]

The work of Ludo Rocher recognizes that the general consensus of Vedic intellectuals firmly upholds the fidelity of the Puranas and refuses to divorce them in any way from the Vedas.[31] Much to the relief of contemporary Vedic adherents, Rocher was able to see that they consider the Puranas, at the very least, as natural continuations and developments of the four Vedas. Even more intimately, though, the Puranas are celebrated as essential companions for correct understanding of the four Vedas. Because the Puranas manifest and demonstrate Vedic truth, the aspiring Vedic devotee is directed to take shelter in them. From Vedic times onward, they exist as companion literature.

Vedic sympathizers are not the only ones to hold that Puranic knowledge originates in the uncharted depths of the Vedic past. Rocher's study surprises us by pointing out that many modern scholars believe lost in antiquity is an original, singular corpus of Puranic knowledge, known as the *Purana-veda*.[32] Indologists sometimes use the Germanized term "Ur-Purana," the original Purana. Rocher points out that in this way, incredulously, a sizeable bulwark of modern scholastic conjecture actually veers quite close to the Puranic version of the Puranas. For example, the *Bhagavata Purana* states that the Puranas as well as Vedic histories like the *Mahabharata* all form the fifth Veda. Along with the foursome of the *Rig-*, *Sama-*, *Atharva-*, and *Yajur-veda*, the *Purana-veda* advented and coexists. In time, the one *Purana-veda* manifested as the various tributaries we recognize today.[33]

Especially in tracking the Puranas, we should remember that we are attempting to grasp knowledge, not so much the linguistic conveyances of knowledge. Certainly the *Rig-veda* is rightly famous for its impeccable tradition of syllabic fidelity, passed down intact over thousands of years, in an astonishingly strict system of memorization and recitation. We should note that the *Rig-veda* serves as a ritualistic sourcebook. In Vedic sacrificial performances for good karma, just one misplaced accent or mispronounced syllable can render the entire ritualistic process useless—or even disastrous. Therefore the *Rig-veda* demands an absolute rigor in the transmission of its language. The Puranic wisdom, however, never claims to adhere to such syllabic strictures. The Puranic treasure is not so much the minute details of communicative expression. Instead, the Puranas put a premium on the original clarity of the purport—conveying content without distortion.

Vedic tradition holds that throughout human history—since time immeasurable—a constant core of Puranic material is reworked and edited. Puranic knowledge is accepted as subject to rearticulation, according to the predominant human mindset for a particular epoch, or expanse of time. Naturally, modern Indologists will not opt for an immeasurable origin of either humanity or the Puranas. Many scholars of Indic Studies, however, do agree that the Puranas as we now know them contain much material of a presently unknown antiquity. Interestingly, the *Mahabharata*, in its *Adi-parva* section, directly attributes its greatness to its being a compilation of previous material.

Alternative-minded readers keen to plumb the Vedic literature for possible clues to humanity's lost history should not be put off by the overblown "Puranas versus the Vedas" storm in a teacup. Both scholars in-the-know and Vedic authorities will inform us that references to Vedic histories do appear in the four Vedas.[34]

The *Rig-veda* describes a world in which learned sages and poets recount histories and sing the glories of great events. Modern scholars have to agree that these are not internal references—the statements do not link to other hymns in the *Rig-veda*. Obviously, the author of the *Rig-veda* assumes his audience is familiar with Puranic-type knowledge, whether in the written or oral medium.[35]

The *Atharva-veda* lends credence to Puranic knowledge as a singular corpus by conspicuously using the word *purana* in its singular form.[36] Also, when the *Atharva-veda* lists the four Vedas, it follows by specifically referring to *itihasa* (Vedic histories) and *purana*.[37] Obviously the so-called "original Vedas" do acknowledge the contemporaneous existence of a Vedic historical and commentative inheritance. Whether as one written or oral work, or as a collection of many works, the Puranas definitely garner only laurels of authenticity and concurrency from what some have mistakenly isolated as "the classic Vedic texts."

LET'S MAKE A SECT

A trip to a public or university library will almost always net the unsuspecting searcher a story that goes like this: Long after the "real Vedic period" of the four Vedas and the Upanishads ended, rival priests wanted to establish the supremacy of their various colorful sects. Some championed Krishna, "the Hindu pastoral love-god;" others rallied around Shiva, "the Hindu god of ghosts;" still others chose Durga or alternative sub-elites of the "Hindu pantheon." The purport of the saga is that the Puranas are recent creations. They are wild and woolly tales constructed by ambitious priests, who set into motion the forerunners of "the modern Hindu sects we know about today."

Hopefully, by now readers of this book will have developed an invaluable sixth sense. Upon encountering any popular notion today about Indology, an alarm bell in the mind should sound: Follow the trail back to the European preceptors of yore. Particularly, we may blame it on the British Empire. Yes, modern Indic scholars do not swallow whole the myths of their early predecessors. But perhaps out of respect for the academic ancestors, they do not publicly censure them. The result of this apparent tepidness in the old boy's club is that the educated public still accepts these outdated fantasies as fact.

H. H. Wilson, from the Boden Chair, led the first campaign to brand the Puranas as sect material. "They are no longer authorities for Hindu belief as a whole: they are special guides for separate and sometimes conflicting branches of it."[38] Continuing his attack, he asserted that the priests had manufactured the Puranas as "pious frauds for temporary purposes."[39]

When the current standard-bearer, Ludo Rocher, underwent his extensive review of Puranic research, he was able to trace the "sectarian Puranas trail" from Wilson and his fellows on up to academics in the twentieth century. For example, in 1840 Eugene Burnouf finished in Paris the first volume of his rendition of the *Bhagavata Purana*. The preface quoted and supported Wilson's verdict, squarely attributing the *Bhagavata Purana* to "modern sects."[40]

Then Christian Lassen, in 1847, published his encyclopaedic survey of Indian civilization. His passage on the Puranas completely depended on the preface of Wilson and, continuing the academic chain, he took shelter in the preface of Burnouf too.[41] Next, in 1852 Albrecht Weber put out his history of Indian literature, and exclusively based his Purana notions on Lassen.[42]

The result of this amusing process? Rocher says that generation after generation of Indologists have imbibed the notion that the Puranas, in Lassen's words, "sind im Interesse und zur Empfehlung dieser Sekten geschrieben" [the Puranas are written for the interest and promotion of sects].[43]

In 1922 the *Cambridge History of India* called the Puranas "sectarian and propagandist." It claimed the Puranas "have become the scriptures of the various forms of later Hinduism."[44] Tidy compendiums like *The History and Culture of the Indian People* carried the same ball into the last quarter of the twentieth century.[45] Now, at the dawn of the new millennium, the notion is still enshrined in public and university libraries—with scant challenge or correction.

The sadly omnipresent idea that the Puranas are recent productions owes its popularity to the first Indologists. They assumed that Vaishnavism and Shaivism are late developments in India— coming long after "the classic days of the four Vedas and Upanishads." Wilson judged that none of the "modern forms of popular Hinduism" could be older than the period of the medieval

Vedic preceptors. He was referring to Shankara (A.D. 788–820), Ramanuja (A.D. 1017–1137), and Madhva (A.D. 1239–1319). To this timeframe, roughly one millennium after Christ, Wilson assigned the Puranas. He opined, "The Puranas seem to have accompanied or followed their innovations, being obviously intended to advocate the doctrines they taught. This is to assign to some of them a very modern date, it is true."[46]

To be sure, both during the heyday of Wilson and later, dissenters had eloquently raised their voice. Vans Kennedy's protests were the most prominent, during Wilson's time. Diametrically opposing the occupant of the Boden Chair, he asserted that "the same system of religion that prevailed in India at least one thousand years before Christ still prevails there today."[47]

Kennedy had the shrewdness to comprehend that, since India lacked any historiography that Western scholars could penetrate, "it must be obvious that there are no means available, by which the date or probable period when each of the Puranas was composed can be determined."[48] But Kennedy became a footnote in nineteenth-century academic history, while the edicts of Wilson became law for generations to come.

In 1879 the German Indologist Georg Bühler expressed his doubts about the party line: "The earlier history of the Puranas, which as yet is a mystery, will be only cleared up when a real history of the orthodox Hindu sects, especially of the Shaivites and Vishnuites, has been written."[49] Now, more than a century later, we are still waiting for that "real history" to be written.

The notion that the Puranas reflect recent sects is entombed in the educated public's mind. For example, let us peek into the current *Penguin Encyclopaedia of Classical Civilizations*. Its description of the Puranas, though relatively subdued, dutifully toes the mainline. Puranic knowledge is attributed to the centuries after Christ. The brahmins concocted it all, to keep abreast with popular trends booming in India around the fourth or fifth century:

The more popular form of Hinduism from the Gupta period (320–ca. 550) onwards has often been called Puranic Hinduism. The Puranas, though composed and edited by brahmins, are very much a manifestation of popular religion: they show that the brahmins have maintained their position as guardians and transmitters of Hinduism only by being receptive, even if reluctantly, to any innovations which achieve a real popular following.[50]

Note that, although Penguin publishes a companion volume on ancient civilizations, it only discusses the Puranas in the volume covering later civilizations. The educated public, no matter to what publication it turns, almost always must swallow the same message: the Puranas, products of later Indian civilization, are brahminical contrivances for capitalizing on a spurt of popular sects.

Today, inside academia, do the few scholars specializing in the Puranas still accept the recent-sect theory? Quietly, no. Rocher concludes his study by noting that among current specialists, "This thesis has, however, not found general acceptance."[51]

NOW LET'S MAKE A DATE

There seems to be widespread agreement among Puranic scholars that the core of the Puranas is a moving target, which existed long before the advent of Christendom. When did the remodelling of this ancient knowledge begin? Did the rearticulation of the corpus proceed indefinitely or did it end at a certain time? These are wide-open questions. Furthermore, what is the complete trajectory of the *Bhagavata Purana*, from recital to its present status as a veritable spiritual encyclopaedia?

To some minds, rearticulation automatically implies deterioration. This assumption holds that, as time marched on, the original Puranic kernel must have accumulated heaps of excess baggage.

Interestingly, Vedic preceptors hold to the opposite: they say that when extraordinary Vedic luminaries re-present the original Puranic nucleus, we accrue not increasing unwieldiness but renewed precision and clarity for our particular era.

Then again, for inveterate Western empiricists and logical positivists, there is Moriz Winternitz's rule of the thumb: the more mind-boggling the content, the more recent the Purana.[52] In other words, "If I can't understand it, and if it completely violates my cherished conceptions of reality, then we must be dealing with a new perversion, a fairly recent distortion of the 'more tidy, original content.'"

Acknowledging the natural desire of Western savants to date the Puranas, Rocher, in his definitive review of the attempt, interjects that it is well nigh impossible. Yet he notes an academic paradox: "Even those who do realize that dating a particular Purana is highly speculative if not impossible, nevertheless propose more or less specific dates."[53]

Wendy O'Flaherty, of the University of Chicago, sums up the futility in this way: "The dating of the Puranas is . . . an art—it can hardly be called a science—unto itself."[54] Rocher concludes his examination of Purana dating without the slightest doubt: "I submit that it is not possible to set a specific date for any Purana as a whole . . . opinions, inevitably, continue to vary widely and endlessly."[55]

THE BHAGAVATA PURANA

Certainly the most popular and famous Purana in India is the *Bhagavata Purana*. Also widely known as the *Shrimad-Bhagavatam*, it is unarguably accepted as having influenced Indian thought and religion more than any other Puranic literature. Vaishnavas—devotees of *Bhagavan* as Vishnu, Rama, or Krishna—consider the *Bhagavata Purana* the natural commentary on the

Vedanta-sutra, the Vedic metaphysical exposition. Both texts start with the exact Sanskrit declaration that the Supreme Personality of Godhead is the source of all emanations and is beyond the material cosmos. Moreover, the *Bhagavata Purana* has been called a commentary on the mantra in the *Rig-veda* known as *gayatri.* The first verse of the *Bhagavata* ends with the same key word that the *Rig-mantra* ends with.

Despite the preeminent status of the *Bhagavata Purana,* scholars cannot agree on a date for it. The first guesstimate came from the earliest Indic scholars, H. T. Colebrooke and William Ward. At the beginning of the nineteenth century they spread an Indian-born speculation that a grammarian named Bopadeva had written the *Bhagavata Purana* six hundred years earlier—in the thirteenth century A.D. The chief argument was based on language. Ward, reiterating what he heard from some Indian pundits, wrote in 1811, "They say, the language is not that of the other pooranus, but more difficult, so much so that not a single learned man in Bengal can thoroughly understand it."[56]

True, Sanskritists past and present have recognized the sublime literary qualities of the *Bhagavata Purana.* Winternitz charitably crowned it as "the one Purana which more than any of the others, bears the stamp of a unified composition, and deserves to be appreciated as a literary production on account of its language, style and meter."[57] Today the popular *Penguin Encyclopaedia of Classical Civilizations* seeks to impress upon its innocent readers that this literary excellence means recent authorship: "The Bhagavata Purana . . . reveals its lateness by the very fact that it is relatively structured."[58]

Back in the nineteenth century, Vans Kennedy disagreed with the notion of recent composition by Bopadeva. Perhaps predictably, H. H. Wilson supported it. Then Wilson's minions, headed as usual by Burnouf and Lassen, emblazoned his judgment upon posterity.[59] By now, however, regardless of what has been fed to the public, Sanskritists have generally—though very quietly—rejected the Bopadeva idea. Investigations have identified Bopadeva as the thirteenth-century author of merely a compilation of verses he extracted from the *Bhagavata Purana*, to illustrate salient points in Vaishnavism. He also wrote a treatise based on the *Bhagavata* called *Harilila*.[60]

Lest anyone doubt the thoroughness of Rocher's study of Puranic scholarship, he provides the vital statistics to evidence his conclusion that no one can tie down a date for the *Bhagavata Purana*. A table of guesstimates from more than thirty scholars allows us to easily see the folly: the thirty or so stabs fill a range of 2,500 years, spanning from 1200 B.C. to A.D. 1300.[61] Remember Winternitz's appraisal of the history of Vedic literature, quoted in Chapter 3: "truly terrifying darkness"?

LOST BEGINNINGS:
THE EGYPTIANS, SUMERIANS, AND OLMECS

Let us ignore, for the moment, the puzzling extraterrestrial scope of Puranic texts, especially of the *Bhagavata Purana*. Nevertheless, we will find that if we choose just to focus upon down here on the ground—concentrating on potentially historical information that the Puranas offer for planet Earth, still we run into mystery.

Semitic religions don't share such a great problem. For example, whether mainstream scholars accept the divinity of Christ or not, most will accept that the sociocultural world of the New Testament is an accurate portrayal of humanity at the start of the first millennium A.D. The archaeological record has been supportive of this general correlation—between what the texts portray and the actual *milieu* of the times.

When we turn to the Vedas, however, we run into a roadblock. Vedic preceptors say that the *Bhagavata Purana*, the *Bhagavad-gita*, and the *Mahabharata* can transport us to the Vedic world preceding 3000 B.C. Have no doubt: few establishment Western scholars will accept that the sociocultural world in these texts really matches humanity at that time.

Furthermore, they gape with amazement upon anyone seriously proposing that Vedic knowledge was the cynosure of the ancient Earth. And don't you dare even think of mentioning the universe. As your head lowers in mortification, you will hear that Vedic literature is standard, legendary, mythical material. Kindly professors may console you, "Don't fret—after all, just consider, for example, the description of Attila the Hun in the Germanic epics. Likewise, the ancient chronicles almost always serve massive myths as the main dish, sprinkled perhaps with a few granules of real history."

Before so handily dismissing the Vedic vision of the world before ca. 3000 B.C., we might reflect upon how much we actually know about the origins of civilization. Ancient Egypt, Sumer, and Mesoamerica have long been exposed to our probes. At least superficially, they are familiar to every high-school student. Yet how deep is our most advanced knowledge of their genesis? Our present information of even "the standard ancient peoples" is more opaque than we think.

Mainstream academia teaches its students that nothing significant in human history happens before 4000 B.C. Consequently your eyes are glued to the past 6,000 years. Calmly munching your milk and cookies, you humbly accept what may soon turn out to be extreme tunnel vision. For now, though, the official story is that outside the 6,000-year dispensation, only simple agricultural settlements existed. When you follow the story further back in time, to around 10,000 years ago, only nomadic hunters and gatherers will you find. These primitive wanderers preceded the agricultural communities. Thus, in reviewing the span of the past 10,000 years, we should accept that a miracle struck around the fourth millennium B.C. Suddenly, ca. 3000 B.C., advanced human civilization broke out.

Recently a spate of alternative research is dragging this embedded notion out into the open. A full exposure of the Big Bang theory of civilization's development is beyond the scope of this book. The curious reader is invited to explore lengthy discussions elsewhere.

Briefly, let us begin with Egypt. Standard history books say that Egyptian civilization began just prior to 3000 B.C., when Menes was to have united the Upper and Lower kingdoms. Before that, only simple farming, or Neolithic cultures, existed. Then abruptly all the famous facets of Egyptian prowess clicked on at once, completely developed. Science, art, architecture, theology, and hieroglyphics all exploded into full bloom. The later dynasties, however, somehow could not match or even equal these initial feats.

For none of these monumental cultural achievements is there any trail of development from primitive simplicity to full-blown, sophisticated complexity. The knowledge encoded in the temples seems to appear out of nothingness. The archaeological record suggests virtually an overnight emergence of a civilization fully formed and fully featured. Violating all conceptions of historical sense, an advanced society pops out of nowhere, fast—devoid of an appropriate transition period. Mainline Egyptologists quietly acknowledge the riddle but, to date, have felt no need to publicly face the implications. Walter Emery, late Edwards Professor of Egyptology at the University of London, pinpoints the problem:

> At a period approximately 3,400 years before Christ, a great change took place in Egypt, and the country passed rapidly from a state of neolithic culture with a complex tribal culture to one of well-organized monarchy. . . . At the same time the art of writ-

ing appears, monumental architecture and the arts and crafts develop to an astonishing degree, and all the evidence points to the existence of a luxurious civilization. All this was achieved within a comparatively short period of time, for there appears to be little or no background to these fundamental developments in writing and architecture.[62]

Both alternative researchers and a few name-brand main-streamers point out that most Egyptian archaeological material from the close of the Paleolithic period to the start of the Bronze Age has come from places other than the Nile delta and valley. The majority of clues to predynastic Egypt have surfaced in areas near the desert or areas bordering the Nile Delta that are higher than the river's floodplain.

Geologist Robert Schoch explains that very little has been discovered in the Nile valley and delta simply because archaeological excavation is extremely difficult there. Before the Nile was dammed, yearly flooding covered the delta and the remainder of the floodplain with soil. Thus, the passage of ten thousand years, since the beginning of the Neolithic period, would have buried the Nile delta and valley under approximately twenty-six feet of river-borne soil. Moreover, part of the Nile has changed course, and much of the inhabitable coast of Egypt several millennia ago is now submerged under the sea. Scientists say that beginning around 8000 B.C., the Mediterranean quickly rose at least 200 feet. Any cities, villages, or other noteworthy sites on the coastline would have slid under the sea.[63]

Prehistorian Mary Settegast has severe doubts about the lack of evidence for civilization in the Nile delta and valley, during the millenniums preceding what we call dynastic Egypt: "It has never seemed logical that the Nile Valley would be almost uninhabited during a period when lands to the east and west of Egypt were experiencing great advances in population and cultural development."[64] Very possibly the answers—cities—lie under the silt deposited by thousands of Nile floods, under the waters of the Mediterranean, or under the sands of the shifting desert.

What the established conception holds as the world's first civilization, Sumer, always receives extensive coverage in nonspecialist publications. Quietly, behind the scenes, however, Sumer is also seen as a puzzle. As in Egypt, suddenly things began to pick up in Mesopotamia just prior to 3000 B.C. Apparently, out of the mist sprang what is considered the first written language and the first wheel, as well as advanced mathematics, metallurgy, and astronomy. Was the boom in Mesopotamia homegrown or an import? Among scholars there is an admitted cloud of mystery. For example, without deviating from mainstream thought, the archaeologist R. Stigler concedes, "The origins, linguistic and otherwise, of the Sumerians is a most complicated and debated question. . . . alternative explanations involving invasions-migrations and in situ development have been put forth."[65]

Meanwhile, very recently, new ruins found in northeastern Syria have completely upset the traditional story we've been taught. Every student, from childhood up, has learned that the Tigris Euphrates—during the Uruk period (circa 3200 B.C.)—is the cradle of civilization. The new discovery, however, has punctured the notion. As of mid-2000, no longer is Sumer credited with the hatching of urban centers in northern regions of the Middle East.

The discovery of the ruins, named Tell Hamoukar and dated at more than 5,500 years old, inspires a new idea that other cities arose simultaneously but independently of Sumer. This northern urban development is now envisioned to have resulted from contact with a Mesopotamian culture preceding Sumer—a forerunner dating to the Ubaid period (circa 4500 B.C.).

Archaeologist McGuire Gibson explains that if the first cities indeed occurred during the Ubaid period, then archaeologists have to wrestle with a tough concept that urban centers appeared before the invention of writing and "before the appearance of several other criteria that we think of as marking 'civilization.'"[66] Gibson, of the Oriental Institute of the University of Chicago, concluded, "We need to reconsider our ideas about the beginnings of civilization, pushing the time further back."[67]

In Mesoamerica, along the southern Gulf Coast of Mexico, the lesser-known Olmec problem nags us. The earliest carbon dates for an Olmec site—found at San Lorenzo—have been 1500 B.C. But how did the Olmecs—Mesoamerica's earliest known civilization—develop? From what, and from where? The Olmecs were no smalltimers. In their carving and manipulating huge stone blocks, they demonstrated meritorious engineering and organizational capacity. In addition to building pyramids, the Olmecs carved out of stone enormous, twenty-ton heads. These negroid-like heads were made of basalt quarried and transported from mountains as far as sixty miles away. Accomplishing such feats demanded extraordinary physical labor as well as administrative expertise.

Olmec society was also distinguished by a dating system, long-distance trade routes, ceremonial centers, and exquisite jade work. According to the standard story, the Olmecs began as a farming community around 1500 B.C., and then somehow, within a period of three hundred years, all their advancement immediately surged forth.

A renowned expert on Mesoamerican cultures, Richard E. W. Adams, gently admits to the riddle of the Olmec rise out of nowhere. A professor of anthropology at the University of Texas, Adams writes in his standard text *Prehistoric Mesoamerica*, "It is clear from the evidence of the Olmec site of San Lorenzo that massive public construction began by 1350 B.C. At this point then we are confronted with the spectacular but somewhat problematic appearance of the Olmecs."[68] The esteemed archaeological team of C. C. Lamberg-Karlovsky and J. A. Sabloff also acknowledges the enigma: "This seemingly sudden growth of a complex society on the Gulf Coast has led to much speculation about the reasons for the rise of the Olmecs."[69]

Perhaps academia should be more forthright in disclosing to the public the perplexing hole in the standard narrative of human civilization. Indeed, the Big Bang theory of the origin of civilization may well be the weakest drama in what we currently accept as human history. Like so much in the Western canon of accepted truth, the mystical leap from primitive hunter-gatherers to the sophisticates of Egyptian, Sumerian, and Olmec societies demands great faith. Alternative-minded scholars contend that a short spell of simple agricultural settlements does not suffice as an intermediate stage. A period of survival cultures based on farming, they say, is not an adequate forerunner to the complex civilizations that followed. And remember, the majority consensus is that the fabled leap happened at least three separate times, in at least three separate places.

Though Egypt and Sumer existed only a few hundred miles from each other, scholars are loath to posit a possible cross-fertilization of one by the other. Certainly some similarities can be found; moreover, no one doubts that Egypt and Sumer were aware of each other. Yet scant archaeological evidence exists for supporting any notion of a direct, causal relationship between these two hallowed cradles of civilization.

Surprisingly, some academics propose an outside agent, a third party, responsible for the booms in at least Egypt and Sumer. The established duo of Lamberg-Karlovsky and Sabloff concedes the existence of this third-party theory: "A minority of scholars have theorized that changes in Southern Mesopotamia, as in Egypt, were so rapid that the invisible hand of an invading culture must have been responsible."[70] For example, the reputable Egyptologist Walter Emery states:

The impression we get is of an indirect connection, and perhaps the existence of a third party, whose influence spread to both the Euphrates and the Nile. . . . Modern scholars have tended to ignore the possibility of immigration to both regions from some hypothetical and as yet undiscovered area. [Nevertheless] a third party whose cultural achievements were passed on independently to Egypt and Mesopotamia would best explain the common features and fundamental differences between the two civilizations.[71]

In theology Egypt and Sumer share almost identical lunar deities. Pointedly steering clear of theories of cross-fertilization, the famous Egyptologist Sir E. A. Wallis Budge opts for the unknown third-party explanation: "The similarity between the two gods is too close to be accidental. . . . It would be wrong to say that the Egyptians borrowed from the Sumerians or the Sumerians from the Egyptians, but it may be submitted that the literati of both peoples borrowed their theological systems from some common but exceedingly ancient source."[72]

Crossing the ocean from Egypt and Sumer to Mesoamerica, we will find that some scholars entertain third-party hypotheses for the Olmecs too. The two senior archaeologists Lamberg-Karlovsky and Sabloff, without submitting to theories of outside influence, definitely acknowledge their existence:

From an archaeological point of view, the Olmec civilization suddenly appeared in a relatively well-developed form around 1200 B.C. . . . There seems to have been no long, slow sequence of local growth in the Gulf Coast lowlands prior to the rise of the Olmecs. If the Olmecs did not evolve in the same area where they later flourished, where did they arise? . . . Although there are suggestions that Olmec civilization might have originated outside the Gulf Coast lowlands of Mexico, the most reasonable position for the moment seems to be "wait and see."[73]

MISSING IN ACTION:
A BRILLIANT CIVILIZATION

In their attempts to solve the mystery of the Egyptian, Sumerian, and Olmec explosion, those mainstream scholars contemplating the third-party solution are tight-lipped about the identity of that unknown civilization. Nevertheless, though established academics hesitate to posit a particular people, non-mainstream researchers are not shy to fill in the blank. Their theories range from inhabitants of the lost continent of Atlantis to ancient astronauts arriving from a distant star. To conservative ears, their alternative explanations are certainly repugnant. Open-minded inquirers, however, should review the miracles of civilization we have to account for—the hidden wonders of history that mainstream academia overlooks. Perhaps what should annoy us more is the penchant of established scholars to ignore these monstrous "anomalies."

Moreover, though alternative theories may sound, at the least, improbable, we would do well to consider that the current dominant notion of human development is itself improbable. Alternative researchers often render a valuable service by alerting us to undeniably contrary evidence. Fingers do point to an advanced civilization, missing somewhere—a forerunner that seeded its brilliance in Egypt, Sumer, and Mesoamerica.

Remember the major archaeological evidence that intelligent humans have existed on this planet far longer than current Western dogma admits. Remember the portolans—potential remnants of an advanced maritime civilization that may have accurately mapped Antarctica at a remote time when the polar continent was free of ice. Remember the advanced astronomical knowledge as well as the mind-boggling construction technology.

And now what? Should we search for the missing civilization under the sea—plumbing the depths for lost continents? Oceanographers tell us that the floor of every ocean has been mapped—no hidden landmasses have been found.

Alternative-research kingpin Graham Hancock, in his runaway success *Fingerprints of the Gods*, reasons that the missing master civilization was much too accomplished to have thrived on just any piece of land.

> Its homeland . . . must have been blessed with major mountain ranges, huge river systems and a congenial climate, and with many other obvious environmental prerequisites for the development of an advanced and prosperous economy: good agricultural lands, mineral resources, and so on. So where could such a landmass have been located, if not under any of the world's oceans?[74]

Hancock admits he knows scientists have found nothing under the seas. Yet, to where else can he turn for the habitat of the lost people? He surmises, therefore, that a huge natural disaster so altered the Earth's geography that any traces of the lost civilization disappeared.

Or should we look to the stars? Some writers do lunge for the ancient astronaut escape hatch. But down here on planet Earth, there is a solution none of the well-known alternative researchers have examined. No one has turned to India. "And why not?" we should ask. The ancient scriptures of India specifically put forth the existence of a highly advanced global civilization—headquartered on the Indian subcontinent.

Contemporary Vedic exponents can establish a very impressive case that Vedic chronicles—the Puranas and Itihasas—indicate a Vedic culture that dominated the world. Rather than immediately dismissing or ignoring the possibility, perhaps we should listen. According to their presentation, the geopolitical division of the world is a relatively recent development. The orthodox Vedic version is that, until approximately 5000 years ago, the whole world was predominated by Vedic culture. The ancient texts say that a Vedic emperor oversaw the globe from his throne in the capital city known as Hastinapura—now New Delhi. Subordinate kings and their states throughout the world paid their allegiance and taxes to him.

We are told that the text *Mahabharata* is the history of the entire planet, but that it describes only the most important persons and events. The ancient Vedas refer to what we call India by the name *Bharata-varsa*. The Sanskrit means "the geographical realm made famous by the rule of King Bharata." Europeans bestowed the name *India* upon the subcontinent. The Vedic appellation, however, refers to more than just the subcontinent—it is said to mean the whole planet.

Therefore, tradition holds, when we say *Mahabharata*, it means, in modern parlance, the history of "the Greater India." The Sanskrit word *maha* means "greater" and *bharata* means what we now refer to as India. Currently one may say "the Greater New York" or "the Greater London," when referring to a city proper and its surrounding areas. Similarly "the Greater India" described in the *Mahabharata* is accepted as what we now call India plus the rest of the world as its surrounding, dependent regions.

Upon the end of the Kurukshetra War, so vividly recorded in the Mahabharata, the global Vedic culture is to have begun its decline. The Vedic version of this battle, accepted as occurring 5,000 years ago, is that the conflict was global in scope, though the actual battle was fought north of what is now New Delhi. Traditional accounts say that all the kings of the world took sides. Afterwards, within the past 5000 years, the worldwide hegemony of Vedic culture was to have rapidly disintegrated. Then the planet underwent the marked geopolitical and ethnic partitioning so familiar to us.

Except for textual information recorded in the Vedas, any

other evidence of a global Vedic civilization has vanished—as far as we know today. According to present perceptions, no physical traces exist. Therefore, to our intimidating list of historical mysteries, we can add the complete disappearance of the worldwide civilization described in the Vedic literature.

Once again, we have to do battle with a nagging suspicion: "Don't the texts merely give us mythology?" The Vedic version of antiquity, when considered in isolation, certainly can seem no more than legend. When severed from the other tremendous mysteries of antiquity, the Vedic accounts of a lost civilization can be difficult to swallow. On the other hand, when we see these same chronicles in a worldwide context of lost human history, then we may credit the Vedic version for opening up extraordinary avenues of possibility.

Emperor Bharata, of Bharata-varsha fame, is said to be the remote ancestor of the Pandavas, the heroes of the *Mahabharata* and the winners of the Kurukshetra War. Most of us would readily agree to overlook the ample and detailed Puranic references to royalty existing millions of years ago. Yet, even the list of kings since the traditional dating of the Kurukshetra War stretches our brains. The literature says that upon the end of that battle, 5,000 years ago, Yudhishthira, the oldest Pandava, accepted the emperorship of the world and was succeeded by several other world-class monarchs.

Though conventional historians today pooh-pooh the assertion, India's traditional accounts and records do not. For example, during the nineteenth century, the famous Jagannath Temple at Puri, in the state of Orissa, held in its archives a list of kings who ruled Orissa during the past 5,000 years. The list was recorded on palm leaves, impressed by a sharp iron pen, without ink. Two respected British historians investigated these palm-leaf records—by way of local pandits under their employ. In the first half of the nineteenth century, Andrew Stirling engaged a staff to assist his study of the list. He published his work in the journal *Asiatic Researches*. Next, native Bengali scholar Bhabanicharan Bandopadhyaya published the list in his work *Purushottama Chandrika*, now a rare book even in Bengal. Then, in the second half of the nineteenth century, the British scholar William Wilson Hunter analyzed the works of both Stirling and Bandhopadhyaya. In praise of the Bengali scholar, Hunter wrote:

> We owe the most successful of these researches to a learned Brahman of Calcutta, who published an epitome of the palm-leaf writings in Bengali in 1843. He informs us that he spared neither labour nor expense; and as one of the most devoted of the modern worshippers of Jagannath, he had special opportunities for the work. I cannot withhold my tribute to the conscientious toil to which the work of this admirable scholar bears witness.[75]

The priests at the Jagannath Temple—still thriving in Orissa today—were not about to let just anyone sift through their archives. Also, it should be noted that, although both British scholars, Stirling and Hunter, published the results of their research into the palm-leaf records, neither personally accepted the information on the earliest kings as necessarily factual. The scholars just dutifully recorded what the natives had recorded about their remote past: "As, however, it will be not uninteresting to those curious in researches into Hindu antiquity, to learn what traditions the natives of this district have preserved regarding their history in the earlier ages, I shall begin my sketch of the contents of their annals from the remotest period to which they profess to go back."[76]

Of course, any high-school student knows the potential flaws of traditional, native knowledge. Ironically, however, at the dawn of the twenty-first century, many university students doubt established Western knowledge.

What follows is the B.C. section of the king list from the annals of Jagannath. The second British investigator, Hunter, collated this presentation from the original work of Stirling and the Bengali scholar. Note that, although the archives at the Jagannath Temple focus upon the area of Orissa, the first three kings on the list are in the Vedic world-class category. These three—Yudhishthira, Parikshit, and Janamejaya—are described in the Vedic texts as global emperors, who not only dominated Orissa but also exacted fealty from subordinated kingdoms throughout the world. The collated list, reproduced in part below, is unique in that it combines traditional records with the adjustments of nineteenth-century scholars.[77]

A Chronicle of the Kings of Orissa
from 3101 B.C. to A.D. 1871

Based on the Palm-Leaf Records of Jagannath, as digested in the *Purushottama Chandrika* by Babu Bhabanicharan Bandopadhyaya, collated with Stirling's Essay in the *Asiatic Researches*, vol. xv (ed. 1825), and his posthumous paper in the *Bengal Asiatic Society's Journal*, vol. vi., part ii, 1837.

B.C. 3101–3089. YUDHISHTHIR, a monarch of the Mahabharata, of the Lunar Race of Delhi. Reigned 12 years. [According to Stirling (*Asiatic Researches*, vol. xv), 3095–3083 B.C.]

3089–2358. PARIKSHIT, a monarch of the Mahabharata, of the Lunar Race of Delhi. Reigned 731 years. [According to Stirling, 3083–2326 B.C.]

2358–1807. JANMEJAYA, a monarch of the Mahabharata, and the patron of that work; sprung from the Lunar Race of Delhi. Reigned 551 years. [According to Stirling, 2326–1810 B.C.]

1807–1407. SANKAR DEVA. Reigned 400 years. [According to Stirling, 1810–1400 B.C.]

1407–1037. GAUTAM DEVA. Extended the Kingdom of Orissa to

the Godavari River. Reigned 370 years. [According to Stirling, 1400–1027 B.C.]

1037–822. MAHENDRA DEVA. Founded the town of Rajma-hendri as his capital. Reigned 215 years. [According to Stirling, 1027–812 B.C.]

822–688. ISHTA DEVA. Reigned 134 years. [According to Stirling, 812–678 B.C.]

688–538. SEVAK DEVA. Reigned 150 years. [According to Stirling, 678–528 B.C.]

538–421. BAJRA DEVA. In this reign Orissa was invaded by Yavanas from Marwar, from Delhi, and from Babul Des—the last supposed to be Iran (Persia) and Cabul. According to the Palm-Leaf Chronicle, the invaders were repulsed. Reigned 117 years. [According to Stirling, 528–421 B.C.]

421–306. NARSINH DEVA. Reigned 115 years. Another chief from the far north invaded the country during this reign, but he was defeated, and the Orissa prince reduced a great part of the Delhi kingdom. The monarch excavated the tank at Dantan near Jaleswar, which exists at this day. [According to Stirling, this prince was called Sarasankha, and reigned 421–306 B.C.]

306–184. MANKRISHNA DEVA. Reigned 122 years. Yavanas from Kashmir invaded the country, but were driven back after many battles. [According to Stirling, this king was called Hansa, and reigned 306–184 B.C.]

184–57. BHOJ DEVA. A great prince, who drove back a Yavana invasion, and is said to have subdued all India. Reigned 127 years. [Stirling's date here coincides with that of the Palm-Leaf Record; and when this is the case, I do not give his figures.]

This remarkable compilation—the product of both tradition and early academia—continues into the years A.D., up to A.D. 1871. We should note that the date the list gives for the first monarch cited, Yudhishthira, is approximately 5,000 years ago. The

Vedas record that at this time Yudhishthira emerged from the Kurukshetra War as the world emperor. We should also note that, aside from the short rule of Yudhishthira, the reigns of the kings between approximately 3000 B.C. and 1000 B.C. are quite lengthy—from the modern perspective. Indeed, the first three kings—familiar to readers of Vedic history—cover an immense span of 1294 years, from 3101 to 1807 B.C.

No Vedic adherent accepts these three monarchs as mere petty rulers. As the historian Hunter appropriately pointed out, "The first king with any pretensions to being [just] a local monarch reigned from 1807 to 1407 B.C." The next major development is that, after 1000 B.C, the reigns begin to shrink. The spans given become more palatable to our conceptions, as the Vedic era of Kali-yuga progresses. As discussed in Chapter 10, in Kali-yuga longevity gradually diminishes.

The full list, not reproduced here, continues into the years A.D. It documents ninety-six kings of Orissa from the first century A.D. up until A.D. 1871. All these kings have spans quite acceptable to our modern dictates. In fact, after A.D. 600, the reigns become brutishly short—seven to fifteen years—as per our modern political experience.

For the paradigm challenger and the connoisseur of alternative history, the Jagannath annals are a stimulating meditation. Needless to say, the list does not prove anything, though so carefully collated from the palm-leaf records of Jagannath and the scholastic adjustments of early scholars. Certainly we are entitled to decree that the remote part of the list is legend and the less distant part is fact.

In the earliest days of Indology, enthusiasm for anything smacking of remote antiquity ran high. Hence, we might choose to safely ignore nineteenth-century research favorable to Vedic remote antiquity. After all, the legendary rigors of modern critical scholarship had not yet fully emerged. To be fair, however, we moderns might do well to apply these same fabled critical skills to our enormous burden of hidden assumptions and dogmas—an all-pervasive network that often binds and chokes our knowledge factories.

Once again, we can turn to anomalies from other civilizations to derive intriguing cross-perspectives. Egyptian, Sumerian, and Mesoamerican societies all have their share of ancient king mysteries too. Whereas the Vedic mysteries of royalty extend far back into the deep past as well as creep up close, to ca. 1800 B.C., the royal mysteries of these other cultures seem only to thrive in far-distant times.

The Sumerians have a king list asserting that in the depths of the unknown past some of their rulers lived thousands of years. Naturally scholars dismiss such statements. Nevertheless, when Sumerian records mention later kings, with respectable lifespans, academia seriously considers their authenticity. As the march of time approaches the beginnings of historically verifiable Sumer, the length of reigns that the Sumerians document becomes easy to digest. Furthermore, archaeological evidence has surfaced to confirm the reigns of some Sumerian kings of the fourth and third millennium B.C.

Egypt tantalizes us with accounts of *Tep Zepi*, "the First Time," a mystical period in Egypt's lost past when extraordinarily powerful personalities flew through the sky in "air boats" and transmitted knowledge to their descendants by establishing a royal chain of Pharaohs. Once again, scholars, of course, must immediately brand the First Time as fable. And once again, we must ask: Why should we, on the one hand, eagerly embrace the Egyptian king lists when they refer to the historically verifiable period, and, on the other hand, turn away from the same sources when they reach back into a lost and mystical past?

Major Egyptian temples contain lists of kings that name every Pharaoh confirmed by modern Egyptologists. Some of these documents attempt to take us back in time farther than the First Dynasty. Breaking out of the confines of our "historical Egypt," these lists seek to transport us deep into remote antiquity. Two well-known lists, stored in European museums, are the Palermo Stone, dated at ca. 2500 B.C., and the Turin Papyrus, dated at ca. 1300 B.C. Then we have the famous history of Egypt compiled by Manetho, a Heliopolitan priest in the third century B.C. His extensive history—preserved in the writings of later chroniclers like Josephus (A.D. 60) and Eusebius (A.D. 340)—gives us king lists for whole dynastic eras of Egypt.

Manetho's accounts, the Palermo Stone, and the Turin Papyrus all share the same fate. On the one hand, they delight us with their information of "historical Egypt"; on the other, they repulse us with their references to the First Time. All three of these major sources make the mistake of violating our modern standards, by their harkening to a mystical period, the *Tep Zepi*, when extraordinary rulers graced the Nile Valley. For example, Eusebius cites Manetho as his source for a predynastic chronology of rulers that spans 24,925 years of lost antiquity.[78]

Interesting it is that, when Manetho supplies thirty dynasties of what can be comfortably accepted as Egypt's "historical period," Egyptologists eagerly lap it up. Archaeology has aided their digestive process, by confirming what Manetho recorded.[79] Yet, when the same Manetho confidently plunges into "prehistory," and provides us with glimpses of a lost golden age, we abruptly jettison him. And, since archaeology has not uncovered corroboration for the strange predynastic chronology, we rest assured that our biases are intact.

THE COSMIC PURANAS

Throughout history, many societies have acknowledged consciousness as something more potent than we have in the West—

as a sieve or receiver and transmitter of communication with forces, not always visible, other than ourselves. The contemporary Western tenet that we are alone in the universe, conversant only with ourselves, is, in fact, a minority perspective, an anomaly. (Dr. John Mack, Harvard University Professor of Psychiatry, from his book *Abduction: Human Encounters with Aliens*)

The debate whether life, and intelligent life, exists elsewhere in the universe may well be an almost uniquely Western neurosis. What's more, the perplexity may turn out to be a complete embarrassment for the West. Later in the twenty-first century, human beings may scratch their heads in disbelief, wondering aloud: How could our predecessors dare entertain the folly that only their planet supported life?

The Puranas, besides contradicting current assumptions about human civilization on Earth, threaten the prevailing geocentric biases against extraterrestrial intelligent life. Furthermore, the Puranas, if taken seriously, challenge the utility of our human senses as well as our technological sensory devices. According to the Vedic information in the Puranas, many planets and realms in the universe are invisible, and many entities in the cosmos cannot be detected by our bodies or our gadgets. Puranic knowledge delights in subtle astral phenomena and then leaves the material cosmos entirely, to bring us the spiritual world, beyond the laws of time and space.

Though moderns can seem to make a fetish out of chronology, Vedic knowledge does not consider chronological order a prerequisite for imparting profound knowledge of the Earth and beyond. This failure to worship at the altar of chronology does work to diminish the prestige of the Puranas—in the eyes of today's established brains. The most prolific Vedic exponent in contemporary times, A. C. Bhaktivedanta Swami Prabhupada, defends Puranic knowledge in this way:

The Puranas, or old histories, are sometimes neglected by unintelligent men who consider their descriptions mythological. Actually, the descriptions of the Puranas, or the old histories of the universe, are factual, although not chronological. The Puranas record the chief incidents that have occurred over many millions of years, not only on this planet but also on other planets within the universe. Therefore all learned and realized Vedic scholars speak with references to the incidents in the Puranas.[80]

Incidents mentioned in the Vedic literatures, such as the Puranas, *Mahabharata* and *Ramayana* are factual historical narrations that took place sometime in the past, although not in any chronological order. . . . Besides that, they happen on different planets, nay, in different universes. . . . We are simply concerned with the instructive lessons of such incidents, even though they are not in order by our limited range of understanding.[81]

Comprehending the Vedic universe is a humbling experience for humans. The Puranas introduce us to a world that in many ways modern science is in no position yet to affirm or deny. When read through the prism of what we consider human, the literature is guilty of hawking to us a cosmos that is predominantly non-human. Since the Puranic reality is often non-terrestrial, it has trouble fitting inside the narrow confines of our scientific framework. Vedic preceptors ask that we not label as myth or magic that which simply is beyond our conceptions and abilities.

We learn that enfolded within the universe are different levels of power and expertise. What is mystical or unbelievable to one species of creatures is routine or humdrum to another. In other words, different regions of the cosmos allow varying degrees of access to the potencies of the cosmos. According to your body (senses), you inhabit a particular realm, with its concomitant abilities and limitations. Therefore, both body and environs restrict the living being—existence is relative to these parameters.

What we call the planet Earth turns out to be a tiny slice of all the action in and around earthlings. The Puranas say that other, generally unseen, dimensions of habitation exist within the Earth, on its surface, and in the space surrounding it. Thus humanoid and other types of "alien beings" are found in parallel realms both nearby and on distant planets. It is not so much that physical distance makes them inaccessible to us; it is more that their particular cosmic niche, their dimension, renders them invisible to our senses.

The Puranas reveal that Vedic Indians had an immense appetite for cosmic knowledge. We may wonder how the cosmic zest apparent in Vedic times compares to the enthusiasm the general public feels, at the moment, for cosmic exploration. The executive head of NASA, Dan Goldin, has defined the prime mission of America's space agency: searching the universe for life and other solar systems. This, he felt, is what the American people want from NASA. At the 1996 annual meeting of the American Astronomical Society, Goldin flew in to fire up the astronomers and astrophysicists for a new millennium of research. Unfurling bold plans to image other solar systems by way of giant inferometers based in space, Goldin implored his troops to devise methods to photograph clouds and mountain ranges on planets resembling Earth but belonging to other solar systems. This, he believed, is what the taxpayers will pay for.[82]

As the twenty-first century opens, most mainstream scientists persist in contemplating life on other planets according to current human conceptions of biochemistry. For example, a prominent planetary scientist at the University of Colorado, Bruce M. Jakosky, assures us that most of his scientific associates now expect extraterrestrial life to be quite common. The theoretical bedrock beneath this apparently radical breakthrough? "There have been key discoveries that suggest life is simple, straightforward and easy—if you have the right conditions."[83]

A chief scientist at NASA pondered the latest knowledge of extremophiles—earthly life forms in extreme environments. His conclusion was to reduce the remaining barriers against life on other planets to just one: no liquid water. "Wherever liquid water and chemical energy are found, there is life—there is no exception," proclaimed Wessly Huntress Jr., the Associate Administrator of Science.[84]

Approximately every two years the orbits of Earth and Mars offer a suitable "window" for spacecraft to leave Earth for Mars. After the launch of the *Pathfinder* and *Mars Global Surveyor* in late 1996, two years later NASA dispatched two new spacecraft, the *Mars Climate Orbiter* and *Mars Polar Lander*. NASA has declared that for the first decade of the twenty-first century, it intends to continue launching pairs of spacecraft to Mars every two years. The last two for the old century shared a specific task: searching for traces of water on Mars. Another NASA science chief, Ed Weiler, assured, "If you want to look for life, either fossilized or even extant life on another planet, you have to follow the water."[85]

For launching in 2003, NASA, in conjunction with Stanford University, is preparing a mission to Europa, the moon of Jupiter. Once again the quest is water. Stanford scientists announced that, if their hunch about a liquid ocean on Europa proves correct, "then the Jovian moon will become one of the hottest spots in the solar system to look for alien life."[86]

From the Vedic viewpoint, such hypotheses are foolhardy. They are human-centric lenses that prevent us from experiencing the full majesty of the cosmos. The Puranas describe a universe comprising natural substances and processes far more subtle than what humans encounter. More is happening in the universe than the liquid water and biochemical reactions that earthlings know.

Similar ludicrousness, according to the ancient vision, is our scientists' scanning the cosmos for signals beamed by alien civilizations. Harvard University has a 250-million-channel receiver listening for radio signals from space. Dare we concede that our most advanced technology may lag eons behind other civilizations in the universe? We may have to accept the futility of searching for extraterrestrial civilizations with primitive human gadgets. Puranic knowledge describes humanoid prowess that easily eclipses the brains of our top scientists. Human beings as we know them are classified as comparatively weak in power.

Furthermore, why automatically posit that "the aliens" are from distant star systems? Puranic information describes that nonhuman intelligent life forms have been near or on our planet for countless millennia—outside the reach of our senses and instruments. Therefore, the Vedic process for acquiring knowledge is based on hearing. That which you cannot see or detect, you can hear about, from advanced sources.

The Puranas, particularly the *Bhagavata Purana*, or *Shrimad-Bhagavatam*, inform the reader that a plethora of planetary systems or realms exist in countless universes, and that the total number of these material universes is just a small fraction of the energy of Godhead. Beyond the clutches of time and space is the spiritual realm, where matter and its interactions have no access.

Within the material cosmos, organisms possess bodies adapted to their specific environment. Birth in a particular realm or dimension of the universe is arranged according to karma from the past life. Each cosmic niche is graded. Therefore, based on the relative superiority or inferiority of the niche, the inhabitants are endowed with corresponding expertise in the gross and subtle manipulation of matter.

A concomitant principle is that bodies designed for Earth cannot ordinarily exist in the atmospheres of other planets or dimensions. Just as when traveling from the tropics to the polar caps, we must change our dress, similarly a transformation of the body is necessary for the living entity to enter other cosmic environs. For example, entrance into some cosmic habitats requires that you leave behind your gross physical frame. Living entities in these realms exist in only their subtle coverings: mind, intelligence, and ego.

Modern humans think of space travel always in mechanical terms. This stumbling block seems to impede their entrance into Puranic knowledge. A typical conundrum we cannot resolve is how entities from distant stars might visit Earth. With our crude, earthling brains we calculate, if the ET's home is a star system, say, a mere 1,000 light years away, that means the creature needs at least 1,000 years to get to Earth. Then, the entity's return voyage requires another 1,000 years. In disbelief we wonder, what kind of species could ever live that long? The creature's communication with home, from Earth, would also require 1,000 years for both the message sent and its reply. Any kind of electromagnetic signal such as radio or television travels at the speed of light. Hence, our verdict: mission impossible!

The Vedic civilization revealed in the Puranas and the *Mahabharata* revels in interplanetary contact and visitations. Space communication and travel was considered a natural part of human culture—at that time. It appears that, just as modern culture strives to honor the libido and unfetter it, Vedic culture recognized the natural desire for cosmic travel and sought to facilitate it. Interplanetary or multidimensional travel was considered an appropriate desire. Certainly the Puranic knowledge, filled with exciting accounts of other globes and realms, stimulated that urge. And the literature makes it obvious that the temptation was not meant to be resisted.

Nevertheless, Puranic accounts show us that no one ever thought to force their way into another realm or planet by way of mechanical contrivance. A cute example demonstrating the folly of interplanetary mechanical intrusion came from NASA scientists working on the Mars Pathfinder project. As their little six-wheeled, remote-controlled rover analyzed the soil on the Red

Planet, the Pathfinder team at mission control allowed themselves a little humor. Mars would make a great playground for children, they announced. Because Mars's gravity is a third of Earth's, our tots could hurdle three-foot rocks with ease. What's more, they could kick up the Martian sand and create mini-duststorms around their legs. All the kids would need is a full suit of protective clothing and an oxygen mask. Without these, sunbathing in the afternoon highs of 4 degrees Fahrenheit would not be recommended.

Our reliance on space vehicles and protective equipment, if at all successful, makes for quick, artificial trips at best—to only the nearby destinations our gross senses can perceive. How to reach the far reaches of the cosmos? And if some ETs hail from distant stellar regions, how do they get to our cosmic neighborhood? In the mind of scientists, the main logistical barrier to interstellar travel is the uselessness of gravitational propulsion.

Any rocket propels itself by burning a fuel in its reaction chamber and then ejecting the exhaust out of a nozzle. As soon as you attempt to apply earthling rocket science to interstellar travel, the Einstein barrier stops you cold. The exhaust speed generated by the fuel is limited to 186,232 miles per second, or the speed of light in a vacuum. Even if a rocket could approach that speed, to reach its distant destination, it would have to store a ridiculously absurd amount of fuel. That is to say, for star travelling, any spacecraft would need to generate for itself more energy than what all the humans on Earth produce every year. The manufacturing bill would surpass the GNPs of the USA, Europe, and Japan—several times over. Hence, mainstream scientists feel secure that interstellar travelling is a physical and economic impossibility. Therefore, they reason, aliens from far-off worlds could never visit us. It is believed that Einstein's hallowed barrier would keep them effectively fenced into their own neck of the woods.

The hope is that exotic fuels or some special astral energy

source would allow sustained travel near the speed of light. For completely breaking out of Einstein's cage, however, "traversable wormholes"—special conduits through space and time—are an attractive speculation. Two scientists from California Tech, Kip Thorne and Michael Morris, along with Igor Nivikov of Moscow State University, have published papers in the distinguished journal *Physical Review* on the physics of time travel and traversable wormholes.[87] Shortcut tunnels through both time and space, these traversable wormholes would serve as time-travel gates. Constructed by advanced ETs capable of astral engineering, the wormholes would allow starships to enter in one locale of space-time and then emerge in another, far-off galactic region of space-time.

Upon turning to the Vedas, we find that Vedic cosmic traveling has little to do with either the most advanced speculations of our scientists or the best technology attributed to the mysterious UFOs. For Vedic cosmic travel, its ancient practitioners knew they had three choices:

- Accumulate a sufficient quantity of good karma and please the *devas,* so that for the next life the qualified could transfer themselves to higher (more luxurious) regions of the universe. Just as the living entity transmigrates from body to body, so it can also relocate from one planet to another.

- Practice mystic yoga so that, at the time of death, an accomplished yogi can transfer to celestial realms of the cosmos. Or, the most advanced yogis could even commute back and forth during the same lifetime, in the present body. Just as humans can tour the continents of their globe, similarly, with the proper method, an expert can tour the planets and realms of the universe. Doing so is simply a question of technique.

- Be a member of a civilization on Earth so advanced that higher entities—*devas* and sages from other realms—are attracted to visit and make themselves visible. By the grace of these empowered visitors, some abnormally qualified humans would receive the ability for interstellar communing, much as modern students can qualify for a university exchange program and visit foreign countries.

For any of the above three methods, preparation is the key. We can enter any planet provided that we ready ourselves, through qualification. Civilizations described in the Puranas excelled in all three methods. In the present debilitated age known as Kali-yuga, however, all non-mechanical space travel has stopped. The expected destination for most denizens of this blighted age, after animalistic life as humans, is an actual animal body in the next birth.

That aspects of reality that humans are ignorant of exist is nothing new. Radio waves, infrared radiation, UV radiation, gamma rays, and X-rays did not suddenly pop into the cosmos upon human discovery. These cosmic attributes were always around, "on the loose," until our gadgets advanced enough to register them. Similarly, in the immense cosmos, other "spectra of reality" lay in the wait.[88] The Puranas explain that the so-called aliens thrive in these unknown spectra—cosmic niches with properties inconceivable to humans. Therefore, extraterrestrial life styles, including their travel and communication, are so dissimilar to what humans expect.

How does the Vedic literature describe travel to other worlds, star systems, or parallel dimensions? Dr. Richard Thompson, in comparing modern UFO and alien encounters to the Vedic accounts, gives good guidance:

> The Vedic literature does not use geometric terms such as "higher dimensions" or "other planes" when referring to this kind of travel. Rather, the travel to other worlds is described functionally in terms of the experiences of the travelers, and it is necessary for the modern reader to deduce from the accounts that this travel

involves more than motion through three-dimensional space. Since people of modern society are accustomed to thinking that travel is necessarily three-dimensional, I will use the term "higher dimensional" to refer to Vedic accounts that cannot be understood in three-dimensional terms.[89]

As the alien issue continues to swell, and as conventional knowledge sources admit their bafflement, the treasure chest of the *Shrimad-Bhagavatam* and other Puranas will become an increasingly attractive option. Even formerly jaded scholars will have sufficient motivation to take another look—humbly and open-mindedly.

No doubt, some mainstream brains will never change their stripes. Yet, we should beseech them to at least consider partially modifying their overall judgment. For so long they have told us that the Puranas—whether describing Earth or alien dimensions—are legend, laced with a few unimportant facts. Soon these same scholars should find it easier to concede that the Vedic seers deserve perhaps a dash of credit for their acknowledging extraterrestrials, unknown ages ago.

Meanwhile, the world is not standing still, in wait. Bold seekers will immediately find that especially the *Shrimad-Bhagavatam* offers an abundance of cosmic and extracosmic insights. Through the *Shrimad-Bhagavatam*, our curiosity about other spectra of reality and their inhabitants will lead deep into the heart of the Vedic mystery.

WHY ARE THEY HERE?
(WHY ARE WE HERE?)

While most mainstream scientists scour other planets for revolutionary signs of water and primitive microorganisms, nonestablishment scholars wrestle with the alien-motive issue. These independent thinkers have already concluded that intelligent humanoids regularly visit Earth. Consequently, for the true believers in extraterrestrial visitations, the riddle is not whether cells exist on other planets. After all, countless earthlings claim to have encountered powerful extraterrestrials. Hence the burning questions of the day: What are their motives? Why are these strangers here? Are they malefic invaders or benign space brothers?

Western ET and UFO researchers can draw upon only their collection of anecdotal evidence and ominous leaks from government sources. They have no complete picture of the cosmos. That means they utterly lack a framework upon which they can hang their assorted random clues. Without an adequate cosmic schema, of course, neither synthesis nor analysis is possible. One consequence of this crippling deficiency is the debate over the nature and motives of extraterrestrial visitors. The issue has become the hottest feud in alternative knowledge.

A serious name in the intellectual fracas, Dr. David Jacobs, a history professor at Temple University in Philadelphia, is convinced by his research that the human species is doomed—the hostile invasion has been under way, while we slept on the lap of ignorance.

> The aliens have fooled us. . . . They lulled us into an attitude of disbelief, and hence complacency, at the very beginning of our awareness of their presence. Thus, we were unable to understand the dimensions of the threat they pose and act to intervene. Now it may be too late. . . . Now I fear for the future of my own children.[90]

The most influential name in abduction research, Budd Hopkins, shares the dark-invader viewpoint. Based on extensive, meticulous interviews with abductees, he has delineated a fourfold alien program: abduction of human specimens; breeding of alien-human hybrids; refining the hybrids to become more humanlike while retaining essential alien attributes; and integration of the hybrids and aliens into human society, to take it over.

On the other side of the fence are "the Positives." They feel that the visitors are clearly wellwishers, who have come to aid our physical and spiritual progress. Stand-out names in this group are Dr. Stephen Greer, director of the Center for the Study of Extraterrestrial Intelligence, and psychologist Richard Boylan, author of *Close Extraterrestrial Encounters: Positive Experiences with Mysterious Visitors*. Positives generally hold that the visitors hail from a type of Galactic Confederation, and are buzzing about Earth to lend humanity a helping hand in a time of planetary trials and tribulation. Furthermore, most Positives feel that the terrifying reports of abduction derive from human paranoia and misunderstanding—not ET crimes. The out-of-towners are here only to assist ignorant earthlings through their crisis of transformation. We should allow them to usher us into a new age of cooperation with the cosmic version of the UN.

The agonizers, like David Jacobs, Budd Hopkins, and others, refuse to sign up for membership in the stellar confederation. They utterly reject the "no worries" interpretation:

> In a way, I wish I could be like the Positives, existing in a naive but happy dreamland, awaiting the coming of the Benevolent Ones who will engulf us all in love and protection . . . [but] I must go where the evidence leads me. I have come to view the alien abduction phenomenon as an asteroid hurtling toward the Earth—discovered too late for intervention. We can track its progress and yet be utterly incapable of preventing the collision.[91]

Are we at the beginning or are we at the end? Is our future doom and gloom, as cosmic slaves, or are we about to enter a golden era of cosmic fraternity? Or, are both the Positives and the

Negatives too extreme in their interpretation and stance? The *Shrimad-Bhagavatam*, or *Bhagavata Purana*, can put these polarities into proper perspective. The universe, as revealed in the Vedic texts, is alive with diversity. Not only are the realms and bodies different, but the motives and behavior are different too. On Earth both ill will and good will are possible, and so it is throughout the cosmos also. The Vedic seers exhort that knowledge is necessary, if we want to navigate the halls and corridors of the cosmos and beyond.

A "Who's Who in the Universe" guidebook would certainly help. Puranic information purports to be just that—and more. On the high end of the cosmic scale are the *devas* and celestial sages. They dwell in realms far more advanced in ability, pleasure, and knowledge. These higher-level residents of the universe do not directly intervene in puny human affairs on Earth, unless the caliber of the particular version of humanity is quite elevated. Therefore, currently, they remain completely aloof. Vedic preceptors hotly deny that any ordinary earthling today is communing with these top-grade controllers and intellects of the cosmos.

Powerful malefic elements also inhabit the universe. They are characterized by their inimical attitude toward any cosmic law and order that leads to spiritual development. Sensual absorption is their main diet, and for pursuing their self-centered agendas, they can determinedly procure subtle, mystic powers and gross technology. Such entities want nothing to do with the *devas* and celestial sages, and they would love to rid the universe of higher, theistic principles. Especially because the *devas* are aligned with the Supreme Controller of all material and spiritual worlds, the malefactors despise them. They violently oppose the direct and indirect efforts by the *devas* to distribute spiritual knowledge throughout the universe.

In Sanskrit these malefic beings are known as *asuras*, demonic fellows. As the *devas* have their heavenly worlds, the *asuras* have their own realms and dimensions—toxic territories of the cosmos, where no spiritual qualities exist. Based from these rancorous and malicious environs, they sometimes seek to interfere in Earth's affairs and alienate humans from higher consciousness. Capable of bedazzling earthlings with demonstrations of their material prowess, these extraterrestrial racketeers and their minions often flaunt astonishing subtle powers, advanced gross technology, and impressive knowledge of the universe. They are even capable of propagating clever bogus "cosmic philosophies," to distract humans from seeking the Ultimate, beyond the material world.

The *devas* and *asuras* are the major players in the cosmos. In between them range a broad gamut of lesser powerful entities. These are usually neutral—that is, they have no interplanetary agendas, whether benign or malefic. They all differ greatly in physical appearance and culture. With the notable exception of Earth's current batch of humans, generally entities in the middling category are aware of one another, and they live cooperatively. Many of these middle-of-the-roaders are said to live in dimensions in and around Earth.

Human beings are classified as the least powerful of this large group, and the most susceptible to outside influence—positive or negative. The Vedic literatures—especially the *Mahabharata*, *Ramayana*, and *Shrimad-Bhagavatam*—relay that, in the remote past, humanoid races visibly frequented Earth. More than just visiting, they would also move in as inhabitants, and even control whole continents.

STAR WARS

Because of the developments of science, all countries on Earth will have to unite to survive and to make a common front against attack by people from other planets. The politics of the future will be cosmic, or interplanetary. (General Douglas MacArthur)[92]

Just a stray musing from a man at the pinnacle of twentieth-century military history? Consider that seven years after this bold statement appeared in the *New York Times*, General MacArthur reiterated his point, in a speech to officers graduating from the United States Military Academy: "You now face a new world, a world of change. We speak in strange terms . . . of ultimate conflict between a united human race and the sinister forces of some other planetary galaxy."[93]

According to the Vedic histories, periodic clashes for dominance can indeed rock huge areas of the universe. The *Bhagavad-gita* explains the sociological and political background of the main adversaries in these intergalactic showdowns: "In the material world," states Bhagavan Krishna, "there are two categories of entities—divine and demoniac."[94] Lesser entities generally fall under the sway of the more powerful. Therefore, the middling peoples of the cosmos, especially earthlings, falls into either category according to which influence prevails over their societies. Sometimes the balance of power in regions of the cosmos veers too much in favor of the demoniac materialists. If the *devas* complain that *asuras* and their influence have gone too far, then, from outside the material realm, Krishna may descend into the cosmos, as an *avatara:*

> Although I am unborn and My transcendental body never deteriorates, and although I am the Lord of all living entities, I still appear in every millennium [Vedic epoch] in My original transcendental form.

> Whenever and wherever in the cosmic system there is a decline in religious practice and a predominant rise of irreligion—at that time I descend Myself. (*Bhagavad-gita* 4.6, 7)

Earth is a frequent hotspot in the universe. The humans are

susceptible to the wiles of demoniac forces; also, pitched battles in other realms can spill over onto the Earthly plane. The *Maha-bharata* describes how malicious, gruesome-looking entities interfered in Earth affairs. They handpicked a future prince at birth to carry out their global mandate for materialism. The designated human, Duryodhana, almost spoiled the plan, however, when, owing to an extreme humiliation, he decided to fast until death. Immediately the *asuras* performed an occult ritual to summon the prince to their realm—a parallel dimension accessible from Earth by appropriate mystic techniques. Using occult mantras, the *asuras* dispatched a sorceress to apprehend the prince and transport him, via subtle-energy conduits, to where they waited.

Once he was in their midst, they revealed to him that they had arranged his birth on Earth specifically to accomplish their purposes. Through their technology, somewhat akin to genetic manipulations, these interdimensional mobsters had tinkered with his body to make it abnormally strong and almost invulnerable to all weapons. Hence, he should not upset the plans for their version of a new world order, by ending his life. They also assured him that fellow *asuras* had taken birth on Earth, as military heroes, to assist him in the campaign. Moreover, the *asuras* would deploy mind control to recruit humans who were normally virtuous, so that they would serve the demoniac cause.

> Other *asuras* will take possession of Bhishma, Drona, Kripa, and the others; and possessed by them they will fight your enemies ruthlessly. When they engage in battle . . . they will give no quarter to either sons or brothers, parents or relatives, students or kinsmen, the young or the old. Pitiless, possessed [by *asuras*] . . . they will battle their relations and cast all love far off. Gleefully, their minds darkened, the tiger-like men, befuddled with ignorance . . . will say to one another, "You shall not escape from me with your life. . . . They will boastfully perpetrate a holocaust."[95]

Ending the pep talk, the *asuras* used the same sorceress to convey Prince Duryodhana back to the site of his now thwarted attempt to starve himself to death. The witch deposited him there, saluted him, and, after Duryodhana officially dismissed her, she vanished. Later, Duryodhana thought the whole event to have been only a dream. Yet, in his consciousness lingered the ominous thought, "I shall wage world war against the Pandus [his own cousins, who were paragons of virtue]."

Though this account has all the makings of a contemporary alien-abduction claim, the timeframe, according to the *Mahabharata*, is approximately 5,000 years ago. Not all the events in the *Mahabharata*, though, purport to have a chronology that is readily identifiable. For instance, the texts relay an account of an interstellar war between the *devas* and *asuras* that resulted in terrorism on Earth. Upon losing to the *devas*, a demoniac space race, the Kaleya Danavas, sought revenge by coming to Earth and wreaking havoc. First they established a clandestine base of operations beneath the ocean. Then, emerging at night from their undersea headquarters, they launched ghastly attacks upon sages and ascetics. Their diabolic goal was to panic human society by cruelly killing its fount of enlivenment, the spiritual guides.

> In the hermitage of Vasistha the miscreant band devoured a hundred and eighty-eight *brahmanas* and nine other ascetics. They went to the holy hermitage of Chyavana . . . and ate one hundred of the hermits, who lived on fruits and roots. This they did in the nighttime; by day they vanished into the ocean. At the hermitage of Bharadvaja they destroyed twenty restrained celibates who lived on wind and water.

> The people did not know about the Daityas. . . . In the morning they would find the hermits, who were lean from their fasts, lying on the ground in lifeless bodies. The land was filled with

unfleshed, bloodless, marrowless, disemboweled, and disjointed corpses like piles of conchshells.[96]

Shrewd researchers, such as Richard Thompson, have noted the similarity with modern UFO accounts. Often the UFOs are reported as having emerged from oceans and lakes. Frequently, the morning after nocturnal UFO incidents, dead farm animals are found, mutilated and drained of blood.

The main theme of the *Mahabharata* concerns an organized attempt by major cosmic demons to invade the Earth. Unlike the scattershot, hit-and-run terrorism by smalltime hoods like the Kaleya Danavas, the grand scheme aimed for a wholesale take-over of Earth. Instead of a D-Day type invasion by alien armies, the preeminent *asuras* schemed to have a huge contingent of their agents take birth in royal families on Earth. Upon infiltrating the governing dynasties, control of the people would be a step away.

Womb warfare was a common technique employed by the *devas* as well. Once the *devas* discovered that the *asuras* were over-loading Earth with their operatives, the *devas* matched them by sending their own special forces into the wombs of earthlings. Eventually, of course, all the implanted *devas* and *asuras* matured into humanlike adults. Hence, the prenatal build-up on both sides directly resulted in a massive clash on Earth, the Battle of Kurukshetra. Bhagavan Krishna spoke the *Bhagavad-gita* (Song of the Supreme) at the start of this eighteen-day war.

PAN-COSMIC FRATERNITY

The Purana par excellence, the *Shrimad-Bhagavatam*, in twelve cantos, contains even more extraterrestrial activity than the *Mahabharata*. The *devas* are there, and the *asuras* are there, but the main focus is *Bhagavan*, the Supreme Transcendence. Krishna, the source of the material and spiritual worlds and their inhabitants, makes Himself extensively known through this fascinating encyclopedic text.

A popular spiritual maxim in India is, "Before you are liberated from material existence, read *Shrimad-Bhagavatam;* after you attain spiritual liberation, go on reading *Shrimad-Bhagavatam.*" Known as the cream of all Vedic literature, the *Bhagavatam* quite nonchalantly presents a Vedic civilization on Earth that was in regular contact with non-earthly denizens. At that time all the protocols and etiquette for interplanetary fraternization were well established. For example, the literature relays that during the reign of King Yudhishthira, celestial sages and *devas* from higher realms in the cosmos would frequent his royal court. Furthermore, in that epoch of Earth's history, the most highly qualified members of human society could visit other planetary systems, without having to change their form. The renowned *Bhagavatam* expert A. C. Bhaktivedanta Swami Prabhupada explains in his commentary: "It is only the spiritual culture that makes interplanetary travel possible, even in the present body."[97]

Yudhishthira, as world emperor, is attributed with all the opulence and natural resources of the globe at his beck and call. Only a monarch of the world-class caliber could marshal the massive, costly materials needed for staging premier sacrificial ceremonies. These gala cosmic events attracted even the prime *deva* controllers to attend. According to the Vedas, such ritualistic performances are now impossible. The *Shrimad-Bhagavatam* predicts that in the present age of debasement, Kali-yuga, the unspiritual leaders will lack the required governmental wisdom and integrity; the people will be flaccid in body and mind; and therefore nature will restrict the supply of natural opulences. What were profusely available in other ages would become rare commodities in the Age of Quarrel.

The Vedic histories reveal that Yudhishthira and his brothers were actually seeded by *devas*, in the wombs of human mothers. This interbreeding was purposely arranged to staff the Earth's rulership with magnificent personalities. The literature portrays a Yudhishthira so powerful and pure-hearted that he could personally contact the Supreme Absolute Truth and present a humble entreaty:

> My dear Lord Krishna, the sacrifice known as the Rajasuya-yajna is to be performed by the emperor, and it is considered to be the king of all sacrifices. . . . I want to perform this Rajasuya sacrifice and invite the demigods to show them that they have no power independent of You. . . . Foolish persons with a poor fund of knowledge consider Your Lordship an ordinary human being. . . . [Therefore] I wish to invite all the demigods, beginning from Lord Brahma, Lord Shiva and other exalted chiefs of the heavenly planets, and in that great assembly of the demigods from all parts of the universe, I want to substantiate that You are the Supreme Personality of Godhead and that everyone is Your servant.[98]

Apparently, the Vedic texts are informing us that controversy about the identity of Krishna is nothing new. Are we to accept that arguments about Krishna existed 5,000 years ago as indeed they do today? The *Shrimad-Bhagavatam* proposes to equip its sympathizers with a window on the spiritual disputes of the time—if, of course, we opt to entertain the Vedic version of ancient history.

To Emperor Yudhishthira's brother, Bhagavan Krishna pinpointed the salient misperceptions about the appearance of the Supreme within the material cosmos. Here are Krishna's own objections, as put forth to Arjuna in the *Bhagavad-gita*:

> The ignorant think I am a human being. They fail to comprehend My transcendental existence. They are unaware that I conduct the creation, maintenance, and annihilation of all the universes. (9.11)

Speculators are convinced that the Ultimate Truth is formless. Not knowing Me perfectly, they think that originally I am impersonal and then—coming to this world—a personality was assumed. Mistaking My body to be made of matter, the unintelligent cannot understand nonmaterial individuality, qualities, and form. Why don't they perceive My exalted personal existence—imperishable and supreme? (7.24)

Deluded by the three modes of material nature (goodness, passion, and ignorance), both earthly and extraterrestrial beings cannot perceive Me, because I am above the modes and inexhaustible [though all energy emanates from Me, I remain complete]. (7.13)

Arjuna, indeed I am the Supreme Personality of Godhead (your confines of time are no obstacle for My knowledge). I know everything, past, present, and future. I know all living entities, but no one knows Me. (7.26)

Emperor Yudhishthira, aware of these most crucial issues of identification, devised a solution—suitable for his times, but impractical for ours. Since interplanetary exchanges were a social norm back then, he thought, why not orchestrate an event that would draw all the important personalities of the universe? If, in their elite presence, the uniqueness of the Supreme Truth could be established, the lesson would endure for all ages, for all planets. Out of pure love for the All-attractive Supreme Person, the Emperor was keen to ratify that Krishna is beyond the laws of material nature. "I want to establish this fact, and I also want to show the world the difference between accepting You as the Supreme Personality of Godhead and accepting You as an ordinary powerful historical person."[99]

Rare was the ruler, terrestrial or celestial, who could muster all the natural wealth and manpower required to carry out the king of sacrifices, the Rajasuya-yajna. Therefore, upon the news that King Yudhishthira had successfully gathered the necessary resources, denizens from all dimensions and planets arrived to witness the rite. Besides the local royalty and sages from Earth, along with *devas* and Vedic scholars from the heavens, the guest list included even Brahma and Shiva.

The cosmic pageantry was overwhelming. During the sacrificial performance, the host, King Yudhishthira, was able to vividly demonstrate the paramount position of Bhagavan Krishna. Satisfied, the interstellar guests departed, back to their various realms. The *Shrimad-Bhagavatam* records: "The demigods, humans, and residents of intermediate heavens, all properly honored by the King, happily set off for their respective domains while singing the praises of Lord Krishna and the great sacrifice."[100]

THE INTERSTELLAR ASSEMBLY

Vedic tradition has no doubts that the empowered sage Vyasa composed the *Shrimad-Bhagavatam* and then transmitted its kernel to his son, the wandering transcendental professor, Shukadeva Gosvami. This spiritually brilliant son of Vyasa then delivered the entire *Bhagavatam* to King Parikshit, approximately 5,000 years ago.

The *Bhagavatam* is celebrated throughout India for its intra-cosmic and extra-cosmic scope. In the world outside of modern India, the numbers of *Bhagavatam* enthusiasts are rapidly increasing, especially owing to the efforts of the International Society for Krishna Consciousness. Newcomers to the *Bhagavatam* should note that the recital by Shukadeva Gosvami to the King, though held on the bank of the Ganges, was an interstellar, cosmic event.

King Parikshit is the grandson of Yudhishthira, the first king, we may recall, mentioned on the palm-leaf records of Jagannath.

Parikshit inherited from Yudhishthira what the Vedic viewpoint considers to have been a global empire. Though an extraordinarily saintly philosopher-king, Parikshit was inappropriately cursed by an uncouth son of a brahmin. Upon hearing that he would die in seven days, the saintly emperor immediately seized the opportunity to prepare for enlightenment. He abruptly relinquished both his global responsibilities and his family duties. Retiring to the banks of the Ganges, said to have flowed by his palace near what is present-day New Delhi, King Parikshit decided to fast until death.

The unqualified son of a brahmin had wrongly misused the mystic power of his family's occupation to condemn the King to death, just for a slight misunderstanding. Parikshit, however, a rare noble soul, humbly adjudged that the foolish boy's fatal prank was entirely his fault. Blaming himself, he welcomed the sudden calamity as an opportunity to leave material existence. Here is part of the account, from the *Shrimad-Bhagavatam*, first canto, Chapter 19:

4. While lamenting his role in the petty quarrel, the King received news of his imminent death. The son of the sage had cursed him to die by the bite of a snakebird. Accepting this death knell as good tidings, he used the sudden disaster to set into motion his detachment from worldly affairs.

5. King Parikshit sat down resolutely on the bank of the Ganges River. There he concentrated his mind in Krishna consciousness. He rejected all other practices of self-realization, because transcendental loving service to Krishna is the greatest achievement—superseding all other methods.

Though an emperor with sovereignty far beyond what current historians will accept, Parikshit immediately took up the life of an ascetic. Vedic commentators point out that actually the King had the personal potency to ward off the boy's mystic attack, but he refused to exercise this immunity. He was aware of a higher purpose for the tragic caper, and readily agreed to participate in this greater plan.

> 8–10. As the news of Parikshit's decision spread throughout the universe, all the greatest spiritual intellectuals and their students began to travel to Earth. The celestial sages offered the plea that they were departing on a pilgrimage to the Earth planet, for bathing in the holy Ganges River. All of them, however, were advanced enough to purify any holy place just by their presence. From different areas and dimensions of the cosmos, they transported themselves to the bank of the Ganges, just to witness the monumental event.

The text records that *devas* from the higher planets also arrived. Also, assorted saintly kings, advanced brahmins, and heads of dynasties famous for knowledge came. Imploring the good will of such an illustrious earthly and non-earthly assembly, the Emperor bowed his head to the ground. Honoring them all, he sought their blessings for his journey out of the material cosmos. Waiting until the guests had seated themselves comfortably, the King humbly presented himself to them. Standing reverently with folded hands, he informed them of his decision to fast until death.

> 13. Emperor Parikshit said: "Most grateful are we kings who have been trained to seek favors from the great saints. Normally you sages deem royalty as refuse—fit for being rejected and discarded in a distant place."

Not assuming any honor for himself, Pariksit gave all credit to his family upbringing. He attributed the extraordinary convocation gathered around him to the careful training he had received since childhood. Moreover, he was sure that the transcendental celebrities had come because of the merit of his forefathers like Yudhishthira and Arjuna, who were all pure transcendentalists. As he rightly noted, saints and sages would generally never become too personally involved with the royalty. Though discharging their duty of imparting perfect advice to the administration, Vedic sages kept their distance from the kings and princes. Their intimate mixing with persons caught up in worldly affairs would be considered suicidal. King Pariksit, however, had been called to return to the spiritual world.

14. The King continued: "The Supreme Personality of Godhead, the controller of both the transcendental and mundane worlds, has graciously overtaken me in the form of a brahmin's curse. I was too attached to my family life. Therefore the Lord, just to save me, has appeared before me in this way. As a result, only out of fear, I will detach myself from the world."

15. "I say to you O brahmins, please accept me as a completely surrendered soul. Let the river Ganges, the representative of the Lord, also accept me in that way. Already I have taken the lotus feet of the Lord into my heart. Hence let the snakebird— or whatever magical thing the brahmin boy created—bite me at once. I only desire that you all continue singing the deeds of Lord Vishnu."

The *Bhagavatam* commentators tell us that material affairs are so entangling and complex that even a great soul like Parikshit had to be extricated by a special divine plan. Even Parikshit, though trained in spiritual cultivation since birth, found the allurements of family and society to be strong. What certainly appears to us as a disastrous turn of events, he saw as special mercy upon him. Because of his spiritual stature, the greatest minds in the universe flew in, to partake of his holy association. The King, however, saw in the visitors the presence of the Supreme—a transcendental favor bestowed upon him in his last moments. He was fearless and ready for his journey beyond time and space.

16. "Again, bowing unto all you brahmins, I pray that if I should again happen to take birth in the material world, I will have complete attachment to the unlimited Lord Krishna. I also pray that regardless of where my next destination is, I may have association with Lord Krishna's devotees and friendly relations with all living beings."

17–18. Exhibiting perfect self-control, the King sat on a seat of straw, situated on the southern bank of the Ganges River. The roots of the straw faced east, and the King himself faced north. Before leaving behind his home, he had handed over the administration of the empire to his son. As he sat, fasting until death, all the *devas* in the celestial planetary systems lauded his actions. From their higher realms they happily showered flowers upon the Earth and beat heavenly drums.

A. C. Bhaktivedanta Swami Prabhupada, in his commentary on Text 18, informs us, fittingly: "Even up to the time of Maharaja Parikshit there were interplanetary communications, and the news of Maharaja Parikshit's fasting unto death to attain salvation reached the higher planets in the sky where the intelligent demigods live."[101]

Amid the shower of flowers from the *devas'* heavenly dimensions, the spiritual scholars gathered around the King voiced their complete approval of his decision to leave the world of matter. Observing the King's absorption in Bhagavan Krishna, they offered bounteous blessings. Parikshit was successfully turning the curse of an unstable brahmin boy into an inestimable benediction.

20. The assembled sages said: "O chief of the saintly kings of
the Pandu dynasty, all who strictly follow the path laid out
by Lord Krishna! The helmets of many subordinate kings
decorate your throne, yet we are not astonished that you
renounced it to attain eternal association with the Personality
of Godhead."

Modern-day political leaders and corporate heads love to cling
to their positions as long as possible, often until the moment of
death. Though none of them have experienced even a fraction of
the grandeur, opulence, and power that King Parikshit wielded,
still they hang on, reveling in their momentary prestige while pa-
pering over massive social problems. Seen from the Vedic viewpoint, they are ruining their precious chance at human life. The
ancient sages would ask: Why squander every moment of life,
until the last breath? Why waste time fomenting political and economic schemes on a planet so insignificant and run-of-the-mill?

The Vedic histories say that Parikshit held sway over subordinate rulers throughout the Earth. Their kingdoms all pledged allegiance to him. Still, unblinded by the splendor of a global empire,
at the right time he walked away from it all to achieve eternal
association with Krishna. As King Yudhishthira had done, leaving
the administration of the world to Parikshit, so in turn Parikshit
did, leaving the globe to his son Janamejaya, the last of the Vedic
world-class emperors.

21. The sages concurred: "We shall all wait here until the foremost devotee of the Lord, King Parikshit, returns to the supreme planet. That paramount abode is completely free from
lamentation. No material contamination exists there."

The hallmark of Vedic civilization is the freedom to travel anywhere, both within the material world and out of it. The living

entity, part of the Supreme Soul, can choose to reside any-where—either in the spiritual sky or in the material cosmic mani-festation. Our existence in the material realm is attributed to a severe misuse of independence. Hence, we incur the limitations of time and space, which spoil our pursuit of continual happiness.

Perfect yogis know the art of departing from their material body and transferring to higher destinations. First they have to determine where they want to go. The *Shrimad-Bhagavatam* and other Vedic texts shatter our geocentrism by alerting us to the reality of countless universes—each with innumerable planets and dimensions. The yogis glean their information from these Vedic texts and then map out their life to achieve a specific abode. Rather than billion-dollar vehicles for quick jaunts into nearby space, the yogis depend on personal mystic power for a lengthy lifetime on distant planets.

The chronicle of King Parikshit departing this world tells Vedic sympathizers that interplanetary travel is nothing new. Since the lost, remote past, human beings have been going and coming, between Earth and other cosmic realms. Some have even left the cosmos of gross and subtle matter completely, to attain the origi-nal home of the spirit soul. That is where the *Bhagavatam* says King Parikshit is heading—not just to the spiritual world, but to the supreme planet in the spiritual world, the personal, intimate abode of Krishna. The exalted assembly of terrestrial and extrater-restrial visitors could foresee his destination; hence they urged him onward, as they awaited his momentous exit.

Contemporary Vedic preceptors judge that the carnal civiliza-tion of today has lost not only knowledge of the soul but also awareness of high-class material pleasure. In the qualitatively higher realms of the material cosmos, the living entity can live for hundreds and thousands of years—compared to Earth time. The Puranic descriptions of the standard of living in these more luxurious dimensions make the most enjoyable holiday spots on

Earth seem like Somalia or North Korea. Those humans who have qualified themselves through a life of either mystic yoga or meticulous karma can transfer themselves to these more materially advanced abodes.

For example, the planet called Siddhaloka is the home of beings perfect at subtle materialism. They are endowed with the natural abilities to control gravity, space, and time. Whereas Earth's scientists struggle with the velocities of air and light, the residents of Siddhaloka—just by virtue of their birth there—have automatically mastered the velocities of mind and intelligence. Entry into this choice locale requires the applicant to leave behind the gross material body. Residents of Siddhaloka have only the subtle covering of mind and intelligence.

King Parikshit, however, adopted the best itinerary. He converted the brahmin boy's ill deed into a ticket back to the spiritual sky, composed of pure spiritual consciousness instead of material elements. Masters of mystic powers cannot enter there. Even the finer, subtle body has to be relinquished. The entry price is complete detachment from even a tinge of gross and subtle materialism, coupled with absorption in transcendental loving service to Bhagavan Krishna. The successful devotee enters the spiritual world in his original, spiritual form—pure, nonmaterial individuality, with eternal activities and qualities.

22. All the words of the preeminent sages were sweet to the ear, pregnant with import, and profound in truth. King Parikshit—yearning to hear the activities of Krishna, the Personality of Godhead—congratulated the convocation of sages.

23–24. The Emperor said: "O great sages, mercifully you have all gathered here from all regions and dimensions of the universe. O trustworthy brahmins, I now inquire from you, what is my immediate duty? Please deliberate fully and then tell me what is the perfect duty for everyone, regardless of the circumstances. Moreover, specifically tell me the duty of persons about to die."

The King's two questions were actually one, because everyone in all cases is about to die—in either a few minutes or a few years. The exact moment we do not know. By divine arrangement, the King received accurate notice that death would strike him in seven days. (Generally, we do not know if we have even seven minutes.) The assembled spiritual scholars glorified King Parikshit for his shrewdly detecting the irrelevance of the relative duration of life. The King—piercing through the ignorance and denial that veils material existence—had deftly seized upon the essential issue: how to die to attain the highest good.

Actually the King already knew the answer to the questions he posed. Bhagavan Krishna had explained the answer when speaking the *Gita* to Arjuna, King Parikshit's ancestor:

> After attaining Me, the great souls, who are yogis in devotion, never return to this temporary world, which is full of miseries, because they have attained the highest perfection.
>
> From the highest planet in the material world down to the lowest, all are places of misery wherein repeated birth and death take place. But one who attains to My abode, O son of Kunti (Arjuna), never takes birth again. (*Bhagavad-gita* 8.15–16)

As the descendant of such extraordinary souls as Yudhishthira and Arjuna, King Parikshit certainly knew to aim outside of the material cosmos, to the supreme spiritual planet. Yet, he wanted to hear the assembled sages resound with a unanimous verdict. After all, the Vedic texts are often said to present many processes of elevation. Therefore the King—a perfect transcendentalist in his own right—was actually arranging that the sages clear any doubts about the Vedas, for all posterity.

Indeed, there was some indecision among the sages themselves. Though Vedic knowledge is forthright about its ultimate conclusion of surrender to the Supreme, it contains many subordinate pre-scriptions for persons under different modes of material nature. Just as doctors may differ in their remedies, so even Vedic sages may differ—until the senior physician, the preceptor, arrives.

Into the scene of the discussion walked the greatest yogi, Shukadeva Gosvami. Though only sixteen years old, he had more transcendental experience than even the elderly sages gathered there, from Earth or abroad. Through the art of physiognomy, the erudite audience could detect his rare level of attainment, although Shukadeva Gosvami tried to hide his advancement. The spiritual scholars, glancing over his beautiful physical features, quickly as-certained his special stature and honored him by rising from their seats. King Parikshit bowed his body low in utter respect, and the entire assembly offered Shukadeva Gosvami the presiding seat.

> 30. Surrounded by saints, sages, and *devas*, Shukadeva Gosvami appeared like the resplendent moon amidst the stars, planets, and other celestial orbs. Radiating an aura of munificence, he was revered by all.

The recital of *Shrimad-Bhagavatam* had begun. From cantos two through twelve, the best professor of transcendental science, Shukadeva Gosvami, would answer all of the Emperor's questions, though not necessarily in the order he asked them. The interplan-etary conclave of saints deferred to the Gosvami and sat in rapt attention to receive what they knew as the perfection of knowledge.

Notes

1 See *United States Journal of Commerce*, 15 July 1997.

2 Direct efforts to firmly authenticate this quote, originally found in a source not renowned for its precision, brought this tactful affirmation from the governor's press secretary, John D. Cox: "I have not been able to confirm that exact quote but I do believe it is mostly accurate."

3 *EIU Country Alert*, Economist Intelligence Unit, 10 September 1997.

4 John E. Mack, *Abduction* (New York: Ballentine Book, 1995).

5 *Brahma-samhita* 5.40.

6 Tom Rhodes, the *Sunday Times*, London, 10 November 1998.

7 Proceedings from the Prophets Conference, presented by Axiom, in Phoenix, Arizona, October 1997; available from World Wide Web at http://www.cseti.org/position/addition/mitchell.htm, 12 September 2000.

8 Ibid.

9 From an article by John Earls, *Sunday Times* (London), 25 October 1998.

10 From an article by Tom Rhodes, *Sunday Times* (London).

11 Ibid.

12 A sampling of the strict laws controlling potential UFO sightings: Air Force Regulation 200–2, "Unidentified Flying Objects Reporting," prohibits the release to the public and the media of any data about "those objects which are not explainable." Joint Army Navy Air Force Publication 146 lays down the law even more severely. It threatens to prosecute anyone under its jurisdiction—including pilots, civilian agencies, merchant marine captains, and even some fishing vessels—for disclosing reports of sightings relevant to US security.
On the lighter side, note *The Fire Officer's Guide to Disaster Control*, second edition—the official manual used by the Federal Emergency Management Agency (FEMA). It is also taught at the seven universities in the USA offering degrees in fire science. The textbook warns of "UFO hazards," such as electrical fields that cause blackouts, force fields, and physiological effects.
"Do not stand under a UFO that is hovering at low altitudes," the book cautions. "Do not touch or attempt to touch a UFO that has landed."

13 The French study, "UFOs and Defense: What Should We Prepare For?", and the political strategies suggested by Admiral Lord Hill-Norton and Edgar Mitchell were reported in the *Boston Globe* by Leslie Kean, 21 May 2000.

14 Lisa Miller, "Body and Spirit" (Special Report), *Wall Street Journal*, Millennium Edition, 31 December 1999.

15 Ibid.

16 From an article by Maurice Chittenden, *Sunday Times* (London), 22 March 1998.

17 Ruth Gledhill, *Times* (London), 29 August 1998.

18 *700 Club* news broadcast on 8 July 1997, commenting on the Mars *Pathfinder* landing four days earlier.

19 Haraprasad Shastri, "The Maha Puranas," in *Journal of the Bihar and Orissa Research Society* 14 (1928): 324.

20 Venkataram Raghavan, "Introduction to the Hindu Scriptures," in *The Religion of the Hindus*, ed. Kenneth Morgan (New York: Ronald Press Co., 1953), p. 270.

21 Raghavan, "The Puranas," in *Sanskrit Literature*, ed. V. Raghavan, (Delhi: Publications Div., 1961), p. 36.

22 H. H. Wilson, trans., *Vishnu Purana, a System of Hindu Mythology and Tradition* (London: Oriental Translation Fund Committee, 1840), p. lxxii.

23 Vans Kennedy, *Researches into the Nature and Affinity of Ancient and Hindu Mythology* (London: Longman, 1831), pp. 153–55.

24 Paul Hacker, "Puranen und Geschichte des Hinduismus. Methodologische, programmatische und geistesgeschichtliche Bemerkungen," in *Orientalistische Literaturzeitung,* 1960, p. 342.

25 Ludo Rocher, *The Puranas* (Wiesbaden, Germany: Otto Harrassowitz, 1986), p. 5.

26 Theodore Goldstücker, *Inspired Writings of Hinduism* (Calcutta: Susil Gupta, 1952), pp. 105–9 at 108–9. This text first appeared in "An English Journal," 1859–63.

27 "Puranism: or the popular religion of India," in the *Calcutta Review* 24, no. 48 (1855): 190, 223.

28 Max Müller, *A History of Ancient Sanskrit Literature* (London: Williams and Norgate, 1859), p. 61.

29 Goldstücker, *Inspired Writings*, pp. 108–9.

30 Theodore Goldstücker, *Sanskrit and Culture* (Calcutta: Susil Gupta, 1955, written in 1862), p. 155.

31 Rocher, *The Puranas*, p. 14.

32 Ibid., p. 17.

33 As cited by Rocher, *Shrimad-Bhagavatam* 3.12.36–39.

34 See chapter 2, note 9.

35 See *Rig-veda* 10.90.9.

36 See *Atharva-veda* 11.7.24.

37 See *Atharva-veda* 15.6.4.

38 Wilson, *The Vishnu Purana*, pp. iii–iv.

39 Ibid., p. vi.

40 Eugéne Burnouf, trans., *Le Bhagavata Purana*, vol. 1 (Paris: Imprimerie Royale, 1840), p. xxxiv.

41 Christian Lassen, *Indische Alterthumskunde*, vol. 1 (Bonn: Koenig, 1847), pp. 479–82.

42 Albrecht Weber, *Academische Vorlesungen* (Dümmler, 1852), pp.179–80.

43 Lassen, *Indische Alterthumskunde*, p. 479.

44 Edward Rapson, "The Puranas," in *Cambridge History of India* (Cambridge: Cambridge University Press, 1922, reprint Delhi: S. Chand & Co., 1962), p. 266.

45 M. A. Mehendale, "The Puranas," in *The History and Culture of the Indian People*, vol. 3 (Bombay: Bharatiya Vidya Bhavan, 1970), pp. 297–98.

46 Wilson, *The Vishnu Purana*, pp. ix–x.

47 *Asiatic Journal*, 1837, p. 244.

48 Ibid., p. 243.

49 Georg Bühler, *Sacred Books of the East*, vol. 2, 1879, pp. xxvii–xxix.

50 John Brockington, "Imperial India," in *Penguin Encyclopaedia of Classical Civilizations*, ed. Arthur Cotterell (London: Penguin, 1995), p. 221.

51 Rocher, *The Puranas*, p. 24.

52 Moriz Winternitz, *A History of Indian Literature*, vol. 1, no. 2 (Calcutta: Calcutta University Press, 1963), p. 465.

53 Rocher, *The Puranas*, p. 103.

54 Wendy O'Flaherty, *Hindu Myths: A Sourcebook Translated from Sanskrit* (Penguin Books, 1975), pp. 17–18.

55 Rocher, *The Puranas*, p. 103.

56 William Ward, *Account of the Writings, Religion, and Manners of the Hindoos*, vol. 2 (Serampore: Mission-Press, 1811), p. 117.

57 Winternitz, *A History*, p. 488.

58 *Penguin Encyclopaedia of Classical Civilizations*, p. 222.

59 Rocher, *The Puranas*, p. 145.

60 Ibid.

61 Ibid., pp. 147–48.

62 W. B. Emery, *Archaic Eygpt* (London: Penguin Books, 1987), p. 38.

63 Schoch, pp. 54—55.

64 Mary Settegast, *Plato Prehistorian: 10,000 to 5000 BC in Myth and Archaeology* (Cambridge, Mass.: Rotenberg Press, 1986).

65 R. Stigler, "The later neolithic in the Near East and the rise of civilization," in *The Old World: Early Man, to the Development of Agriculture*, ed. R. Stigler (New York: St. Martin's Press, 1974), p. 117.

66 Kristin M. Romey, "Sumer Loses Bragging Rights," http://www.archaeology.org/online/news/hamoukar.html. 15 June 2000.

67 John Noble Wilford, "Ruins Alter Ideas of How Civilization Spread," the *New York Times,* 23 May 2000.
The excavation report from the first season at Tell Hamoukar can be found on the Oriental Institute's website at http://www-oi.uchicago.edu/OI/PROJ/HAM/Hamoukar.html

68 Richard E. W. Adams, *Prehistoric Mesoamerica* (Oklahoma: University of Oklahoma, 1991), p. 49.

69 C. C. Lamberg-Karlovsky and J. A. Sabloff, *Ancient Civilisations: The Near East and Mesoamerica* (Menlo Park, CA: Benjamin/Cummings Publishing Co. Inc., 1979), p. 247.

70 Ibid., p. 142.

71 Emery, *Archaic Eygpt,* pp. 31, 177.

72 E. A. Wallis Budge, *From Fetish to God in Ancient Eygpt* (Oxford: Oxford University Press, 1934), p. 155.

73 Lamberg-Karlovsky and Sabloff, *Ancient Civilisations,* p. 248.

74 Graham Hancock, *Fingerprints of the Gods* (London: Mandarin, 1996), p. 489.

75 W. W. Hunter, "Orissa Under Indian Rule," first published 1872 as a chapter in *The Annals of Rural Bengal,* contained in *A History of Orissa,* vol. 1, ed. N. K. Sahu (Calcutta: Susil Gupta, 1956), p. 67.

76 Andrew Stirling, "Orissa: Chronology and History," first published 1822, in *Asiatic Researches,* vol. 15, contained in *A History of Orissa,* vol. 2, ed. N. K. Sahu (Calcutta: Susil Gupta, 1956), p. 225.

77 The list first appeared in W. W. Hunter's two volume *Orissa,* published in England in 1872. It was republished in *A History of Orissa,* vol. 1, pp. 196–97.

78 W. G. Waddell, trans., *Manetho* (London: William Heinemann, 1940), p. 5.

79 For instance, see Michael Hoffman, *Egypt Before the Pharaohs* (London: Michael O'Mara Books, 1991), pp. 11–13.

80 A. C. Bhaktivedanta Swami, *Shrimad-Bhagavatam* (Los Angeles: The Bhaktivedanta Book Trust, 1975) Canto 6, Chap. 1, Text 20, commentary.

81 Ibid., Canto 1, Chap. 9, Text 28, commentary.

82 Bernard Haisch, "UFOs and Mainstream Science," in *The Mufon UFO Journal,* no. 335 (March 1996): 14–16.

83 Associated Press, 14 October 1998.

84 *San Diego Union Tribune,* 19 February 1998, p. A1.

85 CNI News, vol. 4., no. 20, 16 December 1998. Available from CNINews1@aol.com

86 Ibid.

87 See also, Kip Thorne and Michael Morris, "Wormholes in Spacetime and their use for interstellar travel," *American Journal of Physics*, May 1998.

88 The director of the Center for the Study of Extraterrestrial Intelligence, Dr. Steven M. Greer, has presented this appropriate allegory.

89 Richard Thompson, *Alien Identities* (California: Govardhan Hill Publishing, 1993), p. 214.

90 David Jacobs, *What the Aliens Really Want, and How They Plan to Get It* (New York: Simon & Schuster, 1998).

91 Ibid.

92 Quoted in the *New York Times*, 8 October 1955.

93 Quoted in the *New York Times*, 12 May 1962.

94 *Bhagavad-gita* 16.6

95 *The Mahabharata*, books 2 and 3, trans. J.A.B. Van Buitenen (Chicago: University of Chicago Press, 1975), p. 692.

96 Ibid., p. 420.

97 *Shrimad-Bhagavatam*, trans. A. C. Bhaktivedanta Swami Prabhupada (Los Angeles: The Bhaktivedanta Book Trust, 1975), Canto 1, Chap. 13, Text 14 commentary.

98 A. C. Bhaktivedanta Swami Prabhupada, *Krishna* (Los Angeles: The Bhaktivedanta Book Trust, 1996 edition) pp. 170–71.

99 Ibid., p. 171.

100 *Bhagavata Purana* 10.74.52.

101 *Shrimad-Bhagavatam*, trans. A. C. Bhaktivedanta Swami Prabhupada, Canto 1, Chap. 19, Text 18, commentary.

EPILOGUE

~

Everything that has come down to us from heathendom is wrapped up in a thick fog. It belongs to a space of time we cannot measure. We know it is older than Christiandom, but whether by a couple of years or even by more than a millennium we can do no more than guess.[1]

Western views on the remote past have come a long way since the early nineteenth century, when a Professor Rasmar Nyerup of Denmark gave this overview. Nevertheless, despite twentieth-century advances in archaeology, history, and linguistics, when we attempt to glimpse the distant sun that is ancient India, dense billows of fog still obscure our sight.

India's Vedic glory should shine through, in the new millennium. A complete overhaul of Indology is long overdue. A Vedic revision is the need of the day.

Meanwhile, the train of challenges to the Western mainstream version of knowledge rolls on. Considered in the wake of these continual upsets, a call for reevaluating ancient India and its knowledge doesn't seem such an affront to our conceptual biases.

In the year 2001, the surprises continued, both on the land and in the skies. Astronomers, as we have come to expect, added two more planetary systems to what we know as the universe. This time, however, scientists are publicly wondering whether the cosmos contains more types of planets than they could ever conceive of. Moreover, doubts now plague them about the very meaning of the term "planet." The problem: neither of the newly discovered systems resemble each other or anything else in the solar system. One of the new systems contains a star accompanied by an inexplicable object that exceeds the size of Jupiter—the biggest companion of the Sun—by seventeen times.

Dr. R. Paul Butler, of the Carnegie Institution of Washington, said: "This massive planetary object defies our expectations for the largest planets. We never expected nature would make such gargantuan planets, and indeed maybe they aren't planets at all." In the other newfound system, the planets that orbit a small star are normal-sized, but their orbits are completely bizarre. Astounded by the two new systems, Dr. Geoffrey W. Marcy of the University of California at Berkeley, at a meeting of the America Astronomical Society, admitted: "They are unique and frightening. We thought we understood the full diversity of planets."[2]

Closer to our everyday life, the mystery of consciousness also made headlines. The prestigious California Institute of Technology (Caltech) chose to officially hear meticulous medical research that points to consciousness surviving after the brain ceases and a person is clinically dead. The medical study, done in England, threatens to render obsolete the traditional scientific objections to reports of near-death experiences. Previously, skeptics attributed NDEs to hallucinations caused by oxygen deprivation. Other opponents said that NDE memories were produced during the moments the person lost consciousness or regained it.

"The studies are very significant in that we have a group of people with no brain function who have well-structured, lucid thought processes with reasoning and memory formation at a time when their brains are shown not to function," said Dr. Sam Parnia. Does the research suggest that consciousness, or a soul, keeps thinking and reasoning even if a person's life functions have completely ceased and his brain activity is nil? Dr. Parnia replied, "We need to do much larger-scale studies, but the possibility is certainly there."[3]

Down on the ground, the evidence continues to mount that human beings were in North America thousands of years earlier than we have been taught. Chipped tools found in South Carolina combine with evidence from Virginia, Pennsylvania, and Chile to reveal that the continent was inhabited well before the end of the last Ice Age. "It is now reasonable to think of humans living on this landscape perhaps 15,000 to 20,000 years ago," said University of South Carolina archaeologist Albert Goodyear. "It's the dawn of a new chapter in what was already a good book."[4]

The biggest archaeological quake of 2001 produced an entirely new ancient civilization. In Central Asia, in what are now the republics of Turkmenistan and Uzbekistan, Russian and American archaeologists brought to light an ancient civilization that thrived—in a land and time totally unsuspected—more than 4,000 years ago.

The unknown people of that area constructed buildings resembling huge apartment complexes—each larger than a football field and divided into many rooms. Surrounding the residential enclaves were multiple mud-brick walls, some ten feet thick. The people had irrigation systems, bronze-work, fine ceramics, and jewelry of gold and semiprecious gems. Dr. Fredrik T. Hiebert, a University of Pennsylvania archaeologist, at a conference on linguistics and archaeology at Harvard, said about the discovery: "We are rewriting all the history books about the ancient world."

Inscriptions dated to around 2300 B.C. show that the people may have had full-blown writing, or at least were tinkering with a form of proto-writing. Some experts, such as Dr. Victor H. Mair, a specialist in ancient Asian languages and cultures, and Dr. Gregory L. Possehl, a specialist in Indus archaeology—both at the University of Pennsylvania—are confident the inscriptions indicate full writing. Others, such as Dr. Carl Lamberg-Karlovsky, a Harvard archaeologist, are unsure that the inscriptions represent writing in its finished stage. Scholars, however, currently do agree that the symbols bear no resemblance to any other writing system of the time—whether of Mesopotamia, Iran, or the Indus Valley.

The newfound civilization comprises settlements that cover an area in Central Asia 300 to 400 miles long and 50 miles wide. Who the people were or what they called themselves is a mystery. Lacking a name for the culture, archaeologists call it the Bactria Margiana Archaeology Complex, or BMAC. Dr. Mair stated that these ruins of an unknown advanced culture had emerged in a region "where there was thought to be just space and emptiness." The discovery indicated that more than 4,000 years ago Asians were not as isolated as scholars thought, he said, but probably had continent-wide connections.[5]

Why not take a deeper look at ancient India—especially now that a gale of dissatisfaction with the axioms of Western civilization is upon us? Amid this increasing storm, what open mind can fail to notice that the Western paradigm of knowledge twists and totters?

> We are in crisis because we know (within our deeper selves) that the official knowledge, based on the mechanistic metaphor, has collapsed or is collapsing. The whole culture knows instinctively that it has transcended its old paradigm, that our reality is more challenging and more fascinating than we allowed ourselves to believe.[6]

The first half of this new century promises to be both a fascinating and a traumatic epoch. Watch forward thinkers fling off the shackles enforced by the mechanistic approach to life. As the conventional certainties crumble, the general populace will become bewildered. A confused mind is a very dangerous thing. Therefore, heroic and compassionate sages are needed, to ferry people across the turbulent seas of a major paradigm shift. The Vedic texts, seen in a new light, are a civilization-saving beacon.

Whether the folk responsible for Sanskrit and the Vedas originated from within India or without is a current dispute that alternately simmers and boils. But this academic dispute does not reveal the full gamut of the Vedic challenge. Hopefully this book has amply demonstrated that the problem of Vedic antiquity is much greater than the debate over "Aryan origins." Nonetheless, a fair-minded examination of that limited controversy does pry open a Pandora's box of major consequences.

First, the standard story of human civilization becomes suspect. Once you start rearranging the accepted history of the Indian subcontinent, dominos in other areas start to fall. The ancient histories of the Middle East, Near East, and Europe are affected. Moreover, the Vedas and ancient India start to look good. In the nineteenth century, no one wanted this—once the British Raj set in. In the twentieth century, some people did want this; most, however, politely ignored the ancient Vedic challenge. In the new century, bold intellectual pioneers should fare better.

A welcome development is that the colonial and missionary biases underlying the Aryan-intrusion model have faded. These lenses did undeniably blur Indology in the past two centuries. They have finally been shed. Their effects still linger, however, because professors are usually abreast with the cutting edge, the latest trends, only inside their chosen specialty. When confronted with anything outside their narrow focus, scholars cautiously repeat whatever they learned in graduate school—many years before.

The controversial movements of the ancient Aryans will probably necessitate a multi-disciplined task force to resolve. The solution beckons to a convergence of history, historical linguistics, archaeology, astronomy, geology, mathematics, genetics, and botany. Certainly this approach would make the future of Indic studies quite stimulating.

Scholars who feel they have an objective overview of the current indigenous or foreign Aryan debate say retiring it will probably require in-depth, unified knowledge of South Asian archaeology, Central Asian archaeology, Indo-European linguistics, South Asian linguistics, eighteenth- and nineteenth-century European history, as well as Indian nationalist and post-colonial history. Furthermore, mathematics and astronomy—Vedic, Babylonian, and Greek—must be explored.

Some established academics, sympathetic to a revision, muse that the Aryan conflagration may preoccupy a generation of Indologists—to clear the battlefield of conflicting models of history. Other researchers, particularly alternativists, often disagree. Though sharing the excitement of the Aryan quest, they are not always convinced that the problem is so vast. They look to upset the entire edifice of erudite Aryan migration conjecture through a single, pinpointed attack—say through astronomy or geology. Perceiving that one well-aimed cruise missile can bring the whole structure down, they often choose to focus a specialized attack on just one of the complexity's many weak spots.

At the dawn of the twenty-first century, here is the score in the great clash: There is almost no data currently deemed unarguable that allows for indigenous Indians—bearing Sanskrit and Vedic ways—to spill out into the rest of Asia and perhaps beyond. But, at the same time, the incumbent theory that the Aryans brought Sanskrit and the Vedic ways into India from abroad is easily problematized.

Archaeology exposes a significant degree of continuity in South

Asia, stemming back to at least 7000 B.C. The same archaeological record, however, has been notoriously silent on postulated Aryan intrusions from afar. Therefore, to compensate, the official migration hypothesis has been built on a well-woven mat of linguistic data. After fashioning such a successful theoretical basis, Western academia then prescribes that only upon it, the ground of linguistics, can the migration theory be dismantled. Strikingly, however, some top-ranked scholars, such as Edwin Bryant of Harvard University, can demonstrate that all the so-called linguistic evidence supporting Aryan migrationism is actually quite promiscuous. The technical data can be convincingly reconfigured to service other possibilities, besides intrusion into India. That's how pliant, unchaste, the so-called hard evidence for Aryan immigration is.

Brilliant linguistic formulations aside, most educated persons want to see that mysteries of antiquity are finally and firmly solved through archaeological finds—artifacts of clay, brick, and stone. The probes of linguists—relying upon delicacies such as linguistic substrata, linguistic palaeontology, dialectical geography, and loan words—certainly can give clues. Yet many scholars, while appreciating the predictive potential of linguistic analysis, do share the aspiration for some solid ground in Indic prehistory—an earthy solution, something dug up that we can kick with our foot. After all, in our modern attempt at culture, seeing and touching is believing.

Westerners, however, are generally shocked to learn that archaeology in India is still in its infancy—an open frontier. Since the early twentieth century, Harrapa and Mohenjo-daro in the Indus Valley have received the major effort. Sarasvati sites are now enjoying some attention, especially since the rediscovery of the Sarasvati River does make sense of the Vedic literature.

Otherwise, when considering the whole of the Indian subcontinent and its archaeological potential, astonishingly scant work has been done. Though the Vedic literature is full of geographical references to ancient cities and sacred places, few excavations have been attempted—even at high-profile sites associated with the *Mahabharata, Ramayana,* and the *Shrimad-Bhagavatam.* For example, Indraprastha and Mathura, related to the Pandavas and Krishna, have never been adequately explored.[7] An exception is Taxila, a site associated with Janamejaya, son of King Parikshit.

As D. K. Chakrabarti, of Cambridge University, points out in his *The Archaeology of Ancient Indian Cities,* since Indian independence and partitioning at least a half century ago, neither Pakistan nor India has undertaken any exacting, prolonged, and systematically documented excavations to solve the mystery of ancient urban sites. Political and economic realities on the subcontinent have meant no money, time, or organization. F. R. Allchin, still the most influential archaeologist studying India, laments that the population explosion in South Asia has now destroyed many ancient urban sites. Even prime locations undamaged just fifty years ago are now inaccessible to excavation.[8]

The lack of archaeological data available for India's east coast especially illustrates the huge task yet undone. Until recently, no one realized that the coastal area of West Bengal had early urban centres. Chakrabarti comments, "It is imponderables such as these that make all hypotheses regarding early urban growth very tentative."[9]

If we look at archaeological work done in the Middle East, Western capital has matched its religious affiliations by funding extensive digs into Bible history. India, though, has lacked the affluence necessary for costly research into the Vedic descriptions of its remote past. Obviously, Westerners have no mainstream religious motivations that would push deeper their digs into India's mysteries.

Added to the problem of linguistic hypothesis and archaeological scarcity is the puzzle of dating Puranic knowledge. Here, the ground is nowhere near as solid as popular opinion portrays.

Indeed, the footing is quite treacherous, as specialist scholars have attested. And, once the cat of the Purana mystery is let out of the bag, the whole thrust of the Vedic challenge assumes its momentous proportions.

But we should not overlook startling research on Vedic astronomy—a crucial field neglected for almost a century. New, revisionary work, nearing completion, may hurl all Vedic dates several millennia deeper into the remote past. A fresh wave of scientific investigators say that Vedic astronomical references, once thoroughly analyzed, have the potential to spark a revolution in how we see the Vedic times and people.

Surely, a Vedic revision portends a paradigm shift far more consequential than the stir about which way the Aryans moved. Gradually the modern mind is becoming keen to discover the hidden achievements of the ancients. Eventually this curiosity will induce a marked transformation of the way we moderns see ourselves and the universe.

We will understand that ancient civilizations were generally much more advanced than what our traditional knowledge allows. In comparison, we may become embarrassed. Particularly the Vedic literature alerts us to a spiritual basis of organized human life. The Vedic knowledge radically redefines for us what it means to be a human being and what is the actual standard of human civilization.

Besides directly fostering transcendental perfection, the spiritual expertise of the Vedic civilization enabled attendant material benefits of subtle technology. Dare we consider that the subcontinent of India was the center of the greatest wisdom and mystical technology that the Earth has seen? That means the mysteries we find in other ancient lands and cultures may be offshoots of the enormous prowess of ancient India, now hidden away in the Vedic texts. The Vedic knowledge suggests that its jewels are central to the development of high civilization throughout the globe—civilizations with access to subtle abilities beyond the scope of today's comparatively gross technology.

The majority of Indologists have chosen to cram their version of a Vedic Age into a relatively short span of recent time. They fasten upon what they consider as the dark, protohistoric years between the decline of the Indus Valley cities and the appearance of Buddha. That means from anywhere in the second millennium B.C. to about the sixth or fifth century B.C. The top limit depends on varied conjectures for the dissolution of the Indus Valley civilization; the bottom limit rests on academic preferences for what century to place Buddha within. Yet a study of how the chronology of Vedic texts has been constructed will demonstrate the inadvisability of fashioning such an extremely late, limited, and impotent version of the Vedic Age. The entire system of ancient Indian chronology has been erected on flimsy and speculative hypotheses.

In the hands of most Indologists of the nineteenth and twentieth centuries, everything Vedic becomes reduced. Mighty kings become tribal chieftains; great empires become small provinces; the Vedic world influence becomes a local affair—in the five-river region now known as Punjab. Oceans become lakes and river basins. Most significantly, the extraterrestrial becomes earthbound.

The epic *Mahabharata* presents a civil war that consumed all major kings, from a wide geographical area spanning at least the Indian subcontinent. Historians have reduced this massive conflagration to a local brawl among minor princes from the northwestern corner of India.

Why should moderns fight over whether the progenitors of Vedic culture traveled into India or dispersed out of it? They may well have had movements both into India and out from it—and even beyond the planet. When we take into account the undeniable extraterrestrial scope of the Vedas, then the petty migration feuds of conservative academia, borne of obsolete geocentric dogma, fade into the dust of Earth.

Notes

1   C. C. Lamberg-Karlovsky and Jeremy Sabloff, *Ancient Civilizations* (Menlo Park, Ca.: Benjamin/Cummings, 1979), p. 28.

2   John Noble Wilford, *The New York Times*, January 10, 2001. "Found: 2 Planetary Systems. Result: Astronomers Stunned."

3   Sarah Tippit, *"Scientist Says Mind Continues After Brain Dies,"* Reuters, June 28, 2001.

4   *Associated Press*, June 19, 2001.

5   *The New York Times*, May 13, 2001.

6   Henryk Skolimowski, *The Participatory Mind* (London: Arkana, 1994), p. 122.

7   Some research has been done near what is currently known as Dvaraka, but the finds, as yet, do not reveal anything of remote antiquity. To date, the work, by S. R. Rao, has not revealed anything that affirms or denies accounts of the original Dvaraka site in the Vedic literature.

8   F. R. Allchin, *The Archaeology of Early Historic South Asia* (Cambridge: Cambridge University Press, 1995), p. 8.

9   D. K. Chakrabarti, *The Archaeology of Ancient Indian Cities* (Delhi: Oxford University Press, 1997), p. 278.

INDEX